the corporate intranet

Second Edition

RYAN BERNARD

WILEY COMPUTER PUBLISHING

John Wiley & Sons, Inc.

New York ◆ Chichester ◆ Weinheim ◆ Brisbane ◆ Singapore ◆ Toronto

Publisher: Robert Ipsen
Editor: Cary Sullivan
Assistant Editor: Kathryn A. Malm
Managing Editor: Marnie Wielage
Text Design & Composition: North Market Street Graphics

Designations used by companies to distinguish their products are often claimed as trademarks. In all instances where John Wiley & Sons, Inc., is aware of a claim, the product names appear in initial capital or ALL CAPITAL LETTERS. Readers, however, should contact the appropriate companies for more complete information regarding trademarks and registration.

This book is printed on acid-free paper.∞

Library of Congress Cataloging-in-Publication Data:
Bernard, Ryan.
      The corporate Intranet / Ryan Bernard. — 2nd ed.
         p.   cm.
      Includes index.
      ISBN 0-471-24775-8 (alk. paper)
      1. Intranets (Computer networks)   2. Business enterprises—
Computer networks.   I. Title.
      TK5105.875.I6B47   1997
      650'.0285'46—dc21   97-31941
                                                                              CIP
Printed in the United States of America.

10 9 8 7 6 5 4 3 2 1

the corporate intranet

contents

Chapter 6   Harnessing the New Media   239

Chapter 7   Serving Data and Applications   283

PART 3   The Intranet for Managers and Planners   337

Chapter 8   The Internet and the Extranet   339

Chapter 9   Intranet Management Strategies   375

introduction

The first edition of this book was started in late fall of 1995, at a time when the word *intranet* had barely emerged on the scene. As such, it was undoubtedly the first book written on the subject. Two seasons later, as the book was coming off the press and the hullabaloo over intranets was growing to a fever pitch, at least two other books were already making their way onto the shelves.

Yet, what surprised me most—as it did many appreciative readers and critics—was the way that the first edition managed to anticipate with considerable accuracy the complete intranet paradigm as it would unfold over the next 18 months. In fact, it neatly anticipated the concept of "extranets" at a time when that word had not yet been coined. Even now, anyone who reads the first edition of *The Corporate Intranet* will find that most of my original observations still ring true, and most of the explanations and advice will still be quite useful to those who want to understand what intranets are all about.

Time careens forward, however, and many things have changed since late 1995. In particular, none of us could have envisioned how quickly intranet mania would grow worldwide, or how forcefully Microsoft would explode into the market, barreling Netscape aside (at least partially) and jamming its hungry tendrils into every cranny of the technology. Though FrontPage had an early spot in my original first drafts as a favored web-authoring tool (as then offered by a company called Vermeer Technologies), Internet Explorer arrived only as the final drafts were underway. Products like Internet Information Server (IIS) and concepts like Active Desktop were still trapped in the future.

Yet, some of the products that I did recommend for intranets as early as December 1995, like Cold Fusion and HTML Transit, later emerged as solid market leaders in their categories. Of all the recommended tools and vendors, only the frequent mention of the original NCSA Mosaic browser and a company called Spyglass might strike an anachronistic note today.

Despite all the progress in the intranet market, with well over half of all U.S. companies now using the technology in some way, we still have far to go. Many intranets created over the past two years have succeeded dramatically, with documented studies showing return-on-investment (ROI) of 1,000 percent, 2,000 percent, or more. Yet many other efforts fell on hard times because their creators and adopters did not understand what it takes to make an intranet thrive and grow.

Many intranets remain hobbled by the assumptions of the past: that computer networks are something to be restricted and rationed, when in fact they are becoming the most essential pathways for communication and collaboration, not only within the enterprise but between any business and its customers, suppliers, and partners. If there is an underlying message in this edition, then, it is a message that was already central to the first edition, a warning that for your intranet to grow and thrive, you must first "set it free."

Thus, the words I wrote in the first edition's preface still apply. To wit: Over the last 20 years, I have seen a great drive to continuously cut costs and improve productivity. Systems have been reengineered en masse, and organization charts have been streamlined to a fare-thee-well. And yet, despite this tremendous effort, we are still facing many of the same problems that we faced 10 or 20 years ago: how to communicate and manage the vast streams of data and information created daily by millions of office workers, manufacturing facilities, design teams, dealers, sales reps, customers, and suppliers worldwide.

It's amazing, despite the unending improvements in our technology, how little has really changed. When you walk down the hall of any modern corporation, you can still hear the *pop* of the three-ring binder echoing against the walls. Then you turn the corner and immediately stumble across a more recent development: the perpetually gorged recycling bin, where thousands of pages of unwanted information have finally come home to roost.

Despite massive investments in office automation over the past decade and persistent dreams of a "paperless office," corporations still devour trees at an incredible rate. The three-ring binder is only a small part of the problem, yet a prominent symbol of what we're fighting against. The biggest problem is that traditional corporate information systems deal with only a small part of the data processed by the typical business: the mission-critical data that requires priority handling and ironclad security. Much of the rest of the data flowing from corporations begin life in the computer, then go straight to the laser printer, the copying machine, and the mail room for dissemination. As a more extreme and absurd example, consider that much of our business communication still consists of employees reading information from a computer screen to someone over a telephone.

It doesn't have to be so. Intranets, and more recently *extranets,* now make it possible to connect everyone in such a way that information originated in the computer system can glide through the network all the way from source to end user. To use our systems this way, however, we will have to accommodate the extra traffic and make it easier for people to use networks for these purposes. In many ways, it will mean making our data networks as open and easy to use as the in-house phone system.

In late 1994, when I first started circulating the draft proposal for this book, intranets were not a practical way to deliver large volumes of information online. Early intranet publishers had to manually code the HyperText Markup Language (HTML) using a text editor. Early web servers and browsers were rudimentary at best. And if you wanted to do fancy stuff like database queries, you had to hire a programmer with expertise in something called *CGI.* Now, only a few years later, most software applications—and particularly database management systems—come prepackaged with built-in "Internet hooks" that let you easily connect data to the web interface.

Today, Internet and intranet technologies are mainstream, and any business ignoring them does so at its own peril. Most serious-minded companies are already deep into the technology and plowing ahead in a way that will continue to give them a competitive edge. And, since many organizations already have the infrastructure in place that can make an intranet practical, it's clear that the time for this technology has finally arrived.

Theme Song of the Second Edition

When the first edition of this book was released, intranets were a hot new concept, still redolent with "potential." Only about 36 percent of U.S. companies were in the process of developing an intranet. Many people were having a hard time grasping the importance, the value, and the mechanics of this technology. In that sense, *The Corporate Intranet* was tailor-made for its time. It introduced many lay people to the concept and technologies in ways a more technical book couldn't have.

Now, however, studies are showing that over 90 percent of U.S. companies either have an intranet installed, have one in planning stages, or are experimenting with one. Does this mean there is no longer any need for a book that covers the basics of intranets in an easy-to-read fashion?

Perhaps this would be true if we could say that corporations experimenting with intranets have already brought *all their potential users online,* or that everyone involved with intranets already understands the technologies and the business value perfectly. But this is far from the truth.

Unfortunately, one of the main problems with intranets, and what many companies are finding out painfully, is that it is not enough to just establish a prototype or a pilot system. An intranet is not something you can install and then walk away from. It is a dynamic living organism that can and should involve collaboration across the *entire* enterprise. The intranet, then, is not just a tool for IS, as it has been recently portrayed. It is a tool for *everyone.*

In its most fully realized form, the intranet is an open channel through which *all employees* can communicate and learn information about their company operations. "All employees" means not just the developers, IT managers, and technology experts. It means the accounting managers, tech writers, field engineers, sales reps, marketing people, internal newsletter editors, human resource staffers—you name it. That includes a wide spectrum of people, most of whom are *not* technically savvy and don't have a clue about the business value or mechanics of the intranet.

These users represent a "second wave" or "new generation" of intranet acolytes, who are only now coming to the table with their unique requirements and technical questions. Thus, if the second edition could be said to have a theme song, it would be "Let's Move On to the Next Generation Intranet." Companies that have successfully launched their intranets find themselves a year into the project thinking, "Is that all there is? Isn't there something more that we could do with this?" Some people talk about a *second-generation* or *third-generation* intranet, in which online publishing gives way to CGI programming, database connectivity, and then advanced Java programming. There is also ongoing concern about return-on-investment vis-à-vis intranets.

But high-end Java development projects are just a small part of the intranet story and a small part of the forces that can have an overall impact on the intranet. In fact, most of the people who come into contact with intranets are absolutely bewildered by Java. And there are serious questions being raised all the time about its effectiveness and security.

If there is any message that I find timeless, compelling, and worthy of repeating, it is that the success of any intranet is really in the hands of the ordinary user, who can be empowered to fill the Ethernet with a dynamic flow of information using simple, easy-to-use tools that allow not only publishing, but group collaboration, database connectivity at the click of a mouse, easy-to-serve multimedia, and much more. There are many people sitting around thinking all of this is too difficult to bother with, when in fact the right tools and techniques can make them productive almost immediately.

Who Needs This Book

Thus, in preparing the second edition, I kept two types of readers in mind. These are the kind of people I meet nearly every day, who have come to me with questions and requests for assistance and training:

Intranet novices. There is still a large contingent of people who are bursting onto the intranet scene totally fresh, who need to get a quick fix on how intranets can help them, where to get started, and how to proceed. In some cases, these people are not technically savvy, especially with regard to the practical applications of networking technologies. Others may have considerable experience dealing with traditional computer and networking applications, yet may be somewhat muddled in their grasp of Internet-specific technologies such as TCP/IP, HTML, and Active Desktop, and even more muddled in understanding what an intranet can or can't do for them. Most of the acclaim during the first edition came from readers like these, and hopefully this edition will continue to help those who are starting at the beginning.

Intranet improvers. Maybe your company has already created an intranet but isn't realizing the full potential of the technology. Or perhaps you are starting an intranet project and need help finding your way efficiently to the end point. Or maybe you just need a quick reference on "best practices" in the industry. It is my hope you can benefit from this book, even if you already know a fair amount about intranets. In my mind, intranets are about 80 percent human engineering and 20 percent computer engineering. So if you already have a grasp of the technical factors, this book may help you with the human factors—and vice versa.

In addition, you will find this book most useful if your job description fits one of the following profiles:

Managers/department heads. Web technology works best in an environment where upper-level managers clearly understand the technologies and issues involved. This includes not just IT managers, but department and division heads who may end up blindsided not only by the power of the technology, but also by how large these systems can grow and how fast they can become unmanageable. If you are a manager, this book will help you understand the value of the technology and the key management issues involved. If you are not a manager, but are involved in a haphazardly planned or controlled intranet system, please make sure someone upstairs sees this book.

Communicators. Nearly everyone fits this description, since we all have something we need to communicate to others. However, this technology will be extremely helpful to those who regularly provide information or services to the rest of the organization, or those who would like to. In particular, those involved in corporate communications, marketing communications, or technical communications may find intranets an ideal way to distribute information to employees, customers, distributors, or suppliers.

Data guardians.   Those who are involved in managing large databases or data warehouses may find the intranet an ideal way to get more mileage out of the data by opening it up to a wider audience of employees, customers, or suppliers. This book describes both the database-publishing aspects and the security angles.

Work groups.   An intranet system is an ideal way for work groups and teams to publicize their efforts within an organization.

Systems analysts and developers.   A web interface may be the best way to cut down on the work involved in developing GUIs for client-server applications. In particular, you will learn how intranet allows developers to create a single point of access for a wide variety of applications, and how you can roll out self-documenting applications online without much of the effort previously required in developing client-server systems.

Corporate trainers and seminar leaders.   Intranet technology is a new concept for many employees to grasp, especially if they are still trying to learn simple things: like how to get the most productivity out of their word processors. Peoples' understanding of the technology is clouded by their confusion over the Internet—They may not see a clear correlation between the way web sites work on the Internet and the way they can work on the intranet. Most companies will see a necessary period of adjustment similar to what happened shortly after the introduction of early word processors, or after the introduction of Windows 3.1 and other mouse-and-window-based graphical user interfaces. To help ease people into the new technologies, this book may provide an excellent background text for introducing the technology to key employees.

Process improvement teams.   Teams dedicated to improving internal processes may find that intranet technology provides an excellent way to streamline and eliminate many of the costs associated with paper-based information delivery processes.

Where Intranet Technology Fits

Intranet technology is not the best solution for every problem, but it's always amazing to see so many companies using it in all the different ways they do.

In particular, the technology is a natural fit for companies where the following conditions exist:

Internal network running TCP/IP. Web technology is designed for use in a networked environment containing desktop computers, whether they are Macs, UNIX workstations, or PCs—and especially if the network supports a mixture of these operating systems. The main requirement is that these computers be connected into a local or wide area network (LAN or WAN), and that the network support TCP/IP communications. This is not as uncommon as it may sound. Even if your network runs Netware, SNA, or any other protocols, it may already have a TCP/IP overlay on it, and especially if there are UNIX machines being used as servers anywhere on the network. Most desktop operating systems now include TCP/IP as a built-in protocol, including Windows and Mac.

Dispersed but connected work groups. You can use intranet technology productively for the benefit of individual work groups as small as a dozen people working in the same office suite. But it's most useful for improving communications between widely separated work groups—especially those that operate on separate but interconnected LANs or WANs spread across an office building, a campus, or around the globe. The key word here, however, is *connectivity*. Web technology will not work in parts of the network that are not addressable through TCP/IP. Later chapters will explain how this works.

High ratio of desktop computers. Since it is completely online, this technology is of course best used in organizations with a high ratio of computers to employees. To a certain extent, you can work around this by using kiosks in work areas (such as a dedicated or shared web client at the packing station in a warehouse). The user base should be familiar with the use of a mouse, but few other skills are needed with a well-designed interface.

What's in This Book

In case you haven't figured it out yet, let me clarify. This book is emphatically *not* about the Internet or the World Wide Web per se—although you will see them mentioned many times herein. (If you've been to the book store lately, you know there are already far too many books on those subjects, anyway.)

Instead, it is intended to show anyone with a little technical savvy how to apply *the same technologies* used on the Internet and WWW to the typical business enterprise LAN, WAN, *or* Internet gateway. Why? To help you automate and streamline the flow of documents, data, and other mission-critical information in ways they've never been streamlined before. And to share important business data with *all* the people who are important to the success of your business, not only the customers but also the employees, dealers, and suppliers. This *includes* the idea of using the technology on the Internet, but it is by no means limited to that use alone.

To avoid the familiar trap—and provide a fresh viewpoint on the subject—this book takes the position that intranets are perhaps the highest and greatest use of these technologies. Even now, several years into the phenomenon, most people's attention is still riveted on the Internet, and intranet gets only a side mention in computer, business, and technical journals. That is an imbalance this book hopes to correct. Most books on the Internet and the World Wide Web are of little help when it comes to understanding or designing intranets. Although much of the technology is the same, there is considerable difference in the way the technologies are *applied.* The ground rules change considerably when you apply this technology internally versus externally, which is the reason few of the traditional Internet providers and Web design houses get involved in intranet work. And because of these differences, intranets require a completely different approach to the technology, as you will see.

As an added fillip, this book tries to take a holistic approach to the concept of communicating within an enterprise. Too often, people take a simplistic approach to technology that looks at the individual limbs without seeing the whole tree. What they end up with is a system that is harder to use and maintain than it should be. For instance, we are already far beyond the point where people should have to learn an obscure markup language like HTML to publish web documents, just as no one has to code raw PostScript these days to get a nice-looking printout. We are also near the point where we will no longer need programmers to connect intranet systems to external applications like databases.

The other challenge is to take a balanced approach to the use of the technology. Organizations that have rushed onto the Internet, while ignoring their intranet and the potential of the extranet, suffer from a sort of myopia. They're using Internet technology to provide information indiscriminately to the general public, yet denying the same automated online services to other important people: their employees, customers, and business partners. This book will help restore balance by offering an integrated business model that gives proper weight to both the internal and external uses of the technology.

Even for those organizations that have started their own intranets, there is still a sort of myopia because the people who are entrusted with intranet development are usually the most technically savvy, but not always the best communicators. We must never forget that data is "information," and information requires communication, especially in an intranet environment where we can now apply desktop-publishing techniques on the fly and present even the rawest, ugliest data in a pleasing document-like dinner coat.

Though many people already understand how to create Web documents, they may not fully understand all the new approaches to document creation and management this makes possible. Many people instinctively want to apply old paradigms without rethinking the requirements of the new medium. Once we start taking our documents and data online through the intranet, the way we structure them will inevitably change to match the unique capabilities of the publishing medium. Since intranets and the entire client-server environment make it possible to present some information *exclusively* online, we also need to take a look at how that will change the whole way we go about creating, presenting, storing, and retrieving the information. This book explores the idea that documents could become more like data—and data more like documents—so that eventually the two may merge.

Finally, many people who already publish documents on the intranet still don't understand the full power available for delivering high-value information resources. Consequently, this book has chapters devoted to the concept of advanced content delivery, including database, knowledge bases, multimedia, and more. And it makes the assumption that, to get full use out of the technology, you really need to understand how it compares to and interacts with other computing technologies such as mainframe-centric, groupware, client-server, and such.

This book was written to address all these concerns in ways that nearly anyone with a little computer savvy should be able to understand. There's something here for everyone, including writers and communicators, trainers, system developers, designers, network administrators, and managers of every hue and stripe. That's because the intranet itself covers all these disciplines and more. And everyone—management especially—can benefit from a complete overview of both the science and the art involved in creating an intranet.

A Quick Tour of the Book

To help you understand how to get the most from this book, the following presents a "quick tour" of the book's structure and explains the purpose of each section and chapter.

Part 1—The Business Case for Intranets.   This section provides an introduction to the current state-of-the-art in intranet technology, to help you understand the business value and some of the best practices related to intranets.

◆ *Chapter 1: What Every Business Can Learn from the Internet* explains how the Internet model applies to business and gives a first glimpse of the concepts involved; it also explains the progress to-date with intranets and what remains to be done.

◆ *Chapter 2: Understanding the Technology Issues* explains the developments in technology that have made intranet feasible for the enterprise and discusses how it may change the way we all do business in the future.

◆ *Chapter 3: The Intranet in Practice* provides examples of how companies like Sun, Compaq, and Chevron built (and continuously improved) their own intranets.

Part 2—The Intranet for Everyone.   This section tackles the nuts-and-bolts of intranets, explaining what's needed to set up servers and connect users with information. As with the rest of the book, this section is written with the nontechnical person in mind, since it is not just experienced Java programmers who will need to provide information and data on our intranets.

◆ *Chapter 4: Wiring the Business Unit* explains how any department in an organization can use a Web server to create its own "information center."

◆ *Chapter 5: Toward the Paperless Office* explains how to use an intranet as a publishing medium, including how to automate the publishing process.

◆ *Chapter 6: Harnessing the New Media* covers the issues and concepts of delivering multimedia over an intranet.

◆ *Chapter 7: Serving Data and Applications* explains how the intranet can be used to serve data from mainframes and other client-server applications.

Part 3—The Intranet for Managers and Planners.   This section deals with the advanced integration issues facing strategic planners, IS departments, and managers of every type. Included are issues like Internet connectivity, system integration, extranets, advanced development techniques, and technologies.

◆ *Chapter 8: The Internet and the Extranet* explains how to integrate the intranet with the Internet and the extranet.

- *Chapter 9: Intranet Management Strategies* explains how quickly intranets can grow and how to approach the problems of management and strategic planning, especially with regard to corporatewide publishing standards, programming issues, corporatewide access and security, etc.
- *Appendix: What's on the Web Site?* explains what is on the companion web site for *The Corporate Intranet, Second Edition.* Check here for details and also check the web site from time to time for updates on technologies and for information related to the book.

Ryan Bernard
rbernard@wordmark.com

acknowledgments

This book would not be possible without the help of many people. As always, I acknowledge my colleagues John Foster and David Lineman, who collaborated on my first intranet project so long ago in the second half of 1994. Those were the days, guys. Little did we know that the rapid technological growth and universal acceptance of intranets would exceed our wildest dreams and expectations.

Thanks to Joe Rampy for his frequent encouragement over the numerous plates of seafood that we shared while talking business and marvelling at the Internet's growth. Thanks to my business partner, Raymond Smith, for his trust, support, and encouragement during the months it took to put this book to bed. Thanks to all the people at Compaq for their patience, support, and encouragement and for giving me marvelous opportunities to learn and grow, including Seth Romanow, George Favaloro, Larry Griffin, Mike Mata, Stori Carpenter, and Mary Christ. Thanks also to Sharon Sloan, Deborah Scott, and John Hanten at Chevron for their quick response, and to Carl Meske at Sun for his time and attention. Thanks also goes to Lindsay Gabriel for helping me get the early draft in order, and again to John Foster for checking some of the technical matter.

The first edition of this book would not have been possible without the collaborative efforts of my agent, Matt Wagner, who still holds forth quite effectively at Waterside Productions in Cardiff-by-the-Sea, as well as my original editor Phil Sutherland at Wiley, who has since abandoned the ancient world of eyeshades and ink for the startling new world of bits, bytes, and dynamic content. It was Phil's foresight and eye for innovation that led Wiley to sign me up at a time when the intranet concept wasn't even a blip on the IT radar. Thanks to him, we were able to produce one of the first and one of the more successful books on the subject.

The second edition again owes its existence to the indefatigable efforts of Matt Wagner and to the gracious acquiescence and support of Bob Ipsen and Cary Sullivan at Wiley. Thanks to Kathryn Malm and Marnie Wielage for their patient efforts editing and checking the drafts for this version, and to all the other people on the Wiley crew (as listed on the credits page) who helped bring this edition to life.

This edition is dedicated to my parents, Reuben and Alice, who have always been there at the other end of the line. May we communicate for many more decades to come, folks. Of course, my fondest thanks go to my core support team, Diana, Evan, and Claire, for having endured all those late nights of muffled footsteps and clacking keyboards emanating from behind closed doors. And, as always, supreme thanks to Whoever it is upstairs who keeps sending me all these marvelous opportunities.

PART ONE

THE BUSINESS CASE
FOR INTRANETS

◆ This section explains how and why companies are using intranet technology to meet business goals. You will learn why business needs the intranet, why intranets are the culmination of many trends in the business technology world, and tour several companies that have created their own successful intranets.

Chapter One at a Glance

This book explains all the basic information you need to know about the design, building, and management of corporate intranets. But before we delve into the details of intranets, it's useful to start with a common point of reference: the Internet and the World Wide Web (WWW). Only by understanding the Internet and WWW will you come to understand how intranets can also work on private corporate networks. This chapter explains:

- Why the Internet and World Wide Web can serve as a model for business communications, teamwork, and collaboration

- How an intranet works, and why it is useful

- Why most current intranet applications are only the tip of the iceberg, and why some early intranets prematurely failed

- What kinds of "hidden tools" already exist on most computers that make it possible to create intranets

- Why networks are restricted and why that causes problems for intranets

- How intranets may save companies millions of dollars by making it easier for employees to share information, data, and other computer resources online

- Why web technologies will put us light-years ahead on the road toward the "paperless office"

- Why companies need to take a more integrated approach to the design and delivery of intranets

What Every Business Can Learn from the Internet

The growth of the Net is not a fluke or a fad, but the consequence of unleashing the power of individual creativity. If it were an economy, it would be the triumph of the free market over central planning. In music, jazz over Bach. Democracy over dictatorship.

—THE ECONOMIST

You've heard the hype, and it's true. When all is said and done, the Internet will be counted among the greatest success stories in history. Its rise from virtual nonexistence to over 16-million connected "hosts" in the past decade is a growth curve unequaled by any other organization or medium.

This network of networks is like a biological organism that is entirely self-replicating, self-sustaining, and self-governing. No one plans the Internet; no one works to make sure it is properly staffed, managed, or budgeted. It simply happens through serendipity and the cooperative action of millions. The people who make it happen are scattered throughout the globe, are generally unknown to each other, and have little understanding of exactly what the total network looks like or how it truly operates. And yet there has arisen from the Internet the kind of community and culture that can serve as a model for business and other cooperative enterprises well into the next century.

The Internet as a model for business? Eighteen months ago, when I first made that statement in the first edition of this book, the idea could be seen as heresy. Someone saying that business—the paragon of efficiency, profitability, and rigorous management—has something to learn from the wild and woolly Internet?

At first glance, the Internet would seem to be the antithesis of everything that business stands for. Business is orderly; the Internet is chaotic. Business is well planned and managed; the Internet is a free-for-all. Business has leaders, shareholders, and a clearly defined management structure; the Internet, like some kind of asylum for lost souls, has no one in charge and no one to answer to.

If you touted the Internet as a business model in 1994, the business community would have laughed in your face. In 1995, and even 1996, they still might have snickered quietly. But today—especially since the conversion of Microsoft's Bill Gates, Oracle's Larry Ellison, and most other key players in Silicon Valley—*everyone* believes that the Internet is a credible model for business computing. Starting with version 4.0 of Microsoft Internet Explorer and continuing with Windows 98, the web browser has moved from its humble position as "browser-in-waiting" to "king of the desktop." No longer just a way to view web pages, the browser has become—in Microsoft's version anyway—the center of the computing universe. In Sun's version, too, the web has become central to the entire notion of computing, as the intranet-based network computer (NC) replaces the standard desktop workstation.

An acceptable model for business computing, then? Granted. But an acceptable model for business itself? Look again.

First, look at the hundreds of thousands of interconnected web sites out there. Who organized, designed, and built this massive worldwide information system? In reality, it was self-designed and self-organized—not by some massive conglomerate, but by the people who controlled each individual node.

Now look at the new business models evidenced by companies like Amazon.com, the web-based bookseller that keeps little or no inventory of its own and forms only the wispiest of virtual threads between book writer and book purchaser. Then look at the other models unfolding around us: newspapers with no paper, industry consortia with no meeting halls, stock brokerage houses that may someday be run entirely by robotic agents. Come to think of it, maybe a whiff of change is in the air, after all.

Finally, take a look at what is happening in most large, technologically advanced organizations around the globe, including both for-profit corporations and nonprofit institutions. The Internet model is on the rise as a way to communicate within groups, between groups, inside the organization, or outside the organization. People who once interacted primarily through memos, telephone calls, and faxes are finding ways to make the network substitute for the old media of paper and eternal "phone tag." They are learning—bit by bit, but typically with little direct encouragement from management—to hitch their wagons to the Ethernet and conduct their business online in a perpetual state of interactivity.

The more you look, the more you see the burgeoning model of collaborative teamwork first validated by the emergence of *groupware* now being institutionalized by the increasingly pervasive presence of networked computing in all aspects of our lives. In fits and starts, but inexorably, people are learning how to make the network part of their daily routine—the most technically adept first, followed some months later by the more hesitant and less adventurous among us. They are building web sites on their desktops and letting loose a barrage of datagrams that spill over into vast pools of knowledge.

When organized into a computing model, we call the result *intranets* and *extranets,* but it is really the all-pervading spirit of the Internet that we see rising up through the wires and suffusing our institutions with new dynamism. In the future, the boundaries between Internet, intranets, and extranets will blur when viewed on the macrolevel. All will blend eventually into a seamless continuum. But in microcosm, it is still the intranet where most of us will encounter the Internet paradigm—on the job, in the office, as part of our daily routines. And so it is the intranet on which this book must focus.

The Next Generation Intranet

In fact, the intranet is already old hat, some might say. Many companies have tried building intranets over the past few years, and some early experiments lie eerily dormant—failed monuments to inattention and proof that many managers still lack a clear vision of what to do with new technology.

But what we have seen so far is just the beginning. In reality, all the people who have dabbled in intranets to date were just getting warmed up, whether they realized it or not. The best is yet to come. Regardless of initial difficulties and setbacks, the trend is decidedly in the direction of more online connectivity, not less. And in the future, there will be no organizational life that isn't solidly founded on network computing.

So now is the time for those who have tried and failed, or those who have taken the first baby steps, to refocus their attention on what lies ahead. And that, in turn, might be best epitomized by the advent of Windows 98 and the Network Computer. The next generation intranet is not a part of the solution; it is the center of the solution. If it hasn't already, it will become the way we connect with all of our legacy documents, data, and applications. A year from now, we will either call our entire computing system *the intranet,* or the word *intranet* itself will fade away, having outlived its ability to describe something that is separate and apart from the *regular computing environment.* And the *desktop*—to use some new terminology making the rounds—will morph quite subtly into the *webtop.*

For all those intranets that died in the crib, or that are still being born, it's time for their creators to redouble their efforts. If you're coming to the subject fresh or still grasping for the true dynamic of intranets, then it's time to go back to school and learn why and how the intranet is so important to the future of most large technically advanced organizations.

The Ghost in the Machine

Let's begin by talking of LANs and WANs and the interesting secrets they hold. Over the past decade, most major corporations and private organizations have developed their own extensive networks to tie together remote offices no matter where they're located in the world. In most cases, these networks have all the characteristics of the Internet and are capable of carrying the same kinds of traffic, too.

Even local or regional businesses with widely scattered branches, offices, or sales networks have their own local area networks (LANs) and wide area networks (WANs) that can carry Internet-like communications. And in most cases, just like on the Internet, the users of these networks have little idea of what the whole network looks like, how it truly operates, or even that it may already have some components of Internet technology embedded in it—ready to use.

In particular, most computers running UNIX, Windows 95 or 98, Windows NT, OS/2, or Macintosh System 7 or OS 8, have certain Internet tools already built-in, including TCP/IP networking, web-server software, and web browsers that can empower their users to do just about anything currently being done on the Internet. But in most cases, these tools lie dormant because most businesses do not understand how to use them productively to enhance network communications within their organizations. And this is mainly because they misunderstand the fundamental nature of the Internet.

The Internet represents the first truly large-scale experiment in creating a global public network like the phone system, but one devoted to exchanging data rather than voice communications. When you get a phone, you don't have to ask anyone for special permission to call Paris, London, Melbourne, or Tokyo. No one has to reconfigure the system so that you can reach remote areas of the world and chat with tribesmen in Borneo, burghers in Zurich, or gauchos in Argentina. You automatically get access to the entire globe. You can call anywhere in the world and anyone can call you (Figure 1.1).

When you pick up the phone and call Timbuktu, you don't see the complex set of connections made by all the intervening phone companies, state bureaucracies, satellite relays, and fiber-optic links. You don't think of all the treaties that had to be negotiated and technical problems that had to be hurdled to get your voice from point A to point Z. The connection just happens automati-

Figure 1.1   The phone system.

cally. This is now so easy, we all take it for granted. No one sits around all day and wonders, "How do they do that?"

The Internet is a lot like that (Figure 1.2). If you have a computer and an Internet connection, you get access to the entire worldwide public data network without restriction. You can get data and information from Microsoft, IBM, AT&T, CNN, Ford, the *New York Times,* the White House, the Library of Congress, the Australian Parliament, the Vatican, or the World Bank without any additional setup and without asking anyone's permission. If you have the proper setup, you can also *provide* information to the rest of the world. Thus, the Internet, through its World Wide Web feature, in a way supports the same kind of direct point-to-point communication we already get from the phone system—communication that can be one-way, as in fax-on-demand, or communication that can be as interactive as a phone conversation.

It wasn't necessarily planned this way. That's just how it happened. Interactive public networks have evolved—just as free markets evolved—based on their enabling architecture and the way human beings naturally decided to use them. Nowadays, connecting to and exchanging data with a random computer halfway around the world is as routine and easy as clicking your mouse.

The Business Mindset

In our daily work lives, on the other hand, there is a curious (though understandable) dichotomy between the data networks and the phone system.

Figure 1.2   An Internet (or intranet).

When you're hired to do a job, there's a phone already sitting on your desk. You can immediately pick up the receiver and dial human resources, marketing, or any other internal department without further ado. If you want to call a customer or supplier outside the company, you can dial *9* and call outside, too. It's all very simple and it's all done automatically. No one has to give you permission, or set you up specially to communicate with other departments or customers over the phone system. No one tries to control or limit what you have to say.

Why do you communicate with other people? Because you have information to share, and most of it is vital to your job and the health of your organization. Some of the information comes to you verbally through the phone network and some through paper-based communication systems: the copy machine, the fax, or interoffice mail. Together, these communication systems are the glue that holds the business together. The ubiquitous presence of these tools in our daily lives shows the importance we attach to them as means of communication. No one would ever imagine running an organization without them, and no one questions their value.

Things have not always been the same for the computer and the corporate data network, however. Not too long ago, it was a privilege to have a computer on your desk. Network connections were even harder to come by. These days, when you report to work, chances are you'll have a computer sitting on your desk, as well as a built-in network connection that plugs you into the local area network (LAN), or even a wide area network (WAN). Unlike the phone network, however, you can't use the data network to automatically communicate or share data with just *any* department. In fact, you may not be able to share it with anyone at all, except for a few people in your immediate area.

Locked into the Loop

Typically, you may start out being limited to your own local programs and the data on your local hard drive, then have network access added little by little, as you need it. Or, you may be logged automatically to a set of hard drives or *file servers* on a LAN, where data and applications are stored for employees in your group or division. But in most cases, you are locked into a closed departmental or divisional loop. If you want to share information with human resources, marketing, or some other department or division of the company, chances are you'll have to rely on the trusty old phone-and-paper system to do it (or something slightly more advanced, like a floppy diskette shipped through the interoffice mail).

Many companies have tried to remedy this problem using traditional client-server applications such as database management systems (DBMS) and groupware. The idea is that people can share files and data using applications that serve as traffic cops, keeping track of user changes and resolving them in the final version of the data. For example, Oracle software lets multiple users view and edit the same set of data; Lotus Notes does roughly the same thing for documents. This is much more productive than giving people access to a document or database one user at a time, or keeping different versions of the same information on each user's machine.

Still, traditional client-server systems tend to operate in a closed loop. It's as though you had a phone system which allowed you only to talk to the people in your own department or the team members who work on the same project, without allowing you to connect to the rest of the company down the hall. Or as though someone built a gate in the middle of the hallway, and you had to ask a gatekeeper for permission to pass. (Actually, this may not seem so strange to people who work in buildings where every door now requires a magnetic card to get through—just another symptom of our modern-day obsession with security.)

Things are starting to change now, thanks to the success of the Internet and the World Wide Web. Due to the torrent of publicity in the media and trade press in recent years, computer manufacturers and software companies like IBM/Lotus, Microsoft, Novell, DEC, Sun, and Oracle have started building increasingly powerful Internet "hooks" into their operating systems and software. And many of these same companies are leading the way in applying the technologies to their own internal and external business communications.

Back in 1994, when people first started doing it, the idea of installing Internet tools on corporate networks was daunting. Though universally available on UNIX workstations, these kinds of tools were not available on PCs and Macs until the advent of more advanced 32-bit operating systems like Windows 95. Now, however, every new computer is likely to be equipped with essential Internet tools such as web browsers and TCP/IP networking. Because of these developments, the years 1995 through 1997 brought about a second Internet revolution—one that promised to bring true and lasting benefits to the enterprise by *bringing the information superhighway in-house.*

Yet, in some organizations that adopted these new tools, the success of the Internet model was ignored and the intranets were forced into the mold of the old client-server applications, with their limited user bases and rigid login controls. Unlike the Internet, the system was not opened to all comers, and the nodes were not allowed to develop and grow on their own. Those who understood and followed the Internet model, on the other hand, were more likely to nurture the new technology into a self-sustaining role in their organizations.

The World Wide Web We Know and Love

It's important to make a distinction between the global phenomena known as the *Internet* and the *World Wide Web* and the related concept of *intranets* and *extranets.* The words Internet and World Wide Web have been drilled so firmly into our brains that some people may have a hard time separating the original technology from its more recent applications.

The Internet has been around for well over a decade, supporting common applications such as e-mail and File Transfer Protocol (FTP). But the World Wide Web is a fairly recent phenomenon that only started seeing widespread use in 1994. Businesses and their customers started flocking to the World Wide Web in droves soon after the invention of advanced graphical browsers such as Netscape Navigator and Internet Explorer (both cloned from the same common ancestor, a software application named *Mosaic,* which was originated by current Netscape executive Marc Andreessen). These new tools made it possible for any company to transfer graphically rich information—with real type fonts and full-color graphics—across the Internet at the click of a button. Since the browsers were inexpensive, anyone with a computer, a modem, and an Internet connection could easily access the information.

The advent of these new tools, along with the removal of various restrictions on commercial use, created a massive explosion in business activity on the Web. The total number of registered domain names (the unique Internet aliases like *microsoft.com* and *ford.com*) climbed from 17,000 in June 1994 to over 1.3 million three years later, an average growth rate of nearly 1,200 companies a day. By some estimates, there are now over 16,000,000 computers connected to the Internet, and this number is increasing at a rate of 500,000 per month.

These days, there are few companies—from the largest Fortune 500 enterprise to the smallest tamale shop—that don't already have some type of online presence. And anyone who has used the Web knows the wide range of information and services available—from tapping into the Library of Congress to purchasing tickets for the 8 o'clock movie.

To provide these kinds of web services, a company must be set up a certain way. When we say that a company is "on the Web," we usually mean it is connected directly to the Internet through a full-time hookup, which might be either a leased line or dedicated dial-up connection to a local Internet Service

Provider (ISP). The information available on a web site is stored on a desktop computer either at the company's physical site or at a third-party hosting service, which could be anywhere in the world. The transfer of information from web site to customer is handled by web-server software such as a Netscape or Microsoft web server, or any of the dozens of other server products available commercially or free of charge from companies and organizations around the world.

Each web site has its own unique address called a *Universal Resource Locator* (URL), such as the address *www.chevron.com* for the Chevron Oil Company web site. The Internet is set up in such a way that when someone types in *www.chevron.com,* the request is routed directly and automatically to the Chevron web site. When this happens, the server returns a "home page" (Figure 1.3), which contains a series of hyperlinks that the customer can use to access all the other information at the site. The information is stored in text and graphics files, and each embedded hyperlink specifies the filename to be retrieved. Once a site is set up like this, customers can access it anytime from anywhere in the world (Figure 1.4).

To do so, however, customers must have their own Internet connections. For the average consumer, this is a dial-up modem connection provided by a local ISP or an online service such as America Online or CompuServe. Home users pay from $10 to $40 a month for an account they can use to dial in and connect to the Internet. Once the connection is made, the home user can use a web browser to access web sites, an e-mail program to send messages, or a newsgroup reader to tap into bulletin board–style information.

Many people can connect to the Internet at work through high-speed, full-time LAN connections and "proxy servers" that route traffic from the Internet into their company's internal network. Just because an employee can connect to the Internet from a desktop computer at work, however, does not mean that the company has an intranet or an extranet. When this happens, we just say that the employee has "Internet access at work" or an "Internet connection to the desktop." As I will explain later, it takes a lot more than just a work-based Internet connection to give a company its own intranet.

Problems in Paradise

Thanks to the phenomenal growth figures, no one can argue that the World Wide Web hasn't been a complete success. There just hasn't been anything like it to come this far, this fast in a long time—if ever. Not television, radio, telephones, automobiles, or copying machines.

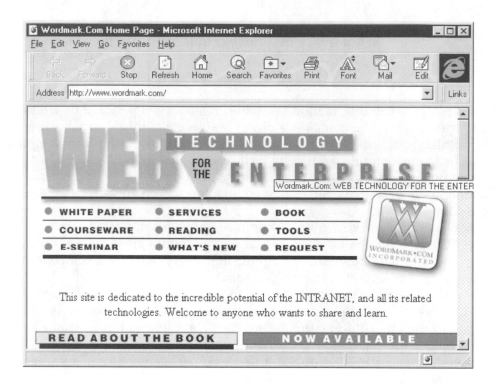

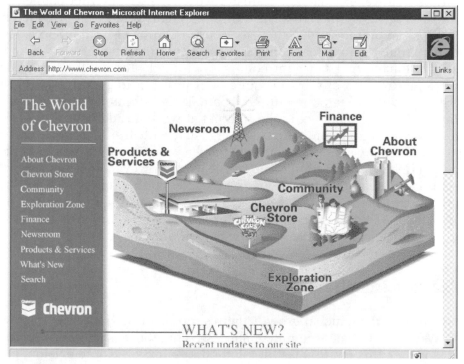

Figure 1.3 Typical business home pages on the Internet.

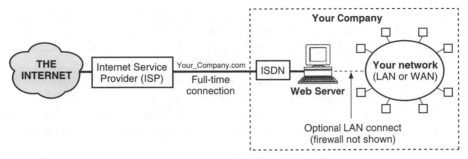

Figure 1.4 Typical business WWW connection.

So what's wrong with this picture? How could we possibly find fault with the success of the World Wide Web? Well, several problems should be immediately obvious to anyone who uses the Web or provides content for others to use.

The first major problem is that, in a sense, web technology is wasted on the World Wide Web, the way great art and gourmet food are wasted on teenagers. A major problem is the connection speed or, as it is often called, the *bandwidth*. The Internet backbone itself—the main channel that links most components of the system—is very fast in some places, passing data along at a rate of over half a gigabit per second (622 Mbps or higher). This is like transmitting a shelffull of books as thick as Tolstoy's *War and Peace* in the blink of an eye. Most major commercial Web sites also have relatively fast Internet connections, ranging from 1.5 Mbps (known as *T1*) to 45 Mbps (known as *T3*).

When the information reaches a home computer modem, however, it's like hitting a brick wall, because the bandwidth narrows considerably. Most users with new home computers have a modem speed of 28.8 to 56 kilobits per second (Kbps), which theoretically should be equivalent to several pages per second—but in practice may be considerably slower. But even if users want to plunk down extra cash for a fast modem, 56 Kbps is the maximum speed currently supported by modems operating over standard telephone lines. This makes it superfast for downloading pages of text, but miserably slow for anything else, including simple graphic illustrations.

The effect becomes even slower when you take into account the phenomenon of "Internet drag," which occurs when too many people hit the same server at the same time, or when parts of the network overload or collapse causing monumental cyber-traffic jams. Faster connection speeds are available through other technologies, such as *Integrated Services Digital Network* (ISDN), *digital subscriber line* (DSL), or cable TV modems. But technical complexity, spotty availability, and high costs frequently put these beyond the reach of the average consumer.

Business users who access the Internet at work benefit from the greater bandwidth of their corporate connections (T1 to T3 is common), but may find their connection slows considerably when it is shared by other employees. Typically, all Internet content at work comes through a single proxy server, which can aid the process by providing a local cache of frequently accessed web pages, but which can also serve as a bottleneck if many users are accessing nonstandard sites. So the true speed of any WWW transaction—at home or at work—is only as fast as the bandwidth at the user end, which in most cases is incredibly narrow.

The data bottleneck at the customer end effectively reduces the Web's power to the lowest common denominator (Figure 1.5). Web site developers must constantly make sure they're not overloading their users with too much graphic information. Customer-conscious site developers check and recheck file sizes and find themselves working overtime to optimize graphics. At 14.4K or 28.8K, text-based offerings such as online data work fine, but multimedia effects such as real-time sound and video are impractical because they are so garbled or of such low-resolution as to be unusable. The effect is slightly better—but still noticeably lacking in fidelity—at the highest available modem speed of 56K.

The latest class of application development tools, such as Sun Microsystem's Java programming language, are stifled by the limitations of the present environment. Many Java sites slow to a crawl or bog down completely when accessed by users with low bandwidth. If a site has the admirable trait of being graphic intensive (pictures being, as we all know, worth a thousand words), it becomes insufferable when filtered through the standard computer modem.

Another problem with the WWW is the sheer unpredictability of what lies at the other end of the connection. Customers may be accessing a web site using a wide variety of hardware and software, including Macs, PCs, and UNIX workstations of varying monitor resolutions. The fact that there are two major competing web browsers on the market (Netscape and Internet Explorer) plus a

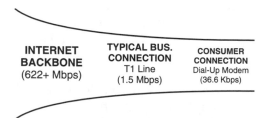

Figure 1.5   The Internet data bottleneck.

minor smattering of others, means that each user's web browser may be inter-preting the same web pages in a slightly differently manner,

The final problem is that the entire business model represented by current WWW use is lopsided (Figure 1.6). The customer is supreme in the business pantheon, and current WWW models rightfully put the customer first. But what about the other people involved in making businesses successful—the employees and business partners who form the organizational food chain that keeps any enterprise alive and kicking? If we can use web technology to smooth the information flow to customers, can't we do the same to benefit these other groups?

The Hidden World of Intranets

As it happens, the answer is yes. One concept that often gets lost in all the Internet hoopla is the idea that many corporate LANs and WANs are already turning into miniature versions of the Internet, delivering home pages, data, services, online documents, and other vital information across departmental boundaries to headquarters, manufacturing sites, and field offices throughout the enterprise.

This is happening because companies are finding ways to take advantage of Internet tools already built into their desktop computer systems. When it hap-

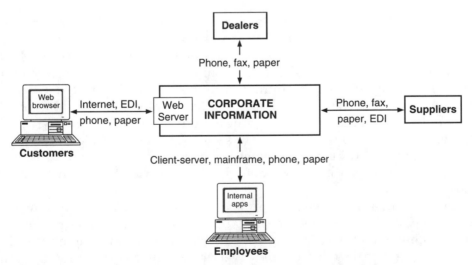

Figure 1.6   A lopsided business communications model.

pens, we call the result an intranet because the communications system is private and exists solely *within* the network boundaries of an organization. The Internet, on the other hand, is a worldwide communications network that provides a connection *between* various organizations. Both intranets and Internet, however, use many of the same tools and techniques, such as web servers and browsers, or e-mail servers and e-mail clients.

Intranets have become so popular over the past few years that most major companies either have them in place or are in the process of building them. These include corporate giants such as General Motors, Exxon, AT&T, Procter & Gamble, IBM, and Microsoft, as well as many other smaller, technically savvy organizations and many that fall in between (Figure 1.7). You never see these sites on the World Wide Web, because they are entirely private and shut off from the rest of the world. These companies may also have Web sites on the Internet, but each company's intranet is a separate realm that exists "behind the firewall"—that is, behind the protective layer of security mechanisms that separate the company's private internal network from the public Internet.

The term *extranet* comes into play when a company allows certain authorized users to access its intranet from outside the company network—either by dialing in directly, or by "tunneling" in through the firewall from various locations on the Internet. With extranets, a company can allow its sales reps, special customers, dealers, suppliers, and business partners to tap directly into its private intranet, without exposing the same information to the general public.

An important concept to remember about intranets is that *an Internet connection is not required.* Your company can have its own intranet without ever having an Internet connection or home page on the World Wide Web. All you need is a network and a set of desktop computers running the correct protocols and software that enable intranets to operate (mainly web servers and browsers, as described in later chapters of this book). Come to think of it, it seems only natural that some companies might want *nothing to do with* the Internet, given the horror stories about security, pornography, and the like. If so, fine: They can still use an intranet for their own internal purposes, without exposing their private networks to the threats posed by full Internet connectivity.

Companies that have taken the plunge and created their own intranets are finding new ways to cut through the communication snags that traditionally shackle their operations. Once grasped, the potential for this approach is truly amazing. Unlike other client-server applications—which require time-consuming login and hands-on involvement by system administrators and programmers—an intranet allows instant, random, and totally unfettered

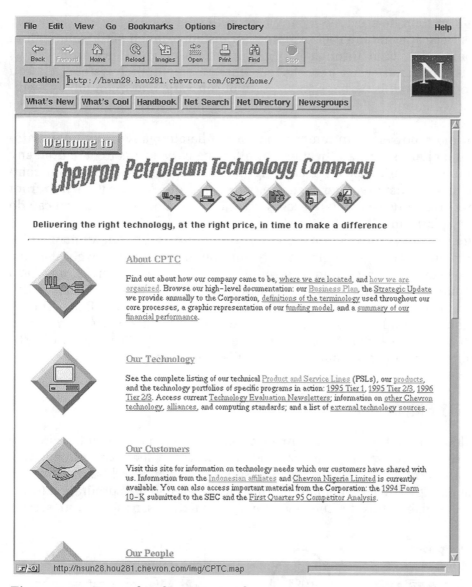

Figure 1.7   Example of an intranet home page.

point-to-point communication between any two nodes on a network without login, setup, or special programming.

By installing a web server on a local computer, any department in your company can become an ad hoc "information center" broadcasting published materials and data to the rest of the network on demand. The published information can then be accessed by any user in the network using web browsers such as Netscape and Internet Explorer. For instance, much of the information now being delivered through expensive custom-programmed applications could be delivered easier and cheaper through an intranet system. All you need to get started is perhaps $500 worth of software, a few commonly available software tools, and a clear understanding of how web technology works (Figure 1.8).

Even more powerful, intranets promise to liberate many traditional mainframe and client-server applications by allowing easy access to data from any seat on the network. Instead of creating special programs to access your company's product database, for instance, you could quickly create a web front end that gives any user instant access at the click of a button. And you can do it on any platform: UNIX, PC, or Mac.

Various studies, have shown incredible return on investment for companies adopting intranet technologies (see results published on the web at home .netscape.com/comprod/announce/roi.html). In one case, International Data Corporation (IDC) studied seven major firms including Lockheed-Martin, Silicon Graphics, Southern California Gas, Deere & Company, and Booz-Allen & Hamilton. The findings showed massive ROI in nearly every case, with average returns above 1,000 percent and some as high as 2,063 percent. Clearly, seen purely as an investment, the intranet is a sure bet.

Visionary Applications

What does an intranet look like? In a typical intranet, there might be a human resources web server, a manufacturing web server, a legal department web server, an information systems (IS) web server—or even a web server for each team or employee who generates information of value to the corporation (some companies using this technology already have thousands of web servers

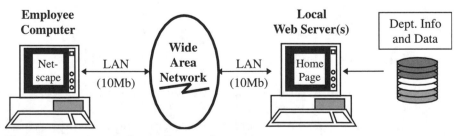

Figure 1.8   Typical intranet web setup.

installed throughout their organizations). A creative webmaster can weave all these different blossoming resources into a central home page with menus and access mechanisms that allow any user to easily browse unimpeded through the company's vast pool of information. Here are a few examples of potential applications:

- Mechanics in an aircraft hangar in Dallas view a drawing of a jet engine and click on any part of it to see detailed maintenance procedures for that part. The information they access is taken from the company's engineering web server in Seattle, where it is being updated daily with new information, including information captured from troubleshooting reports.

- A new employee clicks into a set of pages including an online company orientation seminar, job-specific training, and a follow-up quiz with results automatically graded and forwarded to the employee's electronic file in human resources.

- The company support center is automated, giving employees direct access to troubleshooting information. Instead of getting the information over the phone, they can retrieve it by searching the intranet, thus eliminating phone tag with the help desk and reducing the demand for live help-desk operators.

- The company distributes an online survey to employees nationwide, gathers the results automatically, and stores them in a database for further analysis.

- The company IS department provides a web front end to many of its legacy databases, allowing users to search for information or access computer reports online.

- The company legal department provides employee guidelines on important topics, such as sexual harassment in the workplace, drug testing, and so on.

- Recent addresses by company executives are made available online in text, audio, or video format to all company employees.

- Training videos and manuals are provided on demand through a web-based menu.

- The company sets up a special web server that dealers can access over the Internet. The server is set up to only accept requests specifically from authorized dealer locations, thus creating an extranet just for dealers.

Before the intranet, many such applications could only be created using a variety of online development tools, such as Microsoft Winhelp, Asymetrix ToolBook, and MacroMedia Director. But notice that now, all the listed applications can also be delivered to end users through an intranet web system. Instead of using all these different tools, the intranet solution allows you to put all of them on a single menu accessed through a common interface such as Netscape Navigator or Internet Explorer. Thus, web technology provides the first low-cost, easy-to-use, cross-platform, open standards–based, integratable technology that will allow users to access documents, data, multimedia, and applications through a single interface and do it randomly and universally, on a user-initiated basis, across an entire network.

The Other Shoe Dropping

In fact, the web-based intranet has become "the other shoe dropping" in the Internet revolution. While all the media attention has been focused on the Internet and World Wide Web, many companies have been quietly applying this technology behind closed doors, finding ways to improve internal communications and cut costs in the bargain. The web revolution behind the firewall has not gotten a lot of attention because often it is a grassroots effort led by a few visionary information technology (IT) managers, or applied scattershot by technically savvy employees with a passion for innovation.

One of the reasons for the grassroots nature of this change is the fact that web technology is based on open standards and often inexpensive (or free) tools that are not the proprietary product of a major hardware or software company. For this reason, intranets registered barely a blip on the radar of most corporate MIS departments during the early years of the World Wide Web revolution (1993–1995). The reasons this happened are easy to see. There was no sales force for intranets, as there was for Oracle, or Microsoft, or Lotus products. There were few schools or seminar courses where you could send staff members for training. And (at first, anyway) there were exactly zero squads of consultants from Anderson, Price Waterhouse, et al., swarming across the organization and urging upper management to pour millions of dollars into development of intranets, as they did for other, more lucrative proprietary client-server technologies.

Much has changed in the past few years. With the intranet bandwagon now fully under way, every software product seems to be "intranet friendly" and every grinning VAR salesman seems to be posing as an overt or covert intranet consultant.

Even with all this newfound commercial interest, however, most successful intranets still retain a bit of their original grassroots flavor. This is mainly because—to work properly—they must involve all parts of the organization. Even though the intranet is a computer system, the evolution and maintenance of an intranet can be—and often should be—handled by someone other than the usual crop of computer experts. If the intranet exists to help disseminate information produced by individual departments such as human resources, marketing, and accounting, then those departments will have to participate in building and maintaining it. MIS and its cohort of computer wizards can help, but they cannot possibly substitute for the day-to-day, hands-on development of core information that only the individual data-gathering departments can provide.

Fortunately, the nature of intranet technology doesn't require an MIS expert to make it work. Compared to other types of computer systems, intranets are not only relatively easy to build, they are relatively inexpensive, too. Most of the technologies involved in web development are not the kind of big-budget items that can make or break a departmental budget. They are often simple add-ons or extensions to existing products that make them capable of operating in a different way, like Microsoft's Internet Assistant, which lets Microsoft Word users save their documents in web-compatible format, or the TCP/IP networking features built into Windows 95 and 98. Some components—including web servers themselves—are freeware or shareware that can be tested and evaluated at no initial cost to the corporation.

Guilt by Association

By now, most cutting-edge MIS organizations are fully involved in the intranet fray. But it wasn't always so. Web technologies originally suffered from a poor reputation in the MIS community, because they were mainly known for their association with the wild and woolly Internet. A typical reaction came during a presentation I once gave to upper management of a midsized sales and supply firm. After hearing a half-hour talk on the potential internal applications for this new technology, the company CEO had one pressing question. "Is it *really true,*" he asked, his voice shaking with outrage, "that *children* can actually see *pornography* on the Internet?" The Internet's sordid reputation looms so large that it may be impossible to separate the raw technology from its most unflattering applications, in some peoples' minds.

Until recently, the only way an intranet could be built in a company was if someone took a keen interest in Internet technologies, had a gut feeling for the communications issues involved, had noticed the arrival on the market of these various software tools, and then had a vision of how to put them all together in a way that could facilitate the transfer of data and information across the enterprise. All of these elements had to coalesce first in the mind of an individual or team, and then the people involved had to sell it to management in a way that management could understand.

This, it turns out, still is the greatest hurdle for intranets: getting management to understand the concept, buy in, and accept the idea that the intranet will succeed only if it is treated as an empowering technology that nearly anyone can use to share information across networks. That's not to say that there should be no security controls for truly confidential data, or that all employees should be able to publish whatever they desire on a web server. But it does mean that only confidential information should be restricted, and that in most cases our networks should be opened for easier access and more fluid interdepartmental communication.

The successful implementation of an intranet requires a not-too-hard-to-perform, but occasionally difficult-to-understand paradigm shift in the way information flows across an organizational structure. And it often requires a vanguard team to be empowered in a way that cuts across feudal-era departmental structures. But more on this later.

Why the Web Works Better in Private

Despite the grassroots nature of the intranet webolution, the building of intranets on corporate networks has proceeded at a rapid pace. In fact, most companies that sell web-related software will confirm that the majority of sales are intranet—not Internet—related. If this is true, it indicates that *more computing power is likely being devoted to intranets than to the World Wide Web itself.* Studies consistently show that well over half the corporations in America—and a fair amount of their counterparts in other countries—are already in the process of building their intranets.

When you think about it, private networks are a far better place to use web technology than the World Wide Web itself. Unlike the Internet, where you quickly run up against the brick wall of low-bandwidth consumer modems, corporate LANs have a bandwidth many times greater (10 to 100 Mbps for the typical network interface card, versus 14.4 to 56 Kbps for the average consumer modem). That means not only that text and graphics can move faster through the corporate pipeline, but that it is a bit more practical to serve up exotic content types, such as sound, video, Java applets, and Adobe Acrobat files.

Of course, network bandwidth is always at a premium, even on private networks. There may be a concern from management that web traffic—and especially multimedia traffic—might unduly burden an already overtaxed network infrastructure. And you ain't heard nothing yet: Wait until your company begins to stock up on network computers (NCs) that download their operating systems and applications from the network rather than storing information on local hard drives.

But this is a case where costs and benefits must be carefully scrutinized and weighed fairly against each other. If management hasn't realized it yet, they should be made aware of one important fact: In the future the network will increasingly be the lifeblood of business, and it will have to evolve rapidly to support the advanced modes of communication the new technologies will deliver. For a major organization, this is as important to the business infrastructure as the freeway is to the regional economy. Without the proper infrastructure in place, an organization cannot prosper and grow.

To accommodate these new technologies, networks will have to be rescaled accordingly and grow with the traffic, just as desktop systems have advanced from the dumb terminals and 640KB RAM computers of the early 1980s to the powerful workstations we have today. Any technology that helps shift us from a paper-based model to an online model should be given all the support it needs, because the potential for cost savings is astounding (as shown by the examples later in this chapter).

Admittedly, bandwidth over 10 Mbps was prohibitively expensive for years, but 100 Mbps Fast Ethernet technology is now competitively priced, and is quickly becoming the standard on many corporate networks. Many companies are also evaluating Asynchronous Transfer Mode (ATM) and new Gigabit Ethernet technologies that will increase bandwidth exponentially. So, if your company has to invest to upgrade its network, it may find that the savings and productivity gains brought about by intranets will make it worth the cost and effort.

Unlike some older technologies, web publishing applications may actually *reduce* the drain on network resources because the file size of web documents is typically much smaller than their desktop publishing or compiled online counterparts. Remember that web technology was originally optimized for transport over the much slower public networks of the early 1990s. So the typical web document is stored in a plain text (ASCII) format without the spare baggage of traditional binary file formats such as Microsoft Word and FrameMaker, or even Winhelp and Acrobat. Web-compatible graphics likewise also are stored in the highly compressed GIF and JPEG formats, which are 10 to 100 times more compact than their BMP, PCX, XWD, TIFF, or EPS cousins. As an additional benefit, installing an intranet significantly reduces the number of redundant copies of information across a network. With web server technology, only one copy of the information is needed for distribution companywide.

Unfortunately, some corporate networks are not much more homogenoous than the Internet itself, supporting an unwieldy mix of PCs, Macs, and UNIX workstations. On an intranet, however, you have a better shot at creating an integrated system by developing specifications, standards, and preconfigured installations. You can create templates and style sheets for web authoring, develop a coherent structure for managing the information flow, and automate much of the process of gathering, converting, and distributing information.

For example, you could conceivably specify that everyone on the intranet use a certain version of a certain type of browser, such as the latest version of Netscape Communicator or Internet Explorer. If they don't have the software, you could easily supply them with it. Through a network-based installation utility, you could also include other needed advanced components, such as Adobe Acrobat or RealAudio plug-ins. Once everyone is on the web, you could easily broadcast announcements as system requirements change and provide users with new software components they can download directly through the web browser.

In fact, many of the problems associated with creating the right mix of software for users are addressed directly by the network computers (NCs) and NetPCs being promoted by Sun, Microsoft, and other vendors. With these network-based computers, the end user's desktop software and configurations can be updated on the fly by a remote server on the network. Microsoft also has developed a Zero Administration Windows (ZAW) standard that will perform some of the same functions under Windows NT.

Regarding the potential for security problems, there's no doubt that security is easier to deal with on an intranet than on the Internet, since most intranet users are easily identified internal employees of the company. Of course, sabotage is easier from within than from without, but it is less likely to happen in a controlled environment where the perpetrator's job is at stake.

Most intranets I've seen are open to all comers, with little concern for hiding or protecting any of the data that is served, unless it is demonstrably confidential. That in itself is a powerful indicator of the conceptual paradigm shifts that web technology can bring to an enterprise, opening up the system and exposing to light all the dark, secret corners of the organization.

"We're opening up silos," is how one intranet builder puts it—and that's exactly how it is. At last, an intranet can be used to exhume all those old disk drives and filing cabinets and expose long-hidden information to the light of day. Although there are proprietary data sources that must be protected within an organization, such as customer records and employee files, it is also quite possible to design a web system where confidentiality is fully protected.

Toward a More Well-Rounded Business Model

Putting intranet applications at the forefront of its web agenda—and recognizing their value—is the first step your organization can take toward developing a more well-rounded business model. As mentioned earlier, current web business models focus on the World Wide Web and customer-centered applications, which is great, because customers really *should* be the central focus of any business. But the model is a bit lopsided when you consider all the other ways web technology can be used within the enterprise.

When you look at the whole picture, then consider the Internet as just a component of the overall web system, you have a better chance of restoring balance to the business model, as shown in Figure 1.9. The complete model takes into account not only the customer but all the other players who can benefit from better communication with the core of an enterprise, including employees, dealers, and suppliers.

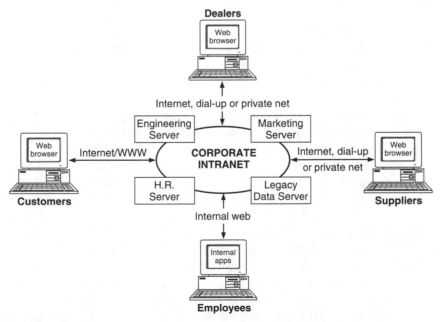

Figure 1.9   A balanced business communications model.

As this model shows, instead of having a single server devoted to customer-oriented marketing applications, the organization might have a group of low-level servers created by different departments of the company to open their channels of information to the rest of the enterprise. At some higher level within the web management structure, the system would be configured so that data from the various servers could be funneled off through different channels to the appropriate constituent groups that have a stake in the organization.

For instance, most human resource data would go only to employees—except job listings, which might be publicized both internally over the LANs and externally over the Internet. Marketing data might be mainly targeted to dealers and customers, but also could be used by employees internally for reference. Transaction processing systems and IS legacy data could be brought into the loop to provide automated information on current business operations to anyone who needs it—with appropriate safeguards to keep parts of it out of the hands of unauthorized users. External Internet access could be provided to employees for researching business topics or competitor information. And internal access could be provided to external users.

An Example: How Web Technology Saves Publishing Costs

Companies that use web technology to distribute documents may experience momentous gains in productivity and incredible cost savings. As with the reengineering craze that has marked the other half of the client-server revolution, converting many paper-based systems to web systems can save both labor and overhead costs within an organization.

Take the simple example of distributing a company policy and procedures manual to employees. Some companies distribute tons of them—enough to fill an entire bookshelf. Typically, the author creates the manual using a program like Microsoft Word, saves it to disk, then prints a master copy on a laser printer.

That is just the beginning of a labyrinthine process that would make Rube Goldberg blush. The master copy is sent to the local repro center or an outside company for printing, where hundreds of copies are made. After the document goes through the printing process, it still may need special collating, binding, or handling. Often it is shrinkwrapped, stuffed into a three-ring binder, and boxed for delivery (Figure 1.10).

Of course, someone must prepare an address label for each box, sort the boxes by delivery zone, and then send them off to be delivered through the company's internal mail system, the national postal system, or a private carrier such as UPS. The end result is that the individual manuals are *hand car-*

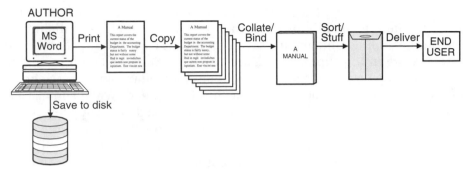

Figure 1.10　Traditional document distribution.

ried—across the building, across town, across the nation, or around the world—to the individual employees who need them.

When these documents reach their destination, what happens then? The manual goes straight onto the shelf, where it may or may not be consulted for days, weeks, or months. Since your company doesn't ever stand still or quit improving its operations, procedures keep changing and soon the manual is out of date. Going through an update cycle starts the whole process over again—still with no guarantee the information is being used.

Meanwhile, look at all the effort and cost—all the paper used and time spent by the mail room and repro center, not to mention your own time and effort—on the chance that the user *might* need this material.

If you've passed the recycling bin on your floor lately, you've seen the logical result of many such efforts. In some companies, the recycling bins are getting to be the size of small Volkswagens. This is great, because it finally brings the problem out in the open and makes obvious to everyone the absurd amounts of paper we are wasting *on the contingency* that someone might have the time or interest to read what we have to say.

The Alternative: Instant Document Delivery

Of course, many forward-looking companies have already discovered the benefits of electronic distribution using advanced media and tools such as Win-Help, Adobe Acrobat, and others. But intranets offer a new dimension to the online equation, going beyond traditional electronic publishing to integrate documents, multimedia, data, and applications into a dynamic cross-platform environment that bridges the gap between the worlds of PCs, Macs, and UNIX machines—and does it all from a single server on the network.

With an intranet (to continue the previous example), the author can still create the document using Microsoft Word or any other desktop-publishing tool. But as soon as the document gets saved to disk, it can be immediately accessible to anyone in the company (Figure 1.11). Joe Schmoe down in engineering can pull it up on his screen and read it anytime he wants to. Jill Schmill in cost subaccounting can read it when she has the time, or when she has a special question. If Joe prefers to read it on a printed page, he can print it on the spot. And if Jill finds the information useful and wants to add an excerpt to one of her memos, she can save a copy to disk or cut and paste at will.

The only difference is that when the author saves the final document, it's saved in a web-compatible format using (for example) the Save As feature in Microsoft Word. And instead of saving the document just anywhere on disk, it's saved in a directory managed by a *web server*—a background process that allows anyone to access the file over the network using a *web client* (also called a *browser*) such as Internet Explorer or NetscapeNavigator. The server is just a piece of software that handles the job of serving documents across the network. It could be easily installed on a special dedicated machine, or even on the author's local hard drive.

Individual users do not have to be set up or configured to "see" the web server as a local drive mounted on their computer, because the web browser can automatically find the information no matter where it's located on the network. So you can hire new employees in the Seattle office and no one has to remember to connect them to every web server in the company (no more than Internet users need to be configured to see each of the thousands of web servers on the World Wide Web). The employee just starts the browser, selects the manual from a menu, and there it is.

Meanwhile, the author can update the manual anytime, and as soon as changes are made and saved to disk, they are immediately visible to anyone reading the document *at that moment.* You don't have to worry whether Joe or Jill bothered to snap their changes into their three-ring binders, because they don't have three-ring binders anymore. The information exists online and no

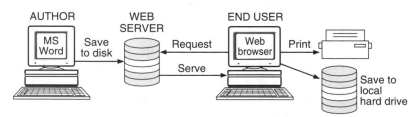

Figure 1.11　Web-based document distribution.

longer needs to be printed. So basically, you can achieve the same goal as before—getting information from the author to the end user—but without using all that paper, ink, and mail-room time or without worrying whether users have the correct server access.

But look what also happens when you start "serving" documents instead of printing and mailing them. Suddenly you've gone from an information delivery model based on *chance* to one based on *demand.* (You might also say that you've gone from a model based on "supplier push" to one based on "customer pull.") Instead of supplying information to people *just in case* they need it, you're making the information available *when they actually need it,* which could be immediately (i.e., as soon as you save it to disk), next week, or maybe never.

If you still want to follow the push model, however, there are now technologies that let you do that too, including the Netcaster feature in Netscape Navigator and the Channel Definition Format (CDF) in Internet Explorer. Thus, you can still deliver documents to users without them asking, but you can do it online so that no paper is wasted if the user ignores the document (although the push model is typically reserved for smaller documents, such as an announcement indicating a new version of the manual is available online at such-and-such a URL location).

If you take this simple example and multiply it times all the manuals, reports, and newsletters your company produces, imagine the tremendous savings in cost, time, and previously wasted resources. Some companies produce literally tons of technical manuals, procedures, specifications, work instructions, and training materials that end up doing little more than taking up space on people's shelves. Imagine sweeping all those shelves clean and making the information available to people online—*whenever* they need it. We are not talking just the cost of a few reams of paper. We are talking major savings in time, money, and frustration.

The question then becomes: If we can publish information universally over a corporate network, what further use do we have for the three-ring binder or the copy machine? If we can publish material cross platform from a single server, what use do we have for platform-specific tools like WinHelp? If we can update online and provide all users with network connections, why limit ourselves to a static version on a CD-ROM? If we can serve compact HTML and other file types through the same browser, why limit ourselves to Acrobat's proprietary file format? If we can serve data and online forms, why use Lotus Notes?

Although there are valid and specific reasons for using any or all of these other tools, the fact is that intranets now give us a single technology that can replace all of them with a single nonproprietary solution that in some ways can be more powerful—and that certainly is more flexible.

Of course, there are things WinHelp and Acrobat can do that the typical web browser cannot. And of course there are things Lotus Notes (and its Domino cohort) can do that the typical web server cannot. But overall, intranets provide the best overall solution for a wide range of publishing and data-sharing problems within the enterprise. And, increasingly they are the conduit for all those other applications.

Interestingly, tools such as Notes, Winhelp, and Acrobat have all been changed radically by the emergence of the intranet. Notes has become highly web friendly, interfacing with the Web and the intranet through its own Domino server platform. Acrobat long ago became a "plug-in" for the Netscape browser and a browsing companion for Internet Explorer. And Winhelp is being replaced by new web-based online help paradigms called *NetHelp* and *HMTLHelp.*

Another Example: The Living Catalog

The globe is dotted with supply houses and sales organizations that daily conquer incredible obstacles in an effort to peddle their wares across broad expanses of territory. Take, for example, a nationwide U.S. distributor of laboratory supplies I once advised. This company was typical in that it spent several million dollars every few years to print a 400-page, full-color catalog of all the products it sold.

The catalog was typed into a publishing program called *PageMaker,* which was used to create a master layout for the book. The typeset pages went to a printing company, where each picture was put through a color separation process, inserted manually into a layout, and burned onto hundreds of printing plates. The book was then printed, cut, collated, bound, shrinkwrapped, stuffed into boxes, and loaded onto trucks headed for the company's activity centers nationwide. From there, stacks of the catalogs were loaded into the car trunks of company salespeople, who went out on the road and hand delivered them to individual customer sites.

The interesting part of this scenario is that these incredibly expensive catalogs were already out of date the minute they went to press. Product prices could change weekly or monthly, and items were continually being added to or dropped from the company's available inventory. By the time the book reached the customer, it was grossly inaccurate. And yet it sat on the shelf for another two years, serving as the customer's main reference to the company's products and prices until the next catalog could be compiled and printed.

Not surprising, a large amount of the company's telephone-based customer support effort went into answering questions about product availability and pricing. So, in addition to the millions of dollars spent on catalog printing, you could add the millions of dollars spent on telephones and customer service operations as the total financial penalty for using this incredibly inefficient system.

My client was no different from hundreds of other sales and supply firms operating in the U.S. Indeed, in their basic mode of doing business, they were virtually indistinguishable from any company that carries inventory, publishes catalogs, and maintains a sales force. Yet all of these companies are ripe for change, specifically change in the direction of web-based electronic commerce. And many of them are already headed in that direction.

There are many examples of this kind of electronic commerce today on the World Wide Web. Check out the Dell web site or Gateway 2000, for instance, if you need a computer. Go to Software.net if you want to buy software, or Amazon.com to buy a book. What is striking is not that there are plenty of good examples on the Web, but how relatively *few* examples there are. Even with home computer users and business users turning to the Web in droves, with web tools on every desktop and on every salesperson's laptop, with modems and wide area networks proliferating like crazy—the fact that so many companies are moving so slowly in this direction continues to amaze me.

The true benefit to a business from this sort of transaction model is not so much the way it makes things more convenient on the *customer's* end, but the way it helps improve internal processes of the *business itself.* These new technologies allow a business to reengineer the entire process of information gathering and delivery to make things incredibly more productive and manageable.

In the case of the lab supply firm, for example, instead of locking catalog data inside of PageMaker files, which can only be used by layout artists, the same data could be collected in a relational or object database that could be continually edited and maintained online by the company's product managers. The database would be stored on a computer accessible to the web-server software, so that information could be transferred directly from the database to the web server, and from there across the network to end-user web browsers.

As the information leaves the database and proceeds to the customer, each field could be wrapped in codes that cause the entire page to display in an appropriate format inside the customer's web browser (Figure 1.12). In effect, the customer would be looking at a fully formatted "catalog page" that had been assembled and published on the fly from the company's product data repository. The fact that the information is so fresh and hot off the press means

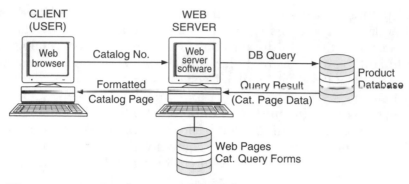

Figure 1.12   Catalog page retrieval process.

fewer calls from customers to verify pricing and availability. So, not only could the company save millions of dollars on catalog printing and delivery costs, it could also scale back its customer support burden, cut back significantly on sales calls, avoid the wasted effort dealing with orders for nonexistent inventory, and keep happier customers in the bargain.

And what about all those salespeople, still wandering about purposefully out in the field? Many companies are finding that they can connect them back to the home base through an extranet. For most of this decade, many companies have given their mobile sales forces the ability to dial in via modem and download information from company servers, including custom-programmed, client-server applications such as Oracle databases and Lotus Notes repositories. The Internet and web technologies add a new dimension to this equation.

With the Internet, field sales reps who work remotely can connect over long distances at much lower cost than the traditional remote phone call using toll-free numbers or direct distance dialing. With new *tunneling protocols* being adopted, it is also possible for authorized mobile workers to surf directly through the company firewall to access data and documents deep within the corporation.

Lessons Learned from the Internet

As you can see from these examples, there are many ways to apply web technology to business problems, and you will learn about more of them as you progress through this book. It should be obvious by now that both Internet and intranet technologies will have a major impact on the way we use corporate networks. The results of this transformation will be interesting, because modern corporations can learn a lot from the Internet and its culture. What the Internet can teach private business, among other things, is:

- How to integrate diverse types of information online in a multimedia environment
- How to finally achieve the much-heralded but yet-to-be-seen "paperless office"
- How to conduct sales and business transactions automatically, without human intervention
- How to design and implement systems that encourage collective action
- How to create collaborative structures that transcend corporate or governmental boundaries
- How to leverage proprietary business knowledge and consulting expertise for external use, business promotion, and financial gain

Models for all these applications already exist in embryonic form on the Internet and in various sectors of the business world. This book shows you how to bring these to the forefront and provide new paradigms for business reengineering well into the twenty-first century.

Where Do We Go from Here?

To fully understand the benefit of intranets, it's best that you understand how web technology is a natural progression from many of the old technologies and how it fits into the current thinking on client-server applications. Chapter 2 starts at the beginning and gives you a technological grand tour that will bring you up to speed on web technology from a business applications point of view.

Chapter Two at a Glance

Many people have a hard time understanding the true value of web technology because they don't understand all its components. Some understand the publishing part, others the network and programming parts, still others the communication and information management parts. But few understand the whole picture. This chapter reviews the trends in management and information technologies that have transformed business over the past two decades, and shows how each component of web technology is a natural outgrowth of these trends. In particular, you will learn:

- How the PC revolution changed the way we manage information
- How the business management revolution helped foster teamwork and information sharing
- How the revolution in desktop and online publishing made it possible for the average person to do sophisticated publishing on paper and online
- How the networking revolution made it possible to share remote computer resources, including files and servers
- How the client-server revolution made it possible to share data and applications across a network
- How the Internet revolution helped expand the coverage of information systems while reducing the administrative burden
- How web technology and the intranet combine all these trends into a single phenomenon and a single solution by inverting the traditional client-server models, opening up network access, and reducing network administration

By learning all these different aspects of information technology, you will be in a better position to evaluate and use intranets as a possible solution to various common business problems.

Understanding the Technology Issues

The dawn of the Information Age happened a long time ago by today's hyperactive standards. And it's only nanoseconds since the World Wide Web was invented. But already, it's high noon on the infobahn and things are getting hotter by the minute, with new technologies coming down the pike at an alarming rate of speed. With so much to learn and so much to evaluate, how do you separate the valuable technologies from all the drivel?

The question is especially crucial in light of phenomena such as the Internet and World Wide Web, which are clearly unlike anything ever seen before. The problem is not just "How does it work?" but especially, "How can you use it to do productive work in a business environment?"

Technology has always been this way, it seems. Perhaps you've heard the story about Alexander Graham Bell and his rival Elisha Gray, who both invented the telephone (independently) at about the same time in the latter half of the nineteenth century. The reason we remember Bell—but not Gray—is because he correctly predicted that people would use telephones to talk, while Gray figured he had just invented a better version of the telegraph. For that error, Gray sank into the mire of history, while Bell went on to stardom. Yet even Bell, with all his vision, could not have imagined the incredible phone networks of the late twentieth century, with integrated fax, cellular, videoconferencing, voice, and paging services.

Web technology is a lot like that. When it first started out, it was intended—and most people perceived it—primarily as a way to share information across the Internet. But others saw that you could use it on private networks, too. Many saw it as a way to serve "home pages" with documents, text, and graphics. Others saw it as a front end for multimedia, data warehouses, and more. Like the argument between Bell and Gray, it's an incredible telegraph, but it's one heck of a telephone, too. You can use it on the Internet, intranet, or extranet.

Anyone who's worked with this technology for a while knows that it is incredibly deep, and we have just begun to imagine all the ways we may eventually use it. Just as the old crank telephone was the precursor to the modern fax, PBX, and pager, so the webs of today are still just rough kludges of tomorrow's cutting-edge information technologies.

Despite all its depth, web technology at its core is not that complex. In fact, the reason for its power and popularity is that it simplifies the process of sharing information across networks, regardless of the computer platform. In fact, this is the one technology that finally brings it all together and gives anybody a way to serve practically *any kind of information to anyone.* In a way, web systems help make possible the grand unification of all types of information, helping us blend documents, data, sound, pictures, movies, messages, and computer applications in ways we never imagined before.

Web is also the only technology to come along so far that simplifies the user's task down to the click of a mouse. You see something, you like it, you click on it. It's like a romp in the candy store. Designers have been working for years to make user interfaces this simple and friendly, to the point that some computers actually grin when they start up. But you can't get much simpler than a mouse click. This, in many ways, represents the end of the road in software design—the Holy Grail of information technology.

In fact, web technology is already changing the way we design computer interfaces. Just as desktop publishing made it possible for the average person to create professional-looking documents, web technology makes it possible for the average person to create actual computer applications that capture or display data.

To help you understand how we got to this point, and how web technology will take us beyond, let's take a tour of long-term trends in business and information technology. As you will see, web technology neatly ties together the loose ends of many developments of the last two decades and points the way to a very interesting future ahead. Even if you already understand a lot about the web technology, you will find the view completely different when you consider the business applications of the corporate intranet.

Revolutions of the 1980s

If you've watched the roller coaster ride of business over the past two decades, you can be excused for feeling a bit queasy. During that time, the modern corporation was wracked by a series of earth-shaking tremors that nearly tore it apart—yet paradoxically left it more sound and viable than ever before. In particular, several trends that began in the late 1970s and early 1980s caused major aftershocks that are still being felt well into the 1990s.

The first major revolution was the one that ushered in the personal computer. Until the PC came along, the computing world was dominated by the bulky leviathans called *mainframes* and the cabinet-sized *minicomputers.* These are the systems that inhabit everyone's nightmares and that—along with that monstrosity we call *DOS* (the early PC's *disk operating system*)—did as much as anything to make people fear and loathe computers.

The problem with mainframes and minis is that they were just this side of inscrutable. Anyone who held a job in the early 1980s can remember the phosphorescent green glow of the early CRTs, which often displayed nothing but mind-deadening rows of numbers. In fact, many people still operate traditional CRTs in anonymous cubicles throughout the corporate world.

The CRT was part of a unit called the *dumb terminal,* which in those days was the only way to communicate with the mainframe (Figure 2.1). These terminals were called dumb because most of the brain power, memory, and data storage was handled by the mainframe—the terminal just gave operators a way to type in the data and view it on the screen.

When the first PCs hit the desktop circa 1981, they were hailed as a force that would revolutionize business by putting incredible brain power on every user's desk. The PC was revolutionary because it united the useful elements of the big computers (processor, memory, disk storage) with the useful elements

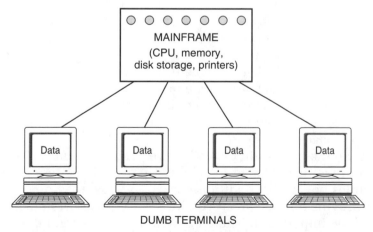

Figure 2.1   Mainframe with dumb terminals.

of the dumb terminal (keyboard, screen) and put it all into a single package that would fit on anyone's desk.

The problem with early PCs was that they were not brainy at all—in fact, they had barely enough power to do anything useful. The first PCs had one hundredth the memory and disk space found on the average home computer today. It wasn't until the development of powerful networked machines using a *graphical user interface* (GUI) that desktop computers finally started living up to their original promise and the PC revolution finally hit its stride.

Business compounded the problem by using the early desktop computers in clunky, unimaginative ways, such as using PCs as dumb terminals for mainframes. With special software called *3270 terminal emulation,* it was possible to create a mainframe display on a PC screen and use the PC keyboard just like the keyboard on a dumb terminal. It wasn't until networks and new types of software came along that we would find better and more productive ways to use the PC.

The Search for Management Formulas

Meanwhile, running concurrently with the burgeoning PC revolution, was a parallel *business management revolution.* Corporate managers began taking a new look at the way they did things, and questioning the standard business models of the past. Various schools of thought arose and vied for prominence on the corporate podium.

Two decades ago, the predominant business religion was management by the *bottom line.* As with everything else, it made sense at the time. In this line of thinking, companies were divided into cost centers, and each department or cost center was judged by its total contribution to the bottom line (that is, to the company's overall profitability).

The mid-1980s ushered in a new way of thinking about business called *total quality management* (TQM), a movement inspired by Japan's successful domination of the international market for autos and electronics. By the late 1980s, with a major recession brewing, western business started fighting back by giving Japan a dose of its own medicine—in effect mimicking many of Japan's own quality management practices.

The quality movement didn't exactly save business from all its follies, and many might argue that it failed to achieve many of its lofty goals. But it did help companies break with tradition, reexamine how they did business, and focus on improving discrete processes. More specifically, it helped companies understand how important it is to *empower employees* and improve the lines of communication between departments, and between the organization and its customers, suppliers, and dealers.

Remnants of the quality movement can still be seen in the current emphasis on interdisciplinary *teamwork* and *collaboration.* Not surprisingly, desktop computers fed these trends, networks catapulted them, and intranets can launch them into orbit.

The Growth of Desktop Publishing

While managers were wrestling with quality issues, yet another revolution was taking place—this one in the publishing arena. When I started my first job in the data processing department of a local company in 1972, we used IBM Selectric typewriters, Rapidograph pens, scissors, glue, and Scotch tape to deliver information to the end user. The office copying machine had just been invented but already was a major part of our effort. Back then, "cut and paste" really meant "cut and paste," and the final draft of a document might well look like one of the stabbing victims at the county morgue.

Over the years, our publishing tools changed rapidly and relentlessly with the development of new technologies. The typewriter gave way to the dedicated word processor, which succumbed to the PC word processor. PostScript was invented, and along with it laser printers and windows-based, desktop-publishing systems such as PageMaker, Interleaf, FrameMaker, and Quark.

The new publishing systems brought the ancient art of typesetting directly to the desktop. As recently as 1969, about the time the Internet was being invented, typesetting was still done using a clattering monster called a *Linotype machine,* that created a product called *hot type.* All the letters on a page were created by tiny molds arranged just so in a tray—upon which was poured a nice steaming batch of hot molten lead.

In the mid-1970s, if you wanted to change fonts in midsentence, you had to open the back of your phototypesetting machine, change a few gears and pulleys, wrap a different font strip around the drum, close the machine, go back to the keyboard, type a few words, then repeat the process all over again. By 1980, we had found ways to automate this process by putting font change and formatting codes into text like this:

```
[Single Space] [Helvetica,14] [bold on]
A Short Report on the Current State of Publishing [Return]
[Times Roman,10] [bold off]by Haiku Kirby[Return]
[Extra Leading 12 pt] [Times Roman,10]
Does this look confusing to you? It does to me, too! There
simply [italic on]must[italic off] be a better and easier
way to publish our documents.[Return]
```

Some popular word processors of the mid-1980s, such as WordPerfect, let you choose whether to hide or reveal the codes. But the result was still rather unenlightening, since you often had to guess how the final result might look on the printed page. There was a "preview mode" where you could see an approximation of the printed page on the screen, but you couldn't edit the text in preview mode. So formatting a document often involved a lot of switching back and forth between preview and editing modes.

One of the greatest advances in authoring technology was the development of WYSIWYG, which means "What You See Is What You Get." Instead of seeing a mess of codes as in the example above, or a monospaced approximation of the final printed result, you could see the document displayed on the screen exactly as it might finally look on the printed page. This seems like a no-brainer now, but it took years for character-based nonwindows applications like Word Perfect 5.1 to slowly disappear from the workplace.

The advent of WYSIWYG was helped by the development of PostScript and software font packages such as TrueType and Adobe Type Manager. These made it finally possible to do typesetting right on the screen. Instead of pouring on hot lead or projecting celluloid alphabetic images onto photosensitive paper, each alphabetic character could be molded individually and instantaneously out of the glowing phosphorescent pixels on a computer screen.

The Birth of Hypertext and Online Publishing

Once WYSIWYG arrived, it brought up an interesting new question. If you could make text look the same way on the computer screen as it does on the printed page, why use the printed page at all? Why not just publish it online and let people read it there? If you wanted to read it in printed format, you could still print it from the screen image. But if not, why bother?

Online publishing had other advantages, such as the ability to use a nifty new feature called *hypertext*. First proposed by Ted Nelson at Xerox PARC in 1965, hypertext was appropriately named because it is a good way of dealing with hyperactive readers. You can read it in a linear fashion like a book, or you can "jump around" reading it in bits and pieces like a puzzle. Key concepts can be highlighted in a such a way that when you click on the highlighted concept, it automatically jumps to a different document (or page) where the concept is discussed in greater detail (Figure 2.2).

Hypertext is great for tables of contents and indexes, because you can browse through them, click on the topic you want to read, and voilà! you're at the correct page. It's great for cross-references, too, because you don't have to

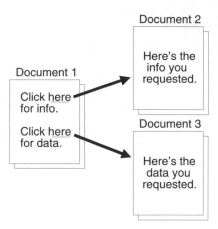

Figure 2.2   The concept of hypertext.

turn to page 42 anymore. You just click on the hyperlinked cross-reference and suddenly you are at page 42, the same way Mr. Spock used to step inside the flux capacitor and suddenly appear on the surface of the alien planet Remulak. (Okay, so I got *Star Trek, Back to the Future,* and *Saturday Night Live* a little mixed up—you get the idea.)

Hypertext started appearing on desktop computers in the early 90s, embedded directly into the operating system of PCs running Windows 3.1. The hypertext system for Windows was called *WinHelp* and is familiar to any PC user who has ever used the ubiquitous "online help system." (Macs had a similar utility called *HyperCard.*) Though it was designed to provide online help for PC-based programs, many people started using WinHelp to produce online newsletters, reports, manuals, and many other types of documents.

Since these tools were bundled with the operating system, they required no other special hardware or software to run. For example, if everyone in your company were running Windows, you could distribute a WinHelp file (.HLP), and they could open it and read it without installing special software on their computer. In a way, a WinHelp file was like a self-displaying document, since it contained not only the document content, but all the buttons and pull-down menus needed to browse through it (Figure 2.3).

The problems with WinHelp were several. First, formatting a document for display involved a final step where you have to run everything through a compiler, just as software developers do to their programming code. Even minor changes required completely recompiling the help file. To make things easier, third-party vendors created online publishing tools like Doc-To-Help and RoboHelp, which helped automate these tasks.

The other problem with WinHelp, of course, was that it only worked under Microsoft Windows. If everyone had a PC, that was great. But what if some

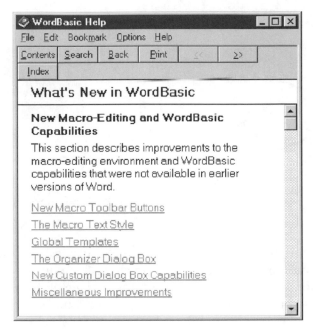

Figure 2.3 Typical WinHelp display.

people used a Macintosh and others had UNIX workstations? WinHelp and HyperCard suffered from a lack of what we call *cross-platform compatibility.* Systems running UNIX didn't even have a built-in online help feature (unless you count the incredibly rudimentary *manpage* utility).

The Move to Cross-Platform Technologies

The market always has an answer to every problem, of course, and it wasn't long before some companies started taking the cross-platform issues into account. In its heyday, Frame Technology Corporation (now owned by Adobe Systems) was one of the leaders in cross-platform connectivity for both desktop and online publishing. With Frame, you could create a desktop-published document on a UNIX workstation, copy the file to a floppy diskette, and then—incredibly—pop it into a PC or Mac and view or edit it with no (apparent) conversion involved.

FrameMaker, Interleaf, and others had their own *interchange formats,* which were plain-text (ASCII) representations of a document that could be moved easily between different versions of the software operating on different plat-forms. PostScript was similarly a *device-independent* printing language that consisted entirely of coded instructions stored as plain text.

FrameMaker was also advanced in the sense that you could create hypertext links and active push buttons directly on the document page. Just underline a word or phrase (or draw an invisible box over a graphic), insert a hidden marker telling where the link should jump, and voilà: hypertext. With a few keystrokes you could lock down the document, hide the regular FrameMaker menus, and create a neat little self-contained online document window, so that the desktop-publishing file and the online-publishing file often were one and the same (Figure 2.4).

Nothing is perfect, of course, and Frame was no exception. Though it beat WinHelp in the cross-platform category, it lost on ease of distribution. If you wanted to distribute your files to a wide audience, you had to buy each user a special tool called *FrameViewer,* which could be used to open, view, and print the online hypertext file—but not edit it. Still, this is better than nothing, as many online authors will readily admit. If all you have to deal with are strictly Macs or PCs, no problem. But in a UNIX or cross-platform environment, there were few alternatives to proprietary products like FrameViewer and Interleaf's WorldView.

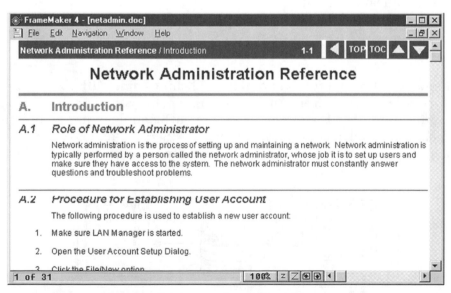

Figure 2.4   Example of FrameMaker help file.

The Viewer/Author Split

Though these products created an extra expense and added another layer of software to the configuration burden, it was a profoundly interesting development. With the advent of inexpensive tools like FrameViewer, software designers were starting to realize the need for a separation between two distinctly different functions: *authoring documents* and *viewing them online* (Figure 2.5).

Frame Technology, for instance, offered two distinctly separate products: FrameMaker as their main authoring tool, and FrameViewer as their online viewing tool—also known as a *browser.* Though you might pay $600 to $1,000 for a copy of FrameMaker with all its bells, whistles, and advanced editing features, you might pay only $30 for a copy of FrameViewer, which would let you directly view the finished document online but not edit it.

Other desktop-publishing products followed this model, in some cases offering a browser for free. In early 1995, for instance, Microsoft Corporation made available a free document browser called the *Microsoft Word Viewer.* This tool lets you open, view, and print (but not edit) Microsoft Word documents—even if you don't have a copy of MS Word on your machine. Theoretically, authors equipped with MS Word are no longer limited to the WinHelp system for online presentation. But, unlike WinHelp or even FrameViewer, the Word files viewed online using Word Viewer are just flat documents with no hypertext features at all.

The Tricks Performed by Acrobat

A more interesting approach to online publishing came with the release of a product called *Acrobat* from Adobe Corporation, the company that developed PostScript in the 1980s and purchased Frame Technology in the mid-1990s. The people at Adobe recognized that their PostScript technology had opened up the field of desktop publishing by providing a freely accessible, widely

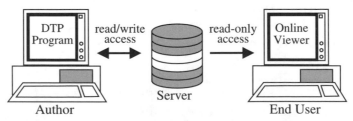

Figure 2.5   The author/viewer split.

available way to print richly formatted documents on any PostScript-enabled device. But PostScript documents were not easy to view online. The file sizes can be massive (especially when they include bit-mapped color graphics), and there was no support in the original PostScript language for hypertext.

To solve these problems, Adobe created a new file format called the *Portable Document Format* (PDF). Unlike PostScript, PDF is a highly compact online publishing format that includes hypertext features. So, as with WinHelp, you can view the .PDF document file online and also hyperlink from one file to another—including web pages.

The most useful aspect of PDF is that it makes it possible to go online from any kind of word processor or desktop-publishing program. To do this, you print the document using a special print driver furnished with the Acrobat Exchange program. The result is not a printed page, but a PDF file that you can view online using Acrobat Reader software (Figure 2.6). Another program called *Acrobat Distiller* lets you actually convert raw PostScript files to PDF. Various tools let you add hyperlinks to the final PDF documents, including hyperlinks to the World Wide Web.

Acrobat and its native PDF format are interesting because they represented the state-of-the-art in online desktop publishing about the time the World Wide Web exploded onto the scene. In fact, you might say the Web stole some of Acrobat's thunder, since it provides not only many of the features of Acrobat, but other useful features such as the ability to access *any* file type (including PDF). Intriguingly, Adobe seemed to be trying at first to position PDF as a possible replacement for the Web browser, but has since decided to coexist. Acrobat now includes plug-ins and controls that let Web users view PDF files *inside* the Web browser window.

The Networking Revolution

During the 1980s, while executives were inventing new management styles and PCs were proliferating like rabbits, more new technologies were emerging

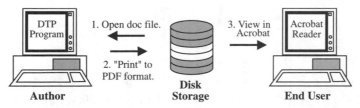

Figure 2.6   How Acrobat documents are converted and used.

that would profoundly change information technology. In particular, net-working technologies have probably done most to make desktop computers the machine of choice for any business application.

PCs and Macs were fine sitting on your desk, but unlike the old mainframe dumb terminals, they were isolated stand-alone machines—cut off from the central repository of data hoarded by the MIS department's gargantuan mainframes. Cut off, that is, until companies such as Apple and Novell found ways to connect desktop computers and mainframes into local area networks (LANs).

The LAN was a convenient way to connect machines on a single floor or in a small building. But a large organization might occupy dozens of floors in an office building, be spread out over a campus, or have geographically dispersed activity centers around the world. Each location might have its own LAN, but these were isolated from the rest of the organization until someone figured a way to connect them into a *wide area network* (WAN), as shown in Figure 2.7. Typically, this was done by simply leasing a line from the telephone company and hooking the LANs together through the leased-line connection.

The WAN made it possible to put the entire company on the same network, no matter how scattered its locations. The network could be spread across a state, a country, a continent, or around the world. Thus, it was possible for global multinational companies such as IBM, Digital, and Chevron to have their own private worldwide networks tying together business locations scattered across the face of the earth.

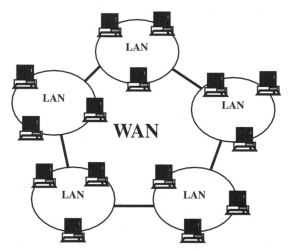

Figure 2.7 Wide area network (WAN) connecting LANs.

LANs and WANs made it possible for business to save money by letting widely dispersed desktop computers share expensive resources. The first things they shared were just hardware components like hard drives and printers. For example, instead of buying an expensive laser printer for each employee, the company might buy one expensive high-speed printer, connect it to a central *print server* on the network, and let groups of employees print to it the same way they might have printed to a local printer on their desktop. Companies also set up network drives or *file servers* that could be used to save data the same way you do on your local hard drive. Instead of being called *drive C,* the network drive(s) might be called *D, E, F, P, X,* or any other letter of the alphabet.

The diagram in Figure 2.8 shows a simplified view of a typical print/file server configuration. Notice that the applications using the server are all self-contained and are installed and run strictly on the users' local computers. The print or file server may not run any applications at all, except the utility programs that control the transfer of files to and from its disk drive(s) and printer(s). Notice also that this kind of setup implies that entire files would

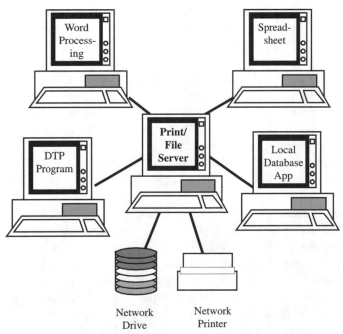

Figure 2.8　Typical print/file server configuration.

have to be shipped across the network from the user's desktop to the server before they can be printed or saved.

The creation of file and print servers begged the question: If you could share hardware such as printers and drives over a network, why not share software and data, too? Of course, it wasn't long before people found a way to do that. The result was a new kind of software application known as *client-server*.

The Client-Server Model

Client-server is a way of designing software that takes advantage of the ability to distribute data and processing chores across a network. And in fact, it is the technology that made the Internet and World Wide Web possible and so successful.

The idea with client-server is that, along with the data itself, you can spread out or "distribute" the pieces of software that handle the data. Even though different parts of an application are scattered across the network, they can still work together very much like a single stand-alone program used to do. (This isn't hard to imagine, since most stand-alone computer applications are just a group of different programs or *subroutines* masquerading as a single product.)

Compare the client-server setup to the file-server configuration discussed in the previous section. With a file server, you might run a database program on your local computer and save the files to the network drive. But this causes problems, since you need a powerful computer to run the database locally, and you must transport the database file en masse across the network every time you want to use it (slowing everybody else down in the process). Compared to client-server, this is a very inefficient way to run a network.

With client-server, instead of running a database locally on each user's machine, you could install the database application and data files on a remote networked computer, then let users access it remotely over the network, as needed.

This is what we mean by client-server. The main part of the application runs on a centralized *server* in another part of the network, and any user can control it using special *client* software designed for this purpose. Instead of transporting the entire database across the network for you to work on it, the server *sends just the parts you need,* and your client software displays them on the screen. If you change the records, your changes are sent back to the server for processing and inserted into the database. (The term *client* can refer to just the software that makes this possible or the entire combination of local machine, software, and user. Likewise, *server* can refer to just the application running on the remote machine or to the entire combination of machine, application, and database.)

In the diagram in Figure 2.9, notice that most servers have multiple clients, and some clients can be set up to access multiple servers. Thus, if you were using both Oracle and Lotus Notes, you would typically have one client program that works with Oracle and another to work with Lotus Notes. As you will see later in this chapter, this entire model may change significantly on an intranet, because you can use a single web client like Netscape or Internet Explorer to access both (see "The Web Browser as a Universal Client" later in this chapter).

In one fell swoop, client-server seemed to solve many of the problems of networked computing using desktop machines. Network traffic was reduced because large database files stayed in one place instead of being shunted across the network. Managers could spend their money on a few powerful servers instead of buying everyone the software, drive space, and computing power to run the full application locally. Centralizing the database made it easier to back up mission-critical data at the network level. In effect, client-server optimized both the network and the individual desktop computers running on it.

Better yet, client-server fit right in with the burgeoning management trend toward employee empowerment, teamwork, and collaboration. Client-server systems and networks became key elements in the *reengineering revolution* that took the business world by storm in the early nineties. Corporate planners found they could use these new systems to reengineer processes, eliminating many unnecessary steps—and jobs—along the way.

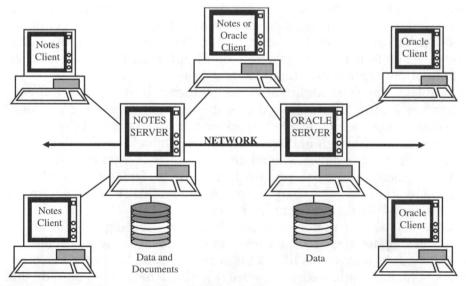

Figure 2.9   Client-server configurations.

The key concept with client-server is the idea of *distributing the work* and *sharing the resources.* Perhaps you've heard computer company slogans such as: "The network *is* the computer." What they mean is the business network has now become like a single giant computing organism with users, desktop machines, clients, and servers all interconnected and working in tandem. Instead of everyone toiling away at his or her own isolated workstations, everyone is now interconnected and sharing data, documents, and many other types of computer resources.

Groupware Emerges

Some of the newer client-server applications were called *groupware* because they fostered this sharing, collaborative approach to computing. *Groupware* is a nebulous term that has come to encompass everything from e-mail applications to databases. It is also one of the hotter buzzwords in some corners of the business world today.

In fact, it is the culmination of many trends in the business world over the past decade, particularly the trend toward empowering teams and work groups to take responsibility for business processes. For this reason, the groupware tag could probably be applied to any software that helps work groups communicate better, including e-mail, online forms, online databases, and common document repositories.

Many people see Lotus Notes as the quintessential groupware application. Notes combines a document database, a messaging system, and configuration tools that let users create their own custom business applications. Like web systems, it supports the custom design of fill-out forms that can be used across the network to capture user input to a database.

Probably the neatest trick that Notes performs, however—and apparently the hardest feature for others to duplicate—is a feat called *replication.* This means that users should be able to work on multiple copies of the same document or data and have all of their changes automatically reconciled across the network. Thus, for instance, you might take a copy of a group-authored document on a business trip with you, work on it on the airplane, then bring it back to the network, and your changes would automatically be reconciled in all other copies of the document in the network.

As the Web became popular and people started dabbling with intranets, one of the hot debates raging in the press and on the Web was whether or not intranets would make tools like Lotus Notes obsolete. A writer for *InfoWorld* intoned: "Eight months ago, there were ten things that Notes could do that the Web couldn't do, now that is down to two." Even IBM, which purchased

Lotus just three months earlier, hosted its own networking forum in which one panelist asked: "Is the Web going to be the death of Lotus Notes?" The predictions haven't panned out, but only because Lotus "embraced and extended" the web with its new Domino server.

The World's Biggest Client-Server Experiment

Amid all these trends, the growth of the Internet turned out to be an experiment in collaborative client-server computing on a global scale. That's because all the major applications that run on the Internet—including the World Wide Web—are based on the same client-server model used by industry-leading applications like Oracle and Lotus. To understand why this is so, you have to understand a little bit about the history of the Internet.

As far back as the late 1960s, during the dark days of the Cold War and especially in response to the launch of the Russian satellite called Sputnik, the U.S. government was looking for a way to counter a perceived Soviet superiority in science and technology. One result of its efforts was the Advanced Research Projects Agency (ARPA), an arm of the Department of Defense that sponsored many projects, among them a search for ways that defense researchers could share computer time and data over packet-switching networks. A key concept of the new networks was "survivability"—the idea that data packets could become self-routing in such a way that they could find their way around any gaps or outages in the network. This technique is now embodied in a network protocol called *TCP/IP,* which lies at the core of the present-day Internet.

ARPA's first stab at such a network was called the *ARPAnet,* naturally enough. When it first started in 1969, this fledgling network connected only four universities: Stanford, Utah, and two branches of the University of California. Within a couple of years, the number of connected organizations had increased tenfold, to 40.

Based in part on the ARPAnet model, other special-purpose networks formed over the next two decades, with names like Bitnet, CSnet, Usenet, FidoNet, NSFnet, and CompuServe. But it wasn't until the early 1980s that they began connecting these expanding networks so that data and messages could be shared freely among them. As these networks began to merge, they formed the beginnings of what we now call the Internet.

In this sense, the Internet is simply an agglomeration of different networks that once existed on their own but now are all connected (Figure 2.10). When you think about it from a business perspective, you might say all these different networks were like separate, isolated LANs until someone connected them into the WAN called the Internet. In this sense also, any WAN could be

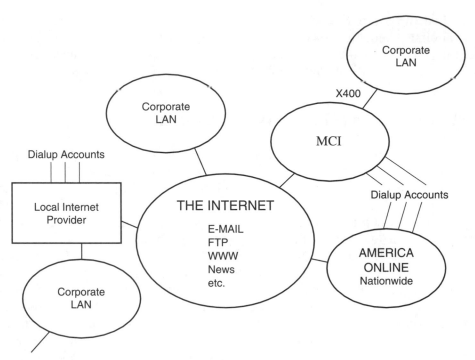

Figure 2.10   The Internet as a group of networks.

considered an internet, because it connects various subnetworks into a unified system. But if the WAN exists solely inside a private company, it's more likely to be called an *intranet.*

Connecting networks into an internet or intranet typically doesn't affect the way people work inside each of the individual subnetworks. It just makes it possible for them to communicate freely with others across the internet or intranet. It's similar to the idea of placing a phone call between different regions of the United States or different parts of the world. Though each region is served by a different telephone company, the local networks are all connected so that the call goes smoothly from a point on one regional network to a point on a different regional network.

The same thing happened in late 1994 when companies such as CompuServe and America Online connected their private networks to the Internet. Now, people who subscribe to America Online can exchange messages with other Internet users. And, when they do, the Internet serves as the bridge between the two systems. The same thing happens every day as more and more individual companies link their own private intranets to the global Internet. When that happens, the people in those companies can send messages to anyone else with an Internet hookup, including not only America Online subscribers but also people who are connected to the Internet through accounts at home or work.

We Pause for This Important Message

Before we go any further, there are a few key points you need to remember about the Internet. I put these here to help avoid some of the most common misconceptions people have about the Internet.

The Internet is nothing but a bunch of wires. The Internet consists of various backbone segments, which are the high-speed core of the network, and many subnetworks that connect to companies, educational and governmental institutions, online services such as America Online, Internet Service Providers, and through them to home users. But at its core, the Internet is nothing but wires: data paths connecting computers, the same way wires connect your computer to others in your local area network at the office.

The Internet would be nothing without applications. It's not the idea of wires that's important. It's what we *do* with the wires. It's the fact that the wires allow us to communicate between computers using applications like e-mail, file transfer, newsgroups, and the World Wide Web. In that sense, any set of wires that look and act like the Internet—including your office network—can run the same set of applications we currently use on the Internet. More about this later.

Nobody "runs" the Internet. The individual networks that came together to form the Internet were based on a decentralized, collaborative model in which each network node is a *peer* to all the others. There *are* administrative organizations controlling individual subnetworks, and there is an organization that handles domain name registrations, but all these administrative structures are quite loosely organized and under no type of central control. What's more, parts can be added without having to reconfigure the whole system. And individual messages or data files exchanged between computers can find their way from source to destination automatically, on their own, without requiring an administrator to make sure the two computers are connected or that the data successfully reached its destination. I call this a *self-administering net-*

work. In some ways, it's like a self-replicating, self-sustaining metabiological organism. Come to think of it, this may not be a bad way to organize our intranets, too.

How Computers Talk to Each Other

The whole purpose of the Internet is to support independent communication between computers. To understand how this works, you need to understand how a network operates and how computers communicate. Every type of communication—whether people-based or network-based—requires a *protocol* to support it.

When you make a phone call, for instance, you always follow a well-known protocol. First, you dial the number and make a connection. The person on the other end answers the phone by saying "Hello." You greet the person, state your name and the reason for your call. Then, you take turns speaking until you're through. Finally, one person says "Good-bye," the other says "So long," and you both hang up.

Of course, the more complex the communication, the more protocols may be involved. Imagine the mass of protocols that surround the meeting of high-level delegations at the UN. There are different protocols for the heads of state, the negotiating teams, the translators, the limo drivers, and so forth. Everybody knows what to say, what not to say, when to shake hands, when to bow, and when to all start dancing.

On a computer network, there may be dozens of protocols operating simultaneously. One protocol controls the physical transmission of electronic signals. Another opens and closes sessions between the chatting computers. Another controls the way data is packaged and handled. Each component of the transaction bows, pauses for a nanosecond, then takes a turn in the dance. These things happen whether the communication occurs on a private LAN or on the Internet.

The key protocol for Internet communication is called *TCP/IP,* which stands for *Transmission Control Protocol/Internet Protocol.* This sounds excruciatingly technical, but it's not hard to understand.

> **TCP handles the packaging and reassembly of data.** It splits large messages or data files into smaller *packets* or *datagrams* that can be sent across the network more easily and independently. Each datagram has a size and sequence number stamped on it, so that the computer at the other end will know how large the packet is and where it fits in the puzzle.

IP creates the "envelopes" which carry each datagram to its destination. On each envelope, it stamps the address of the computer sending the message and the address of the computer that must receive it.

Each datagram is like a paper airplane that one computer wafts toward the other. Once released, each packet must find its way to the target on its own, the way salmon find their way upstream. This happens whether the communication occurs on the real Internet or on the internal kind. It is also employed regardless of the type of data or application that you use.

The process is helped along by intelligent machines called *routers.* A router contains an internal map of the network, recognizes where the packet is headed, and does its best to send it down the shortest or fastest route to its destination. All of this happens so fast and seamlessly, it looks as though the two computers simply connect, exchange data, and disconnect.

TCP/IP communications are not limited to the Internet. This is a native protocol that has been used in UNIX-based networks for years, and later appeared on other platforms such as PC and Mac. Once you have TCP/IP capability on a network, it is possible to run any of the Internet applications discussed later in this chapter.

Calling All Computers

The only part of the TCP/IP you may encounter in your daily life is the IP part. Occasionally, when you are using the Internet or an intranet, you may have to use an IP address to make a connection between two computers. What does this address look like? Well, it looks a lot like a telephone number—and works like one, too.

For instance, when you call a friend in Paris, you dial a number like this, which includes a country code and a city code:

`011-331-8765-4321`

The phone system uses this number to locate the instrument you're calling and make it ring. Likewise, every computer on the Internet (there are millions) also has a unique "phone number" (IP address) that looks something like this:

`193.10.128.45`

So if you want to connect to a computer and send it data, the IP address plays a key role in making the connection.

To make things simpler, computers also use unique monikers called *domain names.* For example, on the Internet, a computer named *sam.abc.com* might be the computer named *sam* at the ABC Corporation. On an intranet, the computer named *cust-serv* might be the database server in customer service.

Domain names were invented to make computer addresses easier to memorize, the same way people use catchy phrases on their license plates. For example, it's much easier to remember *cust-serv* than *193.10.128.45*, even though both refer to the same computer. If you have a choice between using a name or a number, which would you pick? Of course, whenever a domain name is available, few people bother with the IP address.

Even better, the domain name can refer to a permanent logical function rather than a specific computer. So if the customer service data moves to a different computer (at a different IP address), you might still be able to refer to it as *cust-serv,* assuming the network routers are reprogrammed correctly.

What Is an Internet Application?

So far I've talked a lot about how computers communicate, but *what do* they communicate? When we say that networks were created to share data, what exactly is it they share?

Think again of the phone system. When you use the phone system, you are connecting two instruments and using them to exchange information. What type of information? Well, anything encoded as sound. This might be the sound of two people talking, the sound of your company's Muzak lulling a customer to sleep, the warbling of a fax machine as it transmits bitmaps across the line, or the squalling sound of a computer modem as it converts data to sound. In a way, you might think of sound as data, but it is *analog data.*

A data network, on the other hand, is primarily organized to handle *digital data,* which is usually transmitted as discrete packets or datagrams. Typically, the data has a certain length, a beginning and an end. Data can be stored in files on the server end or the client end. The bursts of data transmitted across the network may be in the form of messages or files, but also can include random *character strings* or *commands.* The files you transmit can contain anything you want to share with other people, including messages, documents, graphics, sound, video, and more. How do you share it? On a network, this is typically done using a client-server application. And there are different client-server applications for sharing different kinds of data.

Remember that, on the traditional stand-alone desktop computer, you use specific programs to handle specific applications. You use a word processor to create documents, a spreadsheet program to create financial statements, an accounting program to do billing, and so forth. Likewise, various programs were developed that help people transmit data across Internet-style networks. The most common ones are listed in Table 2.1.

TABLE 2.1   Internet Applications

Application	Protocol	Software Used	What It Does
E-mail	Simple Mail Transfer Protocol (SMTP)	Mail server, mail client (e.g., Eudora, Netscape, IE)	Transfers messages from one computer to another.
Newsgroups	Net News Transfer Protocol (NNTP)	News server, news reader (e.g., IE or Netscape)	Transfers messages to a central server, where they can be read by many people in a group, like a bulletin board.
File transfer	File Transfer Protocol (FTP)	FTP server, FTP utility (or some web browsers)	Copies files to/from a server, plus ability to rename or delete files.
Web	Hypertext Transfer Protocol (HTTP)	Web browser (e.g., Netscape, IE)	Automatically retrieves interlinked documents, graphics, sound, video, data, and other computer resources or objects stored in files on remote servers.

All of these are client-server applications that involve using a server program on a remote computer and a client program on your local computer. When you use e-mail, for instance, you are using an e-mail client to send a message to an e-mail server, which routes it to the person you are addressing. For example, a message to john@abc.com goes to the mail server at abc.com, which stores it in John's mailbox. Likewise, you can use a gopher, FTP, or web client to communicate with gopher, FTP, or web servers.

How does this work? Let's look at a generic FTP session on a UNIX system, which may look something like this:

User Commands	What Happens
`ftp bigfoot`	Log in to the FTP server on the host computer named *bigfoot.*

`userID: your_name`
`password: your_password`
`(connected)`
	Enter user ID and password.

`cd directory_name`	Change to the directory containing the file.
`get file_name`	Copy a file from the host computer to your computer.
`quit`	End the session and disconnect.

Notice in this example that the user actually has to log in and open a session on the remote computer using a unique ID and password. This is typical of most client-server applications in traditional computing environments, because they tend to be tightly controlled. But it's also a lot of trouble, since the person who maintains the server has to authorize a separate user ID and password for each person who might want access to the files.

On a global network like the Internet, this kind of server administration is impossible, so people don't even mess with it. Imagine the administrative nightmare involved if you had to authorize and keep track of a separate password for each of the millions of users who might want to access your site over the Internet. In most cases, it shouldn't be necessary because the information—your resumé or curriculum vitae, for example—is probably something you want to share with everybody. The same should be true of a business sharing product information, a government agency sharing census data, or a university sharing research results within the academic community.

Since the Internet is so massive, ways were devised to make the administrative burden significantly easier. For instance, most public FTP servers support a mode of communication called *anonymous FTP*. With this technique, you still log in, but you can use the word *anonymous* as the user ID and just about anything else as the password.

Thus, instead of having to get into the business of saying yea or nay to every user who comes along, the administrator of an FTP site can let people retrieve information at will, without bothering to ask for permission. As you will see, web technology boils this process down even further and makes it as easy as a single click of a mouse.

The Basics of Web Technology

Client-server Internet tools like e-mail and file transfer have been around since the early 1970s and turned the Internet into a limited success on their own, with millions of users already happily communicating away by the early 1990s. Other Internet applications that we no longer hear about, like *telnet* and *gopher,* were immensely popular for a while. But there is no doubt that the Internet was totally transformed by the arrival of the Web.

The birth of the World Wide Web in 1990 came and went almost totally unnoticed by the rest of the world. As far back as early 1989, Tim Berners-Lee, a then-unknown researcher at the European Particle Research Center (CERN), was writing proposals about a new method people could use to transfer information between computers. The new method took advantage of the hypertext concept proposed years earlier, which was already being used in online publishing applications like WinHelp.

The innovations that Berners-Lee and his colleagues proposed came in two parts:

HyperText Markup Language (HTML).   A way of marking text so that it could be published easily online with embedded hyperlinks, font changes, and other features.

HyperText Transfer Protocol (HTTP).   A communication method that could be used by clients and servers to exchange hypertext documents over a network.

It was just an idea, but it had promise. At first, no one even called it the World Wide Web, but Berners-Lee recognized that if such documents were scattered across the Internet, they would create a "web" of interconnected information that would stretch around the globe.

To understand HTML, think about the codes that we used to see in word processors and typesetting machines (see "The Growth of Desktop Publishing" earlier in this chapter). That's sort of what HTML is like. For instance, a document coded with HTML might look something like this:

```
<TITLE>Short Report</TITLE>
<H1>A Short Report on the Current State of Publishing</H1>
<B>by Haiku Kirby</B>
<P>
HTML still involves coding, but the codes are much
<I>cleaner</I> because most of them specify functional
components of the document, such as headings and emphasis,
rather than specific font changes, spacing, etc.
<P>
HTML lets you add graphic illustrations to your documents,
like the one shown here: <P>
<IMG SRC="picture.gif"><P>
You can also add imbedded hyperlinks, such as the one
<A HREF="resume.html">here</A>.
```

HTML provides a way to mark a document with common desktop-publishing elements such as headings, bullet lists, numbered lists, bold/italic font changes, and so forth. It also provides a way to insert graphic images and hyperlinks that can reference other files on the same computer or even on remote computers. For instance, the <IMG> tag in the previous example inserts an image stored in the file *picture.gif.* The <A HREF> tag turns the words "shown here" into a hyperlink that retrieves and displays the file *resume.html* when selected.

As with the word processors of old, these codes can be inserted by the author but are not visible to the reader. For instance, if you saved the previous example as a file, then displayed it in a web browser, it might look like Figure 2.11 when displayed on the user's screen.

But HTML is only half the picture. Once you create a document using HTML and store it in a file, you still need a way to transfer the file between computers. That's where HTTP comes in; it provides an easy way for a client and server to communicate and transfer hypertext files. This is done using a standard request format called a *Universal Resource Locator* (URL). Anyone who has used UNIX or DOS is familiar with the concept of a *pathname.* In DOS, for instance, the pathname

```
c:\personal\letters\john.doc
```

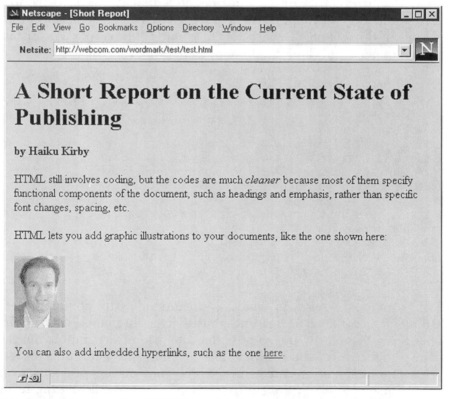

Figure 2.11 Result of HTML codes in web browser window.

indicates that the file named *john.doc* can be found on drive C in the folder *personal* and the subfolder *letters.* A URL works the same way, except it specifies a server type, server name, path, and filename. For instance, the URL

```
http://sam.com/webpages/home.html
```

indicates that the file name *home.html* can be found on the HTTP server named *sam.com* in the folder *webpages.* (Notice that URLs use a forward slash, as in UNIX, rather than the backslash found in DOS.)

When sent from a web client (browser) to a web server, the URL tells the server where to find the document. If you're using a web browser, you just type in the URL and hit the **Enter** key to retrieve the file—the server returns it automatically. The nice part is that each hyperlink has a URL embedded in it, so you don't even have to know the file location or its name. All you have to do is click the hyperlink and the file is retrieved automatically (Figure 2.12).

How the Web Changes Things

It doesn't strike you how simple HTTP makes everything until you compare it with the way we *used to* find information on a computer (in fact, many people *still* do it this way):

◆ Determine where the file is located and what format it's stored in (a process that can take hours, if not days).

◆ Log in to the computer where the file is stored (if you can).

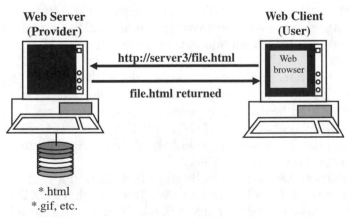

Figure 2.12   Web server and client.

◆ Start an application such as Microsoft Word that can display the file in its native format.

◆ Open the file.

◆ Page down to the desired information.

◆ View the information (print it if desired).

◆ Close the file.

◆ Log out.

Notice how these typical steps are a lot like the FTP session shown earlier in this chapter (see the section called "What Is an Internet Application?"). In a web system, all these steps are collapsed into the single click of a mouse, including the login/logout process. Since the pathname is contained in the URL, there is no interactive session involved in which the user has to tell the server what directory to change to and what file to retrieve. The URL already contains all that information.

It's like a fully loaded guided missile that goes straight to the target and extracts the file in a single step. So what once took minutes or hours now takes only seconds. And the information log jam has been loosened as never before.

The Real Impetus behind the Web

During the first years of its existence, a few adventurous souls used the new HTML/HTTP standards to publish documents on the Internet. But the response from the rest of the world community was a resounding "ho hum." By early 1993, two years after Berners-Lee's original proposal, there were still only about 50 web servers online. Within another two years, however, there were nearly 100,000, with the volume growing exponentially. Obviously, something happened to catapult web technology to prominence in the period between 1993 and 1995.

It's clear that web technology would not exist without the HTML and HTTP standards first proposed by Berners-Lee. But the web, as a technology, did not really kick into high gear until a number of refinements occurred, including more feature-filled versions of HTML and the advent of a landmark web-browser design called *Mosaic*. (It also helped that U.S. government control of the Internet was relaxed in late 1994.)

Actually, Berners-Lee and his colleagues had created a web browser for the NeXT computer system as far back as 1990 (the fact that NeXT systems never sold widely obviously didn't help things). Over the next few years, other browsers came along with long-forgotten names like Viola, Midas, Cello, and Lynx. Of all the browsers that emerged, however, Mosaic—along with its direct descendants Netscape and Internet Explorer—is the product most credited with lifting web technology off the launching pad.

Mosaic was designed by Marc Andreessen and Eric Bina at the National Center for Supercomputing Applications (NCSA) in early 1993. Within a year, the NCSA staff had created versions of the browser for PC, Mac, and UNIX platforms. But Andreessen left NCSA for work in Silicon Valley, and eventually ended up partnering with Silicon Graphics founder Jim Clark to form a new company called *Netscape Communications.* The rest—as they say—is history.

One interesting but rarely mentioned footnote in Internet history is that both Netscape Navigator and Microsoft's Internet Explorer were originally based on the same set of source code derived from Andreessen and Bina's original Mosaic design. In the mid-1990s, NCSA licensed the Mosaic source code to a company called *Spyglass,* which in turn licensed it to companies such as Microsoft and dozens of other companies who repackaged the browser concept under their own brand names. Of all these competing browsers, however, only Netscape and Microsoft eventually obtained significant market share. For this reason, any mention of a web browser in this book and in real life typically refers to only two candidates: Netscape's Navigator product, or the Microsoft Internet Explorer.

The main reason for the success of the original Mosaic design is that it was more or less in the right place at the right time. New versions of HTML and a standard called *CGI* (Common Gateway Interface) were making it possible to create advanced web-based applications such as online forms that could indirectly interface with databases. With these new features, Mosaic and its ancestors would become a lot more than browsers: They would provide a new computing interface that held the promise of replacing all others.

How Web Browsers Beat the Old Internet Tools

The new browsers included a number of advanced features that made them especially powerful information-gathering tools. Unlike other types of client programs, which could only be used with a certain type of server, these were *multipurpose clients.* That means they could communicate not just with web servers (HTTP), but with FTP servers, mail servers, news servers, and others. Thus it was possible to integrate several Internet services into a single interface. To do so, you only had to change the URL to reflect a different server type, for instance:

```
http://server_name/path/file.ext
ftp://server_name/path/file.ext
news:news.group.name
mailto:person@server_name
```

What's more, each additional URL type could be built right into hyperlinks so that users didn't even have to understand that they were using different kinds of servers. If something was available on an FTP server, for instance, the Web page might include a button or a hyperlink that says "get this file" and a single click would bring it straight to your computer.

It's hard to overstate how important this one feature was. Not only could the new web browsers do things better than the old Internet tools, for some purposes they could actually *replace* the old tools. As a result, the web browser became the vehicle of choice for cruising the Internet.

Web browsers added a new level of convenience to file access that had never been seen before on the Internet. For instance, a Web document could contain links not only through words but pictures, too. You could click on a map of the world and see a picture of the selected continent, then click on a country, a region, and a city, zooming in closer with each click to the site you wanted to visit. This was done by associating spatial coordinates on the surface of a diagram with a specific URL, so that if the user clicked the mouse within those coordinates, the browser would retrieve the corresponding web page. Imagine this feature being used in an auto parts manual, where you could click on an engine, then on a fuel injector, and finally on an individual component part and see its exact specifications.

The browsers came with other helpful features, such as the ability to keep track of all the links traversed in a hypertext session and go back to previous links. If you wanted to make a note of an individual page you found useful, you could easily add it to a pull-down menu for later selection.

The last convenience came by way of font selection. In the old publishing paradigm, the *author* was the one who selected the fonts, specifying for instance 14-point Palatino as the user's font. In an online environment, this doesn't make as much sense because the same font might appear differently on different monitors. Most browsers let the *user* select a typeface and font sizes for the visible documents, so that people could adjust the type size for consistent easy viewing at their unique monitor resolution. Even though more recent versions of HTML allow control over fonts, the end user still has the option to control and override fonts for optimum viewing quality.

But these were just the simple, cosmetic things that web browsers could do. For those who understand the technology and how to make it work, there is a lot more depth and power involved.

A Buyer's Guide to Web Technology

Because the typical web browser looks so simple and easy to use it appears that anyone can pick it up and be an accomplished user within minutes. This apparent simplicity, however, conceals an enormous depth and power that may not be recognizable at first glance—particularly the power to serve as a platform for complex, flexible, and highly integrated business applications. To envision the web browser as a business tool, sometimes you need to forget your first impressions of it as a tiny morsel of software you use to "surf" the World Wide Web. Instead, imagine that you are the purchasing agent in a large company and that someone from IBM is trying to sell you this software as a universal solution for all your business applications. As the sales rep rattles off the following list of features, imagine your incredulity that such a simple piece of software could contain so many features. Here are some of the features the sales rep would recite:

- ◆ Inexpensive shareware or freeware
- ◆ Intuitive graphical user interface that reads like a book, menu, or guided tour
- ◆ Requires little or no training (just point and click on interesting topics)
- ◆ Universal browser for any file type (reads file extensions and spawns external viewers, when necessary)
- ◆ Supports full-color, in-line graphics, including animated images
- ◆ Supports multimedia (sounds, video, and other multimedia objects)
- ◆ Supports hypertext links to local or remote documents, including links inside graphics (virtual pushbuttons, clickable maps)
- ◆ Supports SQL queries or other interactive retrieval, display, and updating of database information
- ◆ Supports retrieval/display of reports generated by other applications
- ◆ Supports direct access to mainframe legacy data
- ◆ Supports online forms, data entry, and interactive communications

(continues)

(continued)

- ◆ Supports integration with e-mail applications
- ◆ Supports complex business applications developed using C, C++, Visual Basic, Java, or various scripting languages
- ◆ Supports broadcast of "push" channels containing prepackaged content targeted at specific user audiences
- ◆ Supports organization-wide style sheets which can automatically control the look and feel of all web-based user interfaces on a corporate network
- ◆ Supports secure credit card transactions for online purchase of manufactured goods or intellectual property (e-commerce)
- ◆ Supports automatic downloading or transfer of computer files at the click of a button
- ◆ Contains security features including node access control, user authentication, encryption, and digital signatures or "certificates"
- ◆ Supports Internet services like FTP and newsgroups, even on local networks
- ◆ Supports flexible document/database searches with rank-ordered, clickable, automatically hyperlinked search results
- ◆ Supports on-demand printing of desired documents on local or remote printers
- ◆ Supports online conferencing or "chat"
- ◆ Supports online discussion groups and collaboration
- ◆ Supports usage tracking/analysis (server log)
- ◆ Nonproprietary, platform-independent, open-document architecture based on ISO standards
- ◆ Client-server architecture for optimum performance across networks
- ◆ Saves disk storage space by requiring only one copy of a file, image, or application to exist organization-wide
- ◆ Displays appropriately on any resolution monitor (user adjusts fonts locally for easy viewing)

(continues)

(*continued*)

♦ Works on any computing platform with a graphical user interface (PC, Mac, Sun, SGI, DEC, HP, IBM, etc.)

♦ Works on stand-alone computers, local area networks, wide area networks, or global networks, whether public or private

♦ Configurable as an embedded front-end browser for multimedia CD-ROM applications

The Web Browser as a Universal Playback Device

One of the most powerful features of the web browser is its ability to recognize file types by their extension and trigger "helper applications," "controls," or "plug-ins" capable of displaying the files (Figure 2.13). This is not an entirely revolutionary feature, but it is useful nonetheless. As far back as Windows 3.1, for instance, it was possible to use the File Manager program to associate a file extension such as ".DOC" with an application like Microsoft Word, so that when you double-clicked a .DOC file, it opened Microsoft Word with the correct file displayed inside it.

Web browsers do something similar: They can recognize and directly display certain "native" file formats directly inside the browser window, includ-

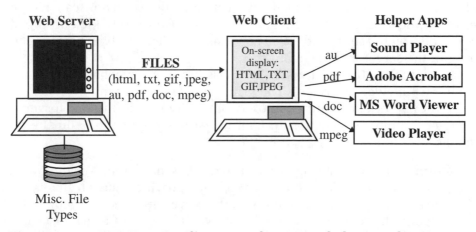

Figure 2.13   HTML native formats and common helper applications.

ing ASCII (plain text), HTML (marked up hypertext document), and GIF or JPEG (inline graphics). But if the URL accesses a different, nonnative file type, the browser can automatically kick off the correct application to display it.

For instance, you might have a button on a web page hyperlinked to a Microsoft Word file. When you click the button, the web server retrieves the file and sends it back to your computer. The browser in turn recognizes the .DOC extension on the incoming file, opens the software needed to display the file (MS Word or Word Viewer), then displays the file so that it can be viewed on your end of the connection. The same might happen for certain types of sound or video files.

Of course, the ability to playback files assumes that the proper playback software and devices are installed on your local computer. For instance, to play back files created using the popular multimedia program called *Macromedia Director,* you need a "plug-in" or "control" provided by a software program called *Shockwave.* This kind of technology not only brings the potential of multimedia to the web universe, but also makes it possible for a web browser to serve as a universal playback mechanism for just about *any file type.*

The Web Browser as a Universal Client

The last feature that made web systems so different was the incredible flexibility built into the HTTP protocol. Earlier, I explained how URLs can retrieve *files* stored on a remote computer. But, in fact, the HTTP protocol can transfer nearly any kind of information that you want between the client and server sides of a web system. For instance, just as a file extension can kick off a helper application on the client side, there are also ways to kick off programs or "scripts" on the server side. You can even pass data freely in both directions between the server and the client.

The original feature that made this possible was a mechanism called *CGI* (Common Gateway Interface). The gritty details of CGI are covered in more detail in Chapter 7, but suffice it to say that CGI made it possible for a person sitting at a client workstation to control various applications on the server side. For example:

Online content search.   Anyone who has used the World Wide Web knows about this one. Many web sites provide a search field you can use to search for information on the server, such as all documents that deal with "cost accounting." The typical result of a search is a clickable list of all matching document titles displayed in your browser.

When you click a title, the corresponding document is retrieved and displayed in the browser window.

Interactive web pages.   Web pages could contain a form with fields that the user could fill in. For instance, you might have a form that could be used to sign up for the company volleyball tournament, by entering name, department, room number, and phone extension. The information entered by the user would be sent to the server, where it could be appended to a file or forwarded to the event organizer in the form of an e-mail.

Interactive database queries.   Web pages could be connected to a customer database, so that if you wanted to view all records for account number 12345, you could type the number, hit **Enter,** and have all the records retrieved. The retrieved records could be formatted in such a way that you could edit them and have the changes written back to the database.

Both examples involve server-side applications that are controlled from the client side. And in both cases, the communication with the remote application is totally transparent to the user because it is handled through the background mechanism of HTML and CGI (see Figure 2.14). In effect, CGI was a way that other applications could be created to interface with the web server.

The interactive nature of this communication is made possible through a feature called *HTML forms* (Figure 2.15). HTML form tags let the web system designer set up pages that look just like a standard dialog box. An HTML form can include most of the standard dialog box components you see in windows-based applications, such as text boxes, radio buttons, pull-down menus, and more.

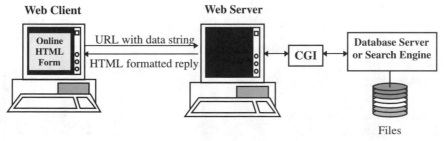

Figure 2.14   Typical CGI configuration.

Information typed into a form (called the *form input*) is passed to the web server and then to the server-side application through the CGI. The reply from the application can come back as straight text or as HTML-formatted text. So the result could be a simple data table, or it could be a data table wrapped inside an explanation, or it could be data with another form embedded for even more feedback from the user. This type of communication can go on indefinitely.

But look what's also happening here. The applications being controlled on the server side may have nothing to do with web technology. They may have been designed for some other purpose entirely. In fact, CGI was first used on intranets, to attach the web server to all kinds of back-end data sources, including legacy data stored on mainframe computers. The Perl scripting language was a frequently used way of creating these early back-end applications. But it was often just as easy to create an application using common programming languages like C and Visual Basic. In effect, with a little back-end programming on the server side, the web browser could be turned into a *universal client:* a dynamic interface for just about any kind of remote application on the network—or a totally self-fulfilling *web application* in its own right.

Better yet, the response from the application could be wrapped in HTML codes on-the-fly as it was sent back to the browser. In effect, the output from a database or interactive process could be published instantaneously online in response to any user query. Instead of getting a flat data readout or a bare-

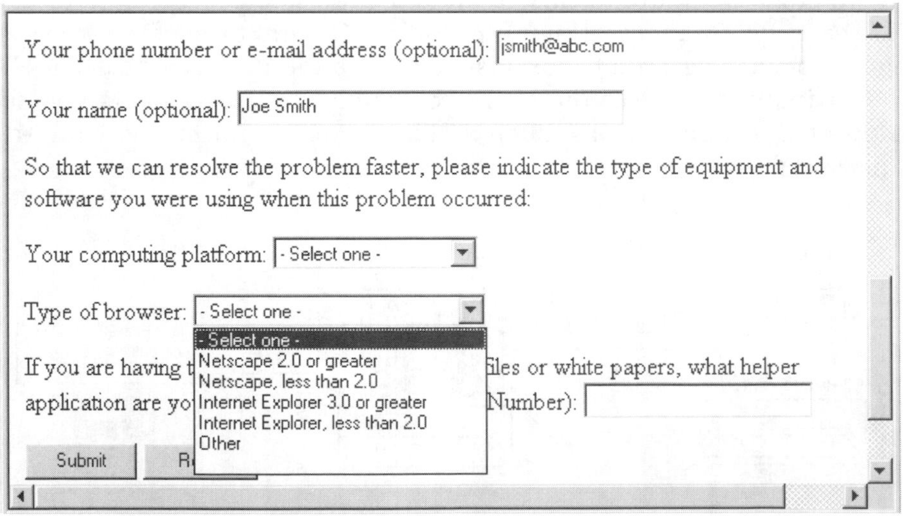

Figure 2.15   Typical HTML form.

bones dialog box the way we used to, we could provide the user with data that was self-explanatory, and dialog boxes that were, in effect, self-documenting. When used this way, web technology blurred the already fuzzy lines between what we think of as *data,* and what we think of as *documents.* Suddenly, online data could be presented within a document-like interface and online documents could be accessed just like data.

What's more, all of this could be controlled from the server end in such a way that the user interface could change week by week, day by day, or even minute by minute in response to ongoing changes in business needs—*without requiring users to change their software, reinstall applications, or retrain on a new system.* A programmer, working on the server side, could update the application and all users who accessed that application through the web would be immediately updated.

Compare this to the static user interfaces you commonly see in most computer programs. These are the result of months of laborious efforts by highly trained and specialized programmers who have to invest a considerable amount of effort and time tweaking massive amounts of computer code until it works just so. Then the code has to be specially compiled, distributed on disks or over the network, and laboriously installed on each user's machine.

Now consider that HTML form tags let anyone with a little knowledge of HTML create a dialog-like interface in minutes. And that a form interface could be wrapped around data dynamically on-the-fly as it emerges from applications anywhere on the network. And that such a form could be called up on demand—just like any other web page—simply by clicking on a hyperlink. This feature alone has revolutionized the way we use networks to get our work done.

The Emergence of Java and Other Advanced Tools

Having accomplished all this, you would think that the people tinkering with web technology would sit back for a while and enjoy the fruits of their labor. Creating a technology that could handle any file type on any platform, that could serve any kind of data, and that could function as a universal client for nearly any type of online application—well, this was a little like creating an antigravity machine that could travel anywhere in the universe in the blink of an eye, using no fuel.

Having done all that, the people in Silicon Valley and Seattle went the web one better, going beyond plain old HTML and HTTP to create advanced programming, scripting, and markup languages that can work their magic through the ever flexible medium of the web—including JavaScript, JScript, VBscript,

VRML, and more. Programming with CGI and older scripting languages like *Perl* wasn't enough. Though CGI provided a useful way to hook back-end programs to the web server, there were significant performance problems.

CGI was not sophisticated enough to provide advanced features such as *multithreading,* which allowed a single process to control multiple data streams. Add to that the fact that CGI was just plain slow and clunky to begin with. For the people who created it, at a time when web servers were still kind of a harmless, gee-whiz technology, it seemed like a nice cool way to extend the functionality of a server. But, as people began to see the benefits of web technology and get deadly serious about it, CGI just didn't hack it.

In 1995, Sun Microsystems of Mountain View, California, emerged with its own solution to the CGI problem—a dragon-killer of a web programming language dubbed *Java.* Originally designed to control electronic devices, Java was retooled to fit the new web paradigm. Sun's idea was that you could write a program once, serve it directly through a hyperlink into the web browser window, and thus have it run automatically on any computer with a web browser (or more specifically, a web browser equipped with a Java Virtual Machine). They even called it "write once, run anywhere," as opposed to traditional programs that must be written and compiled separately for each different machine they must run on.

Java promised not only to enhance web applications—far beyond the original capability of HTML forms and CGI—but to rapidly speed up the time it took to develop computer programs. Though in many ways Java was less powerful, slower, and more limited than languages like C, the trade-off was that applications written in Java could be served to nearly any computer instantaneously through the web. All it took was a web browser equipped with a Java Virtual Machine, which is the piece of software needed to interpret the Java code. Sun at first developed its own HotJava browser for this purpose, but most standard web browsers like Netscape and Internet Explorer now include the JVM as a standard component.

Now almost everywhere you look it's Java this or Java that. "Java saves the World" seems to be a common headline. One wag was quoted as saying, "Java's the solution; now what's the problem?" Still, despite all the hype, many companies are turning to Java as a way to save money and time in bringing computer applications to the desktop—or more precisely to what is now often called the *webtop.*

The main problem with Java, of course, is that it is a full-fledged programming language—an *object-oriented* programming language to be exact. That means that—unlike simpler scripting or markup languages such as Perl or HTML—you must be an accomplished programmer to use it. Fortunately, various companies involved in putting together the web puzzle have created other programming tools, including scripting languages like JavaScript that are not as powerful as Java but that also do not require as much expertise to learn and use.

JavaScript, for instance, was created by Netscape as a way to add functionality to web pages beyond that originally provided by markup languages like HTML. With the client-side version of the scripting language, it is possible to embed JavaScript programming directly inside of web pages. For instance, a phone number or date field on a standard HTML form could contain JavaScript code that would automatically determine whether the user entered a valid phone number or date. Then, the web form would generate an error message informing the user of the problem, as soon as the incorrect entry was made.

Java, JavaScript, and all the others can be considered extensions of the original HTML/HTTP web concept created years ago by Tim Berners-Lee and his CERN colleagues. Even as companies like Sun, Netscape, and Microsoft continue developing more elaborate and useful extensions to the web, Berners-Lee continues to operate in his current position as head of the MIT-based W3 Consortium to develop new versions of the HTML language that continue to push the envelope of what HTML can do.

Yet, even with all these nifty tools, it's important to remember that you can still do quite a lot with the plain old web tools like HTML that were invented back in the Dark Ages—that is, just a few years ago. HTML web pages are still the most predominant form of content on the Internet—or intranets. The good news—thank goodness for all of us—is that you don't have to be a Java guru to share information on an intranet.

How Web Systems Ease Administrative Burdens

Another key concept to understand about web technology—perhaps *the* key concept—relates to the way that users access the system. Unlike other client-server technologies, a web system provides universal access across a network to anyone with a web browser, whether they are authorized to log in to the computer where the server is located or not. That's not to say that a web site can't be protected from unauthorized users, because it can. It just means that most web sites tend to be open to all comers *by default,* unless you specifically protect it.

During the Cold War, people thought of the difference between democratic and totalitarian societies this way: In a free and open society, everything is allowed unless it is specifically prohibited by law. In a totalitarian society, on the other hand, everything is prohibited unless it is specifically allowed.

That's kind of how you might think of the difference between web-based client-server systems and their more traditional counterparts. In a traditional client-server system, people can't access the server unless they are specifically *permitted* to do so—they must either have an account on the server, or it must be installed so that it appears as an accessible application or drive on each user's machine. Most web servers, by contrast, are automatically visible to anyone on the network who owns a web client like Netscape Navigator or Microsoft Internet Explorer. Thus, anyone can access such a web server unless they are specifically *prohibited* from doing so (although there are now some web servers where universal access must be enabled).

This fundamental shift in the client-server model has had an important effect on the way networks are used and administered. In the past, the more users you had for a networked application, the greater the administrative burden. Network administrators had to open an account for each user, or configure user systems specifically to access each server the users needed to do their work. If a company had hundreds or thousands of users who needed server access, this became an incredible administrative chore, easily outstripping the resources of many a harried network administrator.

In this type of system, the network administrator sometimes starts to resemble the old-style Soviet bureaucrat. The system was rigged in such a way that the more services provided, the more work it created for the administrator. In some cases, this administrative bottleneck actually creates a disincentive for people to use the network to get their jobs done. With an open web server installed on a TCP/IP network, however, server access becomes automatic and the converse becomes true: If you want old-style bureaucratic control, you almost have to build it in.

Again, since the technology was originally designed for the Internet, it *had to be designed that way.* Imagine how hard it would be to set up a web site on the Internet if you had to individually authorize each of the 30-plus million users around the globe who have Internet access. Companies like Netscape and Microsoft could not possibly field the millions of requests for information that they get *every day.* Even these companies, however, have protected parts of their sites where you must register to get in.

The New Communications Model

The ability to field massive numbers of requests from any node on the network and disseminate incredible volumes of information is a function of the way web servers communicate. A web server, once installed and started up, really just sits there and "listens" for requests coming across the network. Thus, any web client like Netscape Navigator or Internet Explorer can locate a server no matter where it is located on a network, even if it's on the other side of the world. The hyperlink that you click on the client end contains all the information it needs to find its way to the server and retrieve the correct data. Typically this happens without a visible login and without the user having to consciously understand either the retrieval process or the location of the server.

The information retrieved from the server returns the same way: like a guided missile turned right back around and targeted at the client. The key idea is that the data travels through the network independently, without any lasting connection between the server and the client. As soon as the server reads the incoming URL and returns the data, it's job is finished and it moves along to the next request, even while the retrieved data is still making its way back across the network to the client.

Notice how this communication model differs from traditional client-server communication. In the traditional model (even with Internet services like telnet and FTP), there is a live connection made between the client and the server. The user may manually log on to a server (or a logon may occur automatically on boot up), and when this happens a session begins. If you were sitting at the keyboard on a UNIX server machine, for instance, you could use the WHO command to see all the people currently logged onto the system. The connection between the client and server remains open until the user closes it by logging off (or turning off the machine).

On a web server, typically no such connections occur. Instead, communication between a web server and its clients is more like a set of *discrete transactions*. The server receives a URL from the client, processes the request embedded in it, and returns the requested data to the client. The server is occupied only as long as it takes to fulfill the request and complete the transaction.

The payoff for this approach can be seen when you compare the web to more traditional client-server models. An application such as Lotus Notes may have an upper limit of simultaneous clients it can handle per server. If your users exceed the number allowed, you will need to purchase additional servers to make up the difference. In some cases, you may need a separate server for each LAN, so that users can easily log in for local access.

Now think of how it works on the Internet. A single web server located in Boston, or Tokyo, or Madrid can handle all the users in the world, not all at once but possibly many hundreds of simultaneous requests for documents or data. Thus a web server theoretically can be used by an unlimited number of clients, as long as everyone does not try to use the server at the very same instant. And instead of purchasing separate server and client software for each individual application, the same server and client can support a host of applications. Of course, if it works this way on the Internet, it will easily work the same way on your corporate intranet.

The Role of Authors in a Web System

The last point to understand is how people supply information to a web system and how they use it. Earlier in this chapter, I explained how client-server systems were invented to let users share data and applications over a network. A web system can be used for this purpose, too. But the way it goes about it is quite different from the traditional client-server model.

In a client-server application such as Oracle or Lotus Notes, the system exists for the benefit of a defined group of users (Figure 2.16). Often, the people who use such a system are both the authors and users of the data. In Lotus Notes, for example, people can share documents, which means they can view the documents or edit them. If different people edit the same document, the Lotus Notes software reconciles to the document database the various changes made by the users who are collaborating in editing it. Others may access and view the edited documents, but they are limited to the community of users who have access to the specific server on which the data is located.

In a web system, there is a clear distinction between the *authors* or providers of the information and the *users* of it (Figure 2.17). In this situation, an author develops the information for the benefit of the users. The author has direct access to the server and can use server folders to store documents and data that will be made available to users online.

In this model, however, the users are more passive and more numerous. Typically, they can read the information on the server, but they cannot edit it unless the authors set up some type of interactive mechanism such as a database back-end controlled by a Java application. While this may seem like a

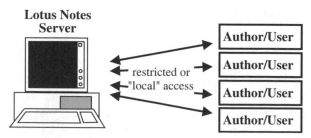

Figure 2.16   Traditional client-server model.

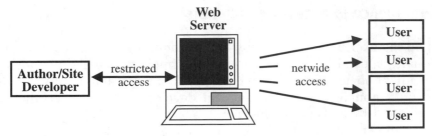

Figure 2.17 Web client-server model.

limitation, it works quite well for information-delivery models where people want to provide free access to their data across a network but don't want just anyone editing it.

Fortunately, web technology lets us have our cake and eat it, too. The diagram in Figure 2.18 shows an example of a web system that is integrated with a traditional client-server application like Lotus Notes. In this case, the Lotus Notes server is still being used by a restricted group of people to author and edit a set of documents. But the presence of a new component, the Lotus Domino web server on the back end, allows the documents to be published across a network to all interested users. The Domino server provides a connection between the application server and the web that automatically converts Notes documents to HTML format, which allows them to be served across an intranet and to be viewed anywhere on the network using a web browser.

Increasingly, vendors of client-server applications are providing these types of built-in web interfaces that make it easy to connect their applications to the intranet. Oracle is just one example, providing web connectivity through its WebServer software. Thus, instead of a team or department taking their information offline and publishing it through paper or other media, widely distributed web users can peer directly into the database and retrieve information on their own.

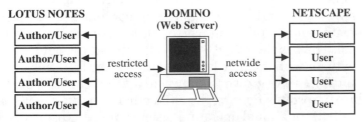

Figure 2.18 Extended web client-server model.

The Emergence of Network Computers

Given all the exciting developments in the computing field over the past few years—and especially in Internet/intranet technologies—it seemed for a while that we might be headed for some kind of intranet nirvana. Funny how things turned out, though. Some of the recent developments threaten the idea of empowerment that I keep talking about, and may eventually plunge us right back into the era of mainframe computers and dumb terminals. If that happens, then we've truly come full circle.

What I am referring to is the concept of the "thin client" and where it is taking us. In a way, "thin client" is the idea of client-server taken to the extreme. In early client-server models, a considerable amount of computing was done on the client side. As servers become more powerful, smart, and flexible, clients have less and less of a burden to do anything at all. We've already seen how Java programs can deliver applications to the web browser window on demand. Those Java programs are installed on the server and never touch the client machine until the moment they are requested. The web browser software loads and interprets the Java program the minute it hits the window.

If we can deliver programs on-the-fly like this to any desktop, then why should we install any programs on the desktop at all? Why not deliver all the software—including even the operating system—to the client "just in time" as needed to do the work. And if we don't need to install software on the client machine anymore, then do we really need that hard drive, that CD-ROM—even that floppy drive—to be there? Why not just strip the desktop PC down to the lowest common denominator: the keyboard, a screen, a little bit of memory. A very thin client indeed.

Does all of this sound familiar? A workstation with nothing but a keyboard and a screen is little more than a dumb terminal with an Intel, or Motorola, or other chip inside. So, if the momentum toward thin clients really played itself out, we would all be staring at a dumb terminal in a few years.

This is a lot closer than you think. Not all that long ago, our friends at Sun, Oracle, and Microsoft announced specifications for a set of machines called either a *network computer* (NC) or a *network PC* (NetPC). These machines are already on the market and being adopted by corporations, in many cases to replace the mainframe dumb terminals of old with a more modern up-to-date dumb terminal. The people over at Sun are already tearing out their UNIX boxes and replacing them with the new JavaStations. Naturally, if this can occur, then all that old software we've grown to know and love will be right out the window.

That's why Microsoft is fighting the NC tooth and nail. The NC is a machine designed to kill off traditional operating systems like Microsoft's. But Microsoft is proposing a NetPC that it feels is the best of both worlds. With the NetPC, you get a stripped down PC that still runs all the old software. There is still a hard drive with copies of Windows and applications like Microsoft Office. But the NetPC is also Java friendly and can accept updates to its operating system and software being provided by network services.

At this point, as this book is being written, it's not certain where this trend will take us. If you're sitting in front of your computer right now, take a quick look at it. Do you still see a floppy drive sitting there? Do you hear that hard drive churning away? A comforting sound, perhaps? Think about that: Some-day—thanks to the same Internet and intranet technologies that made us all into potential global publishers—that sound could disappear completely from the office, to be replaced by the smooth droning hum of the thin client.

The Integration of OS and Browser

The arrival of Internet Explorer 4.0 and Windows 98, in late 1997 and early 1998, herald the beginning of a new trend in operating systems that will see the browser moving from its position as a humble servant in the PC repertoire to the maestro at center stage. Windows 98 will look a lot like Windows 95, with the exception that if you want it to, your web browser will become the central window through which you access all files and information on your local system or on the network.

Remember how file manager programs have traditionally given us a bird's eye view of the operating system, where you could see all the files arrayed in nice little ranks within the folder hierarchy? Now the web browser becomes not just a tool that you can use to surf the Inter- and intranet, but a platform you can use to browse equally and almost transparently all the computer resources you have access to, whether they are located on your hard drive, the nearest file server, or some web server halfway around the world. Windows 98 will also give users the option to see the traditional Windows 95–style background, or use an *active desktop* with web-enabled features such as auto-broadcast of push channels into the Windows background, with transparent icon access to local files, network files, or Internet-based files.

Sun is planning a similar marriage between its HotJava browser and its JavaStation computer, creating a Hot Java Viewer that will provide desktop applications with a view of the World Wide Web and the intranet. Already Sun has converted its own employees to JavaStations, disconnecting them entirely from the UNIX operating system. Even Netscape's Communicator design seems to be an attempt to unify all the major desktop functions into a single, pervasive view. Whether or not these new computing models are successful, it is clear that the desktop may never be quite the same again.

Future Strides in Web Technology

All the features and developments covered so far in this chapter provide the latest on web-related Internet technologies as of the publication date of this book. However, the field of web technology is one of the most explosively dynamic and unpredictable in recent history. In its own disorganized and decentralized way, the ongoing development of the Internet model—including all the money and energy being poured into Internet and intranet development projects through public and private channels worldwide—certainly dwarfs the gargantuan space projects of the late 1960s that ended up putting men on the moon.

The development of this technology has never rested—not a heartbeat—since Marc Andreessen and Eric Bina invented the Mosaic browser, and it is not likely to rest for some time to come. Due to the success of the Internet, dozens of companies have been and will continue to be vying for ways to improve the technology and make it into even more of a "killer app" than it is already. New versions of the Netscape and Microsoft web browsers seem to appear every few months now, even more often than we get new PC operating systems (if you can believe that). Even more important developments still lurk in the future, however, as the intranet moves from a peripheral role in computing to the central foundation on which all computing is built. Here are a few predictions that this author hazards:

The web browser interface will move to the center of the computing universe in new versions of operating systems.   This will be especially true in Microsoft's Windows 98. Rather than just a web browser, the "internet interface" will become the central piece of software through which users view all online content and applications.

Style sheets (CSS) will increasingly make it easier to implement corporate-wide standards for consistent look and feel of web-based content. All pages on the intranet will reference a style that can be defined in a single document. When the style in that document changes, the style in all referencing intranet pages is changed automatically.

New protocols such as PPTP (point-to-point tunneling protocol) built into Windows 98 will make extranets more common than they have been in the past.   This will allow mobile and telecommuting workers to link into the intranet from remote locations off-campus, and may in turn provide a boost to the practice of telecommuting, as companies learn to leverage home-based resources to the service of corporate goals.

Improvements in bandwidth will widen our horizons.   These improvements will include Fast Ethernet and Gigabit Ethernet, along with advanced modem technologies such as DSL and cable modems which will make it increasingly feasible to serve multimedia, video, sound, and large-scale applications across the Internet, intranet, and extranet.

Where Do We Go from Here?

Now that you understand how web technology works and how it fits into the current thinking on client-server applications, let's look at some of the companies that have worked to develop their own intranets and the tools and techniques that they used. Chapter 3 provides a detailed look into three companies and the ways their intranets came into existence and developed into successful enterprisewide systems for interdepartmental communication.

Chapter Three at a Glance

This chapter shows how three major corporations put the intranet into practice, including:

- ◆ Sun Microsystems, Inc.
- ◆ Compaq Computer Corporation
- ◆ Chevron Petroleum Technology Corporation

The Intranet in Practice

Don't take my word for it. Look at what's happening in the real world. Creating an intranet isn't just a good idea in theory, it's already being put into practice extensively at business locations around the globe. If you are just beginning to consider installing an intranet, of course, your main question right now is "How do we get started?" What may be most interesting, however, is not just the methods used by companies to develop their own intranets, but what happens after the intranet is already online. How does the intranet grow, improve, or change over time? For companies that are already far into their first intranet projects, the question is no longer "How do we get started?" but *What do we do next?"*

This chapter takes a look at three different companies that have gone through the various phases of intranet building—from early adoption, to implementation, to growth and improvement. Some of the intranets described here have been online in one form or another for several years now. For that reason, these companies have already gone through their birth pangs and are well on the road to making the intranet an ongoing part of their business culture.

The companies represented here are unanimously large high-tech companies that specialize in applying technological solutions to business problems. But that doesn't mean only technology companies can benefit from the intranet. The ranks of intranet adopters run the gamut, from companies such as clothing manufacturer Levi Strauss, to real estate brokers Cushman Wakefield, to pharmaceutical company Eli Lilly, to many more.

Though most of the companies here are large multinational corporations, small businesses should take heart. If it's possible to implement an intranet in companies with over 10,000 employees, imagine how easy it might be for a company with under 1,000. The only advantage that size may provide is the ability to dedicate extra resources to undertake some of the necessary experimentation that always occurs in the early days of an intranet.

Let's take a look, then, at each of the companies one by one: how they started, nurtured, and grew their own homegrown intranets.

SunWEB: From Zero to 3,000 Servers in Two Years Flat

The intranet at Sun Microsystems, Inc., had fairly humble beginnings for a system that now harbors literally thousands of web servers. It all started as a few pages' worth of progress reports stored on the computer of one Carl Meske in early 1994. Since Meske was the original webmaster responsible for creating the external World Wide Web site for Sun Microsystems (www.sun.com shown in Figure 3.1), it seemed only logical that instead of turning in his progress reports on paper, where they would get buried in someone's filing cabinet, he might instead display them online so they could be viewed by anyone who was interested in his activities.

Meske's online progress reports were mildly impressive to those who saw them, but what got people really fired up was when Meske's team created an internal mirror site for the 1994 Winter Olympics in Lillehammer, Norway. Others took an interest and an informal trend began that saw people building their own intranet sites and viewing them through browsers.

Figure 3.1   Sun's World Wide Web home page.

As time passed, many of the engineers at Sun began using the web to publish their own information, and before long the intranet had 200 different servers running on it. This made it nearly impossible to keep track of all the information available. Web content was becoming increasingly difficult to use and manage. To help solve the problem, Meske created a focus group in 1995 to analyze and solve the problem. Their solution: a professionally designed, central menuing system where information could be listed by category. They called the result *SunWEB*.

Information Categories

The categories originally developed by Meske's focus group and still reflected in the SunWEB main menu (Figure 3.2) cover just about every subject imaginable and could serve as an excellent model for any large-scale business's intranet:

What's New is an essential component of any web site that shows up prominently on the SunWEB home page, providing recent press releases for the company and other announcements.

Campus & Services provides maps to all the different locations and buildings in the Bay Area, including local directories and phone numbers. This area also contains information about commuting, bus schedules, and local company-provided vans. It also shows the location of shipping and receiving areas, food services, reprographic centers, and conference rooms.

Human Resources is one of the larger areas, with information about employee benefits programs, a manager's handbook, a developer's toolkit, and corporate employment information (Figure 3.3). Sun's human resources department manages the area on their own; they even have their own full-time webmaster.

Company Views are located in the upper-right quadrant of the SunWEB menu. There are three different views of the system: an organizational view (the different companies in the Sun worldwide organization), a functional view of the company (corporate, IR, sales, marketing, etc.), and a geographical view (the different Sun locations throughout the world, accessible by clicking on a world map).

Library & Education is the front door for Sun's training effort, including both internal and external training course offerings. This section also includes links to the company's libraries, where employees can access

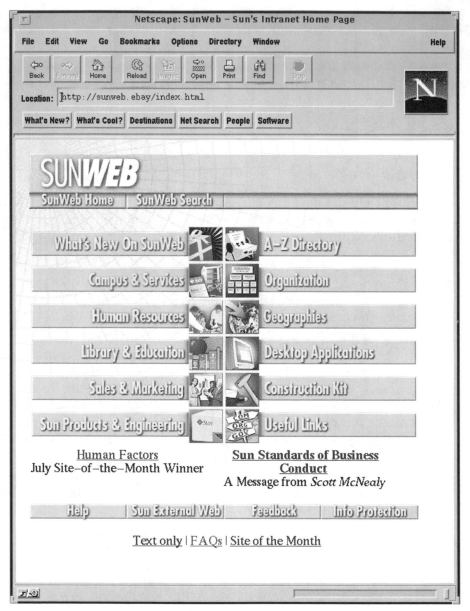

Figure 3.2   Sun's intranet home page.

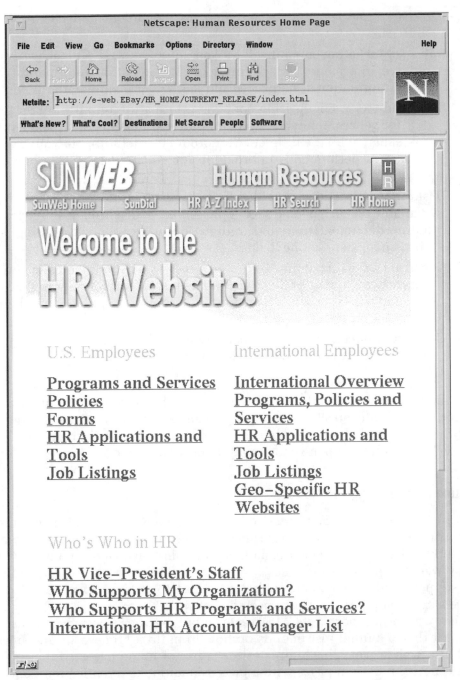

Figure 3.3   Sun intranet—Human Resources site.

research services and locate company document and electronic resources.

Sales & Marketing contains all the marketing and sales databases, competitive information, marketing tools, organization information, and basic information to help sales and marketing people in the field.

Sun Products & Engineering contains information on all the Sun products for general reference by all employees, plus links to the engineering teams for all the different Sun products, including documentation, tools, and performance information for all the engineering organizations.

Desktop Applications provides links to all the software tools that are available on each person's local file server, with a brief product profile, online documentation, and information on how to get training, support, and a stand-alone license.

Construction Kit contains all the how-tos for building web sites on the intranet, including policies and procedures, templates, graphics, clip art, and links to tools (such as FrameMaker applets that handle FrameMaker-to-HTML conversions).

Useful Links contains an extensive compendium of useful links to all types of information both inside and outside SunWeb.

A search option at the top of the screen provides a way to quickly search for specific content on the intranet. Other links at the bottom of the main menu include a "server drop site" where people can register new servers on the central directory, and a comment section that lets people post comments about the web to a newsgroup or send e-mail to the webmaster.

Testing and Refining the Model

To test its original SunWeb interface, the pilot team went looking for certain types of hard-core online communicators. "Anybody who would send an e-mail to the world—such as a message addressed to *all@*—we would jump on them. They were the perfect candidates," Meske says. Then the team worked to gain the support of IR. "They wanted to know the cost, to make sure we weren't going to be a hit on support costs or impact the network."

To lower the support costs, Meske's team put together a basic web construction kit that included instructions on how to build a home page and how to install a web server, plus templates for personal home pages so that people could build their own pages with a professional look. To entice rank-and-file employees to the web, they added information such as that found in the company's human resources handbook. To entice company executives, they put stock quotes online. "We wanted everyone using it," says Meske, "not just engineers."

Typical of their effort was a push to get Sun product information online. "We didn't realize how big a company we were until we started looking at all the products," says Meske. "So we went to the product marketing guys and said, 'We want you to build a web site so we know what you're doing. You've got all these product managers that are managing their products, why not put this stuff online?'

"I wanted to know what other groups were doing, just as they could see what I was doing online. Since we're a fairly large company, it's nice to be able to figure out who is doing what. So we worked with them to build their site, we sent them e-mails explaining how we wanted them to do it. We found that a lot of people are very creative and like to talk about themselves. With our templates you could put up a web site in less than 10 minutes."

A Rapid Explosion

Within a few months, the number of web servers online within the SunWEB exploded rapidly. Within a year, Sun had about 2,000 web sites inside the company, ranging from personal sites, to project sites, to group sites, to functional ones. The result has been savings in time and costs in a number of areas, not just paper publishing.

Today, several years after the original team created SunWeb, Meske's original publishing experiment has become a regular way for employees to communicate across the organization. "It has definitely evolved from where we started to where it is today," Meske says. "We have changed the look and feel of the infrastructure, and gone from a no-management infrastructure to a managed one. We now have a SunWeb Council where we have well-established projects with procedures. Council members are responsible for managing the flow of the intranet—that is driven by the IR organization itself: The CIO and the chief webmaster oversee the entire infrastructure of the SunWeb."

Today, Meske estimates, the total number of web servers online enterprisewide is about 3,000, but not all of them are linked into the SunWeb infrastructure. Some are test machines, while others are project-specific servers that people deploy for use entirely within their own departments.

On SunWeb alone, there are 1,500 web servers, Meske explains. "Every single function has a reference through some entry off our web server. Security, records management, real estate, quality, public relations, purchasing, photocopying forms, the phone directory, payroll, travel services, licensing, production, library, international trade services, investor relations—all the different components of a functioning business can be referenced now through our infrastructure."

Why so many servers? Couldn't everyone use the same server? "The problem with that," Meske explains, "is that our culture is not that way. People don't want to be dependent on IR to keep track of their information. It is also a decentralized, distributed model, so if one piece goes down the whole engine doesn't crash. Also, if a person owns the content and puts it on another machine, then someone else owns it and things get lost. We made the decision to keep the data on the owner's server, so that if there is a problem, it can be updated quickly."

"What we have done too, is make it very simple to deploy a web server," Meske adds. Sun carries site licenses for various Netscape products, though it also makes other web server software available such as the CERN and NCSA servers for UNIX. They use CGI scripts written in the Perl scripting language to handle access to back-end databases such as Sybase, ORACLE, and Informix.

"So if you are going to publish," says Meske, "either you create your own web server or you sign up on this other web server called *Sun IntraWeb,* where they will create a server area for you. Similar to an IR organization, they offer different levels of support and you pay accordingly."

The Publishing Model

To help get information online, SunWEB uses a "gatekeeper" system. A gatekeeper is a person who offers the various content providers publishing assistance, answers to questions, and help getting their content up on the web. They also have webmasters who are responsible for the content of specific large sites such as human resources.

The various operating groups (content providers) have a standard publishing process that involves developing their content and getting approval to put it on the intranet from a gatekeeper inside their own department. "We are trying to develop this infrastructure to let people help themselves, without hiring more people," Meske explains.

Those who want to publish information are encouraged to use the SunWeb templates and publish through the SunWeb infrastructure. Templates are placed online in the Construction Kit area of SunWeb, along with policies and procedures, logo guidelines, and information on how to publish. FrameMaker is the primary publishing tool, along with tools like Netscape Composer for individual web pages—although other tools are also under evaluation.

Once information is published, the content provider can fill out a "link request form" to get the information linked into SunWeb. The form includes the URL, title, and description of the site, plus contact information for the server manager, gatekeeper, and content author. Once the form is submitted, the new content is integrated not only into the web structure, but into the search engines, as well. Sun currently uses the Infoseek search engine to do searching across all of its internal domains.

"If they don't want to be searched," says Meske, "we are coming up with ways to do that. For instance, we can add a file called robots.txt to the document root that specifies which directories are not to be searched."

With regard to the gatekeeping process, Meske says, "We didn't want to build this giant organization, so we pushed the ownership down to the department level. Although the gatekeeping process is formalized, we just wanted to make sure there was someone who was watching the publication process so that information would not get published outside (i.e., on the World Wide Web) that was supposed to only get published inside. Most people can take care of policing themselves, but we wanted to do this, just in case."

Some of the gatekeepers are actually hired now just to be gatekeepers, Meske says, but those are called group webmasters. There are about 20 people in the organization who perform this function, and they have weekly meetings to coordinate policy.

Routing the Intranet

To integrate the intranet with the Internet, Sun uses a number of proxy servers that sit along the firewall, handle requests for World Wide Web content, and cache the information so that multiple requests can be served without having to reaccess the Internet. Each proxy handles a particular internal domain with names like *corp* (corporate), *eng* (engineering), *ebay* (East Bay Area), and *wbay* (West Bay Area). "We have configured the browsers so they point to the caching machines and the caching machines are the ones that do all the work," Meske explains. The arrangement minimizes traffic, so that all employees are not trying to access the Internet through the same node.

Now that the web has grown to take in all aspects of company operations, it shows the superiority of the distributed technology over other ways of serving the same information, Meske says. "Can you imagine what would happen if I tried to gather all these different web sites and put them in one machine? This way, responsibility is distributed and owned by the author. The network is so powerful, why not use it instead of having everything local? If I had to distribute 15,000 copies of everything, the cost and complexity would be prohibitive."

Typically, there is no crossover between internal and external web information, Meske says. "If it's external, then it gets pushed out onto the company's home page at www.sun.com." Sun maintains a special access site for resellers, which is accessed from the regular Sun external web server using a special account that requires the authorized resellers to log in.

As a result of its recent intranet improvements and its simultaneous move to network computing, Sun has placed a considerable investment in upgrading its internal network. "We went from a T1 to a fractional T3 connection to the Internet," Meske says. "Almost all of engineering is 100MB, and our remote offices have links from 56 to 256Kb." The next step is to go from 100MB to 1GB internet. "We are demanding the speed," says Meske. "We are information junkies."

Special Applications

Some parts of the SunWeb intranet are standouts, like the audio report from company president Scott McNealy. "The McNealy Report (Figure 3.4) is an audio interview with people in the company, or customers, or just Scott talking," Meske explains. "There are about 8 or 10 audio segments that people have done. It's a great way for people to stay in touch with the company president. It really has made him accessible to everyone."

To distribute the audio without undue performance drags on the network, Sun places mirrored copies of the files on software distribution servers and accesses them from local servers. "Otherwise," Meske explains, "if 15,000 people download that IMB audio file, you're going to kill the network." Despite the worries of performance drag, studies are being made to convert the audio report to video.

As with any next-generation intranet, the best uses are being seen in dynamic applications, especially those created using Java. "When IR deploys tools and applications, all the tools are created using the Java programming language and are accessible through the browser," Meske says. In fact, Sun was the company that originally created the Java language, and in the meantime has also introduced its own JavaStation—a special-purpose, network-driven computer with no native operating system of its own.

Sun is also experimenting with other advanced intranet uses. "We are making available a lot of information online these days, whether marketing, collateral, or real-time information. That kind of stuff is becoming more accessible and demanded. So, we have agents being developed that you can use to do searches on incoming information. We have an internal tool called Xpresso that searches all these databases on an hourly basis and delivers the information back to you" (Figure 3.5).

Figure 3.4   Sun intranet—The McNealy Report.

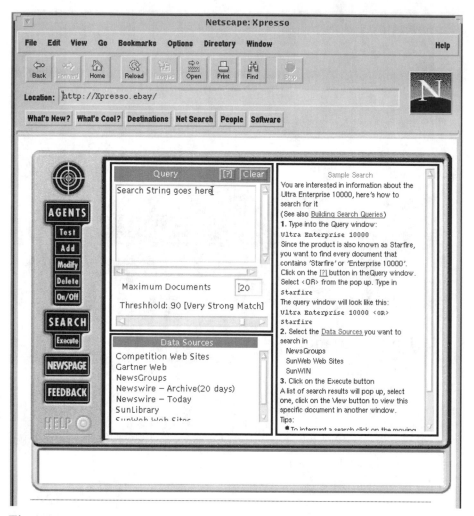

Figure 3.5   Sun intranet—Xpresso agent interface.

Additional Sun efforts are focused on determining the best way to provide training on demand as well as more value-added, web-based services. Says Meske, "SunU has taken a bunch of classes and put them online, and we get training on our products through a reseller web site. We are also looking at providing MPEG video screens so you can listen in on products. To do that, we are working with other video streaming vendors and Java-based video-

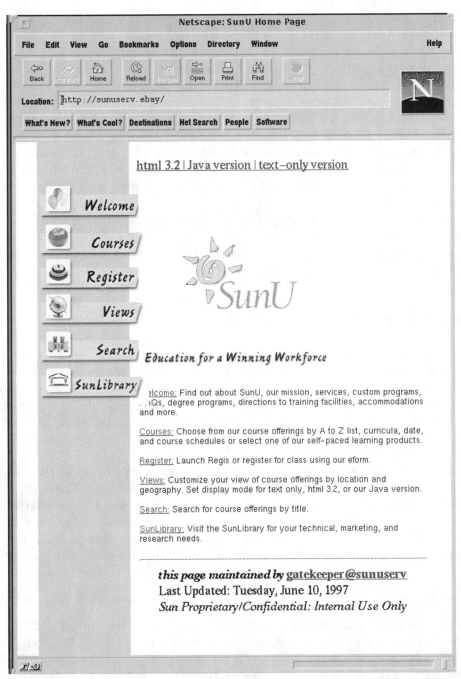

Figure 3.6   Sun intranet—the SunU menu.

streaming applets, so that we can provide more distance-training capabilities. That is a slow process, but we are doing it." (Figure 3.6)

Sun has also made available various tools that let employees update database information online. "We have all different kinds of web site information, plus sales and marketing information, that is database-driven using Sybase and Oracle back ends. We have tools online that are all password-protected for the executives to look at the business. An example is Sun's Capital Asset Management System (Figure 3.7), which allows authorized employees to transfer capital assets between organizations or individuals. This is a Java-based application that requires an employee number and password, then checks them against the corporate databases and dynamically configures a customized menu that the employee can use.

"We are starting to do managed network stuff based on Java, with remote agents, servlets, and applets, which opens up a totally different world," says Meske. "What you can do with Java agents is just awesome. When you start to think the network is the computer, it really starts to make sense."

Compaq Inline: A Worldwide Effort

The Compaq intranet provides an interesting contrast. Compaq Computer Corporation is the world's largest manufacturer of personal computers (PCs), with operations stretching from the western hemisphere, to Europe, and onward to the Far East. Because it manufactures PCs, the vast majority of its internal equipment runs the Microsoft Windows operating system on Intel chips (Wintel). So, whereas the Sun intranet is primarily UNIX- and Java-based, Compaq's intranet is almost entirely Wintel.

In the early days of the Internet—indeed on my first intranet—there simply wasn't much software that would run on the Wintel platform. These days the trend has been reversed entirely to the point that some vendors are starting to develop first for NT. Compaq's experience, then, will echo what many companies are finding. Despite occasional scare stories regarding scalability and security bugs, intranet success is increasingly likely on the Wintel platform.

In the Beginning

The Compaq global intranet got its first real impetus in the spring of 1996. An intranet had existed at Compaq as early as spring of 1995, but that early intranet consisted of a department server that was developed by Compaq's Customer Service department and primarily supported that group's needs. The IT

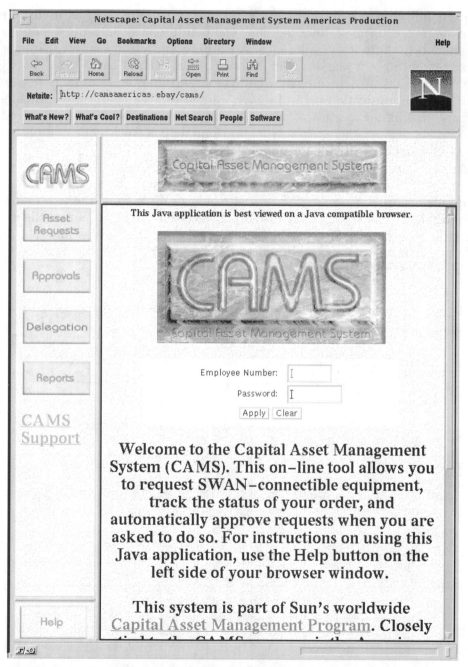

Figure 3.7   Sun intranet—Capital Asset Management System.

department took over the company's intranet effort with the goal to develop a broader, more corporate-focused site. The result was an intranet used mostly by the North America IT audience. According to Seth Romanow, Director of Worldwide Internet Marketing and Communications, in early 1996 "Management decided to take the intranet a little more seriously and put more resources into the communication behind it. We wanted to involve other technical and communications expertise at creating content and creating a presence, so it needed some work there. And, whereas Compaq is a worldwide company, the intranet wasn't worldwide in scope."

Another problem with the early Compaq intranet was that it was an exact mirror of Compaq's external site (Figure 3.8). "They didn't do any custom graphics," says Romanow. "They just used graphics from the external site, which made it hard to tell the difference between the internal and the external site." As a result, the team decided to have a separate design and distinctly separate names: Compaq Online (for the World Wide Web site) and Compaq Inline (for the intranet site).

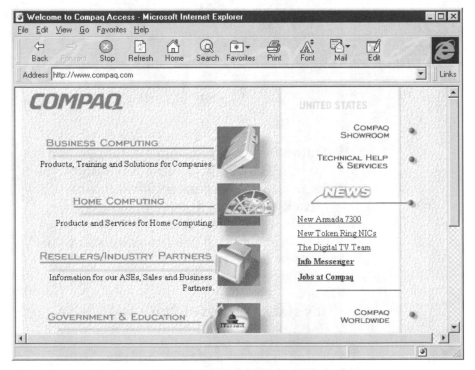

Figure 3.8   Compaq Online—World Wide Web home page.

The major impetus behind the new intranet, however, was "a vision by management that we needed a worldwide communications platform for Compaq to share information with all the teams and all the geographic locations or *geos*—a global employee communications tool." An intranet steering committee was formed representing key business units within the company. The steering committee consisted of Compaq's Chief Information Officer, the Senior Vice President of Human Resources, and the Vice President of Marketing and Communications. This team was responsible for the site's corporate strategy and purpose. Much of the initial research and team coordinating was managed by the company's Director of HR Systems. "She went out and interviewed a lot of companies to study their best practices with regard to their intranets," says Romanow. "To build the intranet Core Team, she assembled key players from the Internet, Product Groups, Human Resources, geos, and other corporate functional groups." The team also leveraged off of Compaq's internal Human Factors group to conduct research on the proposed information architecture, to ensure good navigation and useful content (Figure 3.9).

Larry Griffin, Manager of Inline for the Worldwide Internet Marketing and Communications group, was on the initial Inline Core team and was responsible for managing the design effort for the site, along with developing publishing standards and a process to support users who wanted to publish their content. He also managed a team to populate the site with content for the launch. "The first phase on our launch date, September 10, 1996, was a 'static' web site," Griffin recalls. "We launched with 10,000 pages to a worldwide audience. It took two months of production work. We worked with a local design firm, T1 Design, day and night to get that content populated by the launch date. To be successful, the core team wanted to ensure there would be useful content on day one. The home page had 10 major categories of information and was organized into both functional and logical topics."

The Publishing Model

To ensure that accurate and appropriate content would be published to the site, a team model was developed that consisted of senior editors-in-chief. Reporting to the steering committee, this team made up the Inline core team. Each senior editor-in-chief represented one of Compaq's functional organizations. Under this model, the company's director of Employee Communications leads the Inline Core team to manage site strategy, monitor issues and achievements, and implement work processes. Those senior editors-in-chief have nominated editors-in-chief from the groups and divisions within the organization. The editors-in-chief nominated an identified editor. And, at the

Figure 3.9   Compaq Inline—the original intranet home page.

lowest level—but most important—are the authors who actually create the content. Griffin says, "We enable anyone in the community to publish if they desire, as long as they follow our standards and guidelines and their communication fits within the business strategy of the company." Authors are considered the content experts, and are not required to know how to code in HTML or to know how to build a site on Inline. Griffin's team model acts as a centralized resource to professionally manage site development for business groups who lack the time, resources, or expertise to develop a site.

"When we launched Inline we set up a series of orientations for the authors to communicate the publishing process and guidelines," Griffin recalls. "After we did a couple of those, we relied on the senior editors-in-chief to set up their own orientation sessions within their groups and communicate the Inline strategy and publishing process. In coordination with group orientations, all Inline strategy, policy, and publishing information is posted on the site for reference and is updated as the information changes. Whenever we reengineer a process, we work to orient the authors to understand how the process has changed. Communication is key to making it work. Our list of authors, who access the development server to publish, has been growing since day one—which serves to validate the success of the project. Today, we have about 400 authors worldwide.

"The process of publishing to Inline currently involves using a standardized HTML template with the company's standard tool, FrontPage," Griffin says. "Authors are not required to use FrontPage. They are free to use whichever tool is most comfortable. The goal is to have an environment that is conducive to publishing. By standard tool, we mean software that is supported by our help center. If authors are using the company's authorized tool, and they encounter problems using it, they will get help with that tool.

"Another tool developed internally to help authors publish is the Compaq Web Wizard. This tool allows people using FrontPage to automatically insert the standard required elements without hard-coding them in. We require such elements as meta-tags, header/footer graphics, and a fine-print footer. The fine-print footer contains a confidentiality statement, a link to our corporate Internet/intranet policy, a contact name, and a revise date. Our goal is to keep these elements down to the bare essentials to avoid burdening our authors. To ensure that every person who publishes to the intranet is accountable for the page which they publish, we have a 'contact the editor' tag at the bottom of each page that is basically a mail-to tag that says who is responsible for the page. If you have a question about that page, you know who to contact. All contact is kept at the editor level, not the author level, because we want some accountability."

Creating Web-Based Applications

Just as standards and procedures were used to formulate Inline's first phase, static content, the same approach was used as Inline entered into its next phases of development—dynamic and transactional functionality. The second phase was to make Inline dynamic and able to support global business applications as well as department-specific applications. Inline began to evolve from a reference tool into an indispensable working tool that employees relied on daily. "Looking back, we actually had one application debut on the launch day that served to demonstrate the potential of the tool," Griffin recalls. "It is known as the *Global Graphics Library* (Figure 3.10). Today, it is on its way to becoming a global application, but it really served our North American audience to begin with. It functions as the graphic library of images we use in all our product marketing and other communications. It allows you to use a shopping cart metaphor to purchase images in whatever media type you want and connects you to a third party who fulfills the orders.

"Inline's third phase was to make it transactional, meaning support for actual transactions. For instance, if I wanted to sell a computer to somebody internally, a mechanism needed to be established to support that exchange over the Web.

"To support both of these phases, we had to build the infrastructure to support global and departmental applications. As a hardware manufacturer, it causes you to think about your identity and where this was leading. Suddenly our hardware company was developing software too, because we were building different applications over the Web. The Web forces you to think about yourself in new ways. In addition, we were project managing and developing applications that would hook into our legacy system. So we needed to tread very carefully because we needed to do things that wouldn't bring down the corporate network just because somebody accidentally coded something wrong. Our number one goal was to protect the corporate network from malicious code."

So, to ensure that a consistent process was followed and project efforts were being shared and communicated, a similar process was used to control the development of Web-based applications for Compaq Inline, although, in this process, control is somewhat tighter. "We have a coordinated process to follow," says Griffin. "We need to know whether the Web application is in the best interest of the company's business and communications strategy. Because you are using expensive resources to do something that may affect the company on a global scale, you want company resources used carefully. You don't

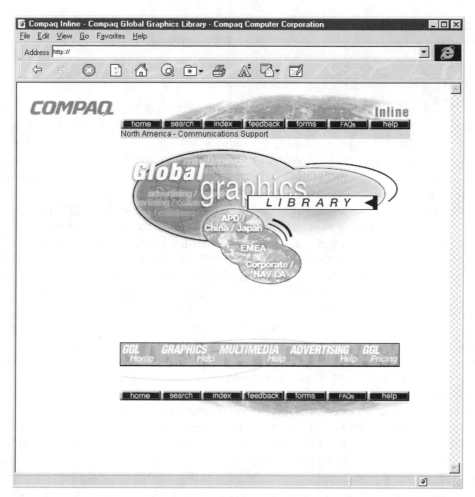

Figure 3.10   Compaq Inline—Global Graphics Library.

want someone in Singapore developing the same Web application that someone in Houston is developing or you'll end up duplicating effort and wasting
resources." By using prescribed development tools based on Microsoft's
Visual Studio suite we are able to manage Web applications better internally.
The team sponsored a Compaq Developer Day, where they pulled in all the
internal developers, business owners, and Compaq-certified Web application
vendors to explain the developer's toolkit and the Web application develop-

ment process. As part of developer education, a site was posted to Inline documenting all of the tools and processes for reference.

Time for a New Design

"As we began to approach our one-year anniversary with the site, and noticed the amount of growth and utility it had achieved and that people were extremely happy with it," Romanow recalls, "we also acknowledged that, as an ongoing effort, it was time to look at improving the overall design and functionality of the tool. We also realized that, with the tool's growth, there was so much information on it that things were getting harder and harder to locate." Even though the intranet had its own search engine, the design of the opening menus was not conducive to easy navigation. "The information was dictated by the organization's structure; so if you didn't know the organization well, you wouldn't know where to go to look for things," Griffin says. "Eventually, as the scope and number of levels grew, we needed to go back to the drawing board and condense the front end so it would not be so overwhelming."

Griffin saw the redesign as crucial. "If the design was too difficult or too involved, the people were not going to see it as an improvement. We wanted to make it interactive and add value to the tool, with a focus on accurate and timely information, but also on applications that people need everyday. We wanted to make sure we took a look at current technologies to enhance the interactivity and communication effectiveness of the site."

An example of the type of content that would be given prominence under the new design included a feature called news.cpq, an employee-oriented news site within Compaq Inline. Every two days, new articles are published to a worldwide community highlighting current company-related events and stories—occasionally happening in real time. For example, when Compaq purchased Tandem computers, the announcement was approved at 10 P.M. Houston time and was up on Compaq Inline by 7 A.M. the next morning so that Compaq employees knew about it first, before the story hit the news wires.

On the home page of news.cpq, marquee-style banner graphics call attention to key news items and encourage people to read the story (Figure 3.11).

Along with the redesign, Compaq will be upgrading everyone to Internet Explorer IE 4.0. According to Griffin, "We wanted to take advantage of the new channel definition format (or CDF, Microsoft's push technology specification) and we want to leverage off of cascading style sheets, object layering, frames, and proactive e-mail notification."

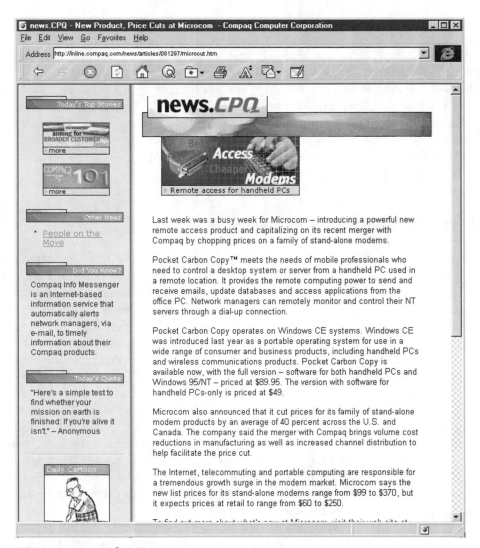

Figure 3.11   The Compaq news.cpq page.

Building Community

"We also wanted to build a stronger sense of the worldwide community," Griffin explains. "The geography that we cover includes North America, Latin America, Europe and the Middle East, Africa, Asia-Pacific, Japan, and China. The goal is to enable sharing of information and collaborating among these groups."

Having learned from past experience, the Compaq Inline management team has developed a somewhat unique outlook on the future. In terms of site redesign, Griffin says, "We should do it on an annual basis. It's an effort, it's not a project. We realize that the Web is changing constantly, and we will totally play to that and try to adopt those changes as they come about. Yet, since it is such a global tool, we need to do it in a very organized and planned, methodical sort of way. We can't say 'This doesn't work, change it now.' We have a process that makes this a scheduled item that we do in the course of our Web lives. We look at what we have, and we look at how we can do it better, and then we plan and make it better."

Chevron: A System in Transition

Like Compaq, Chevron Oil is a truly global organization with a corporate presence in all the major commercial centers of the world. As a company that also prospects for oil and other energy sources, however, Chevron employees are even more far flung than your typical multinational. Chevron crews explore the Siberian tundra and the African veldt, inhabiting base stations from the North Slope of Alaska to the South China Sea. As with every other major company in the world, Chevron has been a denizen of the World Wide Web for years, with its own home page at www.chevron.com (Figure 3.12).

What makes Chevron interesting, however, is not its level of web entrepreneurship, but how closely it represents the average mix of information technologies in the business world in the last half of the last decade of the twentieth century. That is to say, it runs the entire gamut: "We have people that don't use computers at all," says one internal observer. "Then we have people who still think the mainframe is the only way to do things. We have people moving out into distributive processing, and then other people moving back into large server technology on the other end."

That's not to say Chevron is a slouch in the IT department. Some of its operations are very much on the cutting edge, employing the latest RISC and client-server technologies to solve technical problems in oil exploration and production. But as with many companies today, some business units at Chevron still harbor traditional legacy systems, the large mainframe computers still accessed through 1970s-era 3270 terminals. Chevron has already unified its business operations through a global, wide area network that includes satellite links. But some links in the network are decidedly weak, with bandwidth as low as 9,600 baud in some remote areas. In other cases, very small branch offices may not have a network connection at all.

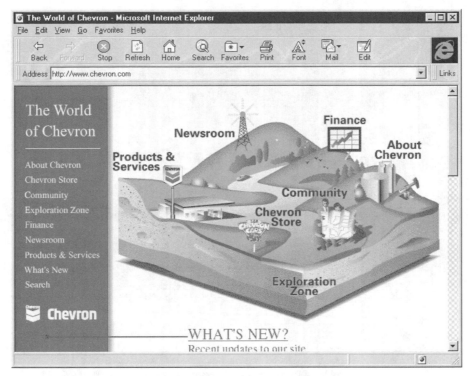

Figure 3.12 The Chevron World Wide Web site.

That an intranet could grow and prosper in such an environment is testimony to its power as a communications tool. Naturally, the web has grown quickest and fullest in areas of the company that have already moved to distributed client-server environments. Chevron technology organizations such as Chevron Information Technology Company (CITC), Chevron Petroleum Technology Company (CPTC), and their London IT group are arms of the corporation that admittedly specialize in applying computer technology to common business and scientific problems, and they are also the earliest adopters. Talking to web proponents in these organizations, you get the feeling it will be only a matter of time before the technology reaches other parts of the global organization as well, and it is these forward-looking business units that are pointing the way.

The Basic Structure

At first glance, many components of the Chevron intranet look just as sophisticated and appear to provide just as much value as anything at Sun or DEC.

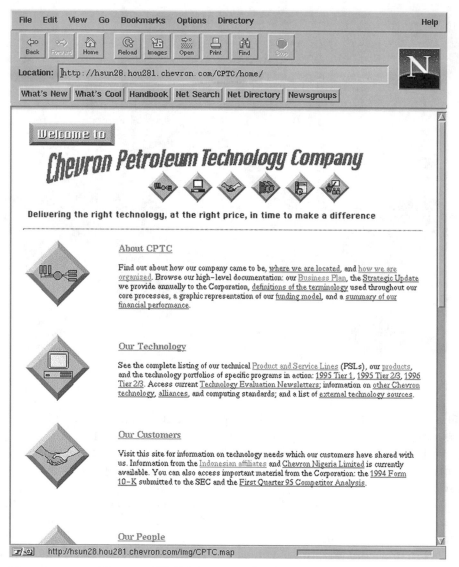

Figure 3.13   Chevron CPTC intranet home page.

This provides clear proof that you don't need every business unit on board before you can start providing value to a wide range of system users. In fact, many business units have built their own semiautonomous intranet web sites, which link to other business units through Chevron's global corporate network in much the same way that autonomous World Wide Web sites link to each other over the global Internet.

The intranet home page for CPTC is a great example (Figure 3.13). Starting at the CPTC home page and drilling down into the web structure, you will find an incredible amount of information about the company, its operations, and its products. Here's a summary of what you will find:

About CPTC.   A history of the company; maps of key locations (Figure 3.14); the company business plan; strategic planning documents; flow diagrams of processes that link to definitions, schedules, tools, improvements; the funding model; financial performance; information on metrics; and a message from the president.

Our technology.   A complete portfolio of the company's technical product and service lines, detail of funding portfolios for each product and service line, information on strategic research, and links to other tech-

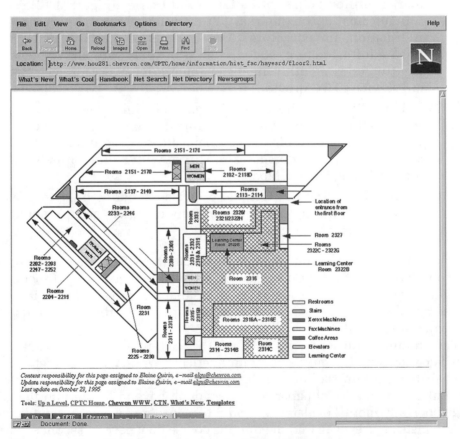

Figure 3.14   Chevron intranet—building floor plan.

nology sources within Chevron and on the Internet. This is the largest and one of the most widely used sections on the CPTC site.

Our customers.   Information on CPTC's internal customers (other business units or affiliates) plus competitor analysis for companies outside of Chevron. This section is provided by people in overseas operations to help CPTC align its operations with their business.

Our people.   Home pages for every employee in CPTC, plus a home page for each business team, including its purpose, charter, and members, with cross-links back to its related product and portfolio pages.

Internal resources.   General communications including corporate bulletins and memos, the company newsletter, and a form employees can use to ask management questions. This page also provides an online library catalog where staffers can search and locate any of over a quarter-million books in the Chevron libraries (Figure 3.12). There's also information on internal job openings; human resource policy information; infrastructure, and all kinds of products and services that are infrastructure related, such as business support services. This page includes monthly financial reports for every project, product, and service CPTC provides.

Training.   Provides course descriptions, schedules, and online registration for all internal training, including the company's geological, geophysical, and reservoir management areas. Descriptions of selected courses from 75 vendors are also shown with a direct link to the vendor's web site, if available.

Other options.   The CPTC home page also contains links to pages explaining web technology, intercompany technical groups, and a companywide search engine.

One thing that strikes you immediately about the CPTC pages is the impressive depth of the information and services available. The library directory and training directory alone are major resources that can provide incredible value to users without the enormous overhead of compiling, printing, and distributing paper documents.

The training directory originally was a 2,500-page paper document that was later converted to online use with Interleaf's WorldView product and now is available only on the intranet by querying an Oracle database. "The web has cut down on a lot of paper, and users don't have to lug around the 2,500-page book any more," explains Sharon Sloan, leader of Chevron's publications group. Instead, users can find the training course they need in seconds, without pulling a book off the shelves. In addition, the information is easier to update through random database entries and—instead of waiting for a "critical mass" or the budget to publish a new 2,500-page edition—each new update made to the CPTC curriculum is available instantaneously over the web (Figure 3.15).

A Study in Experimentation

The story of how the company's intranet came together is an interesting study in experimentation, as always with new intranets. One of the local players in the process was John Hanten, Strategic Planning and Communications Manager at the company's Houston office, who gets much of the credit for the depth and organization of the CPTC web site.

Chevron's ability to create a web benefited from a TCP/IP infrastructure that was already in place, due to the presence of UNIX servers on the network. Before the web came along, the network was already being used for news servers, FTP servers, and file servers. In late 1994, the first components of the intranet began with local experiments at the company's LaHabra, California, facility, followed soon after by a server in London.

By February of the following year, Hanten had "tuned in" to see the offerings of the various servers already on the web. But what he saw was considerably disorganized. "On the Houston page I saw links to neat info, but no real organization at all. At the same time, some of our scientific teams were starting to learn about web technology and were looking for places to see things." At that point, says Hanten, he assembled a small group to design what the overall document structure would look like. "At nights and on our own machines, we started building pages," he said. "We wanted to pack the system with valuable information so people would use it immediately."

Instead of just organizing the information, however, Hanten and his team developed more functionality. "We tapped the resources of Roger Cutler, an experienced Chevron UNIX developer, and found a way to convert some of our legacy databases such as DB/2 to the web format. For example, we had several library card catalogs that we converted completely for access on the web. A lot of information was in obscure legacy systems that only gatekeepers had access to, and we used our programming resources to drain the databases and post the information in web pages."

Within a week, Cutler had converted the card catalogs for all the Chevron libraries and put a search engine on top, so that users didn't even have to contact the librarian to find a book or document. "If you want to check out a document, now you have forms you can use to do that," Hanten says (see Figure 3.16).

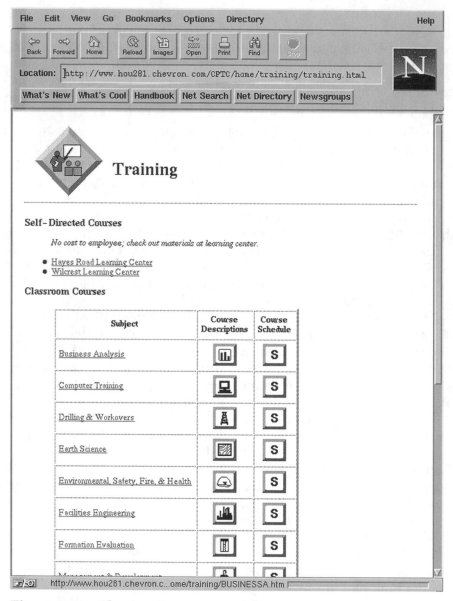

Figure 3.15   Chevron intranet—training page.

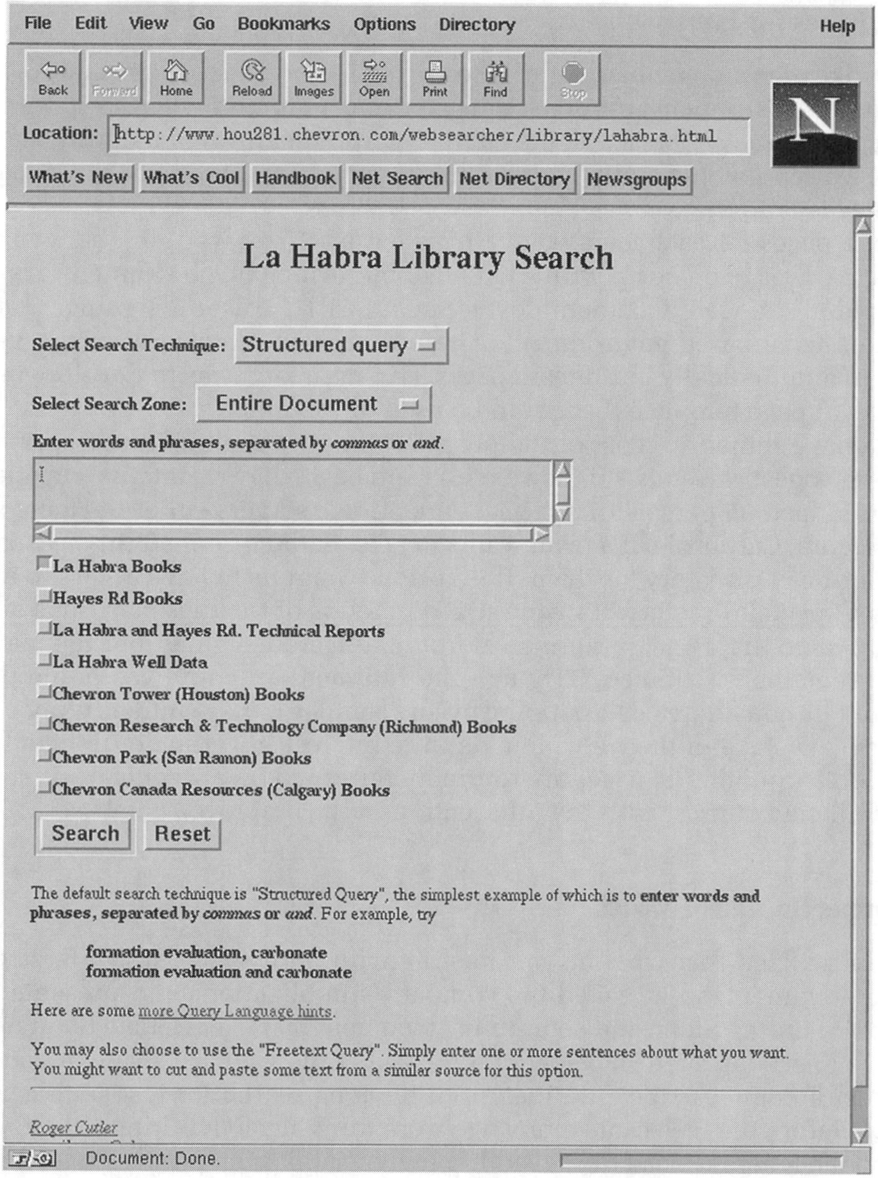

| File | Edit | View | Go | Bookmarks | Options | Directory | | Help |

| Back | Forward | Home | Reload | Images | Open | Print | Find | Stop |

Location: http://www.hou281.chevron.com/websearcher/library/lahabra.html

| What's New | What's Cool | Handbook | Net Search | Net Directory | Newsgroups |

La Habra Library Search

Select Search Technique: Structured query

Select Search Zone: Entire Document

Enter words and phrases, separated by *commas* or *and*.

□ La Habra Books

□ Hayes Rd Books

□ La Habra and Hayes Rd. Technical Reports

□ La Habra Well Data

□ Chevron Tower (Houston) Books

□ Chevron Research & Technology Company (Richmond) Books

□ Chevron Park (San Ramon) Books

□ Chevron Canada Resources (Calgary) Books

| Search | | Reset |

The default search technique is "Structured Query", the simplest example of which is to **enter words and phrases, separated by** *commas* or *and*. For example, try

formation evaluation, carbonate
formation evaluation and carbonate

Here are some more Query Language hints.

You may also choose to use the "Freetext Query". Simply enter one or more sentences about what you want. You might want to cut and paste some text from a similar source for this option.

Roger Cutler

Document: Done.

Figure 3.16   Chevron intranet—CPTC library search.

Home Pages for Everyone

In a stroke of minor genius, Cutler also devised a way to take information from the company's human resources database and *automatically build a starter home page for every person in the company.* To get employee pictures, Hanten says, "we sent people around with a digital camera and then just downloaded the images onto the web."

Home pages for each team were a little harder. "You wouldn't believe how difficult it was to come up with a list of all our team names," Hanten says. "At the time of the web document development, CPTC was undergoing a transition to a team-based environment. The information systems were not yet in place to automatically build team pages. Our approach was to develop a standard team page template that could be used by anyone.

"We have reined in most of the people setting up their own servers—even for team pages," he adds. "If they have a team page, they maintain it on one big server. In fact, 95 percent of our pages are on two servers either in Houston or in La Habra, California. If a team wants to take on the responsibility, we create a higher-level directory for them. If they don't want us to have access to it, we create a special directory. It's centralized in terms of the files being in a single place. We do that to get performance from the search engines, but the maintenance remains distributed." Though the rudimentary employee home pages couldn't be considered eye-popping by any standard, they suddenly gave each employee a stake in the web and a definite interest in getting online and taking a look around. The pages are routinely refreshed on a weekly basis so that they will stay current with the information in the employee database.

Electronic Document Model

Hanten realized that what he was dealing with, in essence, was a large electronic document, so he asked the company's publications and presentations group, including Sloan and soon-to-be document manager Debbie Scott, to get involved early on as the key team for managing the web. He also realized that web technology was the culmination of his long search for just such a set of tools. "Before the web came along, we were thinking about things like Hypercard tools, where we had the capability to hyperlink from page to page. But we didn't have a common platform: We had people on PCs, Macs, and UNIX machines."

CPTC uses the Verity search engine to glean information from any or all of the other Chevron servers, so if you want to quickly search the entire population of servers on the intranet, you can do it using a World Wide Web–style search with keywords. In addition, the Chevron web provides specialized searches, such as a search on technology evaluations, newsgroups, or library documents.

CPTC has added links to its webs so that managers and teams can easily review financial information like the profit-and-loss statements for each project. "In the past," says Hanten, "users would have to learn a series of SQL commands to obtain the information. Now, at the end of the month, we run a batch job and create all the standard reports that the teams might use. This information was originally captured as part of our internal DB/2 billing system and Nomad project management system that most employees found difficult to use.

"The reports are generated in a flat file, automatically parsed and linked using routines developed by Cutler, and presented as preformatted text in the browser window. I monitor team activities, so I look at project financial information for each team for the month, and I also check my own. Customers can call any CPTC project leader or manager and ask how much we have spent on their project year to date. Using the search engine, the project leader or manager can just put in the project ID code and that pulls up the requested information. The old way, you had to run a batch job in a couple of hours or overnight. You never were sure you would get the right thing." Hanten figures his company saves about $200,000 per year in mainframe costs based on avoiding all the extra batch job activity. Most amazing, producing the web applications to generate all this data didn't even require the efforts of a full-time person. It took about a week to do the programming for the financial pages, Hanten estimates.

CPTC uses Lotus Notes for those kinds of applications that require collaborative authoring, security, and the ability to provide different views of information included in the technical and internal service portfolios. Yet, there are only about 200 licenses for Notes in CPTC, and many of CPTC's customers have not adopted Notes as a standard groupware tool. To make this information available, CPTC uses the InterNotes Web Publisher. "Our main challenge with InterNotes," says Hanten and his group, is that "you really need to design your Notes database with the idea that you are going to publish on the web. Some things are very awkward unless you do that."

Managing the Web

To manage the intranet, Hanten created a group called the *CPTC Web Content and Coordination Team*. This team includes representatives from each of CPTC's management teams. "We identified four areas we needed to look at in terms of managing the web document: (1) Is the content appropriate? (2) What kind of style guidelines do we use? (3) What browsers do we have, and how widely are they deployed? and (4) Are employees aware of these things?" In terms of the actual pages themselves, CPTC assigns a content owner and an update owner for each web page. If the people responsible for content don't know how to make the change, they can communicate with someone who does. "We also have some low-key police patrollers who check for bad links," says Hanten. Since the responsible parties have their e-mail addresses included right on the page, it's quite simple for anyone spotting a problem to notify the content or update owner by e-mail.

To improve the management of the overall Chevron web, a similar coordination team was established at the corporate level to study the idea of corporatewide standards for page content, size, navigation controls, helper applications, support for various HTML versions, and other features. One of the first decisions of the corporatewide team was to standardize on the Netscape Navigator browser for all clients. As with many intranet adopters, however, CPTC is now migrating to Microsoft's Internet Explorer product.

For now, the web browser is a standard part of the common operating environment being deployed in many Chevron organizations, which means it is installed by default on every computer in that environment. Hanten and his team are enthusiastic about the payoff from web technology so far. "In the past, our communication with Nigeria has been via e-mail, and with the time differential it was inconvenient. Now, web technology is their preferred method. We stage a lot of technical information out there, so that if they want to see what the current bug release is for a particular application, the team in charge lists it on the web. Instead of contacting a person, users can look it up. In addition, the interested customers can supply us with their thoughts, needs, desires, and problems."

The examples of savings are abundant. "We can document the cost savings we have earned by making the information centrally available. Tangible examples include our financial reports and reduced hard-copy distribution of all types of documents." There are nondocumented savings as well, according to Hanten. "In the past we e-mailed information to all CPTC managers, with the result that we had all these duplicate files lying around on the network that might be current or might not be current. It's intangible things like these that we believe improve productivity and yield the greatest savings," he says.

In terms of costs for the overall environment, the incremental cost of the Netscape licenses was small compared to the added functionality web technology provided, says Hanten. "There's a cost of increased bandwidth, but that would have happened anyway with the normal growth of our network. The cost per byte of bandwidth keeps dropping.

"For a company like ours to be successful," Hanten observes, "we need to tap information sources anywhere in the world and apply the optimum technology solution. We always talk about the collective knowledge of CPTC as an organization, but before there was no way to organize or systematically access this knowledge repository." Of course, as with most other intranets covered in this chapter, the CPTC web provides seamless integration to the external world, including Chevron's own Internet home page at www.chevron.com (Figure 3.12). As with most other external web sites, Chevron's was designed by an external design firm. Since the business of CPTC is research, staffers have found the easy Internet connectivity incredibly useful in their daily jobs. "The real high-tech people can go out on the Internet with different searches and get answers in minutes that used to take people hours to find," says Chevron-Houston webmaster Jim O'Connor.

Looking Back

Now several years into the project, the original team that created the CPTC intranet looks back at the original decisions they made and some of the mid-course corrections since the project first came online. "In a way, it's more of the same, and it has not slowed down," says Hanten. "Maybe the rate of learning about the possibilities has slowed down, but the intranet is expanding and continues to expand—especially in the realm of communications. There is a wider author base, with people learning how to build and maintain web pages with tools such as Netscape Navigator Gold, Microsoft Internet Assistant for Word, and Microsoft FrontPage. We worked with some of the office assistant teams to show them the work flow, and we have templates on our intranet that have navigation buttons and other elements built-in that will allow the page to go live immediately."

Overall the CPTC team has seen a tremendous return on investment, often by incorporating shareware and freeware elements into their intranet, such as a calendar-scheduling package retrieved from the World Wide Web. "The most expensive package we bought is the Verity search engine," says Jim O'Connor, CPTC webmaster. "So the return on investment is taken for granted now. It's just like there aren't studies done anymore of whether you should put a phone in everybody's office. It's just done."

CPTC has also gotten more sophisticated in the way it places content on the intranet. "When the intranet was first started," Hanten recalls, "there weren't a lot of back-end engines to produce web pages dynamically. Now, we have taken great advantage of the Lotus Notes Domino server to dynamically publish Notes databases. We have also experimented with the Oracle web-server tools for ad hoc queries out of our data warehouse." Using such techniques,

Sloan adds that her group of three people was able to publish over 6,000 pages of information in a few weeks.

CPTC has opened its intranet pages to external joint venture partners who have connections to the Chevron global network, such as Hibernia Offshore Canada, Western Australia Petroleum, and others. "Chevron has a strong interest in all of these companies," says Hanten, "but these groups are not allowed through the firewall for IT access." Instead, there is a secured site on the World Wide Web that provides proprietary content appropriate for some of Chevron's business partners. The site is protected by looking at the domain name of the person who is accessing it (rather than requiring a separate user ID and password for each individual trying to access the content). The web server checks the address of the accessing browser and verifies the user's domain name automatically.

Information made available to external business partners includes the Chevron technology catalog, employee lists, project teams, an upstream technology newsletter, and the training catalog with all courses that are open to business partners. In addition, Chevron is building a knowledge base that contains the accumulated knowledge of a small group of key Chevron experts. "Those pages are funded by partners who want to tap into the knowledge base," says Hanten. Some have even contributed their own content, such as interpretation charts and a complete glossary of terms. "For a long time we had help manuals and user guides and frequently asked questions," Hanten acknowledges, "but the idea of having a database to do knowledge capture is something new."

A Tree with Leaves

"In terms of overall intranet content," Hanten says, "there are a few things we did early on that served us well. The original organization of the intranet has changed very little since we set up the model. I see it as a tree, and people are responsible for populating the tree with leaves. Many technical teams now have the capability to build their own pages that are internally linked, but if they want to link off a higher page they work with the publications group."

As opposed to its previous mix of mainframe terminals and desktop computers, the number of dumb terminals in the company will decrease significantly as part of a new project to put PCs on most company desktops within three years. "When we started the intranet, the standard database technology was Nomad, and everyone with a terminal had access to it," Hanten recalls, "That is a legacy thing we are migrating away from."

As part of its new hardware specification, Chevron decided to strongly support mobile computing. Employees will be able to select from a standard desktop configuration or a laptop model. Employees who are on the road can tap into the company intranet through a SecurID system. Meanwhile, the company still copies its intranet onto CD for locations with very slow—or no—network connections.

As before, within CPTC there are still very few password-protected sites on the intranet. "There are some teams who want to make information available only to [internal] paying customers," Hanten says, "but information about our financials is available to all employees, so that they don't have to keep track of passwords and that sort of thing. Our general philosophy is that if it is so sensitive that it could be damaging, it is probably not appropriate for the web."

O'Connor adds, "There were some reports that were protected, but we just don't put them online anymore. There is also protection for calendars. The updating of a site is protected, but not the reading. There are a couple of teams shipping their products [to internal customers] through the web, and in those cases, they give the user the key and then download it. If the user gives the key away, then the user will have to pay for anyone else who downloads the information."

Overall, the impact of the intranet on company operations has been tremendous. "Now, when people are involved in a project, all information describing the project, its vision, its focus, and what decisions have been made are all posted on the web. If people are worried about how some project is going to affect them, they can go to the web to read the status of it. People still hear rumors about what is going to happen, but the web helps get that information out right away so there isn't so much time wasted on 'hall talk.' If there is something they don't like, the web page shows who to contact to get better information." Adds Sloan, "If you tried to manage that using e-mail, it would be a nightmare across the company."

Where Do We Go from Here?

Now that you understand web technology and the way it is used in real business environments, it's time to take a more in-depth look at the tools and techniques used to create the typical web site. The next four chapters cover the major features and applications of the technology, including web-site management, online publishing, multimedia, interactivity, and advanced features.

PART TWO

THE INTRANET FOR EVERYONE

◆ This section can be used by any business unit to create and manage its part of the intranet. It explains what is needed to set up a server and the content that goes on the server, including web pages, graphics, multimedia, and interactive data. The needs of individual business units are different from IS or the strategic planners. Business units are less likely to engage in large-scale, Java-style development projects and more likely to engage in publishing or tool-assisted database connectivity. Even though many companies now have intranets, many business units are still coming online that need help and guidance with the specific technologies to make it all work.

Chapter Four at a Glance

The most successful intranets are not those with the most Java gurus per capita, but those where individual business units have been trained and empowered with the basics: how to bring their own information online by creating simple HTML-based web pages. To assist in this endeavor, this chapter reviews exactly what it takes to set up a departmental web site and begin producing intranet content. This information will best be used by the person(s) responsible for creating and managing the intranet site. You will learn:

- Why it's important to always learn the basics of the technology, whether you are an intranet planner or a content provider

- How to start an intranet from scratch, if your company doesn't have one already

- What any business unit can do to participate in an existing intranet

- What approach to take when planning or enhancing an intranet web site

- How to set up a test server and a *proof of concept* for an intranet site

- What types of information you can share, and the different types of users you can share it with

- Basic tools and work flows you can use to prepare content for the web

- How to structure information on the server

- How to connect your users to the information center or protect your pages from unauthorized users

Wiring the Business Unit

Do me a favor. Before you do anything else, pull out a sheet of paper and write the following words in big block letters. While you're at it, draw a few flowers around the edges, too.

KEEP IT SIMPLE

Now take that sheet of paper, frame it, and hang it on the wall over your computer. This should be the mantra for the intranet, because no intranet will succeed unless you can avoid making things more complicated than they really have to be. Web technology is complicated enough, without you and me adding to the noise level.

Remember that you are not creating an intranet just because you like web technology and think it's groovy. You're creating an intranet because it will satisfy business requirements, make people more productive, open new channels of communication within the organization, and (I hope) make things *easier for everyone.* This means that the system should be easy to use, easy to access, easy to participate in, and easy to administer. Above all it should be easier and cheaper than the current alternatives: the copy machine, mail system, and the bureaucracy-laden network management schemes we use today. Otherwise, nobody will want to use it—nor should they.

That doesn't necessarily mean it will be easy for the people who set up the first few sites or who create the pilot intranet (although it can be, if you use the right tools). There has to be someone who reads this book, getting up to speed on all the concepts and leading the way. As simple as I try to keep things in this book, there are still some subjects that are inherently technical. But the idea is, given this knowledge, you can go out and create a system that will be easy to use *by everyone.*

If you're still stuck in a bureaucratic frame of mind, maybe you'll understand better if I say we need to create systems that are *inclusive, empowering,* and *decentralized.* This is, after all, what the World Wide Web has proven already: You can build a field of dreams and the world will come, as long as you open it up to everyone and keep the bureaucracy at a minimum.

Empowerment is the key to making a web system inclusive and decentralized. Empowerment means people helping themselves, which means having the knowledge, tools, and techniques to do what needs to be done to make the system work. In this chapter and the following, I will try to impart that knowledge to you and show you how to think when you impart it to others.

You may notice something odd about this book that is different from other intranet books. Most books of this kind—by this point—would be deep into a discussion of strategic planning: what to do before you start building your intranet. However, if truth be told, most early intranets—including some of the largest in the world—came into being with very little strategic planning. They simply grew on their own through the initiative of individual work groups who taught themselves the technology and then put it to work. If you read the example of SunWeb in Chapter 3, you should understand how that can work.

That's not to say that chaotic growth is desirable, or that planning is not important—because it is. A well-planned intranet will take you on the straightest (although potentially slowest) path to success. Yet, while planning is desirable and important to success, it is something that is done by a very small cadre of intranet builders. The true action in the corporate intranet is not at the planning level, but at the business unit or departmental level. For it is the individual business unit that must eventually generate the volumes of crucial information that will make the intranet truly useful to everyone.

This chapter, then, begins an in-depth look at all the key technologies that will be employed in bringing your department or business unit online, from setting up a web server, to organizing a web site, to generating published content, to ongoing management of the web site. If you are to be a strategic planner for your budding intranet, you will benefit from wading through this material, because these are all the technologies you should know in detail before you even begin to plan. In addition to the serving and publishing technologies covered here, the next two chapters will continue with additional information related to multimedia and data-driven web applications.

This chapter assumes that a few of you out there may still be building intranets from scratch, but that many more of you are probably struggling to participate in an intranet that already exists on your corporate networks. If you belong to either category, there is something here for you to learn.

If this were like other books, I would jump right into the most technical part of the argument, scare the pants off everyone, and proceed from there. Instead, I am here to tell you that anyone can create an intranet from scratch, or participate in one that already exists. And anyone can provide content that can be served over the intranet. When I say anyone, I mean secretaries, accountants, your boss, people who can't program a VCR, and people with six thumbs on each hand. Not that any of these people will be interested necessarily in setting up their own web sites; but with proper encouragement and a little hand holding, they can at least be motivated to participate.

Above all, I hope to demystify the process of setting up a web site. If there is anything intranets require right now, it is demystification. When approached in the right frame of mind, setting up and using an intranet web site should be no harder than installing and using Microsoft Word. Of course, there may be complications along the way. But let's assume that everything will go right and that you will be successful, then we can talk about what might go wrong.

If we take this approach and treat the intranet like any other run-of-the-mill business application, we can empower any individual, department, or group in the company to become an autonomous *information center,* communicating with users across the enterprise the same way people do on the World Wide Web. This chapter explains what an information center is and how to set one up. And it will show you why we should let many of these centers blossom and grow.

What Is an Information Center?

Information center is the term I use to describe a web site on an intranet. As such, it is the basic unit of organization in an intranet. It can be a person, a group, a department, or a division of a company. The main qualification is that the people involved: (1) work together on the same LAN, (2) have access to the same network drives, and (3) want to share information with other people inside or outside of the company (accessed through the same LAN, through a WAN, through dial-up connections, or by serving across an extranet).

Typically, this will probably happen at the departmental level, since each department has a common set of information to share and a common place to store it. For instance:

Human resources may want to publish employee-orientation materials, benefits programs, company policy programs, and newsletters over the intranet, rather than going through the standard paper distribution system.

Documentation and training groups may want to provide its manuals online through a web rather than in three-ring binders, on CD-ROM, or using other media or tools.

Engineering may want to set up its own servers to communicate product development plans, schedules, and other information.

Marketing may want to distribute continuously updated product information for general reference by employees, dealers, suppliers, or customers.

Tech support could provide troubleshooting tips, access to the knowledge base, and interactive services.

Legal could offer online access to legal guidelines such as those on sexual harassment in the workplace.

MIS could even use it to deliver legacy data from large mainframes or other traditional computing systems, without the traditional programming efforts required by other methods of delivery.

You could say that each of these traditional departments is, by its very nature, already an information center. However, an information center doesn't have to be a department or a traditionally organized group. For instance, a cross-functional team charged with improving productivity in the manufacturing division may have data, meeting notes, and progress reports it wants to share with the rest of the company. Thus, the team itself can become an ad hoc information center providing information to the rest of the enterprise.

At one company where I worked a few years ago, there was a guy who did nothing but cross-reference lists of catalog numbers. For every catalog number the company used, his list showed the corresponding catalog numbers for similar products in competitor catalogs. This information was always in demand, because it was useful not only to customers and customer service reps, but to product managers, sales reps, and even system developers in the company's internal organization. If web systems had existed back then, the guy who maintained that list would have been a natural-born information center.

Maybe *you personally* have some particular information you would like to share with the rest of the company, such as scores of the company volleyball teams, recent sightings of the company president, historical information, troubleshooting tips, software reviews, hard-to-find statistics, or contact information for your department. If you have anything at all you want to share with others in an organization, *you* should consider becoming an information center (Figure 4.1).

What Does It Take to Set Up a Web Site?

With an intranet, it doesn't take all that much to set up a web site, just a computer and the right tools. The main component of a web site is a *web server,* which includes the following components:

Hardware.   A network-connected desktop computer on which the web server software is installed. This could even be the computer you're using right now.

Software.   The appropriate web server software that can be used to automatically send information to any user who requests it. Your company

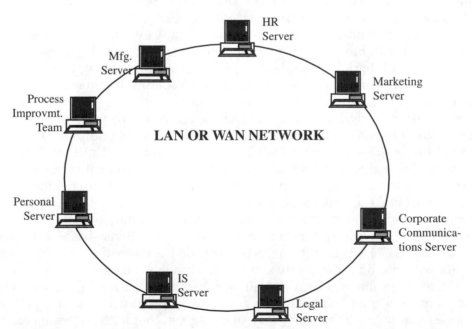

Figure 4.1   Information centers on an intranet.

may already have servers set up that you can use to host your web content. Or it may be okay for you to set up a server yourself. If so, you can get several different types of web servers off the Internet for free evaluation and testing (see the sidebar titled "Where to Find Web Software").

Content.   The information you will serve to the rest of the organization depends on what you have available, but it could be documents, database records, or multimedia files.

Notice the one thing missing from this list that you would need if you were setting up shop on the World Wide Web: an Internet connection. Since no Internet connection is required, this simplifies the process of setting up an intranet web site.

How to Get Started

If your company already has web servers online that can be used for delivering intranet content, a lot of your work has already been done. All that your group needs to do is create the content and put it in the right place for serving. To find out where, ask an existing web coordinator.

If your company doesn't have web servers already available for use and you are entrusted with building an intranet "from scratch," then I suggest you get a web server online right away, before you even begin planning your intranet. Why? Because planning should not occur in a vacuum. If you are the person or team leader in charge of planning, organizing, and building an intranet, you should already have dabbled in the technology yourself, which means you should have created a little bit of web content, put some graphics, sound, or video online, or dabbled in web application development. Until you begin to play with this technology yourself and feel the power you get when you can make it work like a dream, you really have no idea what you are talking about, and you will make a truly lousy planner.

Setting up an intranet web server isn't as hard as it may sound. For example, on one of the first intranets I ever set up (for the Swiss-based European division of a U.S. Fortune 100 company), I carried a shareware web server into the site with me on a floppy diskette. I also brought along an extra diskette containing an evaluation copy of Netscape Navigator. (If you know how large both server and client software has grown over the past few years, you can imagine how long ago this story took place—given that both software components at the time would fit on a couple of floppies.) Neither the server nor the browser software cost me a dime to use for demonstration and evaluation purposes. I didn't preload them or preconfigure them in any way. Here's what I did to get that early intranet fired up:

1. I copied the server installation file onto a PC, unzipped it, and fired up the server.
2. I created a few simple demonstration files in HTML and saved them in the server "document root" (the default folder where web pages are stored).
3. I went to the office of the manager who hired me, installed the Netscape software on his computer, started it up, and let him read the demonstration files I had created. Keep in mind the files were still back on the server computer and he was reading them *across the network.*

Three steps, about 30 minutes worth of time, and voilà—instant "proof of concept." Of course, proof of concept was all it was—as well as the start of what would become a much longer, ongoing development process. But, at that moment, our first intranet web site was already a *fait accompli,* and we were ready to begin the actual development. Although the size and features of the software have changed over the years, the basic principles have not.

Remember that a web server is software that you install on a computer. Typically, the installation will look a lot like any other software installation you might do on the same type of computer. So just about anyone can set up a web server anywhere on a computer network, assuming that doing so is permitted at your company. And once the server is installed and content is prepared, anyone using a web browser should be able to read the content from any location in the network.

The art is not in the mechanical part, it's in the informational part. The art is presenting information to users in a way that provides value, gets people interested in using the system, and then manages the communication explosion that follows.

The importance of these last two factors cannot be overestimated. I know of companies now where the intranet is so popular that some people are using it to put pictures of their *dogs* online. The managers at these companies should be happy (but aren't) because at least their intranets are being used by rank-and-file people to communicate across organizational boundaries (never mind that what they are trying to communicate sometimes verges on the inappropriate). Other places I know have spent a lot of money and put in extensive development work on an intranet, but the employees don't use it, mainly because they haven't been told it exists, haven't been convinced it's important, or haven't been trained to use it. But more on that later.

How to Tell if Your Network Can Support an Intranet

One reason it was easy for me to install an intranet site on the client's network is the network already "had what it takes" to support a web system. The what-it-takes part is the protocol known as *TCP/IP.* I knew that the network supported TCP/IP before I started, or else I wouldn't have bothered. Time was, the only networks that supported TCP/IP were networks that had UNIX servers installed on them. These days, however, most network components, including servers and desktop operating systems, come with TCP/IP already embedded in them.

As you may recall from Chapter 2, TCP/IP is the native protocol that all Internet applications use to communicate. This doesn't mean you need an Internet connection to use it—just that your network must have TCP/IP to run Internet-style applications like web browsers and servers. Without TCP/IP, you cannot create a web-based intranet. So the first thing you may want to do before you even begin to install a server is find out whether the network supports TCP/IP.

Actually, my client was not sure if the network used TCP/IP or not. Keep in mind that this was an IT manager, who normally should know things like this. Originally, he said, "the network uses SNA and Netware." But a quick check with key network administrators confirmed that TCP/IP had also been installed recently to support *other* client-server software running on UNIX servers.

Some people make the mistake of assuming that just because a network uses one type of protocol, it can't support others. For instance, just because your network uses Netware doesn't mean it can't also have TCP/IP. In fact, TCP/IP can sit right on top of Netware without anyone knowing the difference, and web applications can glide across the network on the TCP/IP layer without even causing a ripple in the Netware environment (see the accompanying sidebar, "Running an Intranet on Netware").

That's why it's important—even if someone tells you there's no TCP/IP—to check it out for yourself. Because some of the most knowledgeable people in your organization may not know for sure. When in doubt, it may be easier just to run a quick server test as I did (see the "proof-of-concept" test later in this chapter). But there are also several fairly quick and easy ways you can find out whether TCP/IP is available:

> **People are already using web browsers.**   If you know people are already using web browsers or web servers on your network, skip the rest of this section. That's obvious, isn't it?

People are already using UNIX servers.   If some applications are running on UNIX server, chances are your network supports TCP/IP. When I say UNIX server, I mean something like Sun, Silicon Graphics, IBM RS/6000, or some variant of these.

Your network administrator says so.   Of course, the easiest way to find out may be to check with your network administrator down the hall. Keep in mind that even he or she may not know for sure. On the other hand, the network administrator may have the IP addresses of all networked computers in the building, or even in the entire company, which could be a significant aid if you plan to begin installing and testing a web server.

Actually, this might be a great time to start a dialog with the network administrator about what you're trying to accomplish. Keep in mind that the administrator may be sensitive to unauthorized "tampering" with the network, so it may be wise to clear the project with your manager first. It's important to understand that setting up a web server test will not (at least initially) require anything more involved than installing and running a couple of software programs. You should not have to reconfigure any part of the network, or even any individual desktop machines (see the following section for more details on working with network administrators).

If any of these methods turns up evidence of TCP/IP and you have at least tacit approval from your network administrator and department manager, you can run a server test, as explained later in this chapter. This will be a quick way to test the viability of a web service on your network.

However, if you verify that there is no TCP/IP on the system (and someone in authority says, furthermore, there is no chance you'll have it soon), then you have a larger problem. Not only do you have the chore of creating an intranet, you also have to convince your network people to adopt the basic tools you need to make it work. The main problem here is that you may have to do some serious cost justification. But, with early adopters now reporting up to 1,000 percent return on investment, that job's getting much easier.

How to Handle Surly Administrators

There—did I get the attention of all you administrators out there—network, system, or otherwise? You opened the book, looked at the table of contents, and said "what the . . ." Then you came straight to this section to see what's going on. Great, because I have something special to say to you, as well as to the people who will be working with you.

At this point in history, I expect every network or system administrator with his or her head above water to be fully informed about the intranet and all the benefits it can provide to an organization. Nevertheless, there is still that small percentage of companies out there with IS departments that are still in the Dark Ages. I'm talking about companies where people are still working on networks controlled by LAN Manager, where they are still shepherding massive groups of Windows 3.1 PCs onward through the fog. Or some company where they are still using character-based UNIX applications and people still haven't learned to use e-mail. Or even worse, an organization where the predominant desktop computer is a dumb terminal connected to a mainframe. If your organization doesn't have a mainframe or a PC network yet—well, you shouldn't even be holding this book in your hands: Drop it right now and go back to your typewriter.

If this sounds like your company, setting up intranet web sites may be a lot harder than my description of it in this book. For instance, if you still have Windows 3.1 on your desktops, chances are you may have to install something called a *TCP/IP stack* on each networked computer before an intranet will work. And forget about web authoring—most decent PC-based authoring tools require a 32-bit operating system such as Windows 95 or 98 to work.

Then there are all the in-house experts you may have to deal with. Most companies that are still in the Dark Ages computing-wise are that way for either of two reasons: (1) Management doesn't believe computers are worth the money you spend on them; (2) the internal computer staff is still in the Dark Ages, too. If the latter is the case, you may eventually run across that odd corporate denizen I call "the surly administrator." That's not to say all administrators are surly, or that it's wrong for them to be surly. We all understand that it's the administrator's job to manage both the people and the machines that make the organization drone. And sometimes that means putting up with shenanigans from users who want to do odd things—such as install web servers on the network. When that happens and the administrator's having a bad day, well, let's just say the results could be unpredictable.

In the early days, I was one of those oddball users trying to install web server software on the network, usually by authority of some midlevel manager. And my administrator pals tried their best to understand. But many could not imagine why I would want to put web servers on a private network. There were so many other client-server solutions that seemed so superior to this experimental web stuff, it just didn't compute.

These days, of course, nearly everyone in the IT world has heard about the intranet and what it can do for a company. So now, instead of being the first line of defense *against* an intranet, some administrators are often its biggest proponents. Consequently, I've gone from working at odds with administrators to working with them (or even *for* them).

This brings up some important lessons I've learned that you may want to note as well. The first is for nonadministrators to understand that well-trained, up-to-date network administrators can be your friends and can help you enormously in getting past technical hurdles. More than anyone else, these are the people most likely to have the expertise to help you accomplish your goals. Realize, though, that you may still encounter skepticism, and that you should never ask an administrator to do something that would violate protocol. Having a manager's permission will always be necessary.

If you are a network administrator trying to set up an intranet, you have a different lesson to learn. The main thing is to avoid—as much as your corporate culture will allow—the old mind-set that says everyone must have permission to do *anything.* Remember that people will be using the intranet to communicate. So they will need clear, unrestricted access to a controlled set of directories or folders on the web server. You may still want to impose some control over who can publish on the intranet, but the farther up the chain the decisions must go, the greater the obstacle to the free flow of information. It's best to do as people have done on the World Wide Web and seek wherever possible to *distribute control out to the nodes.*

Whether you are a network administrator, the real opposition may come from someone even farther upstairs—perhaps an upper-level manager or executive who doesn't "get" the whole concept. Often, these people are still conditioned to thinking of IT solutions as *products* the way Lotus Notes is a product. The intranet is a *phenomenon,* not a *product*—and as a result has no sales force gunning for it. So you may need to step in and fill those shoes for the time being.

How Wired Is Your Network?

One last issue before beginning a server test is the level of integration on your network. Previously, I explained that many companies have taken all their separate *local area networks* (LANs) and wired them together into a single *wide area network* (WAN). To install an intranet, it doesn't matter whether you are dealing with a LAN or a WAN, as long as the network supports TCP/IP.

The question of LANs and WANs is not just academic, however. It directly affects how wide your audience will be. If you install a web server on a LAN that is connected to a WAN, then anyone on the WAN should be able to "hit" your server (assuming IP addresses are defined throughout the system). But if

Running an Intranet on Netware

As you can see in this section, TCP/IP is a required component of an intranet. In the early days of intranets, this could cause a problem with networks using the Novell Netware operating system, because Netware was based on a completely different operating protocol (IPX/SPX). As it happened, this included most PC-based networks, since Netware was by far the most popular corporate network operating system in the early-to-mid 90s. That is changing now as Windows NT gains ever greater market share.

Recently, however, and somewhat belatedly in my opinion, Novell has become increasingly friendly toward the concept of intranets, announcing a number of products and initiatives designed to help companies create and operate intranets over Netware-based networks. As mentioned earlier, it is quite possible to run your intranet on a TCP/IP network layer that works independently of (and concurrently with) the Novell operating system. Most desktop operating systems (Win95, MacOS, UNIX, etc.) now support TCP/IP-based communication.

More likely, if you already have a pure Novell solution on your network, you will want to check into the full range of intranet products and options that Novell has to offer, particularly the IntranetWare line of products at www.novell.com/.

your company has not interconnected its LANs, your potential audience will be limited to the people on the same LAN where you installed the server. It's like living on an island: You can drive anywhere you want to on your island, but you can't drive to other islands unless there's a bridge already built between them.

That's not to say web technology is useless on a LAN. I've seen work groups as small as a dozen people use a web system effectively to store and retrieve information. But, of course, the more is always the merrier, and web systems are no exception. Also, if the people down in Cost Subaccounting are the prime target for your web, you'd better make sure they're on the same network that you are before you start building a web site to serve them.

How can you tell if your company is integrated into a single WAN? Of course, the quickest way is to ask a friendly and knowledgeable network administrator. Knowledgeable is the key. But if you can't get a straight answer, it may be time for a quick proof-of-concept that identifies whether you can get a web server to communicate with your target audience.

Creating a Proof-of-Concept Web Site

So if you know there are no intranet web servers already installed for you to use on the network, and you know you will have to install your own, this section explains how to get started with a proof-of-concept web site such as the one I described earlier in this chapter. There are a couple of ways you can do this.

Using FrontPage to Create a Test Site

First, if you are working on a PC, the quickest way to get a test server online may be to purchase a $150 copy of Microsoft FrontPage and install it on your local computer. When you install FrontPage, it automatically installs a web server on your computer as well, which can be used to build and test a local web site. Building a site is as easy as opening the FrontPage Explorer tool and using File/New to create a new site from a template. There are several different templates you can use for departmental or informational web sites, one of which may suit your needs exactly.

In FrontPage 97 or later versions, the software performs one additional key task, which is to identify the name of your machine and show you the correct URL for the home page of the web site. The machine name or host name is typically a network ID given to your machine when networking is first set up. For instance, suppose your machine name is *snoopy* and the web site you create is called *custserv.* You should be able to access your new web site from anywhere in the network using the URL:

```
http://snoopy/custserv
```

If this works, then your proof-of-concept web site is finished and you can begin tinkering with your first web applications as described later in this chapter (see the section titled "What's Left to Do"). However, keep in mind that the web server provided with FrontPage is not considered a heavy-duty production server for major web applications. It may work fine as a personal server for a low-volume web site, assuming your computer has at least 32MB of RAM. It may also help you create some rudimentary form-based web applications using its built-in "bot" feature. But for serious intranet web sites and application development, you will want to invest in (and install) some of the more powerful servers listed in the sidebar titled "Where to Find Web Software."

Using Other Web Servers

If you are not working on a PC or want to use server software other than the one embedded in FrontPage, here are the steps you need to do a proof-of-concept or hello-world server test:

1. **Find a networked computer where you can install the server.** This could really be any desktop computer connected to the network, including your current desktop, assuming it is sufficiently powerful and up to date. At the very least, you can install the server software on your own computer for initial testing and serving and leave it on your computer as long as it seems to be working (that is, if you don't notice a significant drag on performance). A key factor here is memory: Typically, a web server will require lots of it. On a Windows 95 machine, for example, you will want at least 32MB for smooth performance or even as much as 64MB. On a Windows NT machine, 64MB is recommended. If you are doing more than just testing or initial development—for instance, if you are developing a web site that you expect to carry heavy-duty traffic long-term—it's best to start off with the right operating system/server combination, which is probably either Windows NT or UNIX running something like Microsoft IIS or Netscape SuiteSpot, though there are plenty of other choices (see sidebar titled "Where to Find Web Software" for a small sampling).

   Hardware should probably be something equal to or faster than a 133-MHz Pentium PC, Power Mac, or SPARC 10, though slightly lesser models may suffice, depending on the eventual size and traffic load of your site. Older Windows 3.x, PCs or, Mac computers are not recommended in any case. If you are using Windows 95, make sure TCP/IP is installed as a networking protocol in your Control Panel. If you are on a Windows NT network, keep in mind there may be licensing issues that limit the way you can use web servers on an intranet.

2. **Find a networked computer where you can install the client.** Any computer on the network will probably do, as long as it has TCP/IP networking installed and a graphical user interface (GUI). This is where you will install a browser so you can hit the server across the network, the same way people hit servers on the WWW. Ideally, this should *not* be the machine where you installed the server, so you can test the ability to serve across the network. If a suitable client

machine is not available, however, you can install the server and browser on the same computer and hit the server the same way, even though it is located on the same computer. However, this should be done only for local testing. (For proof of concept, you really want a separate machine to make sure your network will carry the client request and server response.)

3. **Obtain appropriate software for the test.**   You can get evaluation software directly off the Internet for free (see sidebar titled "Where to Find Web Software"), or in some cases by contacting the manufacturer. At a minimum, you will need a server and at least one browser. The software you retrieve depends on operating systems of the machines selected in the two previous steps.

4. **Install the server software on the chosen platform.**   Most software you get off the Internet comes in a zipped or compressed format. Create a new folder especially for each software component that you can use for unzipping the files. Installation may be as simple as unzipping or untaring the file (when you do, use the "recursive" option to preserve the directory structure). More likely, after you unzip or untar the file, you may have to run an installation program, such as *setup.exe* (on PC) or *make* (on a UNIX machine). Installing software on a PC or Mac is simple; nontechnical people do it all the time. On the UNIX platform, you may need help from a network administrator unless you install it in your home directory (which may be appropriate for testing purposes).

   If you're installing on a PC, the installation routine should automatically create a set of icons on your desktop (Figure 4.2). It should also create a set of folders containing the server software and various utilities, including such things as sample CGI scripts, icons you can use on your web pages, and possibly some extra web administration tools (depending on the individual server you select).

   For instance, if you install the Website server on a Windows 95 or NT machine, the entire installation may go under a directory like C:\WEBSITE (Figure 4.3). Different subdirectories will contain different types of supporting files, such as the server scripts (\cgi-win or \cgi-bin), server information content (\htdocs), and web administration utilities (\admin).

5. **Create a hello-world test file.**   If you already have some sort of web authoring tool like FrontPage or Netscape Composer, use it to knock off a quick web page for testing. Otherwise, use a text editor (such as the vi editor on UNIX systems, TeachText on Mac, or the Notepad editor in Windows) to create a new file with the following content:

Figure 4.2   Startup icons for a web server.

```
<HTML><HEAD>
<TITLE>Test File: Hello World</TITLE>
</HEAD><BODY>
<H1>Hello World!</H1>
This is a test page for my new information center at
  AnyCompany, Ltd. Here's a bullet list of reasons why I'm
  creating this site:
<UL>
<LI>Easier publishing of information over the network.
<LI>Cost savings over old publishing and information
  systems.
<LI>Ego gratification.
<LI>Excitement/boredom (select one).
</UL>
If you see this test page, give me a ring at my_ext or send
  me an e-mail at my_address.
<HR>
Last updated today's_date. My_Name.
</BODY></HTML>
```

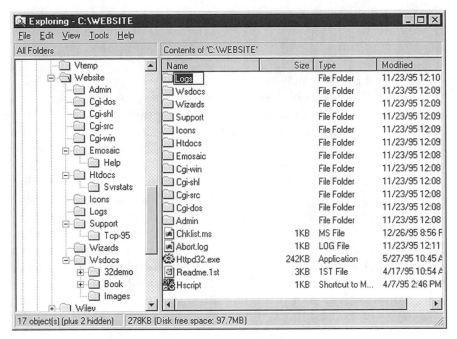

Figure 4.3   Typical server directory structure.

Of course, be sure to change all the italicized parts above to the appropriate values for your situation. Feel free to change any of the text, but be careful about the stuff in angle brackets (< >). This should be all the HTML coding you have to do. In a later chapter, I'll show you some tools you can use to avoid HTML coding.

6. **Save the test file in the appropriate server folder.**   The server will not serve files stored in any folder. Typically, there is only one folder that the server uses for this purpose. This folder is called the *document root* and anything you want to serve must be placed in it. For instance, for a Website server installed on a Windows 95 computer, the document root directory name is *htdocs*. So, if the server is installed on drive C, you would save the test file as:

```
c:\httpd\htdocs\test.htm
```

7. **Fire up the server, if it isn't started already.**   Usually the server software is just a background process, which means either that it

has no real user interface, or that the user interface—such as it is—is *iconized* as soon as you start it. You will see it running in the list of programs, but you will not see it on the screen (other than possibly as an icon).

Starting the server may occur in different ways. On a PC or Mac, the installation should have left behind a program group and startup icons on the desktop, and you can double-click the server icon or executable filename to start the server. If not, you can use the computer's built-in file manager utility to click into the server installation directory and start the executable server program. On a UNIX system, you may need to change to the server installation directory (or add it to the PATH), and start the server executable from the command line.

8. **Determine the IP address or host name of the server.**   This is a key bit of information that will make it possible for you to hit the web site. Typically, in a TCP/IP network, every machine has a unique numeric address, such as 197.34.125.14, and a computer name or host name, such as *sparky* or *viper.* For instance, on a UNIX system, you may see the host name right at the command line, such as this:

```
sparky>
```

If you're lucky, finding the machine name or number may be as easy as checking the command line or /etc/hosts file on a UNIX machine, or opening up the network control panel on a PC or Mac (see Figure 4.4). If you get this right, the name/number you find will automatically work just fine in a URL (such as *http://sparky/test.html* or *http://198.64.12.23/test.html*).

The problem is that some network operating systems like Windows NT can also assign IP addresses dynamically, so that a particular machine may not always answer to the same IP address. The machine may get a new address every time it boots up. So if you are having problems figuring this out, ask a network administrator for help.

Once you determine the correct way to address your server machine, write this down on a piece of paper and tape it to the machine. You don't want to have to go looking for it again.

9. **Install the web browser on the client machine.**   By now, you should have some other machine picked out to test the client-server interaction. Install the web browser software on that machine. As

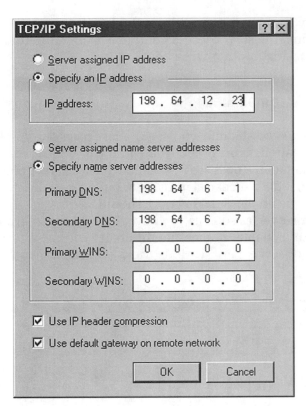

Figure 4.4   TCP/IP configuration panel.

with the server, if you are using a PC or Mac, make sure the machine has TCP/IP networking installed or enabled.

10. **Hit the server.**   Pretend you are on the World Wide Web and try to access the server site across the network. To do this, fire up the web browser, then type a URL in the Location or Address field. For instance, if the server IP address is 197.31.123.14, you would enter:

```
http://197.31.123.14/test.html
```

or, if you know the server name is *sparky,* you might try:

```
http://sparky/test.html
```

If you have done everything correctly up to this point, you should see the server test page (created earlier) appear in the browser window, fully formatted and without the HTML codes (Figure 4.5). If you see this, the server test is complete. Congratulations, you now have a working intranet web site.

What You've Accomplished

If the server test succeeds and you see the test page on the client machine, a hearty congratulations is in order. You can break out a quick bottle of champagne—just don't let the boss see it. You now have a server platform working as part of an intranet that you can start using to build your information center. This means that anyone on the same network should also be able to access the information on your server, as soon as you have some useful information to share.

The rest of this chapter shows the different types of information you may want to consider serving and various tricks you can use to improve the qual-

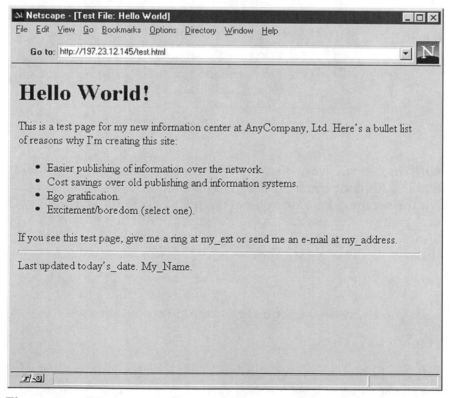

Figure 4.5   Browser window with test page.

Where to Find Web Software

The type of software you use for the server test depends on the type of operating system you have. For a browser, I recommend Internet Explorer on the PC platform, or Netscape Navigator on any platform. For the web server, there are many different choices, again depending on the platform. The following list provides some of the more obvious choices for server software. Your initial test server may not be what you end up using long-term, but these choices should work fine for initial development and testing of your intranet web site. You can move to more powerful or feature-filled packages as your needs grow, without having to redo your existing site content significantly. Each software package can be downloaded from the Internet at the listed URLs. In each case, make sure you just get an "evaluation" or "demo" copy. You still have plenty of time to buy the software, once you verify it fits your needs.

Windows 95 or UNIX
FastTrack   home.netscape.com/comprod/mirror/server_download.html

Windows NT
Microsoft IIS   www.microsoft.com/iis/

Macintosh
Various offerings   www.comvista.com/net/www/server.html

UNIX
Apache Freeware   www.apache.org/

ity of your offering and your own productivity. It also talks about connecting users to your information center and encouraging their participation. Later chapters will give you in-depth examples of how other people are using intranets and how to serve various types of sophisticated content over the web, such as desktop-published documents, multimedia, and data.

What's Left to Do

To finish setting up your information center, however, you will have to take each of the following steps:

What to Do if the Server Test Fails

If you performed the server proof-of-concept test as shown on the previous pages and saw the test page display correctly, skip this section. If not, you may want to consider what might have gone wrong.

No TCP/IP, or Inadequate Connectivity

The most likely culprit here is the TCP/IP connectivity, or lack of it, in the network. Unfortunately, since this is the knottiest problem, this is the last thing to check. It may actually be much simpler, such as one of the other problems listed in this sidebar. A key hint of this problem is getting absolutely no response from the server and never having any real evidence of active TCP/IP usage on the network anyway. For instance, if you did not see TCP/IP-networking installed in the Networking section of your computer's Control Panel, there is good reason to believe the machine is not actively using TCP/IP.

If you think the TCP/IP connection may be the problem, check with your local network administrator. Usually, a good administrator can pinpoint in a minute whether you have the correct protocols installed, and whether the IP addresses are mapped correctly at the server. I have seen cases where the TCP/IP networking on a machine was configured for one IP address, then someone physically moved the machine to a different location and failed to reconfigure the TCP/IP networking to reflect the new address.

Remember that an IP address is location specific, so if the machine moves to a new location it typically gets a new IP address. (This, by the way, is the best argument for using host names instead of IP addresses to refer to machines—*sparky* should always be *sparky,* no matter which IP address it is located at. Unfortunately, though host names are almost always available for UNIX networks, they may not be implemented on some other types of networks unless the people who set up the network were very thorough.)

Server Name or IP Address Wrong

You may have read the wrong IP address off the TCP/IP configuration menu, or you may have typed it in wrong. Double-check it and try again.

If you used a host name instead, it's possible the name is incorrect or spelled imprecisely. On a UNIX or Mac system, for instance, the name may be case sensitive. Thus, *Sparky* and *sparky* are considered two different names.

Part of URL Wrong

Recheck the URL that you entered into the web browser. It may be that you did not type it in correctly. In particular, be sure to use only forward slashes (/), not backslashes (\)—*even on a PC.* Be sure to place a colon and two slashes after the *http.* For instance: http://197.34.127.24/test.html.

Test File in Wrong Directory or Named Wrong

The other problem is that you may have saved the test file to the wrong place or used the wrong name. If this happens, you are likely to get a message back from the server saying it cannot locate the file. If you get such a message, at least you are doing something right, because it indicates the client and the server are actually communicating and the server is trying to find the file.

If you get such a message from the server, there may be several causes. On a UNIX or Mac system, for instance, the filename is case sensitive. So if you save it as *test.html* then try to access it as *Test.html,* the server may not recognize the switch in case. You may also have used *.htm* for the extension, when in fact the actual filename uses the extension *.html,* or vice versa. On a PC, try shortening the extension to .htm. The server may also not be able to find the file because it is saved in the wrong path. If you are unsure which folder to store the file in, you may want to read the server README or Help files to figure out which folder is the server document root. Then move the file to the document root folder and try the test again.

Server and Client Not on Same Network

Unless you know for sure, there is a chance that the machine where you installed the server and the machine where you installed the client are not on the same network. Remember earlier when we talked about LANs and WANs? It may be that you are dealing with two separate LANs that are not interconnected via a WAN. A friendly and knowledgeable network administrator can help you figure this out.

Provide content. So far you just have a single test page on your web server. Next, you will want to start creating (or converting) documents or other information to be served from your site. In the next part of this chapter, I'll show you how to get started. I'll also cover this concept in greater detail in later chapters.

Empower your users. People will not be able to use the information at your site unless they have web browser software installed, such as Netscape Navigator or Microsoft Internet Explorer. If your company already has an intranet, this problem may already be solved. If not, you will have to arrange for them to get a copy of the software installed on their computer. I'll explain how later in the chapter.

Notify your users. One thing you need to understand about a web system: Just because it exists doesn't mean it gets used. Either the system is a regular part of people's lives, or they need to be reminded to use it. In a later part of this chapter, I will explain ways you can do that.

The most important thing to realize is that you have your own information system started here, which doesn't (or shouldn't) require the ongoing involvement or approval of people in other parts of the organization. In other words, you are now empowered.

The web system you installed is now coasting along *on top of* (or should I say *above*) all the other network applications and should not affect or interfere with other network uses, other than to add a slight additional burden to the overall traffic load on the network. In a sense, you have actually hot wired the regular network. And you can use this new system to instantaneously and automatically distribute information across the entire enterprise.

What Can You Share with Users?

Once you've set up a web server, the first question naturally is: What do I do with this thing? (Actually, this question should have occurred to you sooner, but for the sake of argument I will pose it here.)

The answer to this question, of course, is to provide information to users. When you look at the sheer volume of information stored by corporations today—including reams of printed information, such as computer documentation, procedures, specifications, and reference documents—you quickly see plenty of information you can start taking online. Users no longer have time to wade through a shelf full of manuals to find some obscure tidbit of information. And chances are you can no longer justify the cost of printing all this information without any guarantee that users are actually reading it. Then there is the problem of keeping all that printed information up-to-date. So there are a number of information resources and transactions that are potential candidates for your new web site.

Documents

Every company has reams of business information that it must distribute to internal employees or external customers and suppliers. The following list provides examples of the types of documents that companies traditionally distribute:

Policy and procedure manuals

Quality manuals

ISO 9000 work instructions

Employee benefits programs

Orientation materials

Software user guides

Hardware manuals

Quick reference guides

Online help

Style guides and other standards

Training manuals and tutorials

Seminars

Company newsletters and announcements

Scheduling information

Maps and schematic drawings

Computer reports

Customer data

Sales and marketing literature

Specifications

Price lists

Product catalogs

Press releases

Your web site gives you a way to put all of these documents online for instantaneous access by authorized users.

Electronic Resources

Companies also have a number of electronic resources stored on computer that are traditionally distributed by transportable media or by copying across network nodes. These may include:

Test data

Customer data

Spreadsheet templates

Documentation templates

Software applications and utilities

Programmer toolkit components

In the past, many of these resources may have been hidden in rarely accessed cavities of the network. With a web browser such as Netscape or Internet Explorer, you can catalog these resources online for user review and automatically transport them—through a single mouse click—across a network to any authorized user who requests them.

Interactive Communication

Finally, there are various kinds of two-way communication within a corporation that can be facilitated by the new technologies. These include:

Surveys and feedback

Program notification and enrollment

Progress inquiries and reporting

Memo distribution, comment, and reply

Spontaneous data entry and data collection

Interactive database queries against database servers or the mainframe

Product promotion and ordering

Web browsers give us a way to communicate with employees, customers, or suppliers, present information, capture feedback, and process the feedback automatically through databases or scripting mechanisms. They also support spontaneous user searches of information archives or databases. In Chapter 7, we'll delve extensively into how these applications are set up.

How to Share Information with Users

By this time you probably have a good idea what kinds of information you want to share with users. The question now becomes: How do I share it? You may have noticed that the test page created for the proof-of-concept server test was coded entirely using HTML. That's fine for a server test, but you probably shouldn't be doing a lot of raw HTML coding. Intranet content can be created using any number of standard word-processing, desktop-publishing, and illustration tools. But in some cases, you may need or want to adopt additional tools that make it easier to prepare your information for presentation over the intranet.

Table 4.1 summarizes various kinds of information you might serve over an intranet. For each content type, it shows how to prepare the information for the web and some typical tools you might use to do it. It also shows the kind of file you might be saving (.html, .doc, etc.) and the types of situations where the methods are best used.

Notice that in many cases, the second column of the table says something like, "Prepare information as usual, then do *something extra*." If you belong to a group where many people will be contributing to the web, the "prepare as usual" part could apply to the entire group, so that people don't have to give up their regular tools and start learning new ones. The "extra" part could be reserved for a single person who specializes in final-stage preparation of materials for serving over the web, and who makes the extra effort to learn the tools. Such a person is often called a *webmaster* or *web administrator*.

In later chapters, I will show you not only detailed procedures on how to prepare each content type, but also ways you can introduce web production methods while minimizing the disruption to your workgroup.

Setting Up a Home Page

So far in this chapter, you've created one HTML file: a test page called *test.html*. If you wanted to send this file over the network, you would need to type in a URL that includes both the IP address and filename, such as:

```
http://197.34.127.24/test.html
```

TABLE 4.1 Examples of Information Served over an Intranet

Content Type	Preparation Methods	Examples of Tools	Save As*	Best Used For . . .
Documents (layout converted)	Create text with imbedded HTML codes.	Text editor or HTML editor (HoTMetaL, HTML Assistant, etc.)	.html or .htm	Menus, web-based forms, short documents or messages
	Prepare as usual; save to HTML format.	MS Word, WordPerfect, FrameMaker	.html or .htm	Individual documents with straightforward layout using style tags
	Prepare as usual; use web tools to convert document set to a complete web.	Normal authoring tools (Word, FrameMaker, etc.) with conversion programs like Cyberleaf, WebMaker, or HTML Transit	.html or .htm	Large document sets with consistent layout that conforms to a style guide
Documents (layout preserved)	Prepare as normal; print to PDF output.	Acrobat Distiller or Exchange (author); Acrobat Reader (user)	.pdf	Short docs designed for printing or use "as is" (white papers, forms requiring signature, brochures, news-letters, specs, etc.)
	Prepare as normal, serve on web in native format (e.g., MS Word).	Appropriate viewer, control, or plug-in must be installed on user machines, such as MS Word Viewer	.doc (or other)	Limited delivery of docs to small groups, where everyone has correct viewer
Web pages; web sites	Create/edit web sites or web pages directly on the intranet.	FrontPage, Netscape Composer, PageMill, NetObjects Fusion, others.	.html or .htm	New sites/pages that did not previously exist in paper format
Static lists, catalogs, directories	Store information in database or table. Generate static HTML output and store as a document.	Mail merge or database report writer with HTML code wrapped around output fields	.html or .htm	Staff phone directories, small catalogs, price lists, etc.

TABLE 4.1   *(Continued)*

Content Type	Preparation Methods	Examples of Tools	Save As*	Best Used For . . .
Direct database queries	Store information in database or table. Allow user to query directly using HTML form.	CGI scripting language (Perl), programming language (C, VB, Java), ODBC connection (Cold Fusion), database vendor solution (Domino)	.html (form), .pl or .cgi (Perlscript), .exe (application)	Large databases or catalogs
Static illustrations	Create as usual or open existing. Save as GIF (diagrams) or JPEG (photos). Insert into web page or individual hyperlink.	Freehand, AI, Corel, PhotoShop, etc.	.gif or .jpeg	Inline graphics or stand-alone illustrations
	Create inside WP/DTP program; autoconvert to inline web format.	Standard WP/DTP tools (Word, Frame, etc.) converted through WebMaker, HTML transit, others	.gif or .jpeg (created and saved auto-matically)	Illustrations in large docs where images are created/stored inside the document
Dynamic illustrations (clickable image maps)	Create as usual; map coordinates using appropriate tools or HTML.	FrontPage, Mapedit, Webmap, Imagemap Editor, others	.gif or .jpeg (image), .map (map file)	Large illustrations designed to include multiple hot links
Sound/video files	Convert to standard sound/ video formats.	Media conversion tools (RealAudio) Suitable media players may be required on some machines	.wav, .au, .aiff, .mpeg, .mov, etc.	Film clips, sound bites, recorded interviews, etc.
Multimedia; animation	Create as usual; process for web.	Macromedia Director, Shockwave	.dir, .dcr, .dxr	Training programs, tutorials, demos, special effects
Animated GIFs	Create each stage of animation as a separate GIF image; compile into animated sequences.	GIF Animator, others	.gif	Simple animation that loops

TABLE 4.1   *(Continued)*

Content Type	Preparation Methods	Examples of Tools	Save As*	Best Used For . . .
Applications	Create as usual, but design interface using HTML.	CGI or API programming using C, C++, Java, etc. Some visual development environments now available	.html (form) or .exe (executable)	Server-based applications that operate through the web browser

*On an intranet with Windows 3.1 desktops, use three-letter file extensions such as .htm, .mpg, .jpg, etc.

As you create more and more material for your information center, however, you'll need a way users can automatically access all your stuff. Of course, it would be impossible if you put it all on one page, or if users had to memorize the name of each separate file you created. Instead, users should have a clickable list of all the information available at your site, with each different category of information stored in a separate file or group of files. Such a list would be like a *main menu* or—to use a bit of World Wide Web terminology—a *home page.*

Remember that on the World Wide Web a home page is the first thing people see when they get to a site. That's the same concept you should aim for on the intranet. Your information center should have a home page that is the first thing people see when they visit, and it should contain links to all the information available. You can do this by creating either of the following types of home pages:

Single main menu.   You could fill the home page with direct links to every resource available at your site. Clicking a link brings up a document or other resource. A single-page menu can be a problem if you have lots of information to access (i.e., if the menu covers a lot of categories and fills several screens).

Menu hierarchy.   Categorize the various types of information, then create a separate submenu for each category of information. The home page would list the categories and provide a link to each submenu. The submenus, in turn, would contain links to more submenus or to actual documents or server files.

The examples on the following pages show how each type of menu structure might be created.

Creating a Single Main Menu

When you set out to create a web menu, you need to have a good idea how you want it to look. For instance, let's say you wanted to create a document menu listing some of the first documents you created. You may want the user to see something like the test page in Figure 4.6.

Of course, for the home page to work the way it is supposed to, you will have to create hyperlinks to other content. The hyperlink is the underlined word or the live graphic on the page that is set up in such a way that it will retrieve a different web page when it is clicked. See Chapter 5 for details.

You can easily create such a page with embedded hyperlinks by using tools like FrontPage, Netscape Composer, Microsoft Word Internet Assistant, or many of the other programs developed for this application (see Chapter 5 for details).

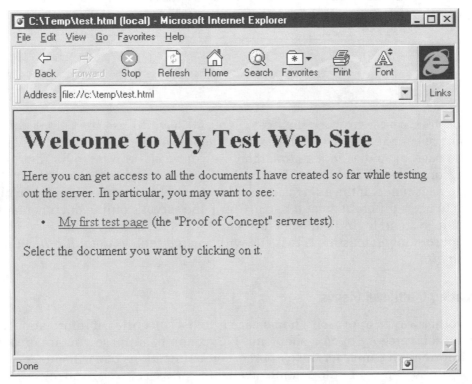

Figure 4.6   Test server page.

The Importance of a Default Filename

Typically, when you create a home page for a web site, you save it as a file called *index.html* (or *index.htm*). This is the default name of the home page for many web servers, although some servers may require a different name, such as *default.html* or *welcome.html.* The home page is defined in the server *by default* so that users can access a site without knowing the exact filename of the home page.

For instance, to see the Microsoft home page on the World Wide Web, you can just type in:

```
www.microsoft.com
```

When you do this, the Microsoft server automatically retrieves the default home page for Microsoft, because its name has already been defined in the server configuration at Microsoft. Likewise, on an intranet you want to be able to just type in an IP address or server name to access your home page, such as:

```
http://197.34.123.14/
```

or

```
http://sparky/
```

For your server to work this way, you will have to use the actual default home page name defined by the server. A good way to check this is to create a home page, save it as *index.html,* then use your web browser to hit the server using only the IP address or host name (as just suggested), leaving out the home page name. If the home page displays correctly, it works. If not, you may have to use a different default name. Check the server's online documentation (or help system) to find out what this name might be, or look in the server document root for an existing HTML file with a name such as *default.html* or *welcome.html.*

Creating Multilevel Menus

The other way to approach a home page is to list categories of information and have each category open a submenu. For example, suppose you are creating an information center for the corporate communications department, and you have three types of information available: press releases, brochures, and newsletters. Your home page might look like Figure 4.7.

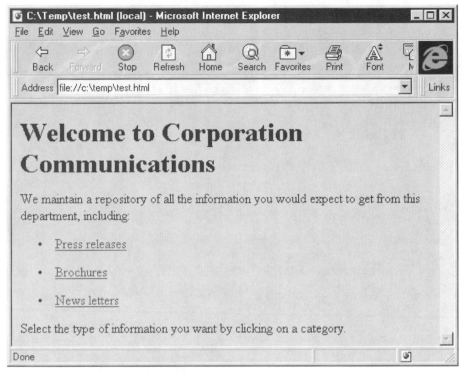

Figure 4.7   Sample home page.

When users click on the Newsletters category, it might look like Figure 4.8. If users select Profiles, they might see another menu listing all issues of that newsletter for the past two years. Clicking on an issue would open the actual document.

Notice that this multiple menu structure implies a hierarchy that looks something like Figure 4.9. In this case, each different menu and submenu is represented by a separate HTML document. In the home page, there is a set of hyperlinks that point to the files containing the submenus. The links in the submenus either point to actual documents (such as the December 3 press release) or still more submenus (Profiles). A standalone document such as a press release might be contained in a single HTML file, but a newsletter might start with a table of contents file, which links to individual files for each section or article.

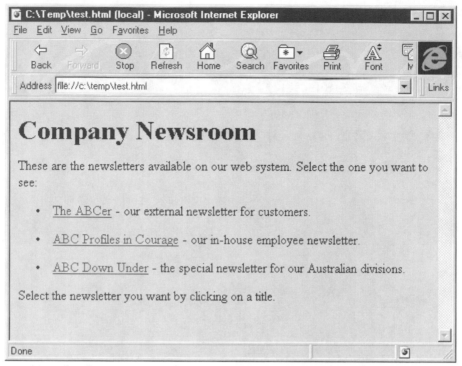

Figure 4.8   Web page resulting from home page hyperlink.

The Rudiments of Site Management

As you can see, with this type of arrangement, the number of interlinked documents proliferates rapidly. The previous diagram implies 16 different menu files (including TOCs), plus about triple that amount of actual documents that can be browsed. This is a fairly simple web site, yet there are already close to 40 separate documents to keep track of (not to mention any illustration files that might be associated with the documents). You can see why people call this thing a "web."

File clutter like this screams out for some form of management, especially as more information continues to be added to the site. Though there are many advanced tools for site management discussed later in this chapter, you can start out with the simplest of all: arranging related files into folders (subdirectories).

The diagram in Figure 4.10 shows the same document structure, but instead of a functional view you are now seeing the actual filenames and link names

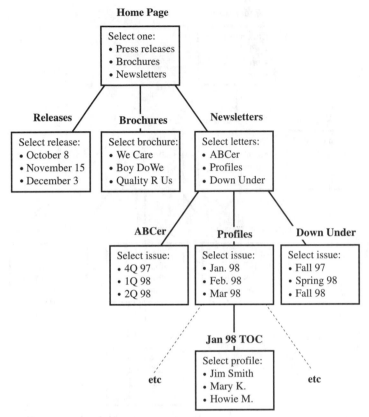

Figure 4.9   Menu hierarchy at a web site.

that might be used. Each box represents a separate menu file, and the label over each box shows the filename for that menu and its location in the path from the server root. Inside the box, you can see the actual reference name used in the hyperlink. Notice that relative links can be used, and a default filename can be used in each directory. So a link to "nws" on the first level would retrieve the default menu file in the /nws folder, which happens to be /nws/index.html. Likewise, a reference in that menu to "abc" would retrieve the default menu file in the /abc folder.

If you looked at this same document hierarchy in a more traditional directory tree structure, it might look like the diagram in Figure 4.11. In this directory tree, notice that as you create each file, it might be saved to a different path. For instance, the table of contents for the January 1998 issue of *ABC Pro-*

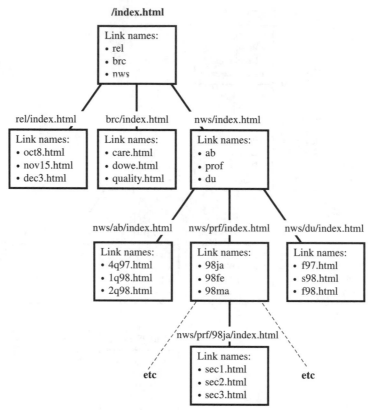

Figure 4.10   Site hierarchy diagram with file and link names.

files might be saved in the following path (assuming the server document root is c:\httpd\htdocs on a PC):

```
c:\httpd\htdocs\nws\prf\98ja\index.htm
```

But the URL used to directly access the same file from a user machine (or via a hyperlink carried on some other server) might be something like this:

```
http://197.34.127.14/nws/prf/98ja/
```

since the /httpd/htdocs part of the path is already implied as the document root, and *index.htm* is recognized as the default opening file for any path.

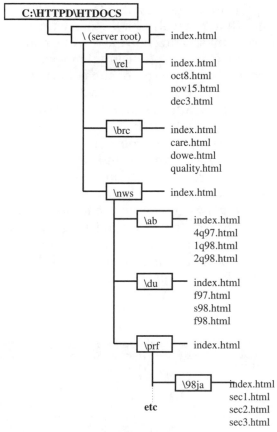

Figure 4.11 Directory tree view of server.

These long URLs are just given as an example, to show the difference between the path when it is referenced on the local hard drive and when it is accessed through a web URL. You need to understand how these URLs work to create appropriate hyperlinks. But the user doesn't need to understand them, because all URLs should be hidden inside the hyperlinks you create.

Now you're asking: What happened to the idea of simplicity? The truth of the matter is, when you set up a web system, you want to think about file and folder configuration because it will make things simpler later on, once you get into a production mode. This complex folder structure might seem confusing at first, but once you install a web publishing system (as shown in Chapter 5), your publishing tools will automatically remember where you store your brochures and where you store your newsletters. And when you create links between documents in different levels of a directory tree, even a tool as simple as Word Internet Assistant should code the relative path changes correctly.

If you plan to do extensive web publishing and site building, however, chances are you will soon need some sort of site management tool. Many web publishing packages now come fully equipped with site management tools, as do some servers. For instance, Adobe's SiteMill, Microsoft's FrontPage software, and Netscape's Livewire all have them.

The main idea behind most of these tools is to provide a graphical view of the web site and an easy way to configure and reconfigure the different files and folders at the site. The FrontPage Explorer, for instance, automatically keeps track of links between various web pages as well as referenced graphics that appear in each file. It can verify the links and notify the web administrator of any links that are broken or of any missing illustrations. FrontPage Explorer shows the links graphically in its web view display (Figure 4.12).

Netscape Livewire is another site management and development tool that lets you use the drag-and-drop capability of most windowing systems to move

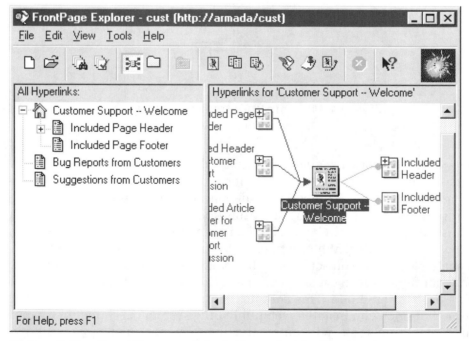

Figure 4.12   FrontPage graphical view of web site structure.

files and folders around, then automatically repairs all the hyperlinks between the files. For example, if you move a file named *brochures.html* from the root directory to the folder named *promo,* the site manager tool would correct any hyperlinks at the site to reference the full path *promo/brochures.html.*

How to Make Your Web Site Look Good

Obviously, the examples of web pages shown so far in this chapter are oh-so-plain and—shall we say it? OK, *boring!* Up to now, I just wanted to show you how to set up a site and get it working. After all, you're probably as busy as I've been over the past year and don't have a lot of time for the niceties. So good design has been temporarily sacrificed to the uncaring god of expedience.

If you are going to be in charge of a web site, however, you should pay at least a little attention to making the site look—if not really, really good—at least presentable. In fact, in some places a site that contains plain, unadorned web pages will get people snickering behind your back. An interesting phenomenon about publishing on the intranet or World Wide Web is that people will spend literally *hours* twiddling and tweaking their pages to make sure that not a single animated GIF or horizontal rule is out of place. In fact, entire books are written on the subject of how to make your web site really impressive. *Killer,* I believe, is the term.

This is something we will all find the energy to do in good time. Especially on an intranet, where there is so much content to put online and so little time to do it. If you have plenty of time to create 25-stage animated GIFs, then by all means plow ahead. I've included some rudimentary information in the next two chapters that should help you address the aesthetic issues. If that isn't enough, you may even want to get your own copy of one of the many books that specialize in web site design.

On the other hand, if you don't have time for aesthetics, I would suggest hiring a good web designer to create an overall "look and feel" for your site, including what I would call "signature graphics" such as a neat, colorful toolbar and emblem you can put on each page. A nice background, a few snazzy animated GIFs for the opening page, that sort of thing. Time was, such designers were hard to find, but by now most decent commercial artists understand a little bit about the web. Then put all that good stuff on your web site and don't tell anyone you hired outside help. See how impressed they will be.

If you find designers too expensive or unruly to deal with, you may want to pick up one of the many web site design packages now on the market that come complete with templates, graphics, and all you need to create a web site. My own modest contribution to this cause is included on the web site for this book at www.wiley.com/bernard. On the site, you will find a prepackaged intranet web site that can be a good starting point for testing, proof of concept, or something even more intriguing.

Why Data-Driven Sites Are Better

Beside making your site look great, it's also good form to make it as interactive and data driven as possible. You may want to have a little multimedia, a little animation, some live database connectivity, and even search engines such as those on the World Wide Web. Intranets that hand their users live data fresh off the silicon are considered much more useful than the kind that just sit there, staring at you.

In fact, later chapters of this book explain how to work with live data sources and get them streaming online. Just so you won't feel too bad about it, however, please keep the following in mind. About 90 percent of the information published on intranets these days is plain old HTML web pages that someone created using a word-processing program or a text editor, or maybe something a little more sophisticated like FrontPage or HoTMetal Pro. Just plain old static web pages.

That's not to say static pages are good or desirable. That's just to state the facts. In today's feverish business environment, many people have good intentions about what they want to put on the intranet, but they lack the time to do it. So a lot of what ends up on the web is just flat, published documents.

Yes, it's a little boring. But that's not to say that published documents can't contain a lot of useful information. You don't need Java to get your point across. And if you consider that hyperlinks allow you to click and choose exactly what you want to see, then perhaps even flat documents are a tad interactive and lively.

But we should never lose sight of intranet nirvana. That means we should always strive to root around in the corporate data bank and dig out all those nourishing little details everyone yearns to consume. Interactive, data-driven web sites *are* worth the small amount of trouble it takes to build them. And it's something you can even do yourself, as you will see in Chapters 6 and 7.

Why It's Important for Everyone to Contribute

If you are starting from scratch to build an intranet that will eventually be used by the entire company, what you've done so far is really just a warm-up for a much larger exercise that lies ahead. Building an intranet may involve many different departments or business units in your company, working together on an initial design called the *pilot project.* The pilot will involve a fair amount of planning and the efforts of a team of intranet builders, of which you may be a member—or even the leader.

Since this kind of project involves strategic planning and management skills, I reserve coverage of it for Chapter 9 of this book. Why the last chapter? Assuming you will have read all of this book along the way, the final chapter will set you on the path you must take to move forward and make your intranet a reality. So keep on reading and we will get to the planning stuff later. Don't ever get the idea you can plan an intranet without first having a basic introduction to all the technologies and techniques involved.

Meanwhile, if you are just setting up a web site for a single department or business unit, you have a much simpler job at hand. But it will still be a fair amount of work to get everyone contributing. Just because you're the person who set up the web site and created the home page and top-level menus, it doesn't mean you have to do all the work and create all the content for the site. In fact, it's much better if you don't. The intranet should truly reflect the communications and knowledge output of your entire department or business unit, and the best way to do that is to get everyone to participate. The best way to get participation, in turn, is mainly through training (as discussed later in this chapter), but also through a little item called *work flow* (also discussed later). People must understand *what can be done,* and also *how to do it.*

In other words, someone (possibly you) will make it easier for people to participate in the intranet by thinking up an easy way for them to move their content from their own desktop computers into the new document publishing arena on the web server. If you've followed along with the directions in the earlier part of the chapter, what you have done so far, and will continue to do, is to create a nice "virtual box" that they can put their goodies into. Designing the site was one part of that. Creating the work flow is another.

Designing an Ideal Work Flow

One of the main tasks involved in getting content up onto your web site is to make sure that all the information people want to put on the site is either created in a web format (HTML) or converted to web format. Put another way, you really have two choices:

◆ Ask everyone to discard their old tools (Microsoft Word, et. al.) and learn some new tools, such as FrontPage or NetObjects Fusion.

♦ Let everyone keep using their old tools (Microsoft Word, et al.) and then just take what they have done and convert it to HTML.

The second method can be the simplest. For instance, if your department is using Microsoft Word now, and you don't want to retrain everyone, just let them keep using Microsoft Word and you can still produce web pages easily from their work. If you are using Word 7.0 or earlier, you can acquire a copy of *Internet Assistant for Microsoft Word,* which is available at the Microsoft web site on the World Wide Web (www.microsoft.com/). With *Internet Assistant,* people who use Word can use the Save As feature to simply save their files in an HTML format that is "web ready." In Word 97, this feature is built-in. If your people use something other than Word, check to see if that word processor or desktop-publishing program has a web extension that allows easy saving or export to web-ready format.

The other way is to use a tool like HTML Transit, which can take multiple Word files and convert them automatically into web pages—a feature especially valuable for large document sets. The document authors don't have to save anything. HTML Transit—and other similar programs—can take any ordinary Word documents or set of documents and use them to generate web pages automatically, breaking long documents up into more "bite-size" files (e.g., at each major heading), hyperlinking all the pages with customized navigation buttons, backgrounds, headers and footers, and a table of contents.

The one crucial element in creating such a smooth publishing work flow is the use of style sheets and templates. Most word processors and desktop-publishing programs these days come with a style tagging feature that lets you tag each paragraph in a document as either a heading, body text, indented text, bullet list, numbered list, or any of a number of other typical style tags. These features help people quickly format documents, regardless of whether those documents are being prepared for the web. Once people learn how to do it—and they do it consistently—every document produced by the group comes with all of its paragraph styles already identified correctly. And that is the biggest amount of work involved in getting a document on the web (Figure 4.13).

Some people quibble about this. You talk to companies that have never used style sheets and templates, and they say it can't be done. Then you talk to companies that use them all the time and they say it's no big deal. The fact of the matter is this: When it comes to creating departmental web sites, you can either (1) ask people to change their habits slightly by adopting templates, (2) ask everyone to learn new tools, or (3) have someone who reformats and decides the styles for every paragraph of every document that needs to go online.

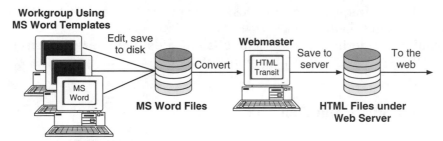

Figure 4.13   Template-based work flow.

Personally, I think it's easier to distribute the workload in such a way that everyone cooperates in maintaining a publishing standard. This helps avoid the retraining that would be involved in a move to new tools, or the rework and doubling of effort required to reformat everything that everyone writes. Style sheets are not all that hard to use: They will make everyone more productive even if you *aren't* doing web publishing. (In fact, I know some companies that win regular annual awards for their technical manuals based in part on the fact that the template design, style sheets, and documentation models almost guarantee an award-winning result.)

The nice thing about style sheets is, if you can get everyone using them correctly (and that's not really such a big *if,* assuming they're well designed and people understand why they're important), documents will go up on the web in seconds. For each set of templates, there will be a set of map files and a tool like HTML Transit, WebMaker, or Cyberleaf that can suck the documents right out of their source directories and turn them into published web documents on the fly (see Chapter 5 for an extensive description of the tools). The important thing is that the templates and the map files be designed to work together by someone who understands style sheets, HTML conversions, the tools involved, and the formatting requirements of the web.

Once all the elements in a template-based work flow are set up and meshed properly, the conversion process is so easy that a single administrative assistant (or webmaster) could easily handle all the conversions required by a work group—or even a set of work groups—without seriously breaking stride. The only steps required for each set of documents would be to open the conversion program, specify the files to be converted, specify the conversion map file to use, and let the conversion run itself. If any given set of documents change often, you may want to find ways to set up the conversion as a time-triggered batch process that runs automatically either nightly or weekly (depending on frequency of updates)—converting the same set of files regularly on a fixed schedule.

If you're wondering how to use publishing aids like Internet Assistant and HTML Transit, see Chapter 5 for more details.

Secrets of Successful Web Sites

At the beginning of this chapter, I plunged right into the thick of things without giving much thought to long-term planning or overall site design. That's fine, because I wanted to cut to the chase and let you see how easy it is to get a server up and running. But creating a web site is more than just a matter of creating web pages. If you can master the intricacies of a WYSIWYG web editor, there are still some other, less-tangible niceties you may want to attend to. Before you go too far in preparing web content, step back and take a good look at where you're going. There are certain quality control issues you'll have to confront.

Remember that you're mainly trying to communicate information. That involves a lot more than just slapping your content online and seeing who reads it (or who doesn't). It's more of an art, like painting or ballet. None of us are born doing the pirouette or the grande jetée. But we can learn to do them with a little practice, improving as we go along (I'm still working at it).

To truly master the art of communication on the web, you may want to study extensively writing, publishing, illustration, graphic design, user interface design, database management, client-server technology, and more. Oh really, you say? Yes, the ultimate web publisher has a bit of all these skills. But that's no reason to get discouraged; there are some fairly basic tricks you can use to make sure your information is well organized, easy to access, and easy to use (remember that mantra). Here, then, are the most basic requirements for successful web sites.

1. Plan Ahead

The best way to plan is to make a list of all the different types of information you could conceivably share over a web. Then go to the nearest white board, get some colored pens and an eraser, and start organizing the information into a hierarchy. Think in terms of big categories instead of specific documents—you will be collecting many documents over time, your big challenge is how to organize them into categories the user will understand.

For example, if you are producing a corporate communications web site, you may realize that the department produces only three types of information:

brochures, press releases, and newsletters. If I'm a user, chances are this is how I'll see it, too. So the main menu might best be arranged by document type. Or maybe the site should be organized by product type instead, because people are more interested in the various widgets your company produces, than in a generic category like brochures. Or maybe you want to organize the information both by both product type and by document type.

To help with your organization, use a storyboard. Draw some pictures showing how you want the different menus to look and work. Spread them out on a table and pretend you're moving from one screen to the next. Show the sketches to users and get feedback. This is usually a lot quicker than setting up each major screen, testing it, then reorganizing it after the fact.

When I created my first intranet, I had a white board the size of the wall on which I drew the entire structure. A good eraser and marker allowed me to constantly update the model as I refined the design. Anyone who wanted to see a clear picture of the intranet structure—or what was planned—could come and look at my wall to see it at a glance.

Creating a good design on the front end will save a lot of work later on, once your site starts accumulating information. You don't want to have to reorganize everything after the fact, rebuilding all the links between documents (although a site management tool like the ones discussed earlier in this chapter would certainly make reorganization much simpler).

2. Chunk, Layer, and Nest Your Subjects

The corporate communications example (see "Creating Multilevel Menus") takes a rather large and diverse set of web documents and breaks it down into nested categories. It even takes an individual document like a newsletter and subdivides it into sections that can be browsed one at a time. This layering actually helps make things easier for the user. Imagine putting all the documents at the site on a single menu, without even trying to arrange them by category. The user would have to scan the entire list to find the desired material, and might not realize that only three types of material are at the site: brochures, newsletters, and press releases.

Dividing large documents into smaller files also helps them load faster. Though this is not as much of a concern on an intranet, very large documents like a technical manual should definitely be chunked into separate files: one per chapter or even one for every major heading. On an intranet, the problem is not loading time, it's scrolling. With a long document file, the user might have to continuously scroll through multiple screens full of details, looking for the desired passage, only to find that it isn't on this page. How much easier, then, to have a quick table of contents for a manual, or even for each chapter, and to click straight into the part of the document you want to read.

One way to improve access within a long file is by putting a table of contents or menu bar at the top, then linking the entries to specific headings in the document.

3. Minimize Clicks; Maximize User Convenience

The danger with dividing your information into categories is that you may end up with too many layers, so that it becomes tedious for the user to click through interminable categories and subcategories of information. On closer inspection, it's easy to see that the corporate communications example (see "Creating Multilevel Menus") suffers from this problem. Instead of having separate submenus for press releases, brochures, and newsletters, wouldn't it be easier to just chunk them all into a single organized menu (Figure 4.14)?

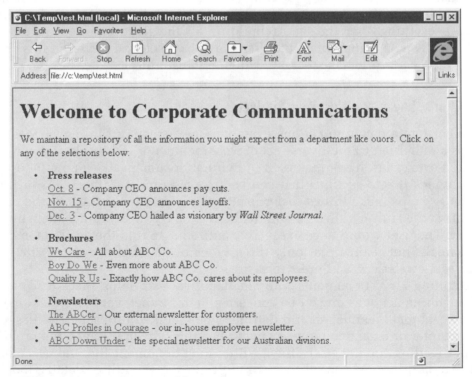

Figure 4.14   Reorganized home page.

Organized this way, the home page eliminates an entire layer of complexity, including three separate submenus. If the separate submenus had been retained, it would take six separate user clicks to see everything that you see in this one page. Though this adds convenience for the user, it's important to strike a balance. If a menu like this eventually expands beyond a few dozen entries, it might be harder to use than three separate submenus.

On the other hand, if the nature of the information is such that the user will always travel vertically in one direction, without a need to travel horizontally across categories, then separate menus might not be so bad. The only way to settle the issue is with rigorous *usability testing.* This sounds difficult, but is actually quite easy. Just show it to some typical users and get their opinion. Then put those opinions to work improving your site.

4. Tell Them What's New

The what's new section is a standard feature of any World Wide Web site, and it should be a standard feature on any intranet site as well. Think about it from the users' viewpoint. Each time users access your information center, they probably see the same menu. There's no way to peer beyond the familiar façade of your home page and guess what might have changed since the last time they visited. The only way is to go poking around through all the submenus, looking for clues. This is not a fun thing to do.

A what's new section puts all the most recent information right up front so the user can see it all at a glance on a single page. The entries in this section should provide a link to new resources in addition to the links already provided on the regular menus and submenus. Of course, going to a what's new page is yet another click for the user, and there is no way to guarantee that every user will do it. Better yet, why not consider just putting all the new stuff right there on the home page (Figure 4.15)? A chatty, newsy introduction is a good way to draw readers into your site. Also check the Netscape home page on the Internet (home.netscape.com/) for a great example.

5. Make It Searchable

Telling them what's new is nice, and it quickly gives users the latest information. But searching is the best way to guarantee that users will locate exactly what they need quickly and easily. There are some easily implemented web search strategies. However, since searching is a somewhat more advanced application, it is covered in more detail in Chapter 7.

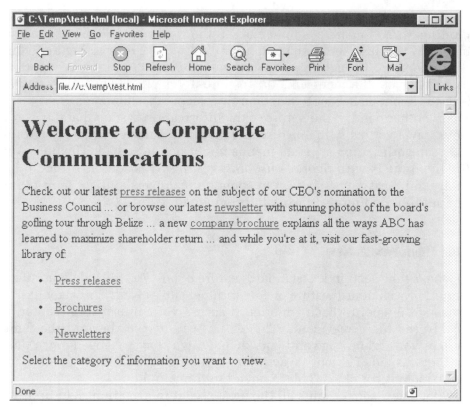

Figure 4.15 Telling the user what's new up front.

6. Provide a Master Table of Contents or Index

The greatest problem with using any large web site is making sure that you haven't missed anything important. Thus, once your site becomes sizable, you should provide your users with a single alphabetical, sequential, or hierarchical listing of everything at the site. I've seen some webs with multiple indexes sorted in different ways, such as by department, by information type, and even by author. Each entry should provide direct clickable access into the material.

7. Make It Look and Feel Consistent

On an intranet, your web pages don't have to be fancy. Unlike the World Wide Web, you're not being judged by a global audience—just by the people in your organization. So before you spend a lot of time on snazzy graphics or mind-boggling applications, spend some time giving your pages a consistent look and feel.

A consistent web page design makes your site eminently more readable and usable, and helps make sure your readers never get disoriented. You'd be surprised how much difference it can make if you pay attention to the following details:

Consistent chunking.   In a web system, larger documents might be split into multiple sections for faster retrieval and scrolling. Each section is stored in a separate file that displays as a separate "page" on the screen. Chunking should be done in logical units and consistently throughout the document (Figure 4.16).

Unique titles on every page.   Each page at your site should have a unique title to identify it, such as "HR Policy Manual, Section 1." Unique titles are absolutely essential to easy navigation. Keep in mind that the user may come to this page in an entirely nonlinear fashion, and the title should answer the question: "Where am I?" Also, in many browsers page titles accumulate on a special menu (such as the Go menu in Netscape) as the user moves through your site. The purpose of the Go menu is to let the user easily backtrack to any previously visited page. If all pages have the same title, it will be hard to tell one from another (Figure 4.17).

Consistent heads within a page.   Each page should have an opening heading that indicates the subject matter on the page. The heading and title may be the same or may complement each other. But a separate opening heading is required because not every user will notice the title at the top of the window (or wherever it happens to be displayed in the browser). For consistent presentation from page to page, the heading

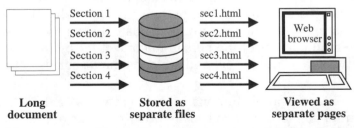

Figure 4.16   How a long document can be chunked.

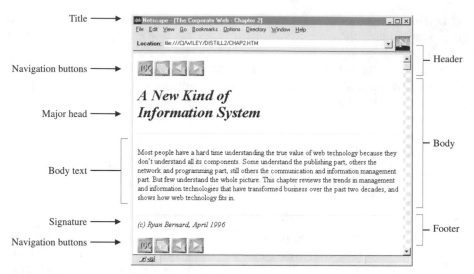

Title

Navigation buttons

Major head

Body text

Signature

Navigation buttons

Header

Body

Footer

Figure 4.17 Typical web page components.

should always be positioned the same way on each page and should always use the same heading level in HTML coding (usually H1). Heading levels should also be used consistently. For instance, never use an H3 level directly below an H1; use heading levels in their intended hierarchy. Many people flaunt these rules, but the result may be visually confusing to the user.

Consistent headers and footers. In an HTML document, just as in a print document, the header and footer are the consistent elements that appear at the top and bottom of the page. The only difference is that a complete web page may not fit into a single window, so that you nearly always see the header as soon as the page loads, but you often don't see the footer until you scroll to the bottom of the page. Certain elements are commonly included in the header, the footer, or in both. These may include a toolbar, navigation buttons, a simple slug that identifies the originating department or group, the date the page was last edited, and the e-mail address of the person to contact for more information. You should always use header and footer elements consistently throughout your site.

Consistent navigation buttons. Most browsers include simple menu controls that let a user go back to previous links or jump to new URLs. But suppose a user links into the middle of one of your documents and wants some way of going backward and forward in the document, or returning to the table of contents (TOC) or opening page. There should be buttons that allow this kind of linear movement or reference, such as a next page/previous page button, a TOC button, or even separate buttons for each major section in the document. Navigation buttons are easy to create in HTML (assuming you already have pictures of the buttons drawn and saved as GIF or JPEG images). This is done by creating a hyperlink on top of an image or web button, which you can do in HTML or by using any web editor. Just insert the button image, select it, then select Insert/Hyperlink or another similar menu function.

A more advanced way of providing navigation buttons is by using a toolbar or a frame. A toolbar is a row of buttons that is saved as a single image and then mapped to a standard set of links using the web's image-mapping feature (discussed in Chapter 5). The problem with this arrangement—as with individual navigation buttons—is that the buttons may scroll off the screen and not be easily accessible. This problem is effectively solved by the frame feature of Netscape (see www.netscape.com/assist/net_sites/frames.html), which lets you display the toolbar or navigation buttons in a stationary window segment that always stays in the same place, even as the user scrolls through the text. The use of toolbars, frames, and image mapping will be discussed in more detail in later chapters.

If you're using an HTML editor to construct web pages, it's hard to maintain consistency, especially when multiple authors are involved. The only way to do it is to publish a style sheet or template and hope that everyone follows the rules.

As it turns out, however, the best way to ensure consistency may be to quit using HTML editors and automate the process of document creation. Some web publishing systems (discussed in Chapter 5) now let you *automatically* include predefined headers, footers, titles, and navigation buttons within every page generated.

8. Make It Easy to Print

Web systems make it incredibly easy to print online documents, as long as the entire document is in a single file. But what if the document has been split into different files, as suggested earlier? To print the entire document, you would have to go to each section and print it individually. For a long document with dozens of sections, this would be prohibitive.

There are several ways to avoid this dilemma. The simplest way would be to produce a print file for the entire document, which can be accessed through a hyperlink, downloaded, and shipped to a local printer. A more advanced way might be to create a simple form for the user to request print jobs. A CGI script attached to the form could kick off a batch print job or notify the local secretary or administrator to kick off a print job and forward the document to the requesting party (see Chapter 7 for details on forms and CGI).

9. Test, Test, Test

You did everything you were supposed to do. You dotted your *i*'s and crossed your *t*'s. But if you don't test your finished pages, you'll never know for sure. There'll always be that little nagging suspicion that something is wrong. So as soon as you are finished creating new pages—or even if you made a few tiny edits—use your browser to quickly review what you've done. Make sure all the hyperlinks still jump correctly. Make sure the illustrations display properly. Make sure the paragraphs all break the way you intended. You never know, you might have forgotten something.

10. Ask for Feedback

You may think you are a web page designer extraordinaire, but why not ask other people what they think? You might be surprised. And you might also be surprised how following up on the critique makes your web site even better.

Power to the People

An old question goes like this: If a tree falls in the forest and there's no one around to hear it, does it make a sound? A more up-to-date question might read like this: If you create an information center or departmental web site, and no one knows about it or uses it, does it really exist?

Sure, you can install a server, save your documents to it, and think up nifty new ways to deliver content and live data to end users. But the web server is only half the equation. You're just spinning your wheels unless you have people actually using the stuff. And the more users you have, the more value you are providing to the entire organization. One of the main tricks to developing a successful information center is capturing the attention of people in your organization (or in the outside world, in the case of extranets) and keeping them coming back. To get there in the first place, they will need certain kinds of tools and access methods, as discussed in the following section of this chapter.

What Software People Need to Reach Your Site

Naturally, people are not going to be able to use your information unless they have the proper tools. Here's what they need:

A browser.   The user needs a web-compatible browser such as Netscape Navigator or Microsoft Internet Explorer (see sidebar). Be sure it is a fairly recent version because older versions may restrict your publishing capabilities significantly. For instance, some old browsers, prior to version 3.0, will not support tables, frames, Java, JavaScript, and other features commonly found on web sites today. Browsers prior to version 4.0 will not support dynamic HTML, push channels, or style sheets. Of course, if you are downloading the software directly from the Internet, you will get the latest version automatically. Keep in mind that you will need a separate copy of the browser for each user machine. So, if you plan to use Netscape Navigator, licensing and cost may be an issue you have to tackle right up front. Internet Explorer, on the other hand, can be distributed freely to all the users on your network who have a compatible computer. Also, keep in mind that older computers using Windows 3.1 will require special versions of the browsers written for 16-bit systems. These also have certain limitations in terms of the complexity of web pages they can view.

A network connection.   The user must be connected to the same TCP/IP network (LAN or WAN) that you are. For users on UNIX workstations, this is typically no problem. Users of aging PCs or Macs (pre-System 7 or Windows 95) may require a special utility called a *TCP/IP stack.* If these aren't already installed, you may have to acquire them and install them. For details, check out the discussion of TCP/IP in Chapter 2 and in the earlier parts of this chapter.

Thus, setting up an intranet may be—at first, anyway—a matter of distributing software. If you work in a company that already has an intranet, or where the employees have the ability and knowledge to retrieve their own browsers from the Internet, so much the better.

If not, you will have to consider different ways of providing users with the software. Most new computers sold these days already have a web browser built-in. In fact, Windows 98 will make the browser an important component of the operating system. So new computers are not the problem, it's all the old ones that will require software.

In many companies, software can be retrieved and installed directly through the network using various installation utilities. Or a support crew may do nothing but go around and install software for people. At worst, you may have to create your own installation diskettes, or put the software on various network file servers where people can access or run it.

Keep in mind that many browsers available for downloading on the Internet are free for short term evaluation, including Netscape (see the sidebar titled "Retrieving Browser Software from the Internet"). However, long-term dedicated use (typically anything over 30 days) requires licensing and payment. Netscape runs about $50–$80 a seat, with lower unit prices for site licenses. Although this is somewhat of an expense, it is still considerably cheaper than almost any other business software you can buy. And once people have it, they will be able to use it in many different ways.

Also, regardless of how you distribute the software, take into account any helper applications, controls, or plug-ins that may be needed with the browser software. For example, if you plan to supply multimedia or Adobe Acrobat files from your web site, users may need special viewer software or plug-ins to make it work. These will be discussed in more detail in later chapters.

What People Must Do to Reach Your Site

Remember how we hit the server during the proof-of-concept server test earlier in this chapter? That's exactly the way all users will be accessing your system. If a full-scale intranet does not already exist, and there is no way to point users to your location through other hyperlinks elsewhere on an intranet, then users will have to type in the IP address or host name of your server.

For instance, someone with Netscape might use the File/Open Location feature to type in the following:

```
http://197.14.123.35/
```

assuming 197.14.123.35 is the IP address of your server, or:

```
http://shorty/
```

if the computer where your web server is installed has the host name *shorty*. Assuming your opening page is set up as *index.html* (or whatever the default filename for your server is), then just typing in the IP address or host name of your computer will bring up your home page or main menu, the same way you did it in the server test.

Please remember that there is no need for users to be logged in to your server, or to have the server drive appear as a local drive on their computer.

That's one of the main reasons you are using web technology, remember? So you don't have to worry about such administrative tasks.

Of course, there are ways to make things simpler and easier for the end user. If yours is the only information center on the intranet, you can set up the browser so that it automatically opens to your home page when the user starts up the software. For instance, the Netscape dialog shown in Figure 4.18 lets you specify the opening page on startup.

Once a browser is set up this way, users don't have to remember *any* IP addresses, host names, or URLs. All they have to do is start the browser software, view your page, and start clickin'. And if desired, you can even save them that step. You can include the browser icon in the Startup group or file so that it starts automatically every time they boot the computer. Thus, the browser becomes an integral part of their everyday desktop environment.

If you plan to set up users this way—so that the browser starts on bootup and automatically opens to your home page—it's best to preconfigure the software *before* it gets installed on the user machine, instead of expecting

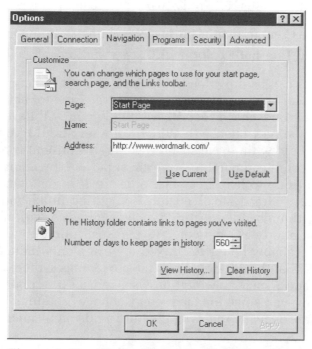

Figure 4.18   Start page setup dialog box.

each user to set it up this way, or having to set it up that way for each individual user. Again, this is just a way to simplify users' access, so that all they have to do is install the software, start it, and immediately connect to the intranet.

Once the user accesses your site, all further connections to information at that site—or to other sites on the network—should be handled transparently through built-in hyperlinks, so that the location and content of the various servers in your company becomes a nonissue. Users should not have to worry about which machines the servers are installed on, how to connect to them, or which file to retrieve. All users should have to do is read a menu, home page, or table of contents, then just point and click to get the information they want.

Retrieving Browser Software from the Internet

Since the birth of the World Wide Web, many different kinds of web browsers have arisen to compete for users' attention. But on the corporate intranet, there are really only two credible contenders:

Netscape Communicator (or just Navigator).   home.netscape.com/

Microsoft Internet Explorer (IE).   www.microsoft.com/

Both browsers can be downloaded for free from the Internet sites listed above. However, you can use your copy of Netscape for short-term evaluation only. If you want to keep it, eventually you will have to pay for it (over $50 last time I checked). Which browser should you choose? It depends. For a long time, Netscape was the preeminent browser, but IE is now considered comparable—or even superior—by many. Both products will continue to leap-frog each other in features over the coming years, and have already evolved into something much more than just a browser, with embedded features such as e-mail or editors. If you are on a predominantly PC network, IE may be your best choice, while Netscape is probably better for mixed environments including companies with UNIX at the desktop. For strategic planners, there may be more important issues, such as which browser will best support Java in the long run. However, since the technology changes so quickly, it's hard to make a fail-safe decision that won't require adjustment somewhere down the road.

Security: Limiting Access to Your Site

An important fact to remember about web servers is that, typically, server access is open by default. That means that—unless you specifically password protect a site—anyone on the network will be able to come in and view your information. If you are in a global corporation, with a wide area network stretching around the world, there may be someone in Taiwan, Luxembourg, or São Paulo viewing your pages right now without your knowledge.

In some companies, this may not be a problem at all. You know right away what your corporate culture is by the way you reacted to that last paragraph. If you recoiled in horror, then yours is probably the kind of organization that takes security seriously. If you are wondering what all the fuss is about, then your company is probably less security-conscious. Either mode is fine for what it is—each company has its own cultural imperatives.

When you put something on the web, assume it's open to the entire network unless you specifically protect it. The major exceptions to this rule are the Microsoft products, which come from a quite different culture than the UNIX servers of old. If you're running Internet Information Server (IIS) on Windows NT, then access is limited by default, and you have to take special steps to open that server to the rest of the world. If you are using UNIX servers, or some of the other Windows platform products, there are ways to protect your site, as well.

Most web servers provide at least a rudimentary way to restrict access to an entire site, an internal folder, or a set of files. Typically you can restrict user access through either of two methods:

User ID and password. For example, you may want to set up a list of authorized user IDs and passwords for people to access the site. When users try to access the site, the browser asks them to enter their IDs/passwords first (Figure 4.19).

IP address or domain. This method works a little differently: It can automatically identify and limit site access by IP address, domain name, or host name so that the site can be accessed only from certain authorized machines. Conversely, most web servers can be programmed to provide open access to all users *except* certain IP addresses, domains, or host names. This method is not too useful in a corporate environment, unless desktop machines are also strictly controlled with their own logins and passwords, so that unauthorized users cannot easily gain access to privileged machines, thereby gaining access to protected web sites. This can also be a good method to use, however, for low-security sites that you want to limit to specific customers, sales reps, or depart-

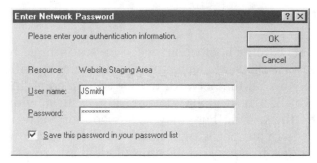

Figure 4.19   Typical user authentication dialog box.

ments. The user would have to be using a machine with an approved address to access the information on your web site.

Some server models also provide additional types of access control, such as group-level control. Access control can typically be put into force on a server level or on a folder level. For example, you may want to restrict access to all files listed under the server. Or you may want to restrict access to just a set of files in a particular folder. Some servers may even let you restrict access to individual files, on a file-by-file basis.

The mechanics of setting up user authentication may vary depending on your server. The best way to determine what is needed is to read your server documentation.

Protecting Your Site through Encryption

Even if you do user authentication, your site is not absolutely secure because there is always a chance that an unscrupulous person has logged in somewhere on the network and knows how to trap user IDs and passwords as they pass through a router or other network-connected device. This situation is of more concern on the Internet than it is on an intranet. On the Internet, you don't know who the person might be who is intercepting the transmission. On a corporate intranet, you are more likely to be able to control and monitor this sort of thing.

Nevertheless, if your site is dispensing highly sensitive data that is subject to snooping, especially in a large corporate wide area network that includes remote business partners and joint venture operations, you should consider further protection in the form of encryption schemes. Encryption is accomplished using a secure server and any browsers that support the same encryption standard. The most common encryption language for browsers is SSL (Secure Sockets Layer), which is spoken by both Netscape and Internet Explorer, as well as by most secure servers sold on the market. Once you have these components, encryption happens automatically. Anything that leaves the server is encrypted on the fly, travels over the network in an encrypted state, and is decrypted by the browser at the other end.

As I said before, though, encryption is normally overkill on an intranet. Most advanced intranets I've seen don't even have user authentication in place, much less encryption. If you are planning to serve some of your data out across an external web, however, encryption becomes more important—especially if the data is intended for viewing only by business partners or field employees. If you plan to use encryption, expect to pay some extra money for your server.

If There Already Is an Existing Intranet

If your network already has other web information servers on it, and you are simply adding yours to the total offering, things become a lot simpler for everyone. For one thing, you probably don't have to worry about distributing software or setting up users. By now, users probably have all the tools they need, and they are already well accustomed to using them. They may also be hooked into a central menu that appears automatically when they start their browsers.

In this case, your job is simply a matter of making sure users can get from other parts of the intranet to your own web site or information center. If there is a central server for the entire company, you will want to tell the people who run it about your new site, so that they can add your information center to any menus or tables of contents they maintain for the company. To make the link, they will have to know your server's network host name or IP address, and they may want a complete list of the content at your site. In the last chapter of this book, I will discuss ways that large webs can be managed to make the notification process easy for everyone.

The Matter of Training

The really neat thing about having an intranet is the way it makes information access so incredibly easy. Assuming your web site is set up right, all the user has to do is just point, click, and instantly retrieve anything on the server. But just because it's easy doesn't mean you can just put it out there and expect people to use it immediately. Some training is *always* required—and if not training, some sort of highly visible publicity about your effort. Rolling out a site on an intranet is not that much different from rolling one out on the World Wide Web. The more people who hear about it, the more "hits" you will get.

As an example, one day I happened to be visiting the headquarters of a major American computer manufacturer that had an intranet already installed, although still in the early stages of development. While there, I broached the subject of the intranet with an employee I was visiting. After I tried describing it in several different ways, this person—who was obviously struggling to connect with the idea—allowed that she had heard of such a thing, but didn't realize it was a web system. She even thought there might be some sort of software on her computer that could access it, but she certainly never had used it.

Since this person never received formal training, she had no way to connect with the concept. Obviously, here was a potentially new and quite efficient way she could get internal information—maybe even do research for her job—but since it was far removed from the normal information delivery channels, she had no way of understanding exactly why or how to use it.

If you want people to start receiving information through the intranet instead of through their normal channels, you may have to lead them the first few steps of the way. If you've already used a web browser, you understand how simple it is to use. But this is not so readily apparent to some of the people who still haven't used one.

What people need is not so much to learn *how* to use a web browser as to learn *why* to use it. There's still a conceptual leap people have to make that they probably won't do on their own unless they've already used the World Wide Web. And even if they have used the Web, there is still a conceptual leap people have to make between the Internet and the intranet. Unfailingly, someone will ask, "You mean we're on the Internet, right now?" "No," you'll reply, "this is an *in-TRA-net.*" Getting people to understand the whys and wherefores of an intranet isn't a major obstacle, but it's a hurdle nonetheless, the same way that getting people to start using a mouse and windows was a minor hurdle a few years ago.

The kind of training I'm talking about could be as simple as a brief luncheon seminar in which you sit people down, get their attention, and do a short demo. In smaller companies or work group situations, it may involve a brief hands-on exercise. Naturally, you may not have much success scheduling the time unless you have management backing, and that may require selling the idea upstairs first.

The success of your effort depends on what you have to show. If it's just a test page with a few pretty graphics, people may ohh and ahh, but go away shaking their heads. If it's company news, hard-to-find statistics, widely used references, online training, or data—in short, truly useful stuff people would kill to get their hands on—you may find that people buy in and start using the system a lot faster.

The best way to get total buy-in, of course, is to rig it so that using some part of the system is required to do their job—such as making the intranet the place everyone must go to turn in their weekly progress reports or get employee benefit information. A good way to get people involved is to provide two-way interaction through forms and database access, so that people will be able to contribute to the system, as well as obtain information from it. Keep in mind that you may only get one shot at this, so you'd better make it good. Be sure you have all your ducks in a row and be prepared to make people go wow.

When explaining the intranet to users, avoid making it sound more complicated than it really is. All they have to know is (1) how to start the browser, (2) how to use it, and (3) what they can use it for—what information is available for access within the company. Under how to use, you should demonstrate the structure of the available web site(s), show them how to browse and navigate, and explain how to save files or print. Since the average browser has a fairly simple set of easily understood features, formal browser training shouldn't take any longer than an hour or two.

But there are other issues to confront. One of the main ones is eliminating the preconceived notions people have about web technology and their confusion about the relation to the Internet. If your intranet happens to be integrated with other Internet applications, including e-mail, FTP, chat groups, and so forth, then there may be a considerable amount of additional training in how and when to use those additional tools.

Getting users acquainted with the intranet is only the first phase of your training effort. An even more intensive period of training will likely occur from a few weeks to a few months after you first introduce the system. The second phase of training is the "publishing phase," when people decide they want to contribute actively to the content of the intranet. At this point, they will need to learn many of the concepts and skills covered in Chapters 5 and 6 of this book.

It's a good idea to have web-publishing tools or add-ons already selected and ready for use by the time this phase occurs. This will happen naturally if you implement a pilot project as described in Chapter 9. You should also have a good idea of the best publishing models for your organization. How web publishing occurs will not be readily apparent to your trainees, nor will the most productive and efficient ways to go about doing it. So in addition to training on tools, you will also want to show work groups how to organize their publishing efforts and configure both their tools and document repositories.

Once you reach the publishing phase, it is important to realize that you are already at a stage where the intranet is poised to achieve maximum value for the organization. Now you have the opportunity to achieve buy-in, empowerment, and full user participation. That's why training is especially crucial at this point: to make sure people are fully empowered instead of being angrily frustrated at their inability to mold the system to their needs. The more you help these people by blazing the trail and predesigning systems they can easily adopt, the simpler it will be for everyone involved and the better the chance that the intranet will grow and blossom within your organization.

Take Your Training onto the Web

Just as the intranet creates additional training problems, it gives us the tools to solve those problems. The term *web-based training* (WBT) has recently crept into the lexicon alongside older terms like *computer-based training* (CBT) to describe training that is delivered online via the Internet or intranet. In fact, when you think about it, it's not hard at all to use the web browser as a mechanism to deliver online training to end users.

Thus, the same kinds of information you see in this book could be presented as a set of bite-size training nuggets that cover all the topics your employees need to know, from configuring the web browser software to web authoring with various tools like FrontPage, to advanced web development with CGI or Java. In some cases, your employees may be able to skip classroom training entirely, if they can tutor themselves on the subject.

If you've checked into training costs lately, you realize that it can be quite expensive—in excess of $300 per employee per day—to train someone in a more traditional classroom environment, especially when you factor in the trainee's lost time away from the job. That's assuming you can even find a suitable classroom training environment that will teach cutting-edge intranet concepts and technologies.

And chances are, the user may have scheduled that classroom time only to learn a couple of key techniques, such as how to create animated GIFs. With web-based training on your intranet, the same employee could look up a special online training module on animated GIFs, read up on it, and even perform a few quick hands-on exercises to build proficiency. In the training industry, they call this *just-in-time training* because the employee gets the training at exactly the moment it is needed, instead of having to wait for a suitable class to be located, scheduled, and paid for.

In the process, however, the employee may have saved your organization over $300 that would otherwise have been spent on classroom training fees. Multiply that times several days of classroom training, then multiply it again times all the people who will potentially use the intranet, and you can see that web-based training promises major savings in training costs within your organization. In companies with more than 1,000 employees, the savings easily mounts into the hundreds of thousands of dollars. If you have more than 10,000 employees, the savings may be in the millions. And this type of training can be applied not just to Internet or intranet topics, but to any other training your employees may need.

In cases where employees still attend a class, web-based training can be used to support and reinforce what they've learned in the classroom, so that your quite expensive investment has a better chance of being preserved. The training industry calls it *online performance support*. Keep an eye on these concepts, because over the coming years they will be increasingly important ways to keep employees proficient in new technologies while significantly cutting the costs of learning.

In fact, this technology is so promising that my company has already developed a set of online training products that do just that, and which are already being used by Fortune 500 companies in the U.S. and by other major corporations worldwide. See www.intramark.com/ for a live demo of the product on the World Wide Web (Figure 4.20).

How to Keep People Interested

Now you have the system running, and you've got everyone interested in it. So how do you keep them interested? This may be the greatest challenge of all (many a webmaster on the World Wide Web would like to know the answer to that one). The answer, dear reader, is what the used car dealer used to say: volume, volume, volume!

The idea is not to have a single web site, or even half a dozen. It is to have as many as it takes to empower everyone to share information across the enterprise. At pioneering intranet sites, such as SunWeb, there are hundreds or thousands of separate web servers running on the internal network (see Chapter 3 for examples). At Sun, the ratio is now nearly one web server for every eight people. That's not to say you need a thousand servers. Some very large companies exist with only a dozen or so.

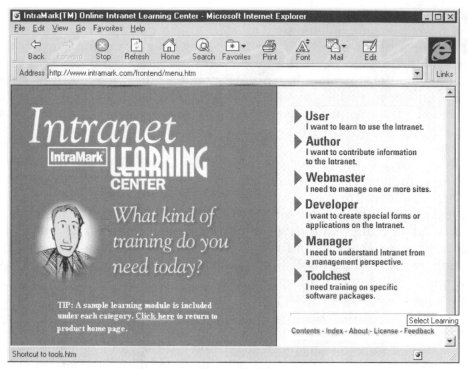

Figure 4.20   Web-based training.

But the more providers, users, and easy server space access, the more valuable the overall web system is to the enterprise. Here's why: Bob Metcalfe is already down in history as the guy who invented Ethernet, the most commonly used network standard for connecting PCs. But he is well known for another bit of wisdom called *Metcalfe's Law,* which (in a loose translation) goes something like this: *The value of a network is proportional to the number of users squared.* If just one person is connected to a network, it's worthless. If two people are connected, that's better. But as you add more and more users, the network's value to the organization grows exponentially.

To Metcalfe's Law, let me add an extra fillip that I'll call *Bernard's Corollary.* Similar to the original law, my corollary applies to the intranet and goes like this: *The value of an intranet is proportional to the number of applications, servers, and users cubed* (beat that one).

Here's what I mean. If you just have one document being served over an intranet and one person reading it, the system has some value because (you hope) you're already saving someone time and money. But, as you add more documents and users, the system's value increases exponentially. This is because you're saving more and more time and money for both the author and the users (since you no longer have to deliver the documents through the old, sluggish repro/mail system).

But the value really starts to expand into a third dimension when you use intranets to deliver different applications running on different servers. For instance, let's say one server is providing documents, another one database access, another one groupware connectivity, and another one is giving users a direct view into the mainframe. Suddenly, you are treating the web browser as a single multipurpose client in a way that makes it very simple for users to surf from one application to the next, all in a single frame.

This saves a considerable amount of time because users don't have to start four different programs to use four separate applications. It also saves software costs and training costs, because you probably won't have to train users for each application. So the net cost saving shows itself in ways you may not be able to fully predict, including software, training, printing, delivery, productivity, help center support calls, systems development overhead, and many more.

The net lesson to learn from all this is simple: The more mileage you get out of an intranet, and the more different applications you can serve, the better. To paraphrase another oft-heard quote: "Let a hundred servers blossom." Most of the companies that have taken full advantage of the intranet literally have hundreds of servers operating simultaneously—and exponentially more web sites.

Where Do We Go from Here?

Now that you understand how web technology works and how to bring a web site online, you've just gotten started. In the next few chapters, we will delve into the specifics of the technology a bit more closely, showing you how to create rich webs of documents, multimedia, and data. Read on if you want to hone your proficiency in web-building techniques.

Chapter Five at a Glance

One of the largest applications for web technology is the online publishing of documents previously distributed using paper-based systems. This chapter explains the ins and outs of online web publishing, including:

- The basics of HTML: how to use it, what its limits are, and why it is essential for web publishing
- A summary of more-advanced publishing techniques, including frames and cascading style sheets
- Various types of software used to create HTML web pages, including web-friendly word-processing programs and advanced authoring tools
- Tools used to automatically convert large-scale document sets to web output
- Tools used to display documents on a web without losing their original layout

Toward the Paperless Office

Document publishing is probably what Internets and intranets do best. When you're surfing out on the World Wide Web, for instance, most of what you see are documents somebody specifically prepared for web viewing. And most of what you do is *read those documents.* That's just the way it is: You shouldn't be using the Web at all unless you like to read things—in very large quantities.

In a corporate environment, this is good news. The fact that web systems enable enterprisewide document publishing means we can avoid the copying machine and start throwing away all those three-ring binders sitting in the closet. With the ability to instantaneously retrieve and view documents across the network, there's no reason we should be generating tons of printed materials anymore—*just in case* someone wants to read them.

An eventual casualty of the intranet revolution should be the compact disk (CD). I have several clients now who have been using CDs to distribute online documents to far-flung field locations, including remote bases in the jungles of Africa, offshore platforms in the North Sea, and instrumentation shacks out on the Arctic tundra. In some cases, there's no recourse: The network connections are too slow or nonexistent for intranet delivery to be totally practical. But think of a CD as "information frozen in time." You record it and it stays that way forever. On the intranet, however, as soon as someone changes a document, everyone on the network will see the latest version the next time it is requested from the server. So if you want to provide your far-flung locations with up-to-the-minute data, then you should do everything you can to bring the intranet to those locations, if it is practical to do so.

Most documents you see on an intranet have one thing in common: They are prepared in HTML format, which makes them load quickly and display nicely inside a web browser. But the ways people prepare the documents vary considerably. Some use common word processors like MS Word that have the ability to save documents directly in HTML format. Others edit the HTML document directly, either in a WYSIWYG or non-WYSIWYG mode. Still others take existing desktop-published documents and run them through various fil-tering devices or conversion programs to produce a finished web automati-cally. And of course there are still a lot of people (masochists, like me) who like to code their documents in raw HTML using a simple text editor.

That's not to say that HTML is the only method for putting information online. Today, there are a host of choices, from VRML (Virtual Reality Model-ing Language) to Dynamic HTML to Microsoft's active server pages and docu-ments generated from databases on the fly, at the moment they are requested. But you have to start somewhere, and for most people that means simple web pages generated using HTML (see Chapter 8 for details on the more advanced methods).

Assuming you start with plain old HTML, which of the methods above is best: raw coding, WYSIWYG editors, or what? The answer depends heavily on your circumstances and preferences. Some people will never be satisfied unless they personally insert every little HTML tag into their own documents. Others will never prepare a document for web consumption if they have to learn a lick of HTML. Still others have such a large volume of documents to "webify" that they can't think of anything but a totally automated solution. Since your needs and inclinations may vary considerably, this chapter exam-ines the whole gamut of web-publishing options, starting with basic HTML and going all the way up to sophisticated work-group automation solutions.

HTML: The Good, the Bad, and the Online

Let me say right off: Coding raw HTML is nasty business. If you have the lux-ury to do so, I say avoid it like the plague. And with the sophisticated tools now available for web publishing (discussed later in this chapter), it's becom-ing increasingly easy to ignore this core bit of web knowledge.

Back in the early days of the Web, of course, we didn't have such luxury. There was no way to produce web documents other than to sit and code them in raw HTML. I always compare it with the early days of PostScript, about 1985 or so. In those days, you could connect a PostScript printer to a PC, but there were no tools yet available to generate PostScript documents.

PostScript tools were first available on Mac only; PageMaker hadn't been invented for the PC yet, and it would be several years before common word processors like MS Word would generate PostScript output routinely. So, sometime back in the mid-1980s I used to sit and code raw PostScript by hand just so I could do desktop publishing on a PC. People chuckle now when I tell them this, but believe me, back in the old days they were ga-ga.

HTML is fast going the way of the early PostScript language. Though not a fifth as hard to use as PostScript was, it's already disappearing behind the slick façades of some quite impressive web-publishing packages. Already you have to examine the innards of HTML files about as often as you look at PostScript files now—which is practically never.

So why bother with HTML? Because, if you really want to understand the document publishing side of web technology, it helps to start with the basics and work your way up from there. Even if you *don't* want to be a publishing expert, you may find it interesting to know the good and bad points of HTML, and why it is such an essential component of web systems.

There are other reasons to learn at least a little HTML. Vendors like Microsoft and Netscape keep extending the language, and many authoring tools can't stay current. Also, no matter how good our tools get, there will always be some sort of tweaking you may want to do behind the scenes to get things to work *just so.* And sometimes, it's a lot quicker (if not easier) to whip out a text editor and slash away at a couple of hyperlinks than go through a bunch of pull-down menus and dialog boxes to achieve the same result. In other words, not everybody needs to know HTML, but *somebody* should. And if you're the person in charge, perhaps you're elected.

Here are a few essential pointers about HyperText Markup Language to get you acquainted fast.

Plain Text: The Basic Foundation

To get started on the right foot, let me say immediately that a document doesn't have to contain HTML to display inside a web browser. Web browsers will display plain text files as well, directly inside the browser window. So if you just want to type a note and put it on the web with no embellishment or further ado, then you can save it as a plain ASCII text file (with the extension *.txt*), serve it that way, and be finished with it. (While you're typing, be sure to hit the **Return** key at the end of each line, so the browser will know where to break your lines. Otherwise, you'll get one continuous line of text.)

Plain text is the simplest type of web document. It's not attractive, but it works. When the text document is displayed in the web browser window, it's displayed in a monospaced Courier font, just the way it might look if you typed it on a typewriter. For example:

```
A Plain Text Document
Here's an unattractive plain text document. Nothing to
```

```
write home about. We can't all be beautiful, can we? It's
quite plain, but you can still read it and get information from
it, can't you?
```

Of course, people are too proud these days to hand out plain text documents. Looks like something somebody did on an old *typewriter*. Everybody wants his or her documents to look sharp—whether they're desktop published or coded in HTML. But it's really useful to think of web documents this way. To get a nice-looking web document, you can start with plain text, then add HTML markup tags to make it look better and better. The more markup tags you add, the better looking your document will get.

Basic Rules of HTML

Don't ever join a poker game unless you know the rules, especially if your partners have been drinking and everyone's packing pistols. That can get you into a lot of trouble. Likewise, if you're going to get into the HTML coding game, you'd better know a few basic rules. They're not hard to learn, but they're essential. And not knowing them may cause a bit of trouble.

The first rule is structure. Every HTML document has the following basic structure:

```
<HTML>

<HEAD>
<TITLE>Title Goes Here</TITLE>
</HEAD>

<BODY>
Main heading and body goes here.
</BODY>
</HTML>
```

Notice how markup tags are used to "bracket" different parts of the document, as well as to bracket text. The entire document begins with <HTML> and ends with </HTML>. The heading begins with <HEAD> and ends with </HEAD>. The body part begins with <BODY> and ends with </BODY>. Bracketing codes like these make it easy to remember because the end code is the same as the beginning code, except that it includes a forward slash (/). Those of you who were born at the PC keyboard, remember to stay away from that backslash key (\).

These structural tags (HTML, HEAD, BODY) have little effect on the look of the document, but are important anyway, because some browsers may not display the document without them. *Note:* To be absolutely cool and technically correct, real webmeisters (like you) include a line at the top of the file that looks something like this:

```
<!DOCTYPE HTML PUBLIC "-//W3C//DTD HTML 3.2//EN">
```

This is a special tag that identifies your document as using HTML 3.2 code based on the document type definition (DTD) created by the W3 Consortium (W3C). Enough said.

Please don't confuse the <TITLE> with the opening heading in a document window. Usually, the opening heading is done with a heading tag, such as <H1>. For instance, when displayed in the browser, the following code looks like Figure 5.1.

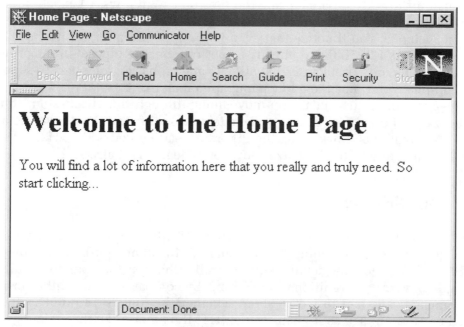

Figure 5.1   HTML code after displaying in a web browser.

```
<HTML>
<HEAD>
<TITLE>Home Page</TITLE>
</HEAD>
<BODY>
<H1>Welcome to the Home Page</H1>
You will find a lot of information here that you really and truly need.
So
start clicking...
</BODY>
</HTML>
```

Everything inside the <BODY> part is intended for display inside the browser window. Everything in the <HEAD> part is just extra information that goes along with the document. For example, the <TITLE> part always goes inside the <HEAD> because it is not intended for display inside the browser window. Instead, it will appear at the top of the window, or inside a <TITLE> field.

The best way to understand HTML, of course, is to start coding a little of it yourself. If you have a browser and a text editor, just create a plain text file and start adding HTML codes to it. You can use the server test file developed in Chapter 3 and add text and codes to it. Be sure to save your file with an *.html* extension (*.htm* if you are storing the files on a Windows 3.1 machine), and use the browser to open it up as a local file and see how it looks.

For instance, you'll notice that even if you type plain text (with no HTML codes) into an HTML file, it already comes out looking typeset in the browser window. The only problem is that all the paragraphs run together. To separate paragraphs, you'll need to add a paragraph break like this: <P>.

Keep tweaking the file as you move along through this discussion, so that you can see how different codes make text look different. While you're at it, you can create headings using the different heading codes (H1, H2, H3) and see how this affects the font size. Hey, you're learning it already!

Look Ma, No Fonts!

One thing that strikes you right off about HTML is the way that you can change fonts without doing "font changes." In other words, a heading tag (<H1>, <H2>, etc.) by default automatically changes the font to a suitable weight and size. In traditional publishing, by comparison, the author or page designer always had to worry about whether the font is 18-point Helvetica bold or 10-point Times Roman regular. HTML is more like the style tags in a word processor, where a "Heading 1" has already been defined as a certain font family, size, and weight.

In the earliest word processors, you had to reset the font manually each time it changed. Nowadays, we use style sheets to define all the different paragraph styles in a word-processing document. But those styles still have the specific font characteristics defined for them. Word-processing style sheets make document formatting easy because you can just point to each paragraph and apply the appropriate style to it automatically. (I still run across secretaries and administrators who haven't yet figured out how to use the style sheets in their word processors and keep resetting the fonts manually all the way through the document . . . what a waste!) Very conveniently, the HTML standard also now includes style sheets, as we will learn later in this chapter.

With HTML, however, the final display font can be selected by the user based on the unique fonts available and user preferences set *at the browser level* (Figure 5.2). For example, in Netscape Navigator the user can choose a set of base fonts for the document under the Options menu (see Figure 5.2). So if Times Roman 12 is the base font for regular body text (proportional), then the browser software scales all the other fonts as some variation of that.

There are ways for the *author* to specify a specific font in HTML (using the <FONT> tag and its attributes), but in the original implementations of this feature, it was assumed that:

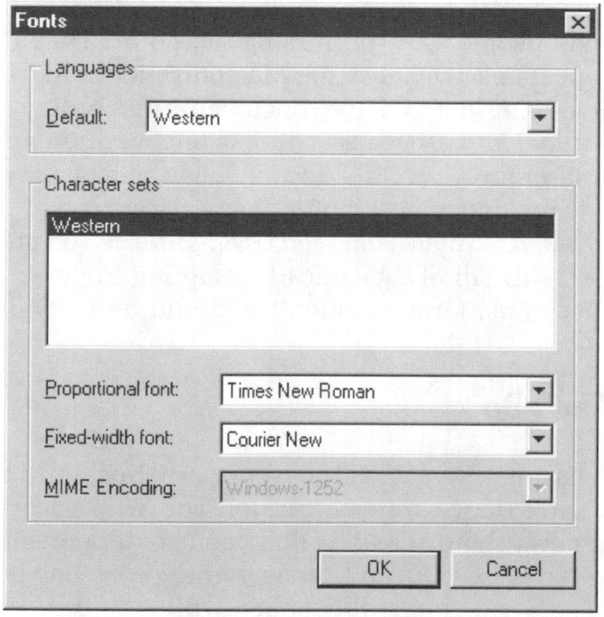

Figure 5.2 Internet Explorer's font setting dialog box.

- The fonts were available on the user's machine, and
- The user hadn't chosen to override the page designer's own font selections.

This override feature was potentially helpful to the user, although often overlooked. HTML files are designed to be transported across the globe to millions of viewers who have an array of different machines with different types of browsers and different monitor resolutions. These differences make it next to impossible to specify an optimal font that all users already have resident on their machines and that will match their screen resolutions precisely. So the people who invented web browsers decided that users should have ultimate font control.

More recent browser designs, such as Netscape Communicator, now include something called *dynamic font support,* which references font files and sends them along with HTML documents, so that the user sees exactly the same fonts that the designer specified. With the increasing availability of features like these, graphic designers have gone from near revolt against the web to a point where many have made their peace with or even enthusiastically adopted the web as a new design medium—learning how to be quite creative while working within the obvious limitations of this still-evolving publishing language.

Unfortunately, when it comes to features like font control and fine design adjustments, some people are still missing the point. They don't understand that what looks great on a cool designer Macintosh looks like breakfast sausage on a monochrome VGA laptop. Paper documents and online documents absolutely *should not look alike,* because paper is one medium and online display is something else entirely. HTML does a lousy job of preserving the font-specific look of paper documents, but it does a decent job of preserving a consistent look *across documents* and *across platforms* when viewed online. HTML also does a fair job of dynamically adapting the web document to the requirements of each platform and monitor resolution on which it is viewed.

What HTML Can't Do

With every discussion of what HTML can do, there should also be a discussion of what it can't do. As anyone can tell you who's worked with it for a while, the good news about HTML is that you can do marvelous online documents. The bad news is, you can't do everything. As time goes by, however, the *can-do* list is growing incredibly larger, while the *can't-do* list is growing considerably smaller.

The first thing to understand about HTML and its features is that you are dealing with a worldwide standard for marking up documents. HTML is based on agreements by international committees who spend a lot of their time arguing about arcane subjects like document type definitions (DTDs) and trying to come up with a set of features everyone can agree on. This shouldn't be all that hard to do, but when you're trying to please everybody in the entire world and accommodate two notoriously competitive companies like Microsoft and Netscape, the process does get bogged down occasionally.

The first versions of HTML (now known as *HTML 1*) were incredibly low on features. Headings, body text, bullets, numbered steps, indentation—these were about the extent of it. You could do fairly simple documents, but more-complex documents were elusive. The next version (now known as *HTML 2*) added the ability to create online forms, among other things. The forms feature opened up the web to interactive database access, e-mail integration, and other nifty features. New extensions created by Netscape in 1995, along with a draft HTML 3.0 specification, soon after brought the all-important feature of tables into existence, so that developers could create column-aligned layouts and more elaborate indentation schemes. The responsibility for setting standards during this period was turned over to a new group at MIT called the *W3 Consortium,* which was headed by Tim Berners-Lee, the original creator of HTML 1.

In late 1996 and early 1997, a period of relative tranquility ensued, in which both the Netscape and Microsoft browsers began to achieve parity, codified in the 3.0 versions of Netscape Navigator and Microsoft Internet Explorer. Soon, however, both companies again started pushing the margins of the technology aggressively with their 4.0 versions, resulting in a flurry of new, incompatible features and product announcements.

Partly in response to these growing disparities, the W3 Consortium issued two new specifications almost back to back in early 1997, called *HTML 3.2* and *4.0.* HTML 3.2 built on the 3.0 draft proposal to codify the markup language for tables, applets, and various extensions that had already become standard in both major browsers. HTML 4.0 added the ability to include richer form features, better table control, more support for objects and scripts, and more special math and international characters.

An interesting sideshow to the standards-setting process has been the way companies like Netscape and Microsoft are always racing ahead with their own extensions to HTML that let you control any number of document-formatting features. It has happened again and again, with features like forms, tables, applets, advanced graphic controls, and much more.

Of course, any standard set by a committee is just that—a standard—until it is accepted and adopted by the software vendors. So just because you read about a new HTML standard or feature on the World Wide Web or in a magazine doesn't mean that the standard will instantly work in your web browser or authoring tool. Typically, the first place a new feature is implemented is in the browsers, which means that a new version of the browser must be issued, downloaded, and installed before the feature will begin to work on the user's local machine.

Sometimes, as in the case of Cascading Style Sheets (CSS, discussed later in this chapter), the standard is implemented unevenly or spottily at first, then browser conformance improves over time. For instance, Internet Explorer was the first to adopt CSS, followed by Netscape.

Even once the browsers adopt new features, there is usually a time lag before the feature appears in most of the common web-editing tools. This is why it is often still necessary to "get your hands dirty" and manually code some HTML on occasion. If you want to take advantage of new HTML features as soon as they are adopted by the browser manufacturers—but before they appear in the editing tools—you will have to code it in yourself.

Even before you use a new HTML feature this way, however, it is important to test it thoroughly in all the browsers that are currently used on your intranet. Once you confirm that the feature works to your satisfaction, you can add it to your repertoire. Keep in mind that your company should already have its own set of standards (see Chapter 10) that specify which HTML features are supported or not supported by the intranet.

What happens if you insert HTML features into a web page that aren't recognized yet by a browser? Most browsers are designed to ignore unrecognized HTML tags (i.e., anything inside open/closed angle brackets that does not follow strict spelling and formatting guidelines). Thus, no harm is done by using an HTML feature before it's time. However, you will soon discover that it is a complete waste of your time.

Getting Framed

Frames are an important and relatively popular feature that was slightly late in making its debut on the web. First announced by Netscape, the technology allowed web authors to actually split the regular web browser window into panels or *frames,* each of which could contain a separate HTML file.

The most typical way this feature is used is to provide a persistent table of contents along the left edge of the screen, or a persistent toolbar at the top or bottom of the page. As I said before, each frame contains its own separate HTML file, so the toolbar might be kept in a separate file, the table of contents might be kept in a separate file, and the main body text might be kept in a third file. In addition, hyperlinks could be used to display new files in specific frames.

To make all this work, you start with an independent file called a *frameset* file and use it to set up the web display. The frameset file not only defines the layout of the frames, but also defines the initial HTML files to be displayed in the frames. For instance, this is an example of a typical frameset file:

```
<html>
<head>
  <title>Wordmark.Com, Inc. - Cool Tools</title>
</head>

<frameset rows="60,*">

  <frame align=center name="toolbar" src="newtoolb.html">

  <frameset cols="120,*">
    <frame align=left name="toc" src="tooltoc.html">
    <frame align=right name="main" src="toolopen.html">
  </frameset>

</frameset>
</html>
```

Notice that there is no <BODY> tag in this file, only <FRAMESET> tags. The first <FRAMESET> specifies a frame layout with two rows (60 pixels high and unlimited pixels high). The first row is represented by a single <FRAME>, but an additional <FRAMESET> divides the second row into two columns (120 pixels wide and unlimited pixels wide). Each column contains its own <FRAME>.

The result is a window with a total of three frames, as represented by the three <FRAME> tags, which also happen to specify the files that will go into each frame, resulting in the following display (Figure 5.3).

Notice in the original frameset file that each <FRAME> was given a name, such as *toc* or *main.* These names can be used in hyperlinks as the "target" of the hyperlink. For example, the whole purpose of the frame setup above is to keep the toolbar and table of contents visible at all times. That means that each hyperlink in the table of contents frame cannot bring up a file in the same frame, otherwise the table of contents would be replaced with the hyperlinked file. Instead, the hyperlink should display the resulting file in a different frame—preferably the main display frame of the window. To do this, the

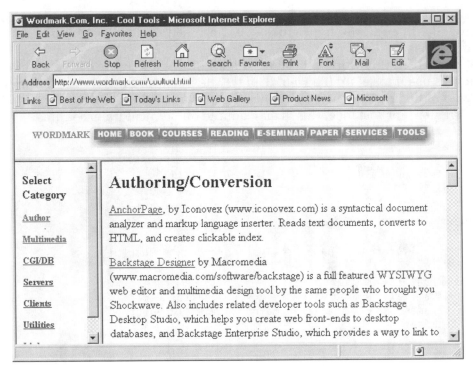

Figure 5.3 Web browser window with frames.

hyperlinks can be pointed to "target=main" to indicate that the result of the hyperlink must be targeted at the "main" frame. This is how it looks in the table of contents file:

```
<HTML>
<HEAD>
    <TITLE>Wordmark.Com, Inc. - Tool TOC</TITLE>
</HEAD>

<BODY BGCOLOR="#FFFFFF">

<H4>Select Category</H4>

<H5>
<A HREF="author.html" target="main">Author</A>
<P>
<A HREF="media.html" target="main">Multimedia</A>
```

```
<P>
<A HREF="connect.html" target="main">CGI/DB</A>
<P>
<A HREF="servers.html" target="main">Servers</A>
<P>
<A HREF="clients.html" target="main">Clients</A>
<P>
<A HREF="utility.html" target="main">Utilities</A>
<P>
<A HREF="links.html" target="main">Links</A></H5>
</BODY>
</HTML>
```

Of course, the preceding layout is just an example. Frame layouts can be varied and sized infinitely to produce the exact kind of layout you need. A caveat: In the past there have been some browser incompatibilities in the way frames are implemented. Before using frames on intranet web sites, be sure to test them in all supported web browsers.

Doing It in Style (Sheets, That Is)

One of the knottiest problems with corporate intranets is providing a consistent "look and feel" when you have dozens or even hundreds of authors collaborating (or not) on all that material out there. For instance, many companies want their employees to consistently put certain signature elements on a page (background color, header and footer with signatures, date edited, toolbars, logos, etc.). There is also the problem of providing a consistent layout, such as a standard indentation, horizontal rule structure before or after certain level headings, and so forth.

Consistency is nice, because if you provide a consistent standard, each page does not have to become a new adventure in formatting. In the past, companies tried using templates to solve this problem, with varying success. The template might be downloaded and used on occasion—sometimes maybe, sometimes not.

Up to now, many people have been slaving to put highly labor-intensive formatting instructions into each paragraph on their individual pages, to indent body text, create different font effects, create indentations, and more. We learned a long time ago—back when we were all using plain, old word processors—that these things were best handled using style sheets. In Microsoft Word and other publishing tools, for instance, you can use style sheet formatting to define *Heading 1* as 18 pt. Times Roman bold italic with eight points spacing above, six points below, and a two-point rule underneath. Once that is defined, tagging a paragraph with Heading 1 automatically makes it a heading with the defined style.

The *cascading style sheets* (CSS) specification published in HTML 3.2 works a lot like that. You can define the same types of attributes and associate them with <H1>, <P>, or any other "primitive" HTML tags. For instance, this is how a style sheet file might look:

```
<html>
<style type="text/css">
   h1 {font: 18pt "Helvetica, sans-serif";
      font-weight: bold;
      margin-top: 30pt;
      color: blue;
      line-height: 26pt}
   h2 {font: 12pt "Helvetica, sans-serif";
      font-weight: bold}
      p {font: 10pt "Times Roman, serif";
      margin-left: 40px;
      line-height: 12.5pt}
</style>
<html>
```

So any time you use <H1> in an associated document, it will automatically set the font to blue 18 pt Helvetica bold with a 30-point top margin and a line height of 26 points. A similar effect would occur for <H2>.

Once defined this way, the style sheet is saved in a file with a .css extension and is enforced across multiple pages through the magic of linking and referencing. It's similar to the idea of referencing an image in a web page: For instance, you might put a single copy of the corporate logo online and have all web pages include that image at the top. With CSS, all the pages on your web might point to the same .css style sheet file, using that single definition to control their layouts.

To reference a style sheet, each web page that wants to derive its style from the CSS must have a link imbedded in its <HEAD> section, such as:

```
<link rel=stylesheet href="stylefile.css" type="text/css">
```

where *stylefile.css* is the name of the style sheet file being referenced. Any time you make changes to the central style sheet, all web pages that reference the style sheet are changed automatically.

Some testing and experimentation may be required to make this work—especially testing the results in all browsers. Make sure you are working with

4.0 or later versions of both Netscape or Internet Explorer—earlier versions won't work. As I said, style sheets won't solve all our problems, but they will take us a long way toward a uniform intranetwide look and feel. Imagine controlling the entire design of thousands of pages on the intranet from a single point—it's mind-boggling.

Beyond HTML: Push, Cascade, and More

It would be fairly simple if HTML were the only way of formatting information for the web, but other models have arisen that can also be delivered to suitably enabled web browsers. I've listed them here in no particular order:

Virtual Reality Modeling Language (VRML). A way of creating three-dimensional graphic displays online that can be tilted and rotated in any direction. The feature has seen some use in organizations that have graphical modeling requirements—for instance, I have seen it used in reservoir modeling at a major client site.

Dynamic HTML. A new method, available starting with the 4.0 browsers, that will allow the web page to change dynamically based on user actions. For example, the user might be able to expand a table by clicking on it, reposition a graphic on a page, or change some of the text fonts—all without pulling down a new page from the server.

Push technology. A way to deliver information to the user desktop automatically via the web. In old web models, the user always has to ask for the data. With push, the information is "broadcast" on "channels" and can be played back on the desktop background, for instance, in Windows 98.

HTML Help and NetHelp. New models for publishing help files on the web. Previously, WinHelp was used on PCs for online help information. WinHelp was a proprietary technology bundled with the Microsoft Windows operating system that turned out to be a very popular feature. All software products on the Windows platform since the early 1990s have used WinHelp for their online publishing model. In the 4.0 versions of Netscape and IE, WinHelp is replaced by new HTML-based formats called HTMLHelp and NetHelp.

Since these are somewhat more advanced features used with differing effect on the corporate intranet, they will be covered in the following chapters of this book.

HTML Essentials at a Glance

Though it may seem a bit awkward at first, HTML is definitely not rocket science. The main complexity involved is the rapid proliferation of tags. Whereas the initial versions of HTML had only a few dozen tags, there are now hundreds of tags and extensions in existence. As with everything else, however, the old 80/20 rule applies. Eighty percent of what you will do with HTML can be done with about 20 percent of the available tags. The most basic tags are listed in the following table (Table 5.1). In my opinion, all the rest are just "icing on the cake." To test them, just create a plain text file with a .htm file extension and test locally in your web browser using File/Open/Browse.

TABLE 5.1   Basic HTML Codes

Text Style	How Used	Example

Heading	Hx, where x is the heading level.	`<H1>Page head or other major head</H1>`
		`<H2>Minor heading</H2>`
		`<H3>Subheading</H3>`

Body text	Requires no special tags except end-of-paragraph mark (<P>) or line break ( ). May have font changes.	`This paragraph has <B>bold</B> and<I>italic text</I> plus an internal line break   and it ends here.<P>`

Ordered list (steps)	Bullets.	`<OL>`
		`<LI>First numbered item.`
		`<LI>Second numbered item.`
		`</OL>`

Unordered list (bullets)	Numbered steps.	`<UL>`
		`<LI>First item in bullet list.`
		`<LI>Next item in bullet list.`
		`</UL>`

Horizontal rule	Separator in text.	`For example, here is text above it.`
		`<HR>`
		`Here is text below it.`

Hyperlink	Go to different file on different server.
	Go to different file on same server.
	Go to marker in same file.
		`<A HREF="http://server/filename"> click here</A>.`
		`<A HREF="path/filename"> click here</A>.`
		`<A HREF="#marker_name">click here</A>.`

(continues)

(continued) Text Style	How Used	Example
	Go to marker in different file, same server. Create a marker in a file.	`<A HREF="path/file#marker_name"> click here</A>.<A NAME="marker_name"></A>`
Inline graphics	Insert a picture at a specific place in a document.	`<IMG SRC="path/filename.ext">.`

Indented text	Block indent a paragraph.	`<BLOCKQUOTE>`
		`This paragraph will be indented.`
		`</BLOCKQUOTE>`

Preformatted text	Computer code, aligned form fields, preformatted columns separated by spaces (not tabs).	`<PRE>`
		`Preformatted text goes here.`
		`</PRE>`

Table		`<TABLE>`
		`<TR><TH>HeadCell1</TH>`
		`  <TH>HeadCell2</TH>`
		`<TR><TD>Row1Cell1</TD>`
		`  <TD>Row1Cell2</TD>`
		`<TR><TD>Row2Cell1</TD>`
		`  <TD>Row2Cell2</TD>`
		`</TABLE>`

Where to Read about HTML Standards

There are plenty of places on the World Wide Web where you can get information about HTML standards. However, the best place to start is www.w3.org/Markup/. This is the official HTML web page for the standard's setting body called the *W3 Consortium,* the MIT-based group created by HTML inventor Tim Berners-Lee, which now coordinates the HTML standard-setting process.

The Best Editors Around

Once you understand the nuts and bolts of HTML, you begin to realize what a bear of a coding task you have on your hands—especially if you want to do something more than just straight body text. At that point you start asking yourself the question, "Aren't there some software tools I can use to make this easier?"

This is the question many people were asking themselves back in the early 1990s, when web publishing was starting to catch fire as a serious pursuit for serious-minded people. Naturally, many software companies responded with the first generation of HTML tools called *HTML editors* (Figure 5.4).

Though there are many other—and often better—choices now for the serious web publisher, lots of HTML whizzes still like to use popular HTML editing programs such as HTML Assistant, HomeSite, and HotDog. Originally, these tools were quite rudimentary, giving the author little more than a rough idea of how the text would look when displayed on the final web page. Headings were bigger and bolder. Bullets (sometimes) looked like bullets. But you would still see the HTML codes sitting right there on the page. For convenience, the codes were often iconized into a single character, so that you couldn't accidentally delete a stray angle bracket while editing your HTML markup tags.

The more recent products, however, have stayed in lockstep with the market, to the extent that many of them now include support for the more

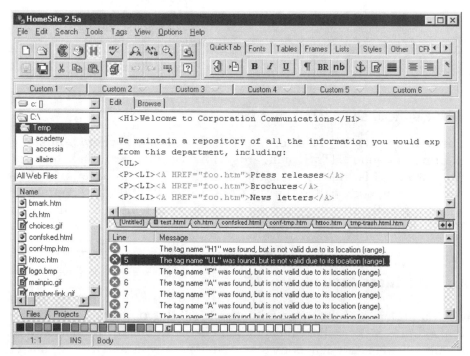

Figure 5.4   The HomeSite Editor by Allaire Corporation.

Where to Get HTML Editors

If the idea of an HTML editor appeals to you, here are some sources on the World Wide Web.

www.zdnet.com/pcmag/iu/author/htmledit/_htmled.htm

union.ncsa.uiuc.edu/HyperNews/get/www/html/editors.html

www.stars.com/Vlib/Providers/HTML_Editors.html

www.starnine.com/development/extendingwebstar/editors.html
(Mac tools only)

---

advanced web technologies including Java, style sheets, frames, and more. By and large, however, these products still provide only an approximation of the final web page, the way that our old word processors used to provide a separate "preview" of the final printed page.

While gung-ho HTML addicts will love the ability to see the codes during the editing process, those who are untutored in the intricacies of HTML may find these tools somewhat less appealing—and even confusing. If you don't want to retrain for HTML, the next category of products may be more appropriate.

How to Create Web Pages without Learning HTML

HTML editors are fine, as far as they go. And if you already know HTML and want to see the codes while you work, they're ideal. But it is already possible to let HTML fade into the background the same way PostScript did. Virtually no one still reads or codes PostScript anymore—it has become a sort of private business conducted between the computer and the printer in a language most people don't understand. But that's okay, because it does its magical work entirely in the background. That's how HTML works (or should work) with the more advanced generation of web-editing tools called *WYSIWYG web editors.*

That's not to say *nobody* has to learn HTML. In every intranet, there must be a few knowledgeable people who can go in and troubleshoot a problem at the HTML level. We call these people *web administrators,* and we put them in charge of keeping the system running smoothly day by day. If you're that kind of person, there are plenty of books on HTML.

But for the masses, you will want to set up the system in a way that allows them to contribute to the success of the intranet without ever learning HTML. There are a couple of good ways to do that:

Give them WYSIWYG tools.   For instance, there are now several add-on products that give everyday word processors like MS Word and WordPerfect the ability to save files directly to HTML format. The latest word processors like Word 97 have web features built-in. Later sections of this chapter show how these work.

Don't even ask them to change tools.   Another way to approach this subject—probably the best way—is to let people continue using the same WP/DTP tools they've always used. That way, no retraining is involved and no one has to break stride. Instead, you just take the documents they create and convert them to HTML using one of the many conversion tools now available. Later sections in this chapter will introduce tools like *HTML Transit* that let you create entire webs from common word-processing documents with only a few minutes' work.

Remember the favor I asked you way back at the beginning of Chapter 4? Is your "Keep it Simple" sign still hanging there? Steering clear of HTML is one of the ways you can keep things simple for the authors in your information center. Some of the best ways to do that are covered in the following sections.

Web-Friendly Word Processors

One way to create web documents without coding HTML is to use the latest version of ordinary word processors like Microsoft Word, Lotus WordPro, Corel Word Perfect—or even other office suite products like Excel, Access, Lotus 1-2-3, and PowerPoint. If you are using a somewhat older version of these products—such as Word 6.0 and 7.0 (Word for Windows 97)—this may require special "add-ons" like Microsoft's Internet Assistant (IA), which you can retrieve off the Microsoft web site. Internet Assistant is just an extra bit of software you can install *on top of* your existing copy of Microsoft Word—or any of the other Office products, including Excel, PowerPoint, and Access—that gives them the ability to create web pages. Word IA is free off the Internet or you can order it directly from Microsoft. If you don't use Microsoft Word, there are other add-on products you can use that work a lot like IA (see "Word Processors and Add-ons").

When added to MS Word, the Internet Assistance product provides the following added features:

◆ The ability to create new HTML documents and forms using the program's standard word-processing features

◆ The ability to read existing HTML documents and edit them inside MS Word

◆ The ability to use MS Word as a web browser to capture pages from the Internet or intranet for editing or to test pages once they are edited

Once you get a copy of it, IA installs just like any other PC program and automatically "adds itself" to the MS Word product, so that all the functions are available from inside MS Word through the standard set of pull-down menus. You don't have to start or learn a different program, you just start MS Word and use it more or less the same way you always did (see Figure 5.5).

With the introduction of Office 97 and later office suites, Microsoft entered a new realm: one in which the difference between "what's on the web" and "what's on the hard drive" is often blurred. Office 97 and other Microsoft

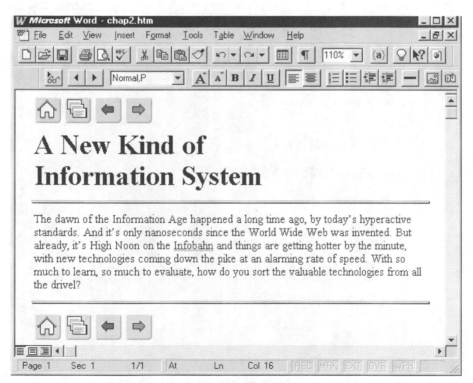

Figure 5.5   Microsoft Word Internet Assistant.

products that immediately followed it—including Internet Explorer 4.0 and Windows 98—were part of Microsoft's strategy to finally integrate web documents and ordinary documents so that office workers can have easy access to *either* source of information for viewing, editing, saving, and printing. Many web-friendly features are integrated directly into MS Office tools like Word, Excel, and others (Figure 5.6), including the ability to:

◆ Create hyperlinks on the fly by simply typing a URL into a document

◆ Allow hyperlinks to call up ordinary documents from the local hard drive or network drive as easily as they call up web pages from the Internet or intranet

◆ Open web pages and edit them

◆ Create new web pages from scratch in MS Word using blank paper, a template, or several wizards that create out-of-the-box page layouts

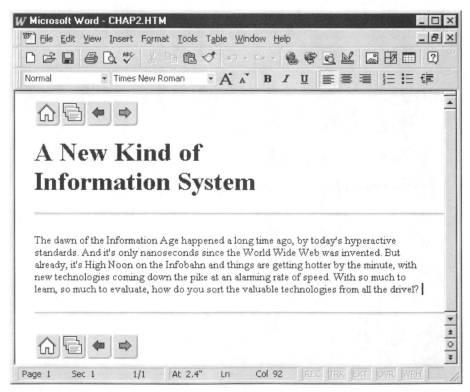

Figure 5.6   Microsoft Word Office 97.

◆ Save office documents automatically to HTML/web-compatible format

◆ Browse through documents using a web toolbar, including a Favorites list

With Office 97, the Internet Assistant add-on products are no longer required. Instead, all the web-friendly features are built-in from the start. The following sections demonstrate how a few of these features work.

Creating a New Document

Here's an example of how you would use Word 97 to create your own personal home page:

◆ Start MS Word the same way you always do.

◆ Create a new document using the New Option on the File menu. The resulting dialog gives you access to several web templates and wizards (Figure 5.7).

◆ Double-click the Web Page Wizard option to begin working with the Web Page Wizard (Figure 5.8).

◆ On the first page of the wizard, select the Personal Home Page option and click the next button.

◆ Fill in all the pages of the wizard with your personal information, as requested. Click the Next Page button after you finish working with each page, and the Finish button after you complete the last page.

◆ When you finish the last page, a personal home page appears in the Microsoft Word window with all your information already entered. You can edit this just as you would any other document.

◆ Click on different paragraphs in the document and notice the "style tag" designation at the upper left on the Formatting toolbar (Normal, Heading 1, Heading 2, etc.). These are the styles you can use to format different components of your document. If you add new paragraphs, you should also select the appropriate formatting style for them, to make sure that the document displays appropriately on the web.

◆ Save the file and if desired move it to your web server (or save it there directly if you have direct write access to the web server from your local computer).

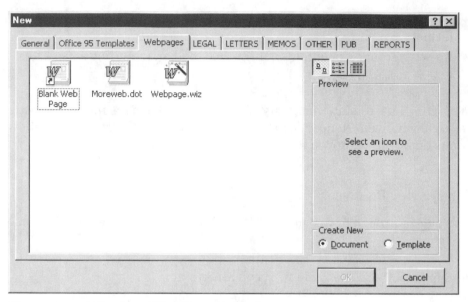

Figure 5.7   Word 97 File/New dialog box.

How Word Saves the File

The previous section showed how to use Office 97 to create a new web page, but you can also turn any ordinary Office 97 document into a web page in one step using the Save As HTML feature on the File menu. When you do this, Office 97 doesn't save it as a normal Word file. Instead, it saves your docu-

Figure 5.8   Word 97 Web Page Wizard.

ment as an HTML file, with all the proper codes to mark the paragraphs you set up as headings, bullet lists, numbered lists, and such. For example, the file you are saving might look like Figure 5.9 when displayed in Word.

But the file saved to disk would actually look like plain old HTML, as shown in Figure 5.10.

Keep in mind, of course, that this assumes the document author has already selected an appropriate "style tag" for each paragraph when setting up the document in MS Word. It's also important to understand that the HTML-coded file is the *only version* of the document that gets saved to disk. There is no MS Word (.doc) file involved at all. If you try to open the HTML file again in MS Word, you still won't see the codes. Instead, Word IA will hide the codes and display the information as WYSIWYG text again. To see the codes, you must use the View/HTML Source option on the menu (not available in IA 1.0).

This is what I mean by a WYSIWYG authoring tool: It is relentlessly WYSIWYG in that it shields the author from seeing most of the actual HTML codes. Microsoft Word, and other packages that work the same way, are built on the assumption that you should be able to use your word processor in just about the same way as you did before, but to do web pages (HTML files) as well as ordinary documents.

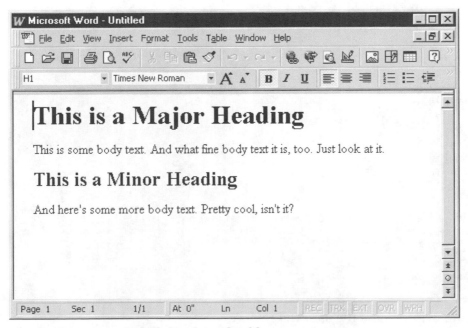

Figure 5.9   How Word displays the file.

Of course, you probably wouldn't hand a tool like Microsoft Word to an advanced web site designer, application developer, webmaster—or even to a desktop-publishing group that is more productive with more advanced DTP tools (and the web-friendly features now built into them).

But today's web-friendly word processors aren't a bad tool for people who regularly use them to create ordinary documents, and who want to begin using them to create occasional isolated web pages for use on intranets. In a case like this, where the web authoring is occasional rather than an intensive ongoing affair, it may not be productive to retrain these kinds of people on more advanced web tools. It's often better to just find the "web hooks" in their existing tools, and then show them how to use them.

```
<HTML>

<HEAD>

<TITLE>Untitled</TITLE>

<META NAME="GENERATOR" CONTENT="Internet Assistant for Microsoft
Word 2.0z">
</HEAD>

<BODY>

<H1>This is a Major Heading </H1>

<P>
This is some body text. And what fine body text it is, too. Just
look at it.
<H2>This is a Minor Heading </H2>

<P>
And here's some more body text. Pretty cool, isn't it?
</BODY>

</HTML>
```

Figure 5.10 Same file as saved to disk.

Word Processors and Add-Ons

In this section, I used Microsoft Word Internet Assistant and Office 97 as examples of the way traditional office suites have evolved to give your rank-and-file employees simple and easy-to-use web publishing capabilities with minimal retraining. Other similar packages are no less feature filled, even if they do get occasional second billing. WordPerfect Office Suite also has added web publishing and collaboration features to its traditional office suite package, as has Lotus with AmiPro and other members of its SmartSuite.

MS Office 95 Internet Assistant www.microsoft.com/msword/internet/ia/

MS Office 97 www.microsoft.com/office/

WordPerfect Office Suite www.corel.com/products/wordperfect/

Lotus SmartSuite www.lotus.com/smartsuite.nsf

Advanced Web-Authoring Tools

The main problem with advanced, web-friendly office suites like Office 97 is that they don't provide all the high-productivity bells and whistles of more sophisticated web-authoring tools, including features like web site integration and true WYSIWYG. Microsoft Word gives you a good idea of what the document will look like on the web, but if you open the same document in a web browser, you'll notice it looks significantly different (compare Figures 5.11 and 5.12). Also, Word and the other office products are great for creating individual documents, but for employees who are involved in direct, hands-on management and updating of web sites, there are many better tools around. Two of the most popular examples are the competing products from Microsoft and Netscape, plus a smattering of other popular web site–authoring tools such as NetObjects Fusion and Deltapoint QuickSite.

WYSIWYG Editing

Certainly one of the most popular tools in this category is FrontPage, a Microsoft product based on a truly inspired original design by a tiny startup

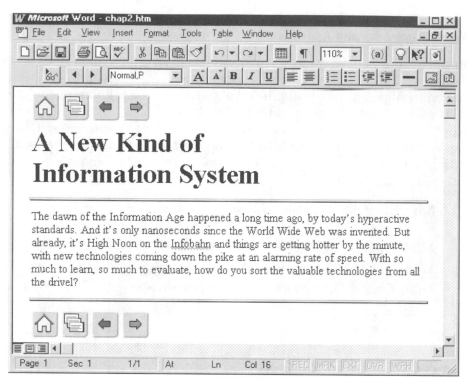

Figure 5.11   Word's not-quite WYSIWYG display.

company called *Vermeer Technologies Inc.* FrontPage was the first integrated suite of advanced web-development tools for PCs, including a totally WYSI-WYG page editor, a visual site-management tool, a built-in web server, and a set of "server extensions" that allowed it to directly control content on nearly any remote web server. *Note:* Please keep in mind that FrontPage is just one example of an entire category of tools that make web publishing easier. It's impossible to cover every one, but some of the other similar tools are listed in the sidebar titled "Advanced Web Authoring Tools."

The best way to understand how the web-editing features of FrontPage works is to install it, start the FrontPage Editor, then open up an existing web page using the File/Open command. When you do, the display looks just like the page as you might view it in a regular web browser (Figure 5.13).

Once the document is open on the screen, you can insert the cursor and start editing. While you're at it, notice how similar the FrontPage document-editing interface is to Microsoft Word and other popular word processors. You

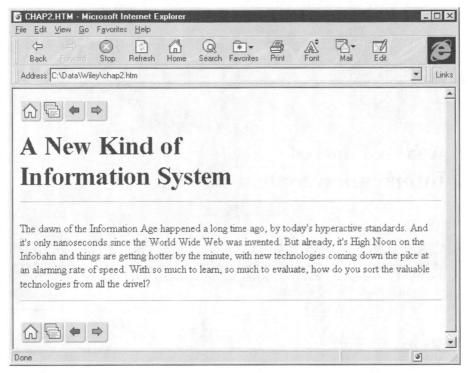

Figure 5.12   A web browser display of same file.

can see many of the same buttons on the toolbar, including those that let you do boldfacing and italics, plus the buttons that do numbered steps, bullets, and paragraph indents. There are all the same buttons for Cut/Copy/Paste and File New/Open/Save, plus the same kind of style tag list you see in the toolbar of Word or Word with Internet Assistant. There is even a spell checker, and a style list that you can use to tag paragraphs with publishing styles that will translate easily into the HTML format once the page is saved.

Of course, if you want to create a new document using FrontPage, all you have to do is use File/New and a clean blank page appears to start with. FrontPage offers a number of standard templates and wizards for various types of web-page design, as you can see from the list in Figure 5.14.

Again, this exactly mimics the way other common desktop applications work. For example, MS Word gives you document templates (memo, fax, report, etc.) and PowerPoint gives you presentation templates (text and graph, table, etc.). Nothing new there—and that's what's good about it.

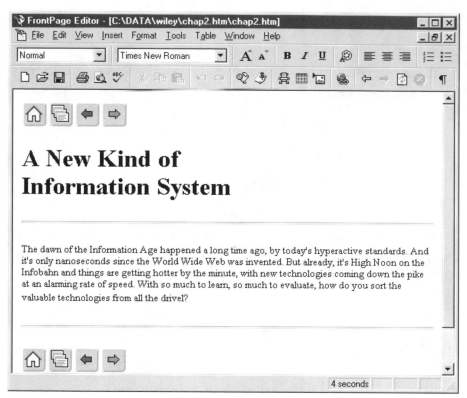

Figure 5.13   True WYSIWYG in FrontPage Editor.

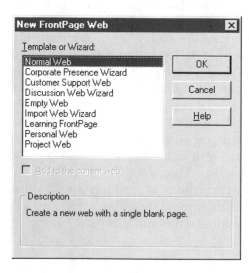

Figure 5.14   FrontPage Editor's New Page dialog box.

Figure 5.15 FrontPage Editor's Form Fields toolbar.

Notice that FrontPage automates many of the special web-creation functions. For example, if you are creating a form to be used online, FrontPage has toolbar icons that let you easily insert a pushbutton, radio button, text field, or pull-down menu directly on your web page (see Figure 5.15 and the detailed discussion of forms in Chapter 7).

If you want to create a hyperlink, all you have to do is shade the text you want users to click, then click on the Create/Edit Link button in the toolbar (or select Link from the Edit menu). When you do, you get a menu like the one displayed in Figure 5.16.

Notice you can easily choose other pages at your site to link to, or select links on the local web or the World Wide Web. If you want to link to a document that doesn't even exist yet, you can do that too by selecting the New Page tab, typing in a page name, then going off to create that document.

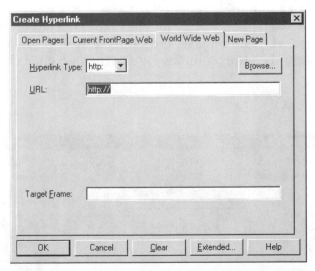

Figure 5.16 FrontPage Editor's Create Link dialog box.

Best of all, FrontPage includes insertable components (called *bots* in previous versions of FrontPage), that work a lot like the field codes in MS Word or the variables in FrameMaker. For instance, you can insert a *Timestamp* anywhere on the current page and FrontPage will automatically insert the current date at that point when you save it to the web. However, there are more advanced components like the *Scheduled Image* that lets you specify an image to be displayed only during a scheduled period of time, or a *Scheduled Include* that inserts the contents of a separate text file during a specified time period. Recent versions of FrontPage include active elements such as a Search Form that makes your site searchable, or a Hit Counter that shows how many times a particular page has been accessed.

Site Management with FrontPage

But FrontPage is more than just a web page editor. In fact, when used correctly, it can be a fairly powerful web site-management tool. The product includes another module called *FrontPage Explorer* that is more likely to serve as the front end of the product for people who are engaged not just in creating web pages but in managing web sites, or *miniwebs* (isolated folders, modules, or sections of a much broader web site). FrontPage Explorer includes templates for a number of different types of web sites, such as a corporate presence web, a customer service web, a discussion web, and a project web.

It includes security features and "server extensions" that allow the author/web administrator to interact directly with the pages on the web server. So instead of creating web pages offline and later copying or moving them to the server, FrontPage lets you manage and edit the web pages directly on the server. This is not only more productive, since the web site is being edited "as

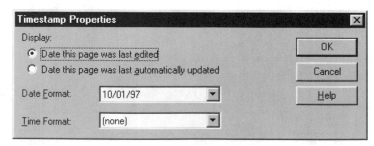

Figure 5.17 FrontPage Editor's Timestamp parameters.

a whole," but FrontPage can take responsibility for verifying the integrity of all links at a site. There are diagnostic tools for verifying links, fixing them, and developing a to-do list of site-management chores. And there are other special built-in tools that let you make the site searchable, create linked-image maps (for dynamic, clickable images with multiple embedded hyper-links), or create dynamic online web forms that can capture user data. There is even a personal web server (Figure 5.18) bundled with the product that can be used to develop and test fully functional web sites offline, on the web author's local machine.

Obviously, these features provide much more depth than many people in your organization may need. And it also takes a considerable amount of train-ing (up to two days) for employees to become power users. Typically, on an intranet, many if not most of the people involved in providing content will do so on a very superficial level, and most people will not want to (or need to) get into the intricacies of web-site management. Instead, you may want to appoint a web administrator in each department or business unit to handle web-management duties and help move content online—especially content cre-ated by people who have little or no web training.

If you have your organization set up that way, it is a simple matter for the vast majority of people to create web-ready pages using tools like Word, the FrontPage Editor, or some of the other editing tools mentioned in this book. Once the web-ready pages are created, the web administrator can easily move them into position on the web server and integrate them with the rest of the web content—creating links to and from the new pages to the existing web.

Figure 5.18   FrontPage Personal Web Server.

Netscape Composer

Netscape's WYSIWYG web editor was originally called *Navigator Gold,* but is now redubbed Composer in the Netscape Communicator suite. With this product, you get both a web browser and editor in one tool.

For instance, when you go to a web page on the Internet or intranet, you have the option to edit it. You can also save the entire web page to your local hard drive, including the images that are included on the page.

The Netscape Composer has many of the same standard editing features of any word processor, including style tags, cut and paste, paragraph formatting, font control, and other HTML-compatible features (see Figure 5.19). Netscape also gives you the option to publish web pages directly to the server. In most cases, this will be an FTP or HTTP server that supports writing to the web-server document area.

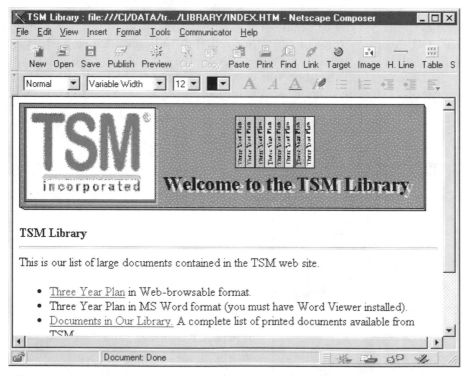

Figure 5.19 Netscape Composer.

Advanced Web-Authoring Tools

In this section, I used FrontPage and Netscape Composer as examples of WYSIWYG web-publishing tools. Here's where to find information on these and other similar tools on the WWW:

Adobe PageMill and SiteMill (Mac)   www.adobe.com/

Claris Home Page   www.claris.com/

Backstage Designer   www.macromedia.com/

HoTMetaL Pro   www.softquad.com/

Deltapoint QuickSite   www.deltapoint.com/

InContext Spider   www.incontext.com/products/

Microsoft FrontPage   www.microsoft.com/frontpage/

NetObjects Fusion   www.netobjects.com/

Netscape Composer   home.netscape.com/communicator/

Moving Finished Documents onto the Web Server

If you followed the discussion in earlier chapters, you understand that each web server has a special place where it keeps all the documents to be served. This area is called the *document root,* and it is typically a folder on the server hard drive that has been defined by default or specially created for this purpose. As a security measure, the server will not allow remote web users access to any parts of its hard drive, except the document root area.

So if you want create web pages using an HTML or WYSIWYG editor, and you want your documents to be viewable over the intranet, they must be stored on the server in this location. To do so, you will need both write access and a physical connection to the server hard drive. On some intranets, FTP servers can be used to allow file transfer between remote parts of the network and the web server. Also, programs like the Netscape Editor and FrontPage can be used to directly interface with servers to directly edit or "publish" edited files into the correct server space.

Once the finished files are deposited into the server document area, they should work fine without any other installation or configuration required, as long as all links have been coded correctly and tested. Web publishing, then, is simply a matter of creating files in the correct format (HTML), then storing them in the right place—either manually or automatically.

Automated Web-Publishing Systems

Tools like FrontPage and Netscape Composer are fine for creating and managing small groups of web pages where each document equals one web page and where the authors of the material actually control the look and feel of the content once it gets up on the web. But what about large document sets being used, created, or updated by a staff of authors who don't want to learn about web pages and HTML? Fortunately, the next category of web tools lets you create extensive sets of interlinked web documents automatically and completely "in the background," which means you don't actually see the documents as they are being processed.

The main benefit of this arrangement is that your authors can keep using their existing tools—programs like FrameMaker, Interleaf, MS Word, Word-Perfect, and others—yet still generate fully functional large-scale web sites without missing a beat. Your staff can continue producing documents just the way that they always have, and you only need one person to take a little time to transfer the documents for delivery on the web. The transfer of documents from paper to web can be automated in such a way that it can become as simple as the click of a button or a scheduled batch process performed automatically. Figure 5.20 shows how the document-to-web conversion process looks.

There are several major tools available for automated web publishing (see the sidebar titled "Tools for Automated Web Publishing"). To show how they typically work, I'll use as an example *HTML Transit,* a PC-based, web-document publishing system from InfoAccess, Inc. (Figure 5.21). HTML Tran-

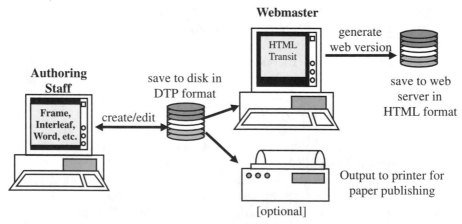

Figure 5.20   Automated web-publishing process.

sit can handle documents prepared in Interleaf, FrameMaker (MIF), MS Word, WordPerfect, AmiPro, Rich Text Format (RTF), Excel, PowerPoint, and other formats. It automatically converts the source documents, with all embedded illustrations, into a web-compatible format, storing the text as HTML files and the graphics in separate GIF or JPEG files. But it preserves the relationship between text and graphics so that the illustrations will still display properly within the documents when they're viewed in a web browser.

While the conversion is underway, HTML Transit can also split long documents into a series of smaller files that are more easily readable in a web environment. For example, you may want it to split a document at every major heading and save each individual section as a separate "web page" (HTML file). HTML Transit can automatically build a hyperlinked table of contents for the entire set of documents or an individual table of contents for each separate web page. A hyperlinked index is possible, too.

Special graphics, navigation buttons, and customized headers and footers can be inserted automatically on every page, along with a time stamp and an

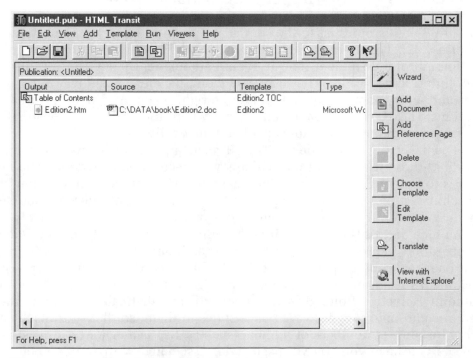

Figure 5.21   HTML Transit main window.

address or signature. All of this happens on the fly as the web documents are being built. The complete processing time for a moderate-size group of documents might be a few minutes to half an hour, depending on the power and speed of the machine and other factors, the size of the document set being converted, and the presence/absence of complex graphics. What's more, you can save the customized conversion template for each set of documents, so that the next time the authors edit or update the documents, conversion becomes as easy as the click of a button.

The person viewing the result of an HTML Transit conversion on the web might first see a table of contents that is completely hyperlinked to various heading levels as desired. The user could click on any title in the table of contents and immediately go to that page. Once on the page, the user would see navigation buttons that allow the reader to progress forward or backward from page to page or section to section in the documents.

To understand how the conversion works, let's walk through key parts of the process. HTML Transit provides a wizard you can use to set up the process for converting your document sets to the web.

For example, the first thing you must do with the HTML Transit wizard is define the location of the files to be used for input and output. In effect, all you are doing is pointing to the source and then pointing to the destination (Figure 5.22). This is important, since it allows HTML Transit to draw information out of a document repository and automatically deposit the finished web into a server folder. That way, you won't have to hunt down individual files and worry about copying them to the right place. And in all future conversions, HTML will automatically know where the source and destination files reside and handle the conversion automatically.

As you specify input files, HTML Transit automatically reads the style sheets of those files to find out which styles need to be converted. The next step is to Define Elements. This includes selecting a style for navigation buttons, but also includes specifying a one-to-one mapping of internal document styles with the way you want them to look on the web page (Figure 5.23).

The nice part of HTML Transit is that it doesn't require the original document authors to use style sheets at all. You can identify certain text patterns or font changes to be mapped to specific HTML tags. For example, suppose a document's major headings are numbered *1.1, 1.2,* and so on, and always use 18-point Helvetica Bold. HTML Transit will automatically recognize these patterns and map proposed web page styles to them, so that—for instance— every instance of number-dot-number (such as *1.1*) as a major heading style.

Once you have your HTML page styles associated with source document styles, it's time to define the look and feel of the final web document. You can

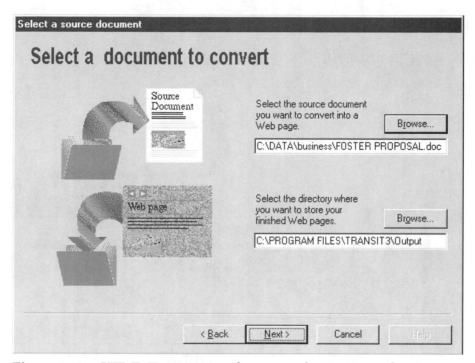

Figure 5.22 HTML Transit wizard—source destination selection.

define the format of your headings (Figure 5.24), as well as the basic layout of body text, tables of contents, and indexes. Tables of contents can be defined for the entire document set or each individual HTML page (local TOC). Part of what you can define is a way of splitting up long documents into shorter web pages and major headings (Figure 5.25).

HTML Transit lets you define the positions of the navigation buttons that will appear on each page (Figure 5.26). You can have buttons that will help users navigate easily to the previous page, next page, table of contents, index, or a specific page. The links can be placed at the bottom or top of each page, or even at every occurrence of a particular web page paragraph style (such as a minor heading). As it builds the web, it will automatically determine the proper link that goes with each navigation button on each page. Imagine the work that would be involved if you had to figure all this out on your own!

Once you're finished setting up the conversion, you can save all of your choices as a "template file" to be used any time you are converting the same—or a similar—set of documents (Figure 5.27).

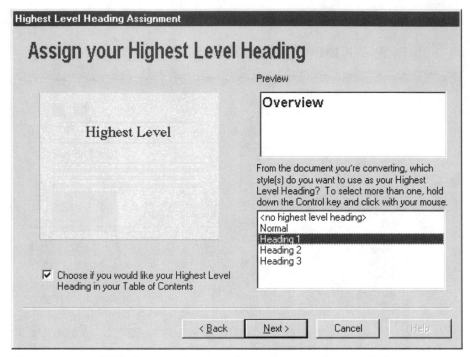

Figure 5.23   HTML Transit wizard—style association dialog.

Next time the authors edit the documents and you need to generate a new set of web files, all you have to do is open the old template file and run the translation. The program remembers how the conversion was set up the last time, and it even remembers where the source and destination files are located. As long as the document files keep the same names and the same source location, you should never have to set up the conversion again—just run it each time you need to move the most recent set of documents up onto the intranet.

Furthermore, if your authoring group is organized enough so that everyone uses the same style sheet consistently in their documents, then the same template file can be applied to any set of documents produced by the same group. This is a great argument for setting up word-processing templates and document authoring standards in your work group, and organizing your authors to work this way. You will only need to run one conversion process any time you want to publish information on the web.

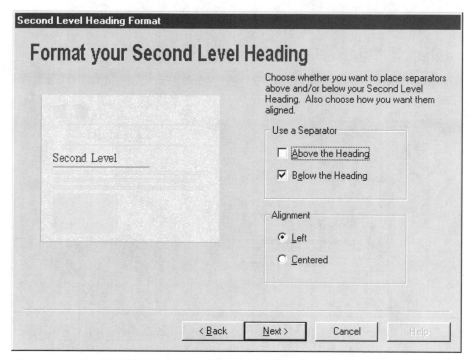

Figure 5.24   HTML Transit wizard—formatting dialog.

Tools for Automated Web Publishing

In this section, I used HTML Transit as an example of an automated web-publishing tool. However, there are several other major tools available on the market now. Here's where to find information on HTML Transit and other similar tools.

> **HTML Transit**   www.infoaccess.com/
>
> **WebMaker**   www.harlequin.com/
>
> **Cyberleaf**   www.ileaf.com/
>
> **SkiSoft Web Publisher**   www.skisoft.com
>
> **Other Tools**   www.stars.com/Vlib/Providers/Translators.html

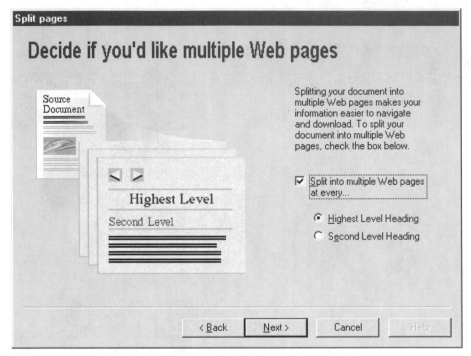

Figure 5.25   HTML Transit wizard—split pages dialog.

Why and When to Preserve Document Layout

Up to this point, we've only talked about ways to create HTML documents for delivery over a web. If you read Chapter 2 closely, you realize you can serve any kind of file over the web—even native word-processing files. But if you've followed my arguments closely, you also realize that HTML files are absolutely the best way to present any web document since they are designed exactly for that purpose. HTML files work better than anything else for display inside web browser windows—mainly because they scale and resize all of their columns (and even fonts) to fit the end user's current window. They also happen to be ideal for network delivery because they involve very compact file sizes.

What happens with HTML delivery, however, is that it permanently changes the look of paper-based documents when you convert them to web format. As mentioned before, users may be able to choose whether they want to see your documents in Helvetica, Times Roman, or dozens of other fonts. Multicolumn documents will typically revert to a single-column format. Page

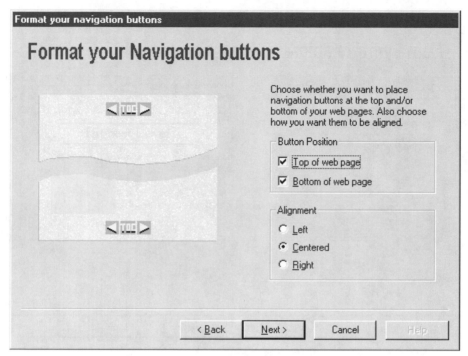

Figure 5.26   HTML Transit wizard—navigation dialog box.

headers and footers designed for 8½ × 11 printing will disappear. Tables will have a different look to them. Navigation buttons may be inserted that didn't clutter the print version of the document but that are essential for online viewing. The net effect is that the carefully designed structure of your print document will be thrown out the window (so to speak) to be replaced by something tangibly different.

As you should know by now, this is a good thing. Documents *should* look and work differently online than they do in print. The end user *should* have some control over the final display. Web presentation is a new medium—and rapidly becoming the *primary* medium for information delivery—so it's best to throw away all those preconceived notions and paper-based paradigms that tell us how a document should or shouldn't look.

Having said all that, there may be many cases where it's actually desirable to serve people documents over the web in the same format as the print version—right down to the last *dingbat,* as it were. There are a number of foreseeable situations where this may apply:

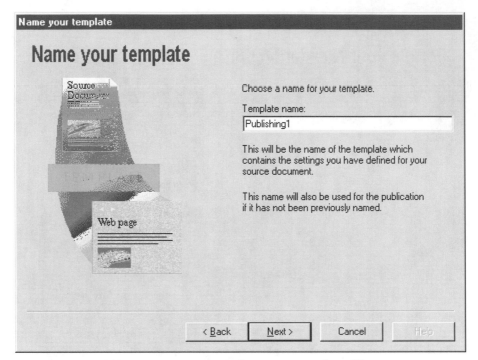

Figure 5.27   HTML Transit wizard—save template file.

Business forms that are still processed as paper.   Every company has plenty of forms that employees, customers, suppliers, and dealers use to conduct business with the organization. Chapter 7 will explain how you can put many of these forms online, getting rid of the paper-shuffling aspects of your job. However, if management still requires the paper forms, if the layout or design of the form is important, or if the form requires a signature, you may want to distribute the form online in a print-ready format so that it can be easily printed and used.

Printable documents.   There may be documents you want to serve over a web that are *meant to be printed* and distributed by hand. These may include white papers, product literature, price sheets, training materials, handbooks, newsletters, and other small documents. Providing printable documents on intranets is a matter of convenience, especially if not everyone in your company has web access. It's easy enough to print any document from the intranet by simply using the Print option in your browser. But when you print a document from the web browser, all you get is the information that's on the current page (i.e., the HTML file that's currently loaded in the browser window). If a web document extends over several pages (i.e., HTML files), the user may have to print each section separately, and for large documents this can be quite tedious. If you have any large documents being distributed exclusively online, you may want to supply a printable version for the convenience of users who prefer to read it in print. On my own World Wide Web site (wordmark.com) I provide a white paper on intranets, so that web users can download it, print it, and hand it out to people who are just learning about the subject.

Notice, in most of the preceding cases, that these are forms or documents that are meant to be printed. This usually isn't a problem, because most documents begin life in print and are then converted to the web. But if the document began life on the web, you may have to reverse the work flow and go backward from a web model to a paper-based model. In other words, the printable version should look like a print document—with headers and footers and nice-looking margins—and not like a web document.

How to Preserve the Original Layout

The main question then becomes: How do you get a document online on the web *without* losing its paper-printable format? There are several ways to handle this.

Use the Original Application

The easiest way is to leave the document in its original format and serve it across intranets that way. Don't even worry about converting it to HTML, just ship the original document files over the network to anyone who wants them. It's not hard to do—just place a link on your web page that references the file directly. For instance:

```
<A HREF="http://server/path/docname.doc">Click here</A>.
```

might be an MS Word file stored on your web server. When the user clicks on such a link, the browser should ask whether the user wants to: (1) open the file, or (2) save the file to disk. The user can then save the file to any desired directory and filename on the local system (see Figure 5.28). Or the user can

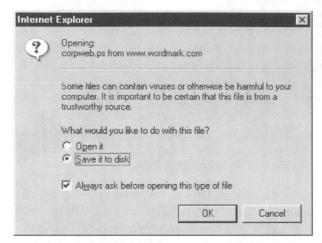

Figure 5.28   Internet Explorer Save/Display option.

automatically open the file in the correct application, assuming the browser has been programmed to work hand in glove with the application.

This assumes, however, that all of your users have the appropriate software to use the file in its original format. For example, if it's an MS Word file, you assume your users have MS Word or MS Word Viewer, which they can use to view or print the file. If it's a PowerPoint file, you assume they have Power-Point or PowerPoint Viewer installed locally.

Users can even configure their browsers to automatically recognize certain document extensions and fire off the appropriate viewing application—thus opening the document automatically when it hits the browser. For instance, it might recognize any file with the extension .ppt as a PowerPoint file, so that when the browser receives a file with that extension, it will automatically start PowerPoint Viewer and display the file. The same might be done with the extension .doc and the MS Word Viewer. In both Netscape and Internet Explorer, there are special options or preference dialogs that let you associate file extensions with the applications used to view them (see Figure 5.29).

Use an Intermediate Application like Adobe Acrobat

The other way to present documents in their original format is to use an *intermediate application* that was designed especially for the purpose. The most commonly used tool for this purpose is the Acrobat product by Adobe Corpo-

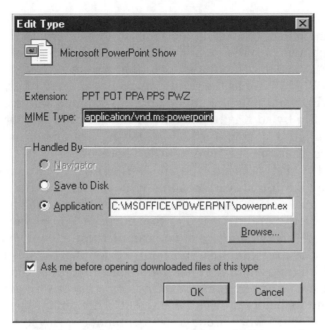

Figure 5.29 Netscape Navigator's helper application settings.

ration. This product allows you to convert the document to an intermediate online format that preserves the original look and feel of the document (more or less) and allows you to view the document online or print it.

Adobe Acrobat uses a proprietary file format called PDF (*Portable Document Format*) that is like a compressed version of PostScript. The difference between PDF and PostScript is more than just file size, however. PDF provides the ability to add hyperlinks to a file, including not only embedded hyperlinks that work in the Acrobat environment, but HTML hyperlinks that access web URLs. Acrobat was originally designed as a product that would allow people to view any kind of word-processing document online. In recent years, the inventors of Acrobat have been working to integrate the product with the web, to the point where a PDF file can now be made to display directly inside a web browser using an appropriate plug-in.

Did you know you can produce a PostScript file from just about any word-processing document by using File/Print to view the standard Print dialog box, choosing a PostScript printer driver, and then selecting the "print to file" option? Well, the Acrobat Exchange product gives any word processor the ability to produce PDF files using the same sort of process.

Acrobat Exchange provides a module called *PDF Writer* that is like an extra printer driver for your computer's operating system. When you go to print, you can select PDF Writer as the print device. But instead of printing, the output goes to a PDF file (such as *mydoc.pdf*). Exchange also lets you edit the resulting PDF file by adding hyperlinks or notes to it. Another Adobe utility called *Distiller* goes a step further by letting you read in and edit raw PostScript files, then output them to PDF. There are other features in Adobe's bag of Acrobat tricks, including the ability to convert scanned documents to PDF and embed a full-text search engine with your online documents.

Once you have a document saved in PDF format, you need a way that users can access it, view it, and print it. For this purpose, Adobe provides free software called the *Acrobat Reader* that you can distribute to all your users. There are also corresponding plug-ins and controls for the Netscape or Microsoft browsers that will cause the Acrobat documents to appear directly inside the browser window. But users must have the correct software already installed on their computers before they can use the PDF document you provide.

Once you've taken a word processing document and saved it to PDF format, you can serve it over the web by attaching it to a hyperlink like the following:

```
<A HREF="http://server/path/docname.pdf">Click here</A>.
```

When the user clicks on the hyperlink, the server automatically retrieves *docname.pdf* (or whatever the PDF file happens to be named) and sends it across the network to the user. What happens next depends on what kind of software

---

Tools for Putting Documents Online

You can use the following World Wide Web locations to get more information about various tools that let you put printed documents online.

Adobe Acrobat Overview   www.adobe.com/Acrobat/Acrobat0 .html

Common Ground   www.hcl.com/cg/

Envoy/Posta   www.twcorp.com/

Net-It-Now   www.net-it-now.com/

the user has and how it has been installed. The document may display directly inside the web browser window, or Acrobat may kick off a second window to be used for displaying the document.

Regardless, the document that the user sees should look almost exactly like the original printed document produced in MS Word, FrameMaker, or any other WP/DTP application. And when the user prints it, the resulting printed copy should look substantially like the original document.

Where Do We Go from Here?

Anyone who's used intranets for a while can tell you that web publishing is great, but it's just the beginning of what you can do with an intranet. The next two chapters will explain other applications, from the simple display of graphics and multimedia files to some of the more advanced database applications.

Chapter Six at a Glance

Multimedia is one of the most eye-catching and rewarding aspects of web publishing. With web technology, you can easily incorporate still images, sound, and moving images into your documents. To help you do it, this chapter explains:

- The most common image formats used in intranets, and how to create them
- How to insert static or dynamic images into web documents, including imagemaps and animation
- How to create image libraries for use by everyone in your company
- How to insert multimedia effects into web pages, including sound, video, animation, synchronized effects, and layering
- How to create push channels for automatic broadcasting of website content
- How to create 3-D models online

Harnessing the New Media

Someday, no doubt, surfing the World Wide Web will be like walking through a giant bazaar. And if you have one of those fully equipped lights-camera-action multimedia computers, even more so.

On any given journey, signs will glare at you, bells and whistles will blare at you. Enticing creatures will beckon from the shadows. Old friends will pop up in online greeting cards, their faces flashing wide grins. An elfin agent or avatar may sprout from the corners of your screen and ask, in plain English (or French, or whatever the local language), exactly what you're looking for today. After a short dialog, the elf may disappear and return seconds later with that elusive item you've been seeking.

A bit dramatized, to be sure, but even today my "giant bazaar" take on the Web is not all that far from reality. There are already "agents" out there to locate things for us—just not many with an elf's crinkly face and squeaky voice. We can already put sound and video online with little or no additional equipment investments—even notebooks now come equipped with built-in speakers and microphones, ready to morph into an instant multimedia presentation platform. And every kid with a CD-ROM drive and a PC has his or her own animated encyclopedia where he or she can listen to frogs croak and geese honk, and watch math problems get solved by themselves.

What's more, we all know a picture is worth a thousand words, and that—when the world is ready and the tools are right—our own online documents will come alive with photos, animation, spoken solutions to knotty problems, or all of the above. We can all look forward to the day when the grand unified theory applies not only to quantum physics, but to data, documents, sound, and video all blended into a nice colorful interactive stew.

Web technology brings all of those things a step closer by making it easy to add images, sounds, and moving pictures to documents. Thanks to HTML, instead of using expensive software, you can now cobble together multimedia presentations with something as simple as a text editor. Of course, if you're the one *creating* the sounds and images, you may need a well-equipped media platform with sound, video, and image-processing capabilities. But these are increasingly available, inexpensive, and common in our daily lives.

Thanks to the flexibility of intranets to serve any kind of file, hypertext can become something more than just hypertext. You can click on a picture of the world to see a country or region. You can see a person's face and click his or her mouth to hear a sound, or press a button inside a document and see a talking head materialize on the screen. That old silent-era web page with the real-time camera shot of someone's empty coffee pot is old hat by now, replaced by pages that come alive with embedded animation and sound. New tools and technologies like RealAudio/RealVideo, NetShow, QuickTime, and Shockwave are making the things you can do with web pages mighty impressive.

In the business world, however, we don't do things just because they're impressive. We do them because they make sense or because they make people more productive. In the typical business network, for instance, many of the technical problems with delivering enhanced media are solved. At potential speeds of 10 to 100 Mbps (or higher), you're no longer limited by the lowest common denominator of 14.4 Kbps, the way you are on the World Wide Web. Online pictures load much faster; even sound and video become more practical. So we know we can serve enhanced media over a network. But the question now becomes—do we want to? Will these new forms of communication really make us more productive and contribute to the bottom line?

In many cases, they already do. Some companies play commercials for their products over the company intranet. The president of Sun Microsystems issues audio reports delivered companywide. If you remember the example from Chapter 3, those reports are one of the main ways rank-and-file employees stay in touch with the thinking of their president. It has truly opened up a new method of communication within the enterprise.

But even advanced intranet sites like those at Sun don't use multimedia extensively over their internal networks. Despite the faster network speeds available on Ethernet (compared with WWW), rich media still takes up so much bandwidth that it can create a serious drag on network performance. Thus, until companies start moving to Fast Ethernet or even faster technologies, any use of video or sound on an internal network will have to be closely scrutinized for its overall value to users. In this environment, a taped message from the president may be fine, but other forms of rich media may have to wait for more powerful infrastructure.

Having said all that, there are many simple ways you can jazz up the information at your intranet site, starting with fancier pictures, built-in pushbuttons, and clickable maps, and progressing all the way up to full-motion streaming video and sound. This chapter is designed to provide you with the extra information you need to incorporate these elements into your web sites if the mood or ability strikes you.

GIFs and JPEGs

The nicest part of web publishing is the ability to incorporate fully illustrated information into your online documents, including color photos, charts, and drawings.

To display correctly inside the web-browser window, the image must be stored and served in an appropriate graphics format that the browser will recognize and display. Currently, the most widely used image format is the *Graphics Interchange Format* (better known as GIF). This a trademarked graphics file format developed by CompuServe for delivering high-quality images in an online networked environment. Since CompuServe was one of the first commercial information delivery services to go online, they needed to create a picture format that was platform independent and highly compact and would take less time to transmit over networks.

Once created, GIF was adopted by the people who invented the earliest web browsers for the same reasons. Notice that the first web browser developers specifically chose the GIF format and programmed their browsers to recognize and display it automatically. Theoretically, web browsers could have been programmed to recognize *any* graphics format, but the only other one they consistently recognize is JPEG (pronounced *jay-peg*).

The JPEG format got its name from the Joint Photographic Experts Group, which is part of the International Standards Organization (ISO). One reason it became a popular standard for web images is because it was supported by Netscape in the early Navigator browsers, which are still the most widely used browsers on the market.

Netscape made a wise selection in adopting JPEG as an alternative graphics format, mainly because it's possible to compress some JPEG files up to 4 times smaller than comparable GIFs, without appreciable losses in quality. And on our already bandwidth-constricted networks, that's a godsend indeed.

When compared to full-color data, the actual compression ratio may be as small as 20 to 1. The reason JPEG can do this is because it lets you actually *get rid of* extra data in the file that isn't essential to the quality of the image. As it turns out, the perception of the human eye is such that large amounts of data in some types of graphics files can be lost without significantly affecting the way it looks to the average viewer (this is why JPEG is called a *lossy* format, because it actually loses part of the data). When compared side by side with the original image, you might notice a little bit of degradation. But for that little bit of degradation you may have reduced the actual file size by 75 percent or more. Figure 6.1 shows the relative file size and image quality if we save the photo as a GIF file versus two different JPEG compressions.

The nice part about JPEG is controling the amount of loss that occurs, squeezing the image to get the optimum trade-off between file size and image quality. If you just want to do a rough thumbnail—say for the table of contents in an image catalog—you can distill the image to its barest essentials and end up with an incredibly small, fast-loading file in the process.

Despite these features, GIF and JPEG both have their respective advantages:

> **GIF is better if image quality is the top priority.** It is also better for sim-
> ple illustrations, like organizational charts and stick diagrams, because
> it is better at compressing large fields of uniform color.

> **JPEG is better than GIF for compressing color or gray-scale images that
> have complex, continuous color variations (such as photos of people
> or natural scenes).** This is simply because GIF is not as good at com-
> pressing such images.

> **JPEG should never be used for sharp-edged images, or images with uni-
> form color fields.** This is because it is not as good as GIF at this type
> of compression and tends to "fuzz" any objects with sharp edges—
> such as embedded text.

Notice how the advantages and disadvantages mentioned above are all somehow related to the image's final file size. In today's computers—even with our massive hard drives and high-speed networks—storage space and bandwidth are always at a premium. The name of the game is getting large files into the most compressed and easily deliverable format available, while preserving acceptable levels of quality. Figure 6.2 shows the resulting file sizes if you take the same image (in this case, a flowchart) and save it as a GIF

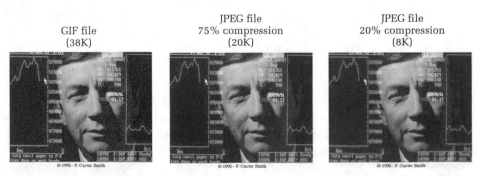

GIF file
(38K)

JPEG file
75% compression
(20K)

JPEG file
20% compression
(8K)

Figure 6.1   Image file size comparison (GIF vs. JPEG).

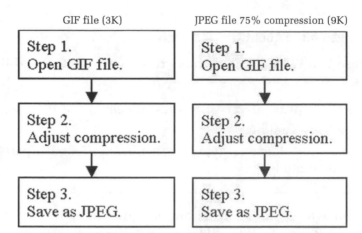

GIF file (3K)   JPEG file 75% compression (9K)

Figure 6.2 GIF and JPEG file size comparisons (same image saved two ways).

versus a 75 percent compressed JPEG. Notice that the GIF results in a smaller file size for the image, because it is line art. If the image were a photo, then JPEG would produce a smaller file size than the GIF would.

So what does this all mean to you, the person who is just trying to get information from point A to point B across a corporate network? If you regularly create images and save them as BMP, PICT, PCX, TIFF, or XWD, maybe it's time to start saving everything you do as GIF or JPEG, if your work is intended for online consumption. Due to the influence of the World Wide Web, most popular image editors and desktop-publishing tools are now almost universally adopting GIF and JPEG as acceptable image formats. So GIF or JPEG will be useful no matter what you do. And they are absolutely essential for use on the web.

Assuming your audience is using any standard, up-to-date web browser that recognizes both formats, it's not necessary to choose one or the other as the standard way of saving images. You can mix and match image formats freely in the same document, so that some images might be presented in GIF format and others in JPEG.

How Will It Look on the Screen?

When creating images for display on a web page, it is crucial to understand the relationship between image size and monitor resolution. Creating an image the wrong size may cause it to look too big on some users' screens, or too small on others.

Where to Read More About GIF and JPEG

Check these WWW locations for more reading on the GIF and JPEG formats.

> home.netscape.com/assist/net_sites/impact_docs/
>
> www.w3.org/Graphics/
>
> www.cis.ohio-state.edu/hypertext/faq/usenet/jpeg-faq/part1/
>   faq-doc-0.html

When you take a picture using an ordinary film-based camera and have it developed at a photo shop, typically the size of the final image is measured in certain standard sizes. The size of the film itself may vary, but is typically 35 mm. When you have a print made in the U.S., you might get what we call a "5×7 print," or an "8×10 glossy."

To produce your printed 5×7 photo, the developer grabs a sheet of photographic paper exactly 5 inches long by 7 inches wide, runs your negative through a projection unit called an *enlarger,* and projects the correct size image onto the photographic paper. To make an 8×10 glossy, a larger sheet is used, and the enlarger scales up the size of the projected image to fit the paper. In effect, the image size can expand from the exact size of the negative all the way up to a sheet the size of a dinner table.

Things are a little different online. When you run an image through a scanner or snap a photo in a digital camera, that image is saved in a "bitmap" format, typically JPEG or some other compressed format. A bitmap is an image made up of tiny dots, and when that image is displayed at "normal size" on a computer screen, each dot in the image will correspond to a pixel on the computer screen. The size of a bitmap image, therefore, can be specified in dots or pixels. So if we say an image is 200×100, that means it is 200 pixels wide and 100 pixels tall.

If you put several computers with different monitor resolutions side-by-side and display the exact same image on each one, you will notice remarkable differences in the size of the image, as it compares to the relative size of the screen. For instance, here are three common monitor resolutions:

VGA	640×480
SVGA	800×600
High-res	1024×768 or higher

In each of these cases, the first number is the width of the monitor display in pixels and the second number is the height. So, for instance, the Super VGA or SVGA monitor resolution is 800 pixels wide by 600 pixels high.

Keep in mind, however, that all three of these resolutions can be displayed on the same screen, within the same area. In other words, it is possible for a suitably equipped monitor to have a VGA, SVGA, or high-res display—depending on the preference of the user. In a PC, you can easily switch the resolution using the Display settings in the Windows Control Panel. As you switch from VGA up to high-res, suddenly you have nearly three times as many pixels crowding into the same area.

Given these differences, what happens when you display a 640×480 image on an VGA monitor versus a high-res monitor? On the VGA monitor, the image takes up the entire screen. On a high-res monitor that is 1024 pixels wide, however, an image that is 640 pixels wide takes up only about half the total width (Figure 6.3).

Understanding this is important for several reasons. If you send a fixed-size image across a web, it will always appear much larger on a low-resolution monitor than it does on a high-resolution monitor. That's why it's important to never make an image wider or taller than the 640×480 dimensions of a VGA screen. In fact, something more like 550×350 may be appropriate, to allow for the incursion of scroll bars, menu bars, and other window components on all sides of the image when viewed on a VGA screen. Otherwise, the end user may have to scroll up, down, or sideways to see your entire image on a VGA monitor.

Also important is creating the image in an appropriate size that will have appropriate visibility at all resolutions. If you develop an image with fine details on a VGA monitor, then attempt to view it on a high-res monitor, the fine details may have shrunk until they are too small to see. On the other hand, a web layout that is perfectly sized to fit a VGA monitor may look like a postage stamp

VGA **SVGA** **High-Res**

Figure 6.3 Same image displayed on different resolution monitors.

when viewed on a high-res screen. Though there are tools, like Netscape's Live-Connect, that allow advanced developers to determine the individual monitor's resolution and respond accordingly, this capability is out of reach of the normal web publisher. It's much easier to simply do pages that take into account all possible viewing resolutions.

This makes the midresolution of 800×600 a good median platform on which to design. On some computers, especially those with high-res monitors, you can easily switch between all three resolutions and visually assess the result. If you have a high-res monitor, a quicker way to simulate this is to display the target page in a web browser and resize the window itself to an approximate 640×480 or 800×600 pixels.

Thinking back to our original paper comparison, remember that graphic images can be resized much more easily than their paper counterparts. Even HTML, as I will show later, gives you the ability to rescale an image on the fly as it hits the browser. The 400×600 image can easily be inserted in a web page with the specification to display it at 200×100, and the browser will do just that, shrinking the image to the desired size for display on the final web page.

However, the problem with rescaling is simply this: When you display an image full size, at its original magnification, the relation of the dots in the image and the pixels on the screen is one-to-one. Every original dot in the image fits into a corresponding pixel on the screen. When you rescale, however, this tidy correspondence is lost.

Suddenly, the image's original dot pattern is condensed to fit into a much smaller area: The image that was 400×600 (240,000 dots) must now fit into an area 200×100 (20,000 dots). The software must suddenly *interpolate:* blending 240,000 dots into this 20,000-dot straightjacket. Inevitably quality is lost. And the poor result is most visible in images where sharp edges don't blend well, such as illustrations containing text.

The lesson here is to create images that are the same size as the screen on which they will eventually appear. For this, you need graphics software that literally measures image size in dots and gives you a chance to compose the art at full magnification. Testing will determine whether the final result fits well into the finished web page under various resolutions.

A final note on monitor compatibility has to do with color. Though 16- and 24-bit color is available on many monitors sold today, there is still quite a legacy of 8-bit, 256-color displays. The more advanced 16- and 24-bit displays do a great job with color, especially photos, but the perceived quality on these high-end monitors degrades significantly once you display the same art in 256 colors. For this reason, especially if you normally develop on a 16- or 24-bit color display, it's a good idea to check how things look in 256 colors before publishing the image. Most computers allow you to switch to 256 colors through the control panel, for a quick check.

Why Web Pages Are Like Putty

Another important point to understand about web displays is how web text interacts with the image and the screen size. Here are a few important exercises:

Open any web page that contains both text and images.   Keep in mind that some text may have been embedded in images by the designer. You can tell the difference between image-based text and web-page text by dragging the cursor across the screen (hold down the mouse button while you drag). Text embedded in the web-page using HTML will be highlighted or "shaded" by the cursor. Text embedded in images will not. Typically, web page text flows down the page in single or multiple columns. Multiple columns are usually created by embedding tables or frames into the web page.

Now resize the web-browser window horizontally by dragging the sides of the window inward.   Notice that any web page text column(s) within the window changes size and shape by "rewrapping" itself within the new dimensions. Image size and font size doesn't change—just the column width. In effect, the web-page text resembles putty that stretches or shrinks to fill the screen horizontally, regardless of the window size. The images, however, are like hard glass—they don't flex.

If the page has a graphic background, notice that it stays the same. The background is typically a static image. In fact, the background graphic may be a tiny sliver of an image that is repeated multiple times or "tiled" across the background area.

Use the font controls in the web browser to change the size of the font. On some browsers, this is controlled by the A button on the toolbar. On others, you will have to use the Preferences or Options menu selections. Notice that the font can be made small, large, or medium.

Scroll up or down the page.   Notice how the text and images move with the scrolling.

What's important about this exercise is understanding the fluid stew of text in which most images float. On most web pages, the image always occupies the same relative physical space and position within the text. The image location is keyed to a spot in the text, so as the text moves through the browser window (i.e., when you are scrolling down the page), the image moves with it.

Having said all of this, let me immediately contradict myself by citing several exceptions. Images may be fixed on the page—and thus not flow with the text—if they are embedded in separate frames, or if they are part of the "background" image. You see this a lot on the Microsoft web site (www.microsoft .com/). In the near future, people who surf the web may also encounter pages created with dynamic HTML that will make it possible to dynamically change the position or size of images or tables in a web page. Also, push technologies integrated into Windows 98 will allow you to have dynamic web content displayed in the overall screen background "behind" the web-browser window.

Now that you understand how images flow (or stay put) inside web pages, let's move on and understand exactly how you create them.

How to Create GIF or JPEG Images

Though GIF and JPEG were virtually unknown a few years ago, they are now carried as a standard export format in popular graphics programs such as PhotoShop and PaintShop Pro. That means you can use any of these tools to create your image and then simply save the image as a GIF or JPEG file. Once the file is saved, you can link it into your documents using the HTML codes explained in the next section, or by using the Insert/Image feature common in many WYSIWYG web editors.

What happens if you have illustrations already embedded in your paper/ electronic documents? For instance, many word processors and desktop-publishing programs—like FrameMaker, Interleaf, and MS Word—have their own suite of drawing tools that let you create graphics right on the page. Typically there hasn't been an easy way to export these kinds of graphics to separate files unless you have the right tools. A web document–conversion tool like WebMaker or HTML Transit will automatically extract the graphic illustrations from the DOC file and save them as separate GIF or JPEG files. Likewise, when you are using a web-friendly word processor such as Word 97 or Word 95 with Internet Assistant 2.0, you can save a file as HTML and all the internal images are automatically saved as separate GIF or JPEG files.

What happens if your illustrations are already saved as separate files, but they're in the wrong format? If you're working on the UNIX command line, the PBM utilities will do nicely to convert from one format to the other. A tool like

Image Magick may work nicely, too. If you're on a PC, look at a tool like HiJaak. Graphics manipulation tools like Photo Shop and LView Pro are handy too, because they let you see the image while it is being converted, so you can use different interactive filtering or size-adjustment techniques and instantly see the result. The most versatile graphics programs now let you open all kinds of graphic images and save them as GIFs or JPEGs. Some tools, like PhotoImpact, even have an optimizer that will take all the extra air out of your image files and make sure they are as small as possible for quick network loading (Figure 6.4).

No matter which format you use, it's important to always make graphics as small as possible—as long as they are easily visible in all the typical monitor resolutions. As mentioned earlier, no image should be larger than about 550×350 pixels, so that it will fit easily inside the browser window or even on the lowest-resolution VGA screens. In fact, most graphics, unless they contain text, are still quite readable even at thumbnail size. Remember: The smaller the image, the smaller the file size, the faster it loads, and the less of a drag it will be on network performance.

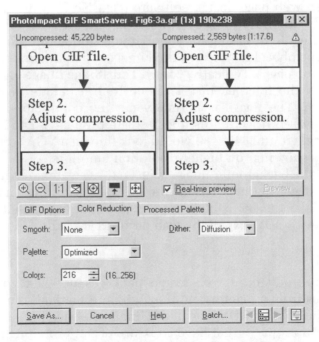

Figure 6.4   PhotoImpact GIF optimizer.

What about Those Backgrounds?

So, OK, what *about* those pesky background colors and images? You've heard me speak about them before. That neat textured stuff in the background that looks a little like a pizza topping. Or that mystical, ethereal mantralike pattern you see on some web pages. Or that dark black, funereal background that some people seem to like so much (especially with that cool, hot pink type overlaid on it.)

On a web page, you can have two types of backgrounds: a solid color or a tiled image. A solid color is just that: a single color that runs uniformly behind everything on the page. This can range from black, to white, to every color of the rainbow in between. In HTML-speak, the color is specified directly inside the <BODY> tag, like so:

```
<BODY BGCOLOR="#RRGGBB">
```

That RRGGBB is not me acting angry; it indicates that the exact color must be specified using a RGB value (which stands for red-green-blue), which is a hexadecimal number such as "#C9F3DD." This sounds complex, but if you own some nice web page design software (e.g., NetObjects Fusion or Front-Page), typically all you do is select the color from a chart, and the program puts in the correct RGB setting for you. Enough said about that.

The other type of background is a tiled image: The pattern or texture you see behind some web pages. Typically, you will create the image on your own, pull one down from the Internet, or select one from a palette in your web page design software. The image is normally not the complete size of the web-browser window—if it were, this might create problems. For instance, a full-size graphic background 640×480 would look fine on a VGA screen, but would have its "edges showing" on higher-resolution monitors.

More likely, the background image is just a tiny swatch of pattern or texture that is repeated many times within the browser window. This repetition is called *tiling.* Like the BGCOLOR specification above, a tiled image is also specified in the <BODY> tag of the web page's HTML file. For instance:

```
<BODY BACKGROUND="pattern5.gif">
```

Again, the more advanced web-design packages now let you select background textures from a palette, and they will automatically insert the correct specification into the <BODY> tag of the final web-page file.

What about those pages that have a texture or pattern along the edge of the screen, and a solid color in the middle? You may have seen some pages that actually seem to have a spiral binding along one edge, with horizontal rules across the page, like a grade schooler's composition book. These types of backgrounds are created using a tiled image. In this case, however, the image is just a horizontal or vertical sliver that has been cut the width or height of the largest possible monitor resolution and that has a texture or pattern along the left edge and a color or other pattern in the middle (Figure 6.5).

This sliver is repeated all the way down the page so that it forms a continuous image with a texture on one side and a color on the other. The web-page text, graphics, and other content is overlaid on this continuous image in such a way that it seems to be framed by it. For instance, the page in Figure 6.6 is actually a large table with two columns and no borders. The left column contains an image (cartoon face) and a menu. The right column contains the main body of the text. The same effect could also be created using borderless frames (see Chapter 5, Getting Framed).

The pages you've seen with spiral binding work exactly like this, except that the slivered image is tall enough to contain a single loop of the binding. The loop is drawn in such a way that it will repeat seamlessly when tiled. Likewise, any background texture or pattern must be carefully constructed so that you don't see the seams at the tiled edges.

By the way, this sliver-tiling effect works as well for vertically oriented slivers as it does for the horizontal ones. Thus, the textured border could as easily run across the top of the page as along the left side. Why not along the right or the bottom? Because tiling starts at the top and left; also, the top and left sides are the only sides of the web page that are guaranteed to show in *any* display. Also, any background image with features that align to the right side of the screen on an 800×600 monitor will be completely off the screen on a VGA monitor or in the middle of the screen on a high-res.

Why Are There So Many Files?

One thing you often hear people complain about is the rapid proliferation of files at a web site. The underlying web page is saved as a file. The background image is saved as a separate file. Each of the individual graphic images on the

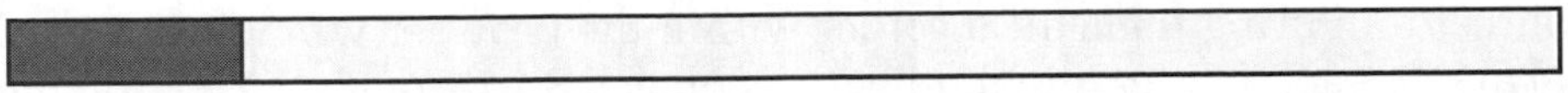

Figure 6.5   A sliver of a background image.

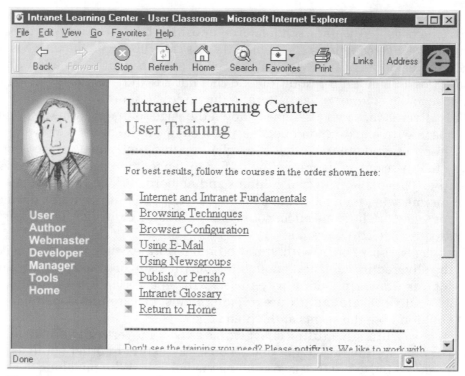

Figure 6.6   A page with same sliver tiled in the background.

page are saved as separate files. If a page has sound and video, these are stored in separate files, too.

On a real cool and graphically rich web site, files begin to multiply like rabbits. In fact, file proliferation is one of the biggest problems adding to the site-management hassles of most webmasters (as discussed in the previous chapter). With other types of publishing formats—like Microsoft Word, FrameMaker, and so forth—all the text and all the images for a given document can be stored in a single file. Why does HTML require you to store them separately and then reference them individually, so that you end up with all these files?

To me, this is a cup-half-empty, cup-half-full question. As you may have guessed by now, I like to think of this technology as a cup half full. Part of the power of web technology is its ability to marshal a wide array of multimedia resources and bring them all together within the browser window, a little like what an abstract painter might do with a collage. So, through the central mechanism of an HTML file, you can pull in and position graphics, sound, video, animation, form fields, live data, or practically any content you wish. In fact, if you know HTML, and assuming you already have created the sound, video, and graphics file to be used in your web display, you can orchestrate a complete multimedia presentation using little more than a plain text editor to specify and position the resources.

When you click a hyperlink on a web-based menu, that hyperlink points to the web page itself—the HTML file (or some of the other web-page file formats you will learn about later). This file in turn specifies all the other resources that must be brought into the web browser to create the web display. So the hyperlink pulls in the HTML file, and the HTML file automatically pulls in all the other elements it needs to create the display. Imagine how hard it would be to create a hyperlink that specified the position and source of all the elements on a page. Besides being impossible, it would make the hyperlink as big as the HTML file itself.

So if you understand why images are stored as separate files, you also understand that creating and inserting graphics into web pages is simply a matter of creating the images and storing them in the correct GIF or JPEG format, and referencing the images using the correct markup tags in the HTML file. Most web-authoring tools now let you do that automatically with a few mouse clicks or even using a quick-and-easy, drag-and-drop procedure.

If all those files really bother you, you may want to take a database approach to web-site management. An object-oriented database or document management software can store all those text and graphic objects in a single file, then merge them into a finished web page on the fly at the moment the user requests the web page (see Chapter 7 for details). For the database-challenged, you may want to use a comprehensive web site–authoring solution such as FrontPage or NetObjects Fusion.

How to Create Interlaced GIFs

When working with GIF images, you can apply some popular tricks for image manipulation that are widely used on the World Wide Web. The main technique for improving the performance of your web page is using *interlaced GIFs.*

Normally, when a picture displays in the web browser, it unfolds from top to bottom, like a window shade coming down. With an interlaced GIF, however, the picture unloads in layers so that it seems to fade in. At first you see a fuzzy rendition of the picture as the first layer loads, then the resolution progressively sharpens as the additional layers kick in (Figure 6.7). Normally, an effect like this would not be a mere curiosity. But, due to enhancements in

---

Where to Find Graphics Manipulation Tools

You can find some of the tools mentioned in this section at the following locations on the Internet. These range from handy little shareware utilities like Lview, all the way up to professional graphics-manipulation packages like PhotoShop.

PhotoShop   www.adobe.com/

PhotoImpact   www.ulead.com/

Shareware.com   www.shareware.com/

PC Magazine   www.zdnet.com/pcmag/iu/author/image/_image.htm

Download.com   www.download.com

---

browser technology, the net effect is to make things much easier and faster for the user.

It's easy to understand why. Instead of waiting for the entire image to download, you can often get a good idea of what's there during the first pass of the GIF. Sometimes, that first pass reveals you are not even on the right page, or it reveals an imbedded button that you can immediately click to go somewhere else without waiting for the GIF to finish downloading.

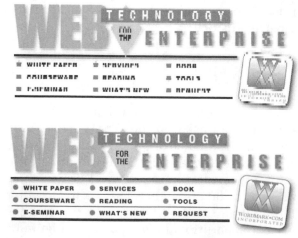

Figure 6.7   Interlaced GIF (before and after).

Despite the obvious convenience factor, interlaced GIFs may not be appropriate for every use. For instance, I never use an interlaced GIF for the human face, because the effect is decidedly weird. It's always distracting, because I sit there waiting for the entire picture to finish loading so that I can tell whether the person is really *that ugly* or not. Human faces aside, interlaced GIF is a great format for large images, especially if the file size is more than 10 KB.

Preparing an interlaced GIF requires the right tools. Some drawing programs and conversion tools give you a choice between GIF 87 and GIF 89 when you are saving (or exporting) the file. GIF 89 is the interlaced format. Others provide a clearly marked option for interlaced GIF. Of course, that's the one to select. If your only export or saving option is GIF, then it's probably just a straight unlaced GIF. In that case, you'll need a new set of tools to produce the desired effect (see the sidebar "GIF Tools on the WWW").

How to Create Transparent GIFs

Normally, when you create a picture and insert it into a web document, it occupies a rectangular space even if the image shape is irregular. For example, if you draw a picture of a target, then display it as a GIF in a web document, you may see the target inside a white box (assuming the HTML document's background color isn't white, too). The white box isn't an element you created when you were drawing the target. It's just the internal background color of the GIF itself.

A nice feature of the GIF format is your ability to make the background color transparent, so that you see right through the GIF background to the background color of the web document. This means that the "apparent" shape of the GIF can be as irregular as the image itself, even if the GIF still takes up more area than it did before. (See Figure 6.8.)

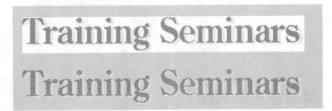

Figure 6.8   Transparent versus nontransparent GIF.

As you can tell, this is not an option that increases user convenience, but it does result in a nicer-looking picture because the image seems to float against the document background. For this reason, you may not want to use transparency widely, but it is nice to use for key images such as logos or opening page graphics.

Again, the key to preparing a transparent GIF image is having the right tools. Some drawing programs now come with the ability to create transparent images—or "mask" background colors (as some software programs put it). Advanced web-authoring tools like FrontPage have a built-in feature that can create transparency in a GIF image. There are even shareware programs like *giftrans* that do nothing but convert regular GIFs to transparent ones.

How to Create Animated GIFs

At this point, you must be getting the idea that the GIF format is quite flexible, and of course it is. One of the most popular ways of handling GIF images is to use them for simple animations. You've seen these: the flags waving on the White House home page, the running tiger on the Exxon site, the occasional web page pushbuttons that shimmer and horizontal rules that glimmer.

Any animation is actually a series of multiple images superimposed on each other. The images play back in such a way that they seem to be moving, when in fact a group of images are simply flipping away before your very eyes, the way a deck of cards might be flipped. Animated GIFs take advantage of the same paging feature that interlaced GIFs do. In this case, instead of seeing layers of the same image, you are seeing multiple images unfold.

Again, the secret to creating animated GIFs is all in having the correct software. A program like PhotoImpact GIF animator (Figure 6.9) lets you pull in a series of images, sequence them, and add special effects to them. This assumes that you have already created each of the individual images involved in the animation. GIF Animator can add its own rudimentary animation to image components (such as "rolling in" or "fading in"), but most of the real action is usually created by the sequencing of your images. The GIF Animator also lets you time the sequence of images, so that each image in the sequence can linger on the screen for an exact amount of time.

How Images Fit into Web Pages

Once you have created GIF or JPEG images, inserting them into your web documents is a fairly simple process. If you are using software that does it auto-

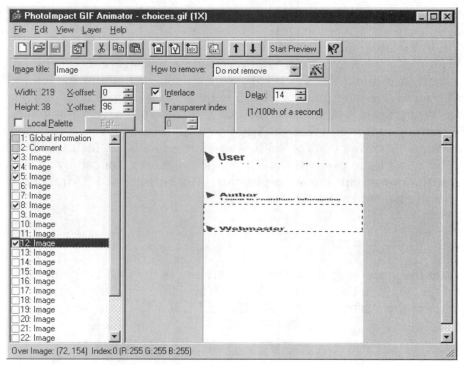

Figure 6.9   The PhotoImpact GIF Animator.

GIF Tools on the WWW

If you're looking for GIF tools to make your image backgrounds interlaced or transparent, look no further than the WWW. Here are some sites where you can find many:

WinGIF (PC)   www.jumbo.com/graph/win/graphics

Giftrans   (Unix)   ftp://sunsite.unc.edu/pub/packages/infosystems/ WWW/tools/giftrans

GIF Converter and Transparency 1.0 (Mac)   ftp://ftp.uwtc .washington.edu/pub/Mac/Graphics

matically for you, like any of the WYSIWYG web editors mentioned in Chapter 5, you can simply use the Insert/Image, Insert/Picture, or Image/Properties option in the program (Figure 6.10).

If you really want to optimize the way your images work, however, it helps to know a little about the way HTML works. Some web-authoring tools allow you to set image-manipulation features in the Insert/Images dialog box (or Image/Properties). Again, when inserting images into a web document, it's important to understand that you can't copy an image into an HTML file and store it there the way you can with most word processors. Instead, the image must be saved as an external file (GIF or JPEG) and referenced by an IMG tag within the document. For example, this little snippet of HTML code references a file named *computer.gif:*

```
Here's a photo of my computer:
<IMG SRC="computer.gif" ALT="My Computer">
```

When the browser sees the IMG tag, it retrieves the SRC image file (such as *computer.gif*) from the server and inserts it into the displayed document at the location of the IMG tag. Notice that the ALT extension tells the browser what

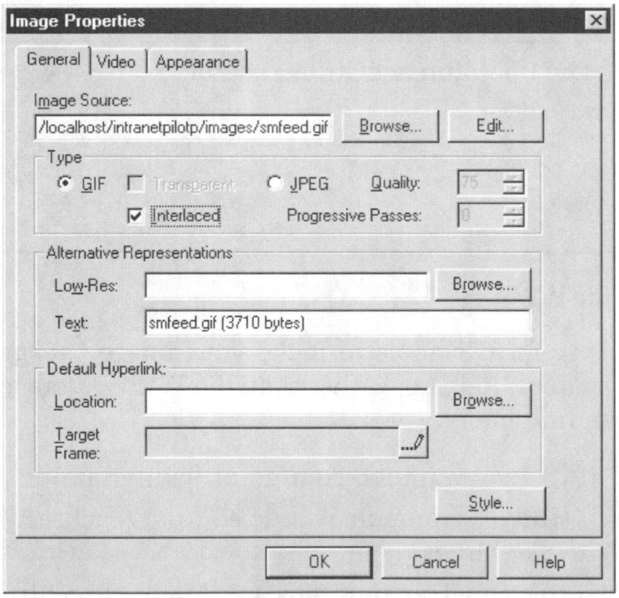

Figure 6.10 Typical image insertion dialog (FrontPage).

to display in case—for some reason—the browser can't find the image or fails to load it properly. Figure 6.11 shows the result of a broken image with ALT text imbedded in it. In some browsers, ALT text will also display in a pop-up message when you move the pointer over the image.

Typically, when you insert an image into a web page, you can also specify its exact height and width. Thus, for instance, an image that is 300×200 could be rescaled automatically to 150×100. This doesn't mean that the source file changes. It just means that the web browser—at the time it loads the image—recalculates the image size, interpolates all the pixels, and displays the reconstituted image within the specified area. Height and width specifications can normally be set in the Insert/Image dialog box in any web-authoring program. In HTML, it looks like this:

```
<IMG SRC="big.gif" WIDTH=150 HEIGHT=100>
```

As mentioned earlier, rescaling the image may cause some degradation, especially for images containing sharp edges, such as embedded text. Photos are not degraded as much as diagrammatic images.

Interestingly, the HEIGHT and WIDTH extensions also help speed up the velocity at which web pages load into the browser. This is because they immediately clue the browser how large the final image will be, so that the browser can reserve the space for the image as the web page loads. Otherwise, the web browser must poll the server an extra time to get the information, then rebuild the page to fit around the correctly sized image frame(s).

Wrapping the Text

Normally, when an image is placed in the text it appears in the exact spot where you inserted it (or, in HTML lingo, where the <IMG> tag occurs in the text). In

Figure 6.11 ALT text displayed before image appears.

early versions of HTML, text did not wrap around the image. Instead, the image was treated as though it were a single object inserted into the flow of text. If the image was in the middle of the paragraph, it would be base-, middle-, or top-aligned with the adjoining text. In HTML, that might have looked like this:

```
Text before the image. <IMG SRC="big.gif" ALIGN=BOTTOM> Text after the
image.
```

To separate the image from the text, you would have placed hard carriage returns (paragraph tags) ahead and behind it. For instance:

```
Text before the image.
<P>
<IMG SRC="big.gif">
<P>
Text after the image.
```

Current versions of HTML now support the idea of wrapping text around graphics. In HTML, the ALIGN=LEFT and ALIGN=RIGHT extensions allow you to float the image at the left or right margin in such a way that text wraps around it. In most web-authoring programs, you can control left or right alignment (or any of the other alignment styles mentioned above) when you go to insert an image using the Insert/Images option.

Serving Other Kinds of Image Files

Earlier, I made the point that GIF and JPEG images are the only kinds of images you can display in a web browser. This is technically correct if we are talking about *inside the browser window.* Actually, you can serve any kind of image (or any other kind of file) over the web if you really want to. The only difference from other image types is that they cannot display inside the browser window.

For example, suppose you have a Windows bitmap file (.BMP) or a TIFF file (.TIFF) that you want to serve over the web without converting it to GIF. You would not use the IMG tag for this purpose, because the IMG tag would try to insert the illustration directly into the web document (and cause an image load error). Instead, you would put a hyperlink into your document that references the image file. For instance, if the image filename is *diagram3.tiff,* the HTML code might say:

```
Click here to see the <A HREF="diagram3.tiff">flow diagram</A>.
```

When the user clicks the words *flow diagram,* the web browser retrieves the TIFF file and prompts to determine whether the user wants to open the file or save it to disk. To open it, the user must have the correct application (in this case, a program capable of displaying TIFF files) already installed and associated with the TIFF file extension. So when the browser receives the file, hopefully it will recognize the file extension, open the helper application, and display the image.

Naturally, this is an inconvenient way to serve random files, unless you know that all the browsers on your network have the appropriate software to read the file format in question. If the application is not configured to work with the browser, users may have to save the image to disk, then open up the application to read it. (There is also the additional problem that formats like TIFF are not the optimum way to transmit graphics online in the first place.)

The advantage of a corporate intranet is that we can preconfigure browsers for special files types, if doing so saves time and money, since (theoretically) we have more control over the end-user configuration. Something like this would be a lot less practical on the World Wide Web. On the other hand, the GIF and JPEG image types are used for a good reason: They provide high-quality images in a small package for easy transport across bandwidth-constricted networks.

The Pushbutton Effect and Clickable Images

Occasionally, when scrolling through a web document, you may encounter a pushbutton sitting right there on the page—even right in the middle of a sentence. When you click the pushbutton, it brings up something completely different. This kind of effect is just a variation of the old text-based hyperlink. Remember that in HTML, a text-based hyperlink looks something like this:

```
<A HREF="newfile.html">Click here</A> to see something completely different.
```

but a clickable button might look like this:

```
<A HREF="newfile.html"><IMG SRC="button2.gif" ALT="Something Completely
Different"></A>
```

Notice that this is simply a graphic image (<IMG>) with a hyperlink wrapped around it (<A HREF></A>). On the web page, this would show up as a button (*button2.gif*) that when clicked brings up the file *newfile.html*. If the button fails to appear for any reason, you see the ALT text "something completely different."

Most web-authoring tools allow you to insert any type of graphic image and then make that image clickable. Instead of a button, you could have a clickable picture of a product, any type of icon—even a mug shot of your boss. You would use the Insert/Image or Insert/Picture option in your web-authoring program, then select the image again and use Insert/Hyperlink to create the hyperlink effect on top of the button. In some web-authoring programs, the hyperlink can be specified in the Insert/Image dialog box.

Another type of image hyperlink is called the *imagemap,* which is any image that has multiple hyperlinks imbedded in it. For instance, you might have a floor plan for your office that lets you click on any room and see who works there. Or you might have a picture of a product that allows you to click on different parts and see the specifications for those parts. Or a toolbar represented by a solid bank of buttons, with each button wired to produce a different effect.

The idea behind a clickable imagemap is defining each part of the graphic image as a separate *hot zone* so that when the user clicks on it, the browser retrieves something from the web server. The hot zone areas—and what they retrieve—are defined directly inside the web page using an HTML sequence. For instance, this map defines hot zones on the surface of a 350×60 image:

```
<MAP NAME="toolbar_map">
<AREA SHAPE="rect" COORDS="1,1,120,60" HREF="file1.html">
<AREA SHAPE="rect" COORDS="121,1,220,60" HREF="file2.html">
<AREA SHAPE="rect" COORDS="221,1,310,60" HREF="file3.html">
<AREA SHAPE="rect" COORDS="311,1,350,60" NOHREF>
</MAP>
```

The four <AREA> tags define three clickable areas and one "dead" area. To understand how this works, think of the image as rows and columns of pixels—in this case 350 columns and 60 rows. The first hot zone begins with the pixel in the first column, first row (1,1) and ends in the 120th column, 60th row (120,60). When the user clicks inside this zone, it brings up the file named *file1.html.* The second and third zone work the same way. The last zone, defined as a dead area, doesn't reference any web page (NOHREF).

Once such a table is defined, all that remains is to insert the actual image and refer back to the table for clickable zones. The following HTML tag inserts the image *toolbar.gif* into a web page and makes the image clickable using the specifications in the <MAP> table above.

```
<IMG USEMAP="#toolbar_map" SRC="toolbar.gif" WIDTH=350 HEIGHT=60
ALT="Toolbar">
```

The main problem with creating imagemaps, of course, is identifying the correct pixel coordinates for each hot zone on an image. You can do this manually—many graphics tools display the coordinates dynamically when you move the mouse over the image, or when you click on a point. It's much easier, however, if you use imagemap editing tools.

Some web-authoring programs, such as FrontPage, provide a built-in imagemap editor that works like a drawing tool (Figure 6.12). You can insert an image in the current web page, then "draw" the hot zones directly onto the surface of the image. After drawing each hot zone, the imagemap editor asks you to specify the URL to be associated with the hot zone. The hot zone rectangles disappear, of course, once the file is saved and displayed on the web. If your web-authoring program does not have a built-in imagemap editor, there are special utilities you can use for this purpose.

The Power of Referenced Images and Image Libraries

One powerful feature of HTML is the ability to pull your images from any source on an intranet. Thus, for example, if the image is stored on a different server somewhere within your organization (or on the World Wide Web), you can reference it directly from any HTML document without having to copy it to your own local disk. In HTML, this means an <IMG> tag where the source image is specified, using a full URL, such as:

```
<IMG SRC="http://server_name/file.gif">
```

Most web-authoring programs should now let you specify a complete URL as the image source.

The URL retrieves the image from the server and file specified. The power of referenced images can be seen if your company keeps a centralized image library. Thus, someone in your company might keep a single set of common images like logos, building photos, or executive photos that everyone can access across the web by referencing the image in their documents.

But the same power applies whether the images are centralized or widely dispersed. For instance, human resources might store on its web server a copy of the most current organization chart for your department. Instead of copying the organization chart to your local disk drive, you can just insert an IMG tag into your local document that retrieves the organization chart directly from the human resources server.

Figure 6.12   FrontPage's built-in imagemap editor.

Where to Find Imagemap Editors

Many author and serving products now come with their own imagemap editors. However, if your software doesn't include these handy tools, you can still find easy-to-use imagemap editors on the Web at the following locations:

MapEdit   www.boutell.com/mapedit/

LiveImage   www.mediatec.com/

PC Magazine Image Tools   www.zdnet.com/pcmag/iu/author/image/_image.htm

Virtual Library   www.stars.com/Vlib/Providers/Imagemaps.html

---

Think about that for a while. If you copied the organization chart to your local disk drive, it would go out of date as soon as Human Resources revises the chart (for example, as soon as your boss is fired). But if you reference it instead through a web URL, then your document *always has the latest version of the organization chart,* automatically delivered direct from the source to your document.

In other words, if users view your document on the web, they will actually see the very latest organization chart as it is currently stored on the computer in human resources, even though the document using it is one you created. And if human resources updates the chart 5 minutes from now and someone opens that document again, *it will automatically contain the new chart,* even though the document itself did not change.

The same can be done for engineering drawings, product photos, schematic diagrams, or any kind of image that is widely used or referenced by people in your company. In fact, you could even use the web as an excellent way to catalogue all these illustrations: Let everyone keep his or her own web-based repository of images for public use, and then have a central web menu where people can go to access all the different image libraries. Thus, the care and maintenance of images can be distributed to all the departments in your company, but the *access to the images* can be centralized through hyperlinking.

Arranging things this way could produce all kinds of unseen benefits. Instead of having 5,000 copies of the official logo floating around on all your company's hard drives and file servers, you could have just one copy on the web server in corporate communications. Instead of doing the old file-chase routine every time you need that image, you can check the image library, find the correct URL, and insert it in your document. You've not only saved the company a great deal of disk space, but you've saved everyone a great deal of time as well.

So, if you're creating an information center for your local department or work group, why not throw away all those outdated organization charts, logos, product photos, and drawings? Get other departments to bring their images online on the web, then start using fresh stuff, direct from the source.

A Sound (and Video) Proposition

A picture is worth a thousand words—that's how the old saying goes. But if a picture is worth a thousand words, then full-motion video with sound must be worth about a million. Genuine multimedia is something we all yearn for in our communications. It's just that, up to now, it's been so hard or expensive to produce that it hasn't been worth the trouble.

Fortunately, web browsers already have incredible sound and video features built right into them, with the ability to play back both video and audio in multiple formats, directly inside the browser window (or through the use of helper applications, plug-ins, or controls). But it's not the browser technology that's holding us back, it's the speed of our networks. Even on an intranet, where the bandwidth is measured in megabits per second, allowing employees frequent access to large sound or video files can bring the network to its knees.

Still, multimedia is becoming an increasingly popular way to convey information within the corporation, especially for training purposes, where a picture really is worth a thousand words. And, chances are, if you aren't doing multimedia today, you *will* be doing it before long.

Assuming the sound and video files are already available, you can insert these types of multimedia into web pages quite easily. One way to do this is to create a hyperlink that points to the file. When the user clicks the hyperlink, it will retrieve the file. For example, the following snippet of HTML code references a file called *toot.wav,* and serves it to the browser when the user clicks the words "hear the horn":

```
Click here to <A HREF="toot.wav">hear the horn.</A>
```

Likewise, the following line of HTML might serve up a video file in MPEG format called *greeting.mpg:*

```
Click here to see a <A HREF="greeting.mpg">greeting from our president</A>
```

Clicking either type of hyperlink retrieves the file from the web server and sends it to the browser. When that happens, assuming the user has the appropriate browser configuration, the file should play back automatically in a separate window (such as the one shown in Figure 6.13), with its own controls for stopping and starting the multimedia clip.

Another way to handle sound and video clips is to embed them directly into the surface of the web page (as shown in Figure 6.14) using the <EMBED> tag. For instance:

```
The following film clip contains a short history of the company:
<EMBED SRC="history.mpg">
```

This snippet of code embeds the video in the web page and lets the user control the playback. However, the video could be set to start itself automatically and/or loop repeatedly by including extra attributes in the <EMBED> tag, such as:

```
<EMBED SRC="history.mpg" AUTOSTART=TRUE LOOP=TRUE>
```

How about a background theme song for a web page that starts automatically on loading and plays repeatedly? This can be done using the HIDDEN attribute to hide the multimedia controls:

```
<EMBED SRC="themesong.midi" HIDDEN=TRUE AUTOSTART=TRUE LOOP=TRUE>
```

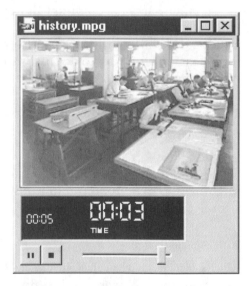

Figure 6.13 Multimedia playback device.

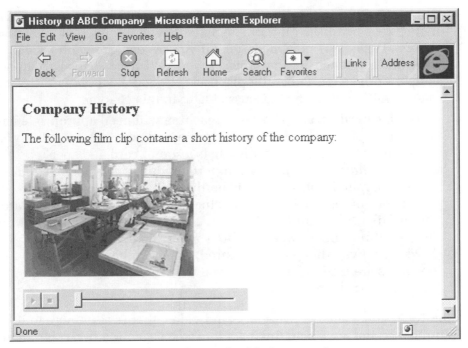

Figure 6.14   Multimedia clip embedded in a web page.

It truly can be that simple. Of course, advanced web-authoring tools will let you embed multimedia in web pages without having to code the sort of HTML just shown. And there are more sophisticated controls available with <EMBED>, such as the ability to set the height, width, and alignment of the video frame—or with sound, to set the start time, end time, volume level, and types of controls that display. JavaScript also gives you methods to build in custom-made controls to play, stop, rewind, or seek both video and audio. In addition, you may want to take a look at the Dynamic HTML features covered later in this chapter (see "Getting Dynamic with HTML").

Overall, you would be surprised how easy it is to get most sound and/or video formats to play in the browser. Having said that, it is not guaranteed that the sound or video that you prepare will play back on just any computer on your network. There are two components that need to be available to make it work:

Compatible software.   The first requirement for playing back a multimedia file is a web browser that supports the audio/video format being used. For instance, Netscape has its LiveVideo component, which plays back AVI files on the Windows platform, and LiveAudio plays WAV, AIFF, AU, or MIDI. Microsoft's ActiveMovie component plays back MPEG, WAV, AVI, and QuickTime. If you are using an audio/video format not supported by the browser, you will need a special client or helper application to handle playback. A good example is the Shockwave multimedia format discussed later in this chapter.

Compatible hardware.   The user's machine will need appropriate hardware to support the playback of audio and video. Interestingly, the most likely hardware to be missing is a sound card and speakers. Your computer already has the most important video component: a monitor. Some computers have built-in hardware-based video decoders, but this is not necessary if you are using an advanced multimedia architecture like Microsoft's ActiveMovie. ActiveMovie can decode MPEG video entirely in software, without requiring special video-decoding hardware. Even though not required, however, hardware-based video decoders are nice to have, because they will always work much faster than software-based ones.

Naturally, if you want to serve sound and video, there's a lot more to it than just putting it on the server and linking it into web pages. Mainly, you will have to create the content, or obtain it from somewhere. It's beyond the scope of this book to delve into the details of audio and video production—if you want to do it and be good at it, there are plenty of books on the subject. Suffice it to say that you can produce sound and video files rather easily if your system is equipped with a sound card, a video card, or similar multimedia hardware.

Many systems being sold today already have sound- and video-recording features built-in. For others, these features may be added easily. Assuming you're not working with older equipment, you should be able to plug microphones, tape recorders, video cameras, or VCRs directly into whatever sound or video cards your computer may have installed. With recording devices plugged in, you can transfer sounds or images directly to the hard drive or to other media. In most cases, the multimedia hardware also comes with software and instructions on how to capture the sound and video from external devices and save it in various digital formats on disk. If the formats used are not those compatible with the web browsers on your network, then you may require special software to convert it.

However, once you are able to capture the sound, save it to disk, and store it in the appropriate format, you can easily serve it over the web. Just make sure the file has been stored in the appropriate server directory using the appropriate file extension (such as .au, .aiff, or .aif). Then be sure to add the multimedia file to the appropriate web page using hyperlinks or embedding.

Streaming the Media

Most common multimedia formats—like MPEG, AU, AIFF, and even Quick-Time—were developed before the World Wide Web became so explosively popular. Just a few years ago, the idea of serving multimedia over a network was not even a consideration. For this reason, the traditional approach to multimedia has been to install it on standalone computers or on computers connected to a network file server, where it can be read directly from disk and played back to the local machine. If you try to serve such files across a network, there is a characteristic pause as the browser waits for the entire file to download and then starts up the application to play it in.

In direct response to the popularity of the web as a multimedia platform, several companies have developed new ways to deliver multimedia to the desktop across TCP/IP networks. These new formats are called *streaming audio* and *streaming video* because they are designed to be received and played back in a stream, rather than all at once. If you think of network-delivered multimedia as a stream of packets being shipped to the user in a specific sequence, the web browser in effect is opening each packet as soon as it comes through the door, rather than waiting for the entire shipment to arrive. Thus, playback can occur almost immediately, as soon as the first packets in the stream begin to reach the browser.

RealAudio/RealVideo

One of the first—and still the most widely used—streaming formats is the RealMedia technology produced by Progressive Networks. This company introduced RealAudio technology for audio streaming in 1995 and later supplemented it with a video-streaming technology called *RealVideo*. The two combined are referred to as *RealMedia*.

Originally this technology was used to create, store, serve, and play back sound and video files in a special format developed by Progressive Networks. However, the definition of RealMedia has been expanded to provide synchronized streaming of a wide array of data types, including text, audio, video, animation, images, and presentations—all in their native format, without conversion to a proprietary format. To do this, Progressive built a complete development environment (as represented by a software development kit called *RealMedia SDK*), which allows web designers to combine all these content types into a synchronized online presentation that is streamed out on-demand to all the participating end users on the network.

Naturally, this requires several tools that were developed by Progressive Networks, including a RealPlayer and a Real Server. The RealPlayer (Figure 6.15) is free for downloading from the Internet and can be distributed freely to all the users on your intranet. But the RealMedia Server is where Progressive *really* makes its money, charging incrementally based on the number of simultaneous streams that the server is enabled to produce. So if you have a large audience that uses the server frequently, you may have to pay for ever-increasing loads of simultaneous streams.

Interestingly, software companies like Vivo (www.vivo.com) have since developed inexpensive software that gives multimedia streaming capabilities to nearly any ordinary web server. However, the Vivo product does not provide the extensive development environment offered by RealMedia. If you plan to offer synchronized multimedia presentations through the intranet, it also might be a good idea to pay close attention to Apple's Quick-Time product.

NetShow

Though Progressive Networks was one of the first on the scene with its Real-Media products, it's increasingly hard to find any part of the Internet software market that hasn't been commandeered by Microsoft. Streaming multimedia is no exception. In mid-1997, Microsoft pulled a major coup in this field by either purchasing or partnering with each of the major players in the streaming-video market in such a way that would make its own NetShow product the standard for all future generations of streaming multimedia.

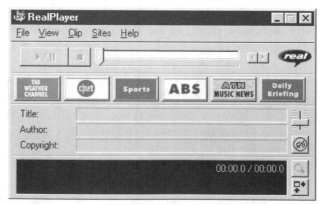

Figure 6.15   RealPlayer from Progressive Networks.

Like RealMedia, NetShow is a combination of technologies designed to provide streaming multimedia over networks. NetShow is based on a standard called *Active Streaming Format* (ASF) that Microsoft touts as "an open, standards-based file format that prepares multimedia content for streaming." The NetShow product includes the following components:

NetShow Server produces the streaming effect. This server does a neat trick, which is to allow either "unicasting" or "multicasting" of streams. With unicasting, a user can start a stream and control it, just the way people can start a movie and control it on their VCRs. Multicasting works more like a broadcast TV show, in the sense that any number of people can watch it, but they all have to watch it at the same time, and they cannot control the progress of the show. Naturally, unicasting takes considerably more server resources than multicasting. With unicasting, a separate stream must be transmitted to each user. With multicasting, a single stream can be addressed simultaneously to any number of users, kind of like a group e-mail.

NetShow Player is the software module needed to receive the streams at the user/client end (Figure 6.16). This can be used as a separate piece of software (helper application), or it can be embedded directly into a web page in IE or Netscape browsers.

NetShow Tools let you convert existing content to the Active Streaming Format (ASF) that is the native language of NetShow. These tools include a real-time encoder, editor, various conversion utilities, and a product called *NetShow Presenter* that allows a PowerPoint presentation to be broadcast as a live video stream.

Microsoft's Active Streaming Format (ASF) is the core of the technology, and any browser equipped to decode ASF streams can receive a NetShow

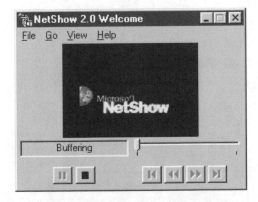

Figure 6.16 The NetShow Player from Microsoft.

broadcast. In fact, several companies have agreed to use ASF as the "native format" in their products—including Progressive Networks (which is now partially owned by Microsoft, and may be wholly owned by the time you read this). That means that ASF—barring divine intervention—will be the predominant format for transmitting Internet multimedia and that any serious video-streaming tool will have to be compatible. Conversely, Microsoft's Net-Show Player will also have the ability to play back RealMedia streams, so that NetShow users will have access to the considerable amount of "legacy" multimedia still out there on the Internet—or on the intranet.

Getting Dynamic with HTML

One powerful aspect of the latest web browsers is their ability to handle an ambitious new feature called *Dynamic HTML,* which gives web designers the ability to marry the traditional web-page infrastructure with more dynamic and interactive elements. Up to now, web pages have been fairly static affairs with images, tables, frames, sound and video elements all mingled together— yet locked into place, in the sense that each embedded element is confined to a fixed piece of screen real estate.

For instance, if you have a video element embedded in a page, the <EMBED> tag places the element at a specific location in relation to the text. As the text moves, the video element moves with it. Moreover, the video is confined to a fixed box of a certain height and width, and runs entirely inside the box.

Where to Find Multimedia Applications

You can use the Internet to download evaluation copies of various multimedia software and plug-ins. Try the following locations:

RealMedia   www.real.com/

Streamworks   www.xingtech.com/

NetShow   www.microsoft.com/netshow/

QuickTime   quicktime.apple.com/

VDOLive   www.vdolive.com/

Vivo   www.vivo.com/

Shockwave   www.macromedia.com

With Dynamic HTML, the strict relationship between text and embedded elements is broken. Designers get to specify the exact x,y positioning of elements on the screen, and the ability to layer objects in three dimensions. It also could give end users the ability to actually manipulate objects in a web page: tugging on the edge of a table, for instance, to enlarge it or reposition it. Obviously, this ability is far outside the range of traditional document publishing—even online document publishing—and inhabits the territory somewhere between multimedia and interactive web-application development.

Dynamic HTML will work slightly differently, depending on the web browser being addressed. Netscape, for instance, uses a <LAYER> tag to specify the upper left *x, y* (left,top) coordinate of a set of content. For example, the following markup code positions the top left corner of a layer (i.e., a section of web-page content) exactly 100 pixels from the top of the page, and 200 pixels from the left:

```
<LAYER ID=layer_name TOP=100 LEFT=200>
All the content that goes in this layer, including normal HTML markup tags,
images, and/or multimedia components, sits right here between the LAYER tags.
</LAYER>
```

Notice that the layer is given a name. Netscape has modified its JavaScript language to include methods that can control the layers dynamically. It is also possible to control layers using the *cascading style sheet* feature of HTML discussed in the previous chapter.

Microsoft's version of Dynamic HTML is built around something called the *Dynamic HTML Object Model,* which was proposed to the W3 Consortium as a standard. Microsoft's version includes a number of features that are enabled *inside the web page* without requiring a trip back to the server or any special applications running in the background on the web server side:

Dynamic styles and content, meaning that it is possible to switch color, size, or style of text automatically, or to change text, images, or multimedia shown on the page.

Dynamic positioning, which includes not only the ability to specify the exact position of an element on the page, but to change that element's position dynamically.

Data binding includes the ability to embed a set of data inside the web page, so that users can manipulate and process locally, without relying on additional help from the server.

Like Netscape, Microsoft's Dynamic HMTL Object Model would allow web-page designers and developers to control the dynamic objects on a web page using scripting languages (VBScript, JScript, JavaScript) or cascading style sheets. The object model also includes support for multimedia elements like sound, video, images, and animation.

Riding the Shockwave

Many third-party companies have provided popular multimedia development and presentation tools that can be used to good effect on an intranet. A perfect example is Shockwave, a multimedia playback device for special interactive content developed by multimedia industry leader Macromedia. Shockwave gives you the ability to play back movies, animations, and presentations—either outside or inside the web browser window. Instead of having a web page with a static image of a product like a car, you might have a web page that contains a video or animation of the car actually moving down a highway. There might be various buttons or animations overlaid on the video or combined in such a way that they produce an interactive multimedia experience.

The most recent versions of Shockwave support streaming content, so the Shockwave file can be delivered incrementally to the web browser across the intranet without having to wait for the entire file to download. In addition, Shockwave supports Dynamic HTML, which means that the various elements in a Shockwave animation can be dynamically positioned or layered across the screen in any manner.

To deliver a Shockwave file to the end user, you must first use Macromedia products such as Flash, Director, or Authorware to create the interactive presentation and save it to disk in Shockwave format. Once the Shockwave object is stored on the web server, you can link to it from a web page (and kick off Shockwave as a separate window), embed it in a page using the <EMBED> tag, or layer it in using Dynamic HTML.

Where to Read About Dynamic HTML

If the advanced features of Dynamic HTML appeal to you, here are the places where the major browser manufacturers tout their competing visions:

Microsoft   www.microsoft.com/ie/ie40/features/ie-dhtml.htm

Netscape   developer.netscape.com/library/documentation/ communicator/dynhtml/

In fact, Shockwave is quite a powerful development tool that includes its own programming environment. For instance, a Shockwave movie can be programmed to contain interactive buttons and text fields that accept keyboard input from the user. You can also program a movie to access information from the network and open other URLs on the web based in different user interactions.

Naturally, to make these effects available to your users, you will need to make sure each user has Shockwave software installed on his or her local machine, or a web browser that supports the Shockwave format, such as Internet Explorer 4.0. As always, this should be a lot easier to do on an intranet than on the World Wide Web, since you probably are dealing with a known group of employees, customers, or suppliers.

Giving It That Extra "Push"

You may recall the big deal I made back in Chapter 1 about how great the intranet is, because it creates a "pull" model where users can get the information they want, rather than having it "pushed" on them? Many of our publishing models these days involve printing reams of paper and then sending it out to people who just *might* be interested in reading it—but probably aren't.

Remember what happens then? They toss it in that big, perpetually gorged recycling bin down the hall. In fact, haven't most of the trees in the Amazon gone into our efforts to make sure we adequately cover every subject with mounds of paper?

So "pull" is great, right? Because it lets users go in and get *exactly* the information they need, without having lots of extra, unsolicited information dumped on them. Of course, wouldn't you know it—as soon as I make that kind of statement, someone comes along and invents a hot new web technology called *push*. If you were alive and breathing circa May 1997, you could not turn a corner without getting whacked in the head by another article explaining how wonderful "push" technology is. Push came into its own later with the introduction of the 4.0 versions of Netscape and Internet Explorer.

Actually, push is not all that new. Way back in 1995, Netscape—in its 1.1 version, in one of its periodic bursts of HTML creativity—invented a tag that would let you poll a web site regularly. They called it "dynamic documents" using "server push" and "client pull" (home.netscape.com/assist/net_sites/pushpull.html). Netscape found that adding a simple <META> tag to a document allowed it to be updated regularly and automatically over the network. For example, you might have a stock quote page that updated itself every 10 minutes or so.

Then a company called *PointCast* came along and made push more than just a fancy trick: It developed a whole new technology and publishing model, as well. With PointCast, you could "subscribe" to "channels" containing all kinds of different content including news, stocks, weather, sports scores, and content from CNN, CNNfn, *Time, People* magazine, *Money Magazine,* and others. What's more, you could have these different information sources broadcast as a screensaver on your local PC. But even PointCast's push was just our old friend pull hiding behind a frumpy mask. The remote channels didn't actually broadcast themselves to your browser. Instead, the browser (or in this case, PointCast's special client) was programmed to automatically hit certain sites every so often and pull down the content.

Soon after PointCast, many other companies flooded the market with products like Castanet, BackWeb, and Arrive. Fortunes were made and lost overnight, as they always are in Silicon Valley. But all of these required special browsers or helper applications to receive the channels.

Leave it to Netscape and Microsoft to jump in and steal the show. Microsoft first, as always, with its Internet Explorer 4.0 channels and its Channel Definition Format (CDF). Netscape right behind with its Netcaster component in the Netscape Communicator product. Naturally, being in competitive mode, both developed their own push models, which were not so much incompatible as just plain *noncognizant* of each other.

In the Netscape push world, there are two types of content: *channels* and *webtops.* A *webtop* is a background display with web capabilities, reminiscent of our current *desktop* with its familiar background pattern and program icons. Clicking a link or icon on a webtop opens a new window with web content. A *channel,* on the other hand, is a specific web site that users can subscribe to. In effect, the user says, these are the web sites that I want to serve as my push channels, and I want those web sites to be updated on my machine every day, or every hour, or every 25 minutes. Defining a Netscape channel, however, requires extensive knowledge and use of JavaScript—especially that part of JavaScript that interfaces with the Netcaster component.

Microsoft's own Channel Definition Format (CDF), by contrast, will be understandable to anyone who knows how to read HTML. In the Microsoft push world, a channel has three general components:

Normal content.   A home page and other pages that provide the content of the channel. These can be an existing web site, which can be simply repurposed and linked into the channel delivery feature.

Special graphics.   A logo that can be used on the special Channel Bar (Figure 6.17) and an icon that can be used on Internet Explorer and Windows menus.

Figure 6.17 Internet Explorer 4.0 Channel Bar.

CDF file. A special file that defines the hierarchical structure of web pages contained in the channel.

Of these three components required to implement the Channel Definition Format, the only learning involved is how to construct the CDF file. The code in a CDF file looks something like this:

```
<?XML version="1.0"?>

<CHANNEL HREF="http://myserver/mypages/index.htm">
<TITLE>The Name of My Channel</TITLE>
<LOGO HREF="http://myserver/myicons/channel5.ico" STYLE="icon" />
<LOGO HREF="http://myserver/images/channel5.gif" STYLE="logo" />
```

```
<ITEM HREF="http://myserver/mypages/item1.htm">
<TITLE>The First Subpage in My Channel</TITLE>
<ABSTRACT>A group of information in one subject matter category.</ABSTRACT>
</ITEM>

<ITEM HREF="http://myserver/mypages/item1.htm">
<TITLE>The Second Subpage in My Channel</TITLE>
<ABSTRACT>A group of information in a different subject matter
category.</ABSTRACT>
</ITEM>

</CHANNEL>
```

Though this may look somewhat forbidding at first, it is actually quite easy to understand. The <?XML?> tag identifies the following code as Extensible Markup Language, rather than HTML. The <CHANNEL> tag shows the location of the main page of the channel. The first <TITLE> and <LOGO/> tags define the channel name, logo, and icon that will appear on menus in the user's web browser or Windows interface (notice the odd closing syntax of the <LOGO/> tag). The <ITEM> tags identify all the subpages in the channel, along with their titles and a short abstract of the information contained in them. Both the main page and the subpages can be existing web pages on a site, so you can gather random pages into your channel by simply pointing to them. If you find this kind of code unappealing, FrontPage 98 includes features that let you build these files quickly without coding.

The CDF file is saved with a .cdf file extension and is placed on the web server alongside the graphics and the content that it references. The last step is to create a hyperlink on the desktop that points to the .cdf file, so that the user can subscribe to it. Once the user subscribes, the channel appears on the Channel Bar and inside the menus of Internet Explorer (or on the Windows 98 desktop).

The channel content is automatically downloaded on a schedule decided by the user at the time of subscription. For instance, if the user specifies that the channel should be updated hourly, the pages in the channel will be checked on the original web site, and any changes will be stored (cached) on the user's local computer. When the user goes to view the channel, the channel contents are retrieved directly from the local cache, so there is virtually no delay.

Modeling with Virtual Reality

Before I close out this chapter, I want to put in an extra word on behalf of the Virtual Reality Modeling Language (VRML) and all the wonders it can perform. VRML is a way to create 3-D worlds inside a web page. Huh? Yes, with VRML you can use the web-browser window to peer into a 3-D universe where solid objects seem to float and rotate like the teacups in the Mad Hatter's party. Drag your mouse in one direction and the objects rotate this way; drag it in the other direction and the objects rotate that-a-way.

So what good is VRML on the corporate intranet? That's the kind of question I was asking myself when I wrote the first edition of this book. At the time, the most creative use of VRML was to build 3-D web pages where your options were arrayed across a landscape, and you could "fly through" the scene to pick the option you wanted. Way cool, but pretty useless when you consider it's much easier to nail a hyperlink cold on a good-old flat 2-D page. (After all—given the average daily commute into the office—I think we've all seen enough of hurtling 3-D objects by the time we reach work.) Keeping in mind, also, that when you venture into the realm of virtual reality, you are in the company of people whose idea of cool stuff is something like "Maze Girl in the Dungeon of VRML."

Nevertheless, since writing the first edition, I have come across engineering and design environments where VRML was put to good use. Typically, the people most likely to use VRML are those who work at Silicon Graphics (SGI) workstations. These are the people most likely to do 3-D modeling of products or processes (although many people also use Sun, DEC, and—increasingly—Pentium Pro machines to do the same). Examples of real-world situations where VRML might apply include architecture, aviation, medicine, finance, engineering, scientific research, applied physics, or any other field that requires advanced data visualization.

As its name suggests, VRML is a language used to model objects in space. For instance, the following statement will produce a rectangular box that can be viewed and rotated in 3-D by simply dragging the mouse and moving various window controls:

```
#VRML V2.0 utf8

Shape {
      geometry Box { size 20 45 80 }
}
```

What's nice and easy about this is having such a box, viewed inside a VRML browser, come already equipped with its own 3-D environment and controls. In other words, if you type the preceding statement, place it in a file with a .*wrl* extension, and open it in a VRML browser, the box will be the lone object in the 3-D world, but it will rotate and move in response to your mouse commands, without any further effort or programming on your part.

Of course, this is the very simplest of examples. Building a complex scene—with detailed colors, textures, and component interactions—can become quite a programming chore. Fortunately, as in the workaday reality of HTML, the world of VRML is increasingly accessible through advanced authoring tools that take away the pain of the coding process, much the same way as normal drawing tools make it possible to create sophisticated 2-D drawings without coding PostScript.

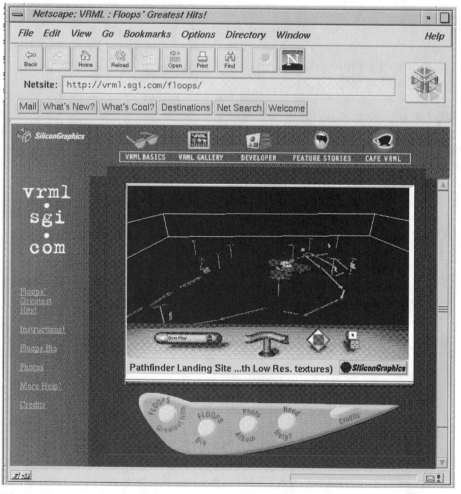

Figure 6.18   Cosmo Player from SGI.

Where to Find VRML on the Web

Microsoft   www.microsoft.com/vrml/

Netscape   www.developer.com/

QuickTime VR   qtvr.quicktime.apple.com/

Cosmo Worlds   cosmo.sgi.com/

VRML tutorial   developer.netscape.com/news/viewsource/pesce_
vrml.html

VRML tools   www.zdnet.com/pcmag/iu/browse/vrml/_vrml.htm

The first version of VRML was great for creating these kinds of virtual worlds. But VRML 2.0—and any later versions that come to market after this book is published—will really make VRML incredibly useful for 3-D modeling on the web. The VRML 2.0 specification, announced in August 1996, is integrated with Java and JavaScript in such a way that these programming languages can be used to provide sophisticated interactivity between the model, the end user, and any back-end data sources.

Normally, as just suggested, in addition to authoring tools, you will need a specially equipped VRML browser for each of the users on your network who plan to view your content online. Fortunately, such equipment is standard—or easily acquired—with the 4.0 versions of Netscape and Internet Explorer. Additionally, there are plenty of third-party browsers and related VRML development tools, including the Cosmo Player browser and Cosmo Worlds authoring system from Silicon Graphics (Figure 6.18) and QuickTime VR from Apple.

Where Do We Go from Here?

Now that you understand the power of the web to deliver published documents and multimedia, only one more uncharted area remains: data and applications. The next chapter will explain how you can use web technology to create interactive forms that help users tap into databases, run remote client-server applications, and perform other astounding feats.

Chapter Seven at a Glance

The most powerful aspect of intranet technology is its ability to provide users with interactive access to data and online applications across a computer network. This chapter introduces the various technologies and how they fit into corporate intranets, including:

- ◆ How HTML forms work, and how they can be used to communicate with users over a web
- ◆ How CGI programs work, and why they're useful for interactive communication
- ◆ How to create virtual documents through on-the-fly web publishing
- ◆ How to use development tools like Perl, JavaScript, Java, and ActiveX to add interactivity to web sites
- ◆ How to use some of the most common database access tools
- ◆ How to set up search applications for web sites
- ◆ What groupware has to offer on a corporate intranet

Serving Data and Applications

Web technology has evolved quite a bit since the day the idea first popped into Tim Berners-Lee's head. In the beginning, HTML was primarily a way to deliver documents. Somewhere along the way somebody decided that the Web should do something more than just serve nice-looking online documents, so they wrote an extension to the web protocol called CGI—the *Common Gateway Interface.* And they invented extra HTML tags that allowed a web page to act like a regular online form or dialog box, with pull-down menus, radio buttons, check boxes, scrollable lists, and text fields.

Suddenly, the web became a two-way street (or an information superhighway, depending on your metaphorical preferences). Sure, you could ship all the information that you wanted to users. But at the same time, users could talk back to you. You could send users data, and they could send data right back. It was nifty and neat, but it was something more than that. It represented a whole new way that data and applications could be delivered.

CGI was only the beginning and was quickly recognized as a fairly slow and clunky way to deliver data across an intranet. The proposed replacement: a web-oriented programming language called *Java* that is still struggling in many ways to prove its mettle in the corporate workplace. Not to mention the others: JavaScript, VBScript, and all the other ways of jazzing up web pages with something more than just static images and text.

All these new tools can be used as ways of taking the intranet into the next generation, producing web applications that work a lot like our traditional computer programs. With these new tools, we have reached a state of affairs where nearly all computer resources and applications can be delivered directly into the web browser—so that this simple tool does indeed become a universal GUI (graphical user interface). So, while online publishing and multimedia are two of the neatest things webs can do, programming and interactivity are where the real action is these days. And, more than anything else, this is where the promise of the intranet lies.

Understanding the Options

The fledgling web developer—and if you're reading this chapter, I assume you are one—has a real landslide of options available today, ranging from the relatively simple to the dauntingly complex. As a matter of fact, there is no way that this chapter—or this entire book, or even any single book of any reasonable length—can tell you everything you could possibly know about developing web applications. The technologies have gotten very deep, very quickly.

Is that any reason to despair? Not really. You have to start *somewhere,* and if you want to start learning about web applications this is as good a time as any. I can't show you everything, but I can at least show you some of the most common tools and techniques people are using to create interactive applications on the web, so that you at least can determine which ones to use and where to go to learn more.

To aid your journey, I have arranged the material so that it takes you into the water a step at a time. First you dip your toe, then you're wet up to the knee—before long you're swimming in deep water.

The first sections of this chapter talk about why it's good to create web applications in the first place. Then I follow with a discussion of forms and CGI, because this is the way web interactivity got started, and these tools can still be quite useful to anyone who wants to create web applications from scratch.

Next, I delve a little deeper into Perl and JavaScript, which can lend complex interactivity to web forms and web pages. Though a little more complex than HTML, these are still languages that even nonprogrammers can use and manipulate. Shortly after, however, I get into slightly deeper discussions of Java, JDBC, and some other fairly complex web application development tools. And that's it for the programming web application side.

At the end of the chapter, I move back into shallower water with discussions of other advanced tools you can use to make your intranet more useable, like search engines, groupware, and intranet suites. If you *can't* make it all the way through the technical areas in between, at least do yourself a favor and jump to the closing sections at the end.

So sit tight while I take you on a tour of web interactivity and show you the possibilities one by one. By the end of this chapter, hopefully you will have learned enough to start creating web applications on your own.

The Advantages of Web-Delivered Applications

Web is not the first technology to capture information from users over a network. That's what all client-server programs are designed to do, including widely used applications such as Oracle and Lotus Notes. But when you add a web component to a traditional client-server application, you gain a few things that traditional client-server programs typically don't provide:

Cross-platform compatibility.   Web browsers have been designed to run on practically every computing platform available. Since they use machine-independent languages that are interpreted by the browser, such as HTML and Java, applications can be delivered instantaneously to any platform in a network, without having to develop special-purpose clients for each different type of machine. This takes a lot of the work out of the traditional application development process.

Universal access.   Web forms can be accessed from *any node* in a network through a simple hyperlink, creating an application that often requires no user setup or login. The applications can even be inserted right into the middle of a web page, so that they appear as part of a document ("You like my newsletter? Tell me about it . . .").

No installation required on client side.   Web applications are installed on the server and then referenced over the network by anyone with a web browser. Unlike traditional applications, users don't have to call you and say, "I want to use your application. Can you come and install it on my local machine?" Instead, the application is made available just like any other part of your web site. The user clicks a hyperlink and the application is delivered instantaneously to the user's browser.

Universal GUI.   The web browser can be used to deliver any kind of web-based client-server application, and can be reused endlessly for hundreds of other applications. And, since all applications can be viewed throughout the network using the same web-browser tool, there is no need to set up and train users on a separate tool for each individual application.

What's more, creating web applications is often simpler than you might think. Especially if you have a WYSIWYG web-publishing tool like Internet Assistant, Office97, Netscape Composer, or FrontPage. Or a web-oriented development tool like Cold Fusion, Visual J++, LiveWire, or Visual InterDev.

Web Forms: The First Step toward Interactivity

In the early days of the World Wide Web—about the time Marc Andreessen and his colleagues were developing their original Mosaic browser—someone got the bright idea that web pages should be more than just a way to publish information. They should provide a way to *gather* information, too. That way, instead of the Web being a one-way street with authors providing information for other people to read, the people at the other end of the pipe would be able to provide information too, and send it *right back to the authors.*

How would they do that? With HTML tags that allow web page authors to include text fields, radio buttons, check boxes, and selectable lists right in the middle of a web page. If you've used a computer any time in the last century, you've probably clicked your share of radio buttons and filled in your share of text fields. This is a commonplace experience for any computer user these days. The people who invented some of the early versions of HTML recognized this and thought nothing of building the capability right into the markup language itself.

When you create a web page with these types of elements in it, the result is called an *HTML form* or a *web form* (Figure 7.1). In fact, web forms were at the heart of the first web-enabled applications to make their appearance on the World Wide Web—and later on the intranet.

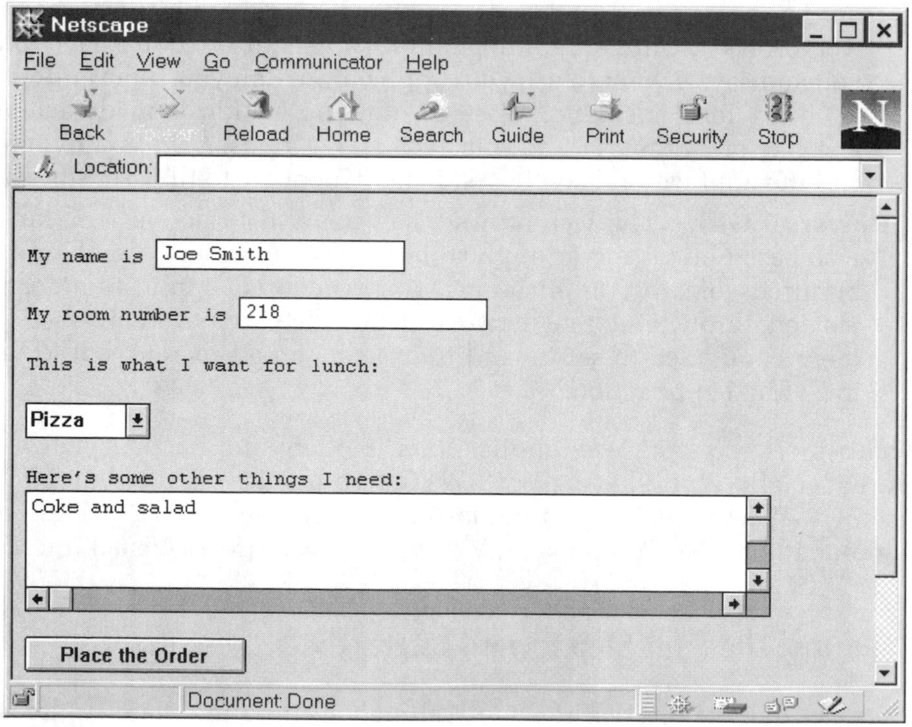

Figure 7.1   Typical web form.

Once you created a web form and collected data from the user, however, you still had to do something with it. The web server was a fairly nifty piece of software, but its main job was to serve files from a web site, not to process random data coming back from the user. To deal with this sudden influx of data from the user's end, the early Web inventors created a way to add some intelligence on the back end.

The result was something we call *CGI,* or the *Common Gateway Interface.* Assuming the web server can't think, or do things intelligently on its own, we can put other programs or applications behind it and use the CGI as a way of passing the data back and forth between these "back-end applications" and the server.

Here's how the web forms and CGI work together on a typical web site (see Figure 7.2):

1. The web site author creates a web form and stores it on the web site so that it is available to anyone who visits the site. For instance, on an intranet, human resources might create a web form to allow users to register for a corporate benefits program.
2. Any user can visit the site and access the web form, just like any other web page.
3. The web form appears in the user's browser, just like any other web page.
4. The user fills out the web form and clicks the Submit button. The information entered by the user goes back to the web server for processing.
5. The web server passes the data through CGI to a "back-end application" such as a script or a database program that is programmed to handle the user's input.
6. The back-end application sends a response back to the user: either a simple "thank you for registering" or something more complicated,

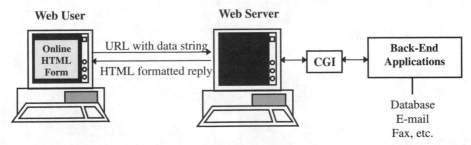

Figure 7.2 How CGI works with web forms.

such as an intelligent response based on the information the user provided. For example, user selections could be used to query a database and return a query result to the browser. In other cases, the user response could be passed on as e-mail or simply stored in a database with no further processing or interactive response.

This sort of CGI/form-based interactivity was the Web's first step toward real, full-fledged applications. Like any baby's first step, however, it was a little slow and awkward—so much so, that over the years it has fallen into some disrepute. Does that mean we should toss CGI onto the ash heap of history? Not at all. In fact, CGI still can be quite useful for many purposes on the intranet.

If you are an advanced developer creating high-volume, high-traffic web sites for mission-critical applications, CGI is probably too slow and rudimentary for you. However, if you are a typical web site developer, just trying to create a web form that people can occasionally use to provide you with information, CGI may be just what you need. Yes, CGI is slow when you are trying to handle multiple simultaneous access by many clients. But for occasional access by the casual user, it is no slower than any other process. The next few sections of this chapter will help you understand a little better how CGI and web forms work.

How to Create a Web Form

A simple web form is not all that hard to create. In fact, using nothing more than a plain text editor and a few simple HTML codes, you can create one in minutes. Start your text editor now, open a new file, and type in the code as shown below.

```
<FORM>
<PRE>

My name is <INPUT NAME="name">

My room number is <INPUT NAME="room">

This is what I want for lunch:

<SELECT NAME="lunch">
<OPTION>Pizza
<OPTION>Burger
```

```
<OPTION>Chicken
</SELECT>

Here's some other things I need:
<TEXTAREA NAME="extras" ROWS=4 COLS=60>
</TEXTAREA>

<INPUT TYPE="SUBMIT" VALUE="Place the Order">
</PRE>
</FORM>
```

Notice the <FORM> tags indicate the beginning and end of the form. Save the form as a text file using the name *myform.htm* and open it up as a local file in your browser (using File/Open). If you did your typing correctly, you should see the Form dialog displayed in a WYSIWYG format as shown previously in Figure 7.1.

Notice in Figure 7.1 that some words were already filled in. Go ahead and fill in the same words, then click the button labeled "Place the Order." If you're using Netscape Navigator, you should see the form get spit right back at you as it is in Figure 7.3. (Internet Explorer will not do this, because it reacts a bit differently to our form. That's okay, if you don't have Navigator, just watch this example.)

Notice that this form isn't complete enough to produce a real result. We haven't done the back-end programming yet. So why bother with this example? Well, you can see that the original HTML codes in *myform.htm* have already created the "user interface" for our fledgling web application.

But take another look. Don't look at the jumble of form fields on the screen. Instead, check out the line of codes after the question mark in the Location field at the top of Figure 7.3. In Netscape, you should see something like this (if your own browser doesn't do this, don't worry, just look at the example here):

```
name=Joe+Smith&room=218&lunch=Pizza&extras=Coke+and+salad
```

This is how data looks when it is extracted from a form and passed back to the server. In a sense, the browser has taken what you typed in on the form and packaged it into a single string of communication that—translated into broken English—means something like this:

```
"the name is Joe-Smith & the room is 218 & the lunch is Pizza & the extras
are Coke-and-salad."
```

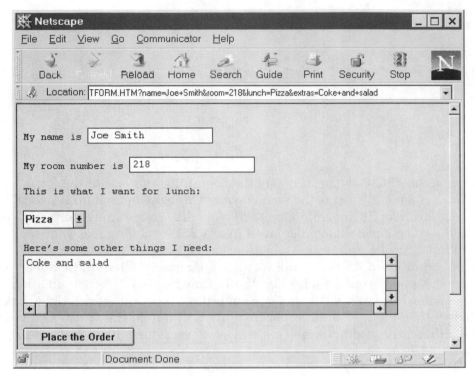

Figure 7.3   Netscape result of clicking the button.

If you were dealing with a real form on a real web server, this is the kind of message your browser would send to the server for processing. And the server, in turn, might read the message, process it, retrieve the data contained in it (Joe Smith, 218, Pizza, Coke and salad), and send an e-mail to the cafeteria (assuming they do deliveries, of course), saying:

```
"Joe Smith in Room 218 wants a Pizza with a Coke and salad."
```

Then it might turn around and add a record to a database like this:

```
Date: 02/15/98
Employee Name: Joe Smith
Lunch Selection: Pizza
Extras wanted: Coke and salad
Cost: $7.95
```

FAX

To: Company Nurse

From: Web Server, Food Services Dept.

Total Pages: 1

Subject: CHOLESTEROL ALERT!

Please be aware that the following employees ordered pizza five days in a row:

- John T. Harris
- Vera Landry
- Joe Smith
- Barney Taylor

Please schedule them immediately for a complete physical, including lab work and a treadmill test.

Signed,
Your Friendly (But Concerned) Local Web Server

Figure 7.4   One possible result of a web form (tongue-in-cheek).

It might also do a few calculations, put two and two together, and send an urgent fax to the company nurse with the startling news shown in Figure 7.4.

Of course, let's not forget about the poor guy who ordered the food. The web server might send a custom-generated HTML form back to the browser that looks like Figure 7.5.

Notice that this could go on indefinitely. The user fills in a form, the server replies with a request for more information. The user supplies extra information, the server responds again until the transaction is complete. The interactivity can be as simple or as complex as you want.

In the previous examples, I showed how to use HTML markup tags to create a web form. Keep in mind that there are many tools you can use to create web forms as well, including common web-authoring applications such as Netscape Composer or FrontPage. With these programs, you can use toolbar icons to build all the components of a dialog, including text boxes, radio buttons, pull-down menus, pushbuttons—you name it. Just place your cursor in the document where you want a pull-down menu to be inserted, then click the appropriate icon on the toolbar (Figure 7.6).

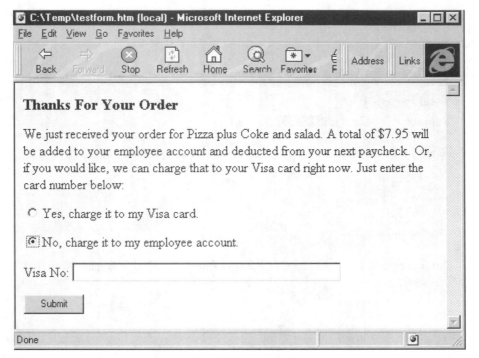

Figure 7.5   Another example of form result.

CGI: The Other Half of the Puzzle

Notice in the previous examples that the web server did some fairly fancy stuff. First, Joe Smith ordered a pizza, Coke, and a salad. No surprise there: That's probably what Joe orders every day. The surprising part is all the different things the web server did with Joe's order. In particular, the server:

◆ Sent an e-mail message to the cafeteria manager
◆ Sent a fax to the company nurse
◆ Created a database record
◆ Sent Joe a thank-you note and asked for more information

Figure 7.6   Typical toolbar for creating web forms.

So, You Want to Be a Form-Coding Expert . . .

Present day WYSIWYG web-development tools have taken a lot of the sting out of creating HTML forms, providing—as they do—complete templates that let you create forms in seconds. If you want to learn more about coding web forms in HTML, there are places where you can learn about it on the World Wide Web.

> **A great place to start is:** union.ncsa.uiuc.edu/HyperNews/get/ www/html/guides.html
>
> **California-based Web Communications also has a good introduction to forms and many other aspects of web development in its Comprehensive Guide to Web Publishing at:** www.webcom .com/html/tutor/forms/start.shtml
>
> **A somewhat technical and laborious discussion of forms is offered by the people who originally brought you Mosaic:** www.ncsa .uiuc.edu/SDG/Software/Mosaic/Docs/fill-out-forms/overview .html
>
> **The latest on forms from W3 Consortium, as of HTML version 4.0:** www.w3.org/TR/WD-html40/interact/intertop.html

♦ Took a Visa card number from Joe and charged the order to Joe's Visa account

Of course, the web server is not a superhuman organism that automatically knows how to do all this stuff. These things are arranged using back-end applications including databases, e-mail programs, or other applications that communicate with the web server using the CGI interface discussed earlier in this chapter, or using web server application programming interfaces (APIs).

Assuming that you need a back-end application to do all this, the question becomes: Can you buy one of these things, or do you have to program it yourself? In the old days, if you built the form, you had to program the back-end application, too—or hire a programmer to do it. Increasingly, however, web servers are coming with built-in programs or tools that do a lot of the fancy stuff for you. So all you have to do is create the form (naturally, since you want to be able to control how it looks), then configure the back-end application to do something with the form data.

To give you a complete tour of the possibilities, however, I want to show you some of the ways people have done it in the past, including ways that you may still want to use today. Even though you may never have to do CGI programming, it's still instructive to understand what CGI is, so that you understand more about the inner workings of web applications.

Speaking in Tongues

By now, you understand that the CGI component of an intranet is just a humble servant that sits between the web server and back-end application and does all the work of passing information back and forth between them. Actually, let's say this is a humble *multilingual* servant. Any CGI program must speak two or more languages: the language of the web server and the language of any back-end applications, so that it can take information from the web server and convey it to the back-end application, and it can take information from the back-end application and convey it to the web server.

For instance, in our previous example, Joe Smith placed an order for pizza that was sent to the web server as a message looking something like this:

```
name=Joe+Smith&room=218&lunch=Pizza&extras=Coke+and+salad
```

The web server takes the message pretty much as is and passes it along to the CGI program. The CGI program has to take the message apart piece by piece (parse it in programmer lingo) and do something with it. If it's communicating with an e-mail system, it might cram the information into an e-mail message and ship it out using the command-line interface for the local e-mail program (notice form data in bold):

```
To: Inez@Cafeteria
From: Web Server No. 2
Subject: HUNGRY GUY
Joe Smith in Room 218 wants Pizza for lunch with a Coke and salad.
```

Notice that the CGI program has taken information originally communicated in web server language and translated it into e-mail language. In fact, you could say that it "repackaged" the data—took it apart and wrapped it inside an e-mail message. If the back-end application is a database, the CGI program could communicate using *Standard Query Language* (SQL).

CGI is not rocket science. It's just a way of taking standard input from a web server, extracting the data, then passing it along to the back-end application. This is so simple that in the early days people didn't even use compiled programs to do this—they just used simple scripts written in uncompiled languages like *Perl*.

Now that the vendors of back-office applications have caught on—people like Lotus and Oracle—they've developed their own web servers or supplied data interfaces to handle communication between third-party web servers and their databases. Third-party software developers have jumped into the breach as well, and they're selling multipurpose CGI programs that can talk to a variety of back-end applications. People are even selling web servers that already have databases integrated with them. Likely, these types of integrated packages will become increasingly prevalent until they merge into single products: databases that do e-mail, speak Web-ese, and publish online documents.

How CGI Talks Back to the User

The nice part about CGI is not only that it can receive data from the user and transfer it to the back end, it can also take data from the back end and send it to the user.

How to send it back? Well, if the CGI program is lazy, it might just take the raw output from the database and transmit it back as a simple stream of text. But that wouldn't be too friendly. More likely, any CGI program with a little self-respect will take the data and make it look nice, wrapping it in HTML codes so it displays magnificently on the screen. Figure 7.7 shows how that might look when diagrammed.

Notice how the data is extracted from the database and inserted into the middle of an HTML document. In the example above, the HTML document would always look the same, but the *variables* (bold words in the middle

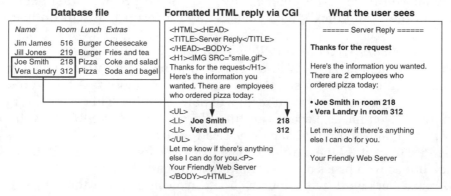

Figure 7.7   Simplified diagram of form data processing.

panel) would change. Of course, there's more to it than that. The CGI program itself, when you look at the raw source, contains a lot more than just this swatch of HTML. But somewhere in there, there's a place where it spits out this kind of HTML code with variables inserted in the middle.

Does this look familiar? In effect, the CGI program is sending users something like a form letter with key data variables inserted into the appropriate slots. The CGI program passes the finished form letter to the web server, which passes it back to the web client, which displays it on screen as a nice-looking, helpful reply to the users—pretty much the same way a traditional form letter gets delivered on paper through snail mail.

In web lingo, we call this kind of action "HTML coding on the fly." In a single motion, the CGI program retrieves the desired data from the database, wraps HTML codes around it, and delivers it back to the browser the same way the web server delivers any preformatted HTML document. Users, sitting there on the other end of the line, may not even realize they're viewing web documents that were generated on the fly. They may not realize that *the document didn't even exist until the actual moment it was requested.* They just see a document that happens to contain exactly the information they're looking for.

Using Perl to Handle Interactive Forms

In the early days of the Web, people used a scripting language called *Perl* to handle the data in web forms. As I mentioned earlier, this way of handling web data has gotten a bad name, simply because tools like Java are potentially better and faster working. However, if you are not a Java programmer and you're not considering handling a dozen transactions per second, Perl may be just what you need. Even people with little or no programming experience may find they can quickly hack together a Perl script that will do just what they need.

Perl (*Practical Extraction and Report Language*) was originally created by a programmer named Larry Wall as a way to process text files. With Perl, for instance, you can create a script that opens one or more text files, processes the information, and writes out results to new text files. This is ideal for interacting with web forms, because all the information received from web forms is plain text, and the HTML language itself is also plain text. So it is possible to use Perl to capture the plain-text data from web forms, process it, then write it back out as web pages or other plain-text formats.

To make Perl work with your web site, you must have the Perl software installed somewhere on the web server computer. If the server is UNIX-based, there's a good chance it has Perl already (enter **which perl** at the command line to see if it does). If your server is NT-based, there is something called *NT Perl* that may already be installed or that you can download from the web and install. See the sidebar titled "Where To Get Perl Info Software" for details.

Figures 7.8 and 7.9 show a web form and a Perl script designed to act together. Figure 7.10 shows how the web form looks when displayed inside a browser. The web form is called *testform.html* and is stored in the document area of the web server, along with the rest of your web site. The Perl script is called *testform.pl* and is stored in the cgi-bin area of the server. To understand how these work together, let's look at them one by one.

Notice that the form is very simple: It contains only a single text field (INPUT NAME="user_name"), which allows the user to enter his or her name. There is also a Submit button the user can press to submit the data (Figure 7.10).

Notice how the ACTION part of the <FORM> tag in the web form (Figure 7.8) actually points to the Perl script (Figure 7.9). When the user clicks the Submit button, the web server opens the Perl script named *testform.pl* and passes the data to it. Remember, as shown earlier in this chapter, that the data leaves the web form as a string. For instance, in this case the user's name would get passed to the Perl script in the following format:

```
user_name=Joe+Smith
```

The script shown in Figure 7.9 takes this data, reads it in (Section 1), splits it up at the equal sign and the plus sign (Section 2), and formats it so that it can be handled as a variable called *$user_name,* which in this case is equal to "Joe Smith." The Perl code in Sections 1 and 2 of Figure 7.9 is fairly standard and can be duplicated verbatim in any script you create. These statements will turn all of the form input fields from any form into named variables that

```
<FORM METHOD=POST ACTION="http://server_name/cgi-bin/testform.pl">

Enter Your Name Here: <INPUT NAME="user_name">

<INPUT TYPE="SUBMIT">

</FORM>
```

Figure 7.8   Example of a simple web form.

```perl
#!/usr/bin/perl

################################################
# SECTION 1: Read in data from the web form
################################################

read(STDIN, $buffer, $ENV{'CONTENT_LENGTH'});

################################################
# SECTION 2: Split data into named variables
################################################

@pairs = split(/&/, $buffer);
foreach $pair (@pairs) {
    ($name, $value) = split(/=/, $pair);
    $value =~ tr/+/ /;
    $value =~ s/%([a-fA-F0-9][a-fA-F0-9])/pack("C", hex($1))/eg;
    $value =~ s/<!--(.|\n)*-->//g;
    $contents{$name} = $value;
}

################################################
# SECTION 3: Save the user output in a file
################################################

$targetfile = "c:\server\htdocs\names.htm";

open (NAMEFILE, ">>$targetfile");
print NAMEFILE "<B>User Name: ",$contents{'user_name'},"</B>";
print NAMEFILE "\n<P>\n<HR>";
close (NAMEFILE);

################################################
# SECTION 4: Send a message back to the user
################################################

print "Content-Type: text/html\n\n";
print "<H3>Thanks for Your Input</H3>\n";
print "<A HREF=\"http://server_name/names.htm\">Click here</A>";
print "to see your entry.";
```

Figure 7.9 Example of a Perl script.

Enter Your Name Here: | Joe Smith | | Submit |

Figure 7.10   How the web form looks inside the browser.

you can use to create various types of output, as explained in the following paragraphs.

Once the data comes into the script in Figure 7.9 and is turned into named variables, the script defines the name and location of an HTML file to which it can append the data (Section 3). Then it opens the file, writes some HTML codes into the file, and closes the file. For example, the lines:

```
print NAMEFILE"<B>User Name:",$contents{'user_name'},"</B>";
print NAMEFILE"\n<P>\n<HR>";
```

actually add the following lines to the bottom of the file called *names.htm:*

```
<B>User Name: Joe Smith</B>
<P>
<HR>
```

This is just straight HTML coding, which will look like Figure 7.11 when the HTML file is opened in a web browser.

Notice in the *print* statements (Figure 7.9, Section 3) that anything in quotes is printed literally into the *names.htm* file (the \n inserts a carriage return). Also notice that $contents('user_name'} inserts the current value of *$user_name* into the file. Since it is not literal text, it is put "outside the quotes" in the *print* statement.

Once the user data has been written to *name.htm* on the server (Section 3), the last part of the Perl script generates a new web page "on the fly" and sends it back to the user's browser (Section 4). In this case, no file is opened. Instead, the last few *print* statements ship a stream of HTML code directly back to the user's web browser, which then displays it just as it would any other web page (Figure 7.12).

User Name: Joe Smith

Figure 7.11   Result of Perl print statements.

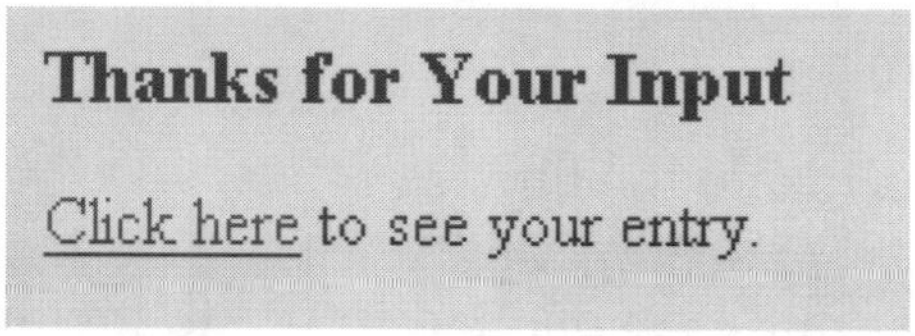

Thanks for Your Input

Click here to see your entry.

Figure 7.12 HTML page content delivered on the fly.

The first line of code in Section 4 is crucial; you should always use this as the first line of code for any web page you generate on the fly, because it tricks both the server and the browser into thinking this is an actual web page you are sending back. Notice that the remaining lines of code actually create the display in Figure 7.12, right down to the hyperlink that links back to the file *name.htm*. In sum total, the script has done the following: (1) allowed Joe Smith to enter his name; (2) inserted Joe's name into a web page; and (3) given Joe a hyperlink to click to see the web page with his name on it.

Once you've complete a Perl script, you should check it visually for syntax errors (e.g., semicolon at the end of each line). Then test the script using the operating system command line, for instance:

```
testform.pl
```

Or, if this doesn't work, include the entire path to both the Perl program and the script, such as:

```
/usr/bin/perl /server/cgi-bin/testform.pl
```

If the script works okay, you will see no error messages, only the output from the script that is to be sent back to the browser (Section 4 of the script). If this happens, you can test the web form inside a web browser and it should work too. Remember, however, that it will not work if you are trying to do something with the script that the system won't allow, such as open and write to a file in a folder where the web server does not have write permissions.

Naturally, there is a lot more you can do with Perl than I've shown in these examples. For instance, you could check the data for validity (e.g., format of date entries). Or you could have a script that takes different kinds of actions based on certain specified conditions (if-then-else statements). Instead of appending to a file, you might write new files, create e-mail messages, or interact with databases using *Structured Query Language* (SQL) commands. But this example should be enough to give you an idea how Perl and CGI works. For more details, see the following sidebar, "Where to Get Perl Info/Software," or check your local bookstore for books on these subjects.

Where to Get Perl Info/Software

There are many locations on the Internet where you can get more information about current versions of the Perl software and download the appropriate interpreter software. Be sure to download the version of Perl that is written for the specific type of platform where your web server is located.

> **General information about Perl.**   www.Perl.com/Perl/index.html
>
> **Download the UNIX Perl software.**   www.Perl.com/Perl/info/software.html
>
> **Download NT Perl software.**   website.ora.com/software/extras.html
>
> **Download Perl for Win32.**   www.Perl.hip.com/

A good book on Perl is the *CGI/Perl Cookbook* by Craig Patchett and Matthew Wright (John Wiley & Sons, Inc., 1998).

How to Do Interactive Forms without Programming

In the previous example, I created a Perl script to handle the data from a web form. In a way, the script acted a lot like a computer program, because it read the data, processed it, and created various kinds of output with it. So the script acted like a customized computer application that I wrote myself.

Now imagine if someone had created a CGI program for you, and had already tested it thoroughly so that it was guaranteed to work. All you would have to do is plug in that program, the same way I plugged in the Perl script in the previous example. The executable program would be stored on the server and triggered by the ACTION statement inside the web form, just as the Perl script was. It could be any kind of program designed to handle input or output from a web server through the CGI, including programs written in the C language or Visual Basic.

Most sophisticated web editors now let you create forms from templates and either provide their own back-end scripts or let you plug in your own. For instance, FrontPage Editor has its own Forms Wizard that lets you create a form just by answering a series of questions (Figure 7.13).

Once you have answered the questions and selected all the desired options for the form, you can specify whether the form data should be saved to a web

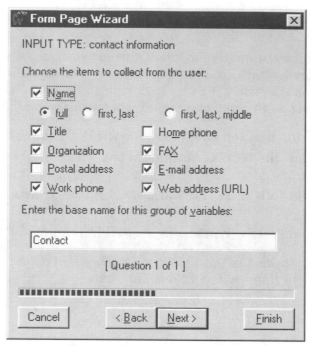

Figure 7.13   Forms creation wizard in FrontPage.

page, in a text file, or processed using a custom CGI script that you have written. Once you answer all the questions in the wizard, FrontPage creates the form automatically and displays it in the FrontPage Editor (Figure 7.14).

There are other programs that help you process the user input from forms, and they come in all shapes and sizes. They range from simple form-processing applications like Polyform, to some of the insertable components in FrontPage, to database access and form-processing programs like Cold Fusion. Even search engines follow this model, as you will learn later in this chapter.

Controlling Web Page Dynamics with JavaScript

In the previous examples, you saw how Perl makes it possible to provide interactive forms using a scripting language, which is somewhat simpler than creating a full-fledged computer program. However, the Perl software as well

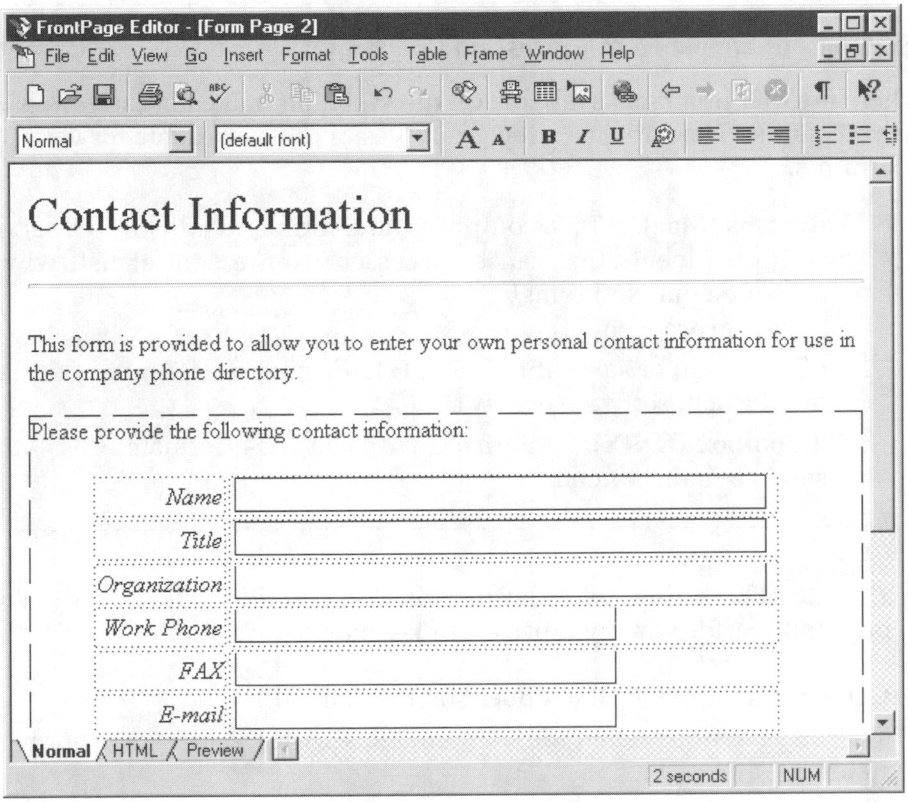

Figure 7.14   Completed form in FrontPage Editor.

as the Perl script itself has to be installed on the server. This is fine if you are a web administrator and have full access to the server environment for developing and testing scripts. But it's quite a bit less convenient if you are a web-page author and simply want to add a little interactivity to your pages.

There are other drawbacks to server-side scripting. Consider the fact that—if you use a Perl script to check the user's input for validity—the user can completely fill out a form and press the Submit button, and it isn't until the user's data hits the server that any errors are caught. How much better it would be if you could check the user's input as soon as the cursor leaves the form field. Yet, there is nothing in HTML that lets you add this kind of error checking directly into the web page.

That's why JavaScript was invented. JavaScript is a rudimentary scripting language developed by Netscape that lets you insert programlike features

---

Examples of Simple Form-Processing Programs

There are CGI programs available on the Web that you can easily plug in to your server. Here are just a few examples of tools available for various platforms.

NetForms (Mac).   Takes output from a form and adds it to a set of web documents that can be accessed from a central list. www .maxum.com/NetForms/

PolyForm (PC).   Takes output from a form and uses it in the body of an e-mail or saves it to file in HTML, comma-delimited, or flat text format. software.oreilly.com/

W3 Toolbox (UNIX).   Interfaces with flat files, formats in HTML, sends e-mail. w3.com/

---

directly into HTML files. With JavaScript, you can add extra functions to a web page that perform many types of tricks, such as:

◆ Controlling messages that appear on the status line
◆ Triggering actions when the user interacts with hyperlinks or form fields
◆ Issuing alerts based on user actions
◆ Checking user input and generating error messages
◆ Spawning new windows or web browsers based on user actions
◆ Spawning user prompts with dialogs, messages, or options
◆ Sophisticated frame control
◆ Dynamic HTML control

Since JavaScript can be added directly to the web page, there is no need to have access to special server folders—any web author can imbed JavaScript in a web page and make it work. Though JavaScript provides extensive programming capabilities that can be used to create fairly complex applications, it is also possible for nonprogrammers to learn and use JavaScript to do simple but useful things. *Note:* Netscape provides a more advanced scripting language called *LiveWire JavaScript,* which is compiled into a bytecode format like Java and used for database access and special server-side programming. This chapter does not cover server-side JavaScript, but you can probably find whole books on the subject, if it interests you.

Unlike other programming tools, JavaScript does not require a compiler or an interpreter. It is interpreted automatically by any JavaScript-capable browser, including both Netscape and Internet Explorer. All you have to do is add JavaScript code "between the lines" of your ordinary HTML pages—or you can reference a file containing JavaScript code, the same way you reference an image.

To show you how this works, add the following lines to the bottom of any web page.

```
<SCRIPT LANGUAGE="JAVASCRIPT">
document.write("Last modified on ")
document.write(document.lastModified)
</SCRIPT>
```

This is a segment of JavaScript, which is marked off by a beginning and ending <SCRIPT> tag. The first line of the JavaScript writes three words into your current document. The second line inserts the document modification date. If you save the file and reload it in your web browser, you should see a message such as the following at the bottom of the file:

```
Last modified on Mon Jan 5 13:32:24 1998
```

If you do not see a message like this, check the Options dialog in your web browser and make sure the JavaScript option is "enabled." Then try again.

Without the SCRIPT tag to hide it, the JavaScript lines might be interpreted and displayed like ordinary text. Instead, the SCRIPT tag hides the scripting language from the user and only displays "the result" of the script.

Yet, the SCRIPT tag is not the only way to insert JavaScript into a web page. You can also insert certain JavaScript commands inside existing HTML tags. These types of commands are typically called *event handlers.* For instance, in most web pages, whenever you move the cursor over a hyperlink, the status line at the bottom of the window shows where the hyperlink is pointed. If you don't understand what I'm talking about, try it now and see.

With a JavaScript event handler inserted into the hyperlink, you can change the message that appears when you move the mouse over the link. For instance, if you were creating a web page for rank novices and didn't want them to see that confusing "http" or "shortcut" message, you might change the message on the status bar by adding an *onmouseover* event to the hyperlink's opening tag. Here's how that might look, inside the opening tag of the hyperlink:

```
<A HREF="newpage.htm" onmouseover="window.status='Clicking here will take
you to a different web page.';return true">
```

If you add the *onmouseover* event to any hyperlink on one of your web pages, you should see the following message on the status line of the current page when you move the mouse over the link:

```
Clicking here will take you to a different web page.
```

Event handlers provide an excellent way to make things happen in your HTML pages based on user actions. For instance, something might happen when the user loads a page, moves the mouse to a certain part of a page, clicks on a part of a page, or moves to a different page. There is an event handler for each of these actions and more, as shown in Table 7.1.

Event handlers can be used to create alerts that pop up when certain things happen on the page. For instance, you may have a welcome message that appears when the page loads (Figure 7.15).

This is done by inserting an event handler into the web page's main <BODY> tag like this:

```
<BODY onload="alert('Welcome to the JavaScript test page!')">
```

TABLE 7.1   Event Handlers

Event Handler	When Triggered	Where Used
onload	page loads	<BODY>, <FRAMESET>, or <IMG> tags
onunload	user exits page	<BODY> or <FRAMESET>
onmouseover	mouse moves over hyperlink	hyperlinks
onclick	user clicks on a button or hyperlink	hyperlinks, form buttons, radio buttons, check boxes
onfocus	mouse moves to a form field	select fields, comment fields, text boxes
onchange	form field is changed	select fields, comment fields, text boxes
onblur	mouse moves away from form field	select fields, comment fields, text boxes
onselect	mouse selects text in a form field	comment fields, text boxes
onsubmit	user clicks Submit button	<FORM> tag
onerror	image fails to load	<IMG> tag
onabort	image loading aborts	<IMG> tag

Figure 7.15   Typical JavaScript alert.

If you have been working with computers for any time at all, you're quite familiar with the confirm dialog, which looks like Figure 7.16.

In a confirm dialog, the user has an option to continue (OK) or quit (Cancel). The confirm dialog just shown may be part of a hyperlink that will take you to a different page. For instance:

```
<A HREF="http://www.microsoft.com/" onclick="confirm('Warning: You are
leaving the test page. Do you want to continue?')">
```

The things you do with JavaScript can get quite intricate. For instance, you can create conditional statements (if-else-then) that work in different ways, depending on user actions or inputs. You can also do various types of looping operations that repeat themselves. The *while* statement lets you test a condition to see if it is true while a loop is being repeated.

One of the most valuable tasks you can perform with JavaScript is to check for errors in user entries on a web form. For instance, the following JavaScript code checks to make sure the user entered either M or F in the Gender field on a web form:

```
<SCRIPT LANGUAGE=JAVASCRIPT>
<!--
 function checkGender() {
  var Gender = document.forms[0].elements[2].value
  if (Gender == 'M')
  {}
  else {if (Gender == 'F')
```

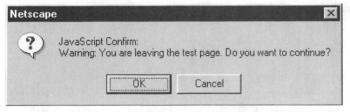

Figure 7.16   Typical JavaScript confirm dialog box.

```
        {}
        else {alert("Gender must be M (Male) or F (Female).")}
    }    }
//-->
</SCRIPT>
```

The function defined above is called by adding a special event handler to the appropriate <INPUT> tag on the web form. For instance:

```
Gender (M or F) <INPUT NAME="gender" SIZE=2 onchange="checkGender()">
```

When this rule is violated, the JavaScript will pop up the alert shown in Figure 7.17.

You can also use "operators" to compare values, add them together, and so forth. These are quite flexible, as long as you use the correct syntax. For instance, a simpler way to phrase the gender comparison in the last example would have been:

```
if ((Gender != 'M') || (Gender != 'F')) {
alert("Gender must be M (Male) or F (Female).")}
```

With JavaScript, it is possible to "look up" and dynamically control the value of any property on a web page, including link colors, background colors, border sizes, image dimensions, image source, document title, form fields and buttons, and dozens of others. For instance, the following HTML code would produce a series of buttons labeled Blue, Green, and Red that would respectively change the body background color to blue, green and red when clicked.

```
<FORM>
<INPUT TYPE="button" Value="Blue"  onclick="document.bgColor = 'blue'">
<INPUT TYPE="button" Value="Green" onclick="document.bgColor = 'green'">
<INPUT TYPE="button" Value="Red"   onclick="document.bgColor = 'red'">
</FORM>
```

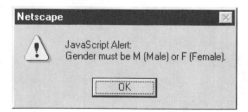

Figure 7.17   Example alert.

You can also use methods to produce a specific action related to any component of a web page. For instance:

```
window.close            /* Closes the current window
window.history.back     /* Moves back one page in the history
document.forms[1].submit /* Clicks the Submit button on second form
```

Typically, if there is a problem with your JavaScript code, you will see an error message like Figure 7.18.

The error message is an opportunity to correct your mistakes. Typically the message indicates what went wrong, although the exact cause may not be totally obvious. The previous message was generated because there was a carriage return in the middle of the alert message. If you've used the World Wide Web for any length of time, there's a good chance you've seen dozens of messages like this already. JavaScript is a finicky beast, and should be thoroughly tested in all the browsers you think your script will encounter.

What's All the Fuss about Java?

Web forms and CGI worked fine for a year or so after the first Mosaic browser was released. But about the time Netscape hit the market, a company called Sun Microsystems was working on a revolutionary new programming language called *Java.* First developed as a way to program household appliances (and originally code-named *Oak*), the Java language was quickly retooled as a way people could reprogram the web browser to handle applications far beyond simple online document publishing.

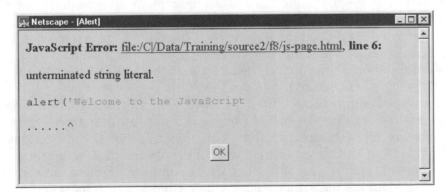

Figure 7.18   Typical JavaScript error message.

Where to Learn More about JavaScript

If you want to use JavaScript extensively, you should acquire one of the many reference books on the subject. In particular, check out:

The *JavaScript Sourcebook* by Gordon McComb. www.wiley .com/compbooks/

The *JavaScript Cookbook* by Yoseph Cohen. www.wiley.com/ compbooks/

The *Official Netscape JavaScript Book* (Netscape Press). www .netscapepress.com/support/javascript/

You can also find more information at the following World Wide Web locations:

JavaScript Guide. home.netscape.com/eng/mozilla/3.0/handbook/ javascript

JavaScript Help Manual. www.jchelp.com/javahelp/javahelp .htm

JavaScript FAQ. www.freqgrafx.com/411/jsfaq.html

JavaScript Resource Center. jrc.livesoftware.com/

Small Java programs called *applets* can be inserted into a web page, in much the same way that you might insert a picture. For instance, when you display a web page with an embedded image, the IMG tag retrieves the image from the server and displays it at a certain spot in the text. With Java, however, there may be an APPLET tag embedded in the page that retrieves a small bit of executable Java code stored on the web server. When this code is retrieved, it runs automatically as soon as it hits the browser. Any display produced by the code displays right there in the text, at the location of the APPLET tag (Figure 7.19).

But Java can also be used to replace the entire contents of the web-browser window with a complete user interface that looks and works like a dialog box, a set of controls, or even (in an odd reincarnation) a traditional web form. Java programming has advanced to the point that traditional applications like Corel's WordPerfect Office Suite are now being offered in Java format.

Think about that for a second. Normally, a computer application resides on the hard drive of the individual user. With WordPerfect, for instance, you go to the store and buy a copy of the program. Then you take it back to your com-

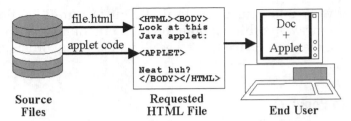

Figure 7.19 Diagram of Java applet retrieval.

puter, install it, and run it. If your favorite computer program becomes a Java application, that means it can be installed on a remote web server and accessed by your local machine at *just the moment you need it.* And not just you, but anyone who has access to that web server. What's more, it works a lot like a web page: If someone puts a new version of the Java program on the server tomorrow, then the next time you use it you will be using the new version.

The software, in effect, is being used without even being installed. It takes up no long-term space on your hard drive because it is used only as needed. And the program itself, even though it plays back locally, is totally network delivered.

The most incredible aspect of Java is the way it has threatened to turn the entire established order of the computer world on its ear. Java was initially hailed by analysts as the "magic bullet" that might someday kill off industry giants like Microsoft Corporation. Soon after those early forecasts, Sun Microsystems and its business partners tried to make the Microsoft death wish come true by launching their own set of Java initiatives. Their goal? To replace the "fat client"—running a traditionally massive operating system like Microsoft Windows—with a "thin client" running nothing but a slim Java-based kernel (JavaOS).

The ultimate thin client proposed by Sun, Oracle, and others was a machine known as a *Network Computer* or *NC*—an odd device running almost entirely on Java and Java applications, with no hard drives, no CD-ROM, and no other peripheral devices. The first NC, with its locked case and total lack of peripherals, looked eerily like the old mainframe dumb terminals we all cut our teeth on so many years ago. Not to be outdone, Microsoft announced it's own NetPC, which is like an NC that also happens to run Microsoft Windows—and of course all the other Microsoft software offerings, most of which are not Java-based.

Oddly, even though the intranet brought the idea of empowerment and distribution of labor to the forefront in information technology, the NC threatens to shove all those ideas once again into the back seat. It is possible that someday you may walk into your office to find your feature-filled desktop computer snatched away and thrown onto the junk pile of history, to be replaced by a soundless, diskless device that takes all its marching orders from central command.

Why Is Java So Popular?

Amazingly, the people who should be most strongly opposed to this turn of events are also the biggest Java boosters. Over the past few years, the Java wars waged by many of the leading Silicon Valley firms has become an anti-Microsoft crusade in much the same way that the Apple Macintosh was.

Microsoft has reacted to all this flak rather coolly, falling back on its traditional "embrace and extend" policy that served it so well in past software battles. Microsoft has embraced Java totally—figuring it's quite alright as long as people don't get the idea that Java should replace the traditional Windows operating system anytime soon. Somewhat to the chagrin of its detractors, Microsoft's Java support and Java development tools are now among the best in the world.

With all the current noise about Java, the phenomenon and world-improving crusade, it's rather sobering to take a good unbiased look at the source of all this hullabaloo: the programming language itself. One of the reasons—possibly the main reason—Java is so popular is its promise to greatly speed up the process of developing and delivering computer applications to end users.

This is possible because Java differs significantly from other programming languages that must be compiled individually on different machines. If you write a program in C language, it must be compiled separately for UNIX, Mac, or PC. You cannot run the UNIX version on a PC or the Mac version on a UNIX machine. Java, on the other hand, is an "interpreted" language that is read and interpreted by the browser as it comes across the network. The language is compiled in a generic *bytecode* format by the Java programmer (Figure 7.20). But once it reaches the web browser it is decoded and—in some cases—may even be compiled on the fly into native machine language using a *Just-In Time* compiler (JIT) that sits on the user's local machine.

Since all the major web browsers on all platforms can read and interpret the same Java bytecode, then theoretically it is possible to "write once, run anywhere" in the words of its creators. In other words, you only have to compile Java once to run it on any platform.

In practice, however, this is not always the case. To get more power and functionality out of their programs, some Java developers include platform-

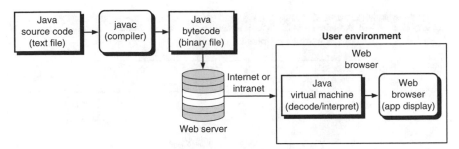

Figure 7.20 Steps in Java creation and use.

specific features—especially those related to Windows platforms. For this reason, Sun and its business partners launched a "100% Pure Java" initiative in 1997, a campaign that quickly turned into an anti-Microsoft roadshow.

Interestingly, despite its great popularity with World Wide Web developers, Java gaining acceptance more slowly on the corporate intranet than on the Web. A 1997 survey done by *Computerworld* showed many IS managers taking a wait-and-see approach, with only 20 percent of those surveyed involved in Java development. Certainly this imbalance will be corrected over time, as Java becomes more of a proven development model.

How to Do Java

Naturally, since Java is a programming language as detailed as C, there is no way you're going to be able to create Java programs unless you are a programmer or you hire someone who has Java experience. To some extent, you may be able to acquire Java applets that do just what you need done, and embed them in your web documents. When that happens, all you have to know is how to use the APPLET tag to embed an applet in your document.

The markup below is an example from the Java site (java.sun.com) that inserts a spreadsheet into a web page. Notice that the APPLET tag works like the IMG tag, with a width and height specified for the applet area. PARAM tags define initial settings for the applet. The result of the applet is shown in Figure 7.21.

```
<APPLET CODE="SpreadSheet.class" WIDTH=320 HEIGHT=120>
<PARAM NAME=rows VALUE="4">
<PARAM NAME=c3 VALUE="fC1+C2">
<PARAM NAME=c2 VALUE="fA2*B2">
<PARAM NAME=c1 VALUE="fA1*B2">
<PARAM NAMEitle VALUE="Example">
```

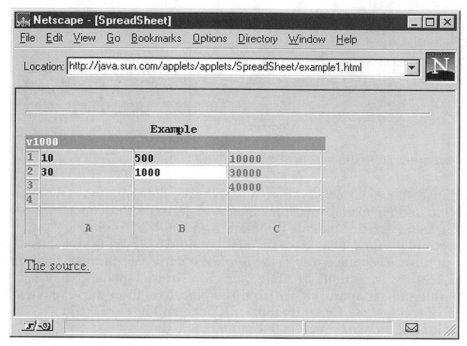

Figure 7.21   Result of Java applet (spreadsheet).

```
<PARAM NAME=b2 VALUE="v1000">
<PARAM NAME=b1 VALUE="v500">
<PARAM NAME=cols VALUE="3">
<PARAM NAME=a2 VALUE="v30">
<PARAM NAME=a1 VALUE="v10">
</APPLET>
```

Notice that the PARAM tags set up the initial operating conditions for the applet, and these will vary widely from applet to applet. In this case, the values define the number of columns and rows and the initial contents of each cell in the Java spreadsheet.

If you want to program in Java, you will need to download and install a *Java Development Kit* (JDK), which you can obtain from Sun Microsystems free of charge (see sidebar titled "Java Sites"). You can code the Java program using any text editor, but many visual development tools are also available. Java is an object-oriented programming language in which each object inherits its properties from various similar classes. The following sample shows a simple applet that sets up some text for display inside the web browser:

```
import java.awt.Font;
import java.awt.Graphics;
import java.awt.Color;

public class hello extends java.applet.Applet {
   public void paint(Graphics g) {

/*

   get parameters
*/

   String txt      = getParameter ("txt");
   int size        = Integer.parseInt( getParameter("size") );
   String ufont    = getParameter("ufont");

/*

   define a font
*/

   Font f = new Font(ufont, Font.PLAIN, size);

/*

   set background and foreground colors.
*/

   setBackground(Color.lightGray);
   setForeground(Color.blue);
   g.setFont(f);
   g.drawString( txt, 10, 25);
      }
}
```

The first two lines import the Java classes needed to choose a font and paint a message to the screen. The IMPORT command in Java serves a similar function to the *include* statement in C or FORTRAN. Import allows you to make use of Java library functions that are built into the Java Virtual Machine which is bundled with the web browser.

Note that the class name (*hello*) defined on the fourth line must match the class name referenced by the APPLET tag on the web page. The rest of the fourth line is standard Java syntax for defining an applet. Everything after the fourth line defines the behavior of the applet.

The preceding applet would be saved as a plain text file called *hello.java* and then run through the Java compiler to produce a bytecode file called *hello.class.* It is this bytecode file that is stored on the server and referenced by the web page. Any time the web page is opened, the Java applet will be retrieved from the web server and begin running inside the page.

That's all for now about Java. For more details, pick up one of the many books on Java programming, or see the "Java Sites" sidebar.

The ABCs of ActiveX

Any discussion of web application development should include a mention of ActiveX. And so here it is. ActiveX is an updated version of Microsoft's original *Object Linking and Embedding* (OLE) technology, which allowed components of one program to be embedded in another. With OLE, for example, you might have part of a Microsoft Excel spreadsheet imbedded inside a Microsoft Word document, so that the document would be updated each time the spreadsheet changed.

In late 1995, due to the explosive popularity of the Internet and World Wide Web, Microsoft began inventing ways that the OLE concept could be used within web pages. The result became known as *ActiveX*. Compare this to two other technologies used for web applications: plug-ins and Java. Netscape allows other companies to create plug-ins for the web browser, such as Acrobat by Adobe. ActiveX is similar to this concept but works in Internet Explorer instead (although there is a plug-in available that allows ActiveX controls to run in the Netscape browser). A Java program or *applet* is somewhat like a plug-in because it is an object embedded inside a web page. And so is ActiveX.

ActiveX provides web developers with a number of key benefits, which has made it immensely popular for developing web applications on the Windows platform:

Java Sites

The Java Development Kit is available for free at the Javasoft web site. Gamelan provides additional Java information, tools, and example applets. Helpful websites include:

Javasoft Home Page.   www.javasoft.com

Java Development Kit.   www.javasoft.com/products/jdk/1.1/index .html

Gamelan Java resources.   www.gamelan.com

Self-contained program. An ActiveX module is a self-contained binary executable program, much like any other. It can start and stop itself on its own.

Accessibility/ease of use. ActiveX modules can interface with other programs, including exchanging input and output with other programs, without you having to recode (or know the code of) the other programs.

Internet/intranet enabled. ActiveX was designed for the Internet and intranet, which are fast becoming the most popular ways to deliver information and applications to end users. ActiveX controls can be embedded directly inside web pages "by reference" and can send output to other applications across a network.

Rapid development and deployment. There are now many off-the-shelf ActiveX applications you can borrow or license to create the web applications you need. New ActiveX applications can be developed rapidly.

Upgradable/retroactive. An ActiveX module may contain legacy components that can be used with different versions of the same program.

Like its predecessor OLE, ActiveX is based on the idea of having small reusable modules (objects) called *ActiveX controls.* These small, self-contained controls can be linked and shared "by reference" across the Internet or an intranet, in the same way that you can reference images or other objects located on a network. To work properly, ActiveX controls must be installed in an ActiveX host, which is usually Microsoft Internet Explorer (IE). The IE program has several ActiveX controls already installed with it that give its web pages the ability to display special features, such as scrolling marquees.

If a control is not preinstalled with IE, the web page using the control should have enough information embedded in it to automatically locate the appropriate control on the network. This is what the HTML coding looks like for an ActiveX control in a web page:

```
<OBJECT ID="Menu1" WIDTH=0 HEIGHT=0
CLASSID="CLSID:B1234C56-D78E-90FG-H12J-345678900000"
CODEBASE="#version=1,2,3,4">
<PARAM NAME="_Version" VALUE="54321">
<PARAM NAME="_ExtentX" VALUE="1234">
<PARAM NAME="_ExtentY" VALUE="9876">
<PARAM NAME="_StockProps" VALUE="0">
</OBJECT>
```

Notice the beginning and ending <OBJECT> tags define the location and size of the control, its ID (reference name), and its CLASSID (unique ID number), along with any parameters used to control the behavior or appearance of the control. Instead of coding all this by hand, you can use Microsoft's ActivoX Control Pad, which lets you specify the size, location, and parameters for a control without tedious manual coding. ActiveX controls can be manipulated by scripting languages such as Microsoft's VBScript and JScript (which is similar to JavaScript).

Database Solutions for the Intranet

One of the most useful aspects of the intranet is the way it allows you to leverage existing content stored in legacy databases—all the places where we stored data before the web came along. Using various mechanisms, including HTML, CGI, *Open Database Connectivity* (ODBC), or *Java Database Connectivity* (JDBC), you can use the web browser to access practically any kind of database, including Oracle, Sybase, Microsoft Access, SQL Server, dBase, Lotus Notes, and many others.

Not surprisingly, the field of web-enabled database access methods has exploded over the past 2 years. In this section, I will take you on a tour of some of the most obvious database tools and access methods.

Microsoft Access

As part of the regular Microsoft Office suite of office automation products, Access is one of the more widely used database tools—as well as being one of the easiest to use. The most recent versions of Access have the additional virtue of being web enabled.

Where to Find ActiveX

Look at these resources for information on ActiveX and for access to some prebuilt ActiveX controls.

    ActiveX Home Page at Microsoft. www.microsoft.com/activeplatform/default.asp

    CNET ActiveX Site. www.activex.com

Even before intranets, Access allowed users to create relational databases containing data tables, queries, forms, and reports. For instance, you could create a database for your company that contains information on suppliers, customers, employees, products, and sales. Data could be entered using a form like the one in Figure 7.22. Unlike web forms, however, data entered into Access traditionally was available only to other users of Access—unless you printed the data as a paper report.

Recent versions of Access have added web-enabled features that let you publish the contents of Access databases in various ways. For instance, selecting the Save As HTML feature on the File menu in Access brings up the web publishing wizard (Figure 7.23), which lets you create web pages from table, query, and form datasheets, and from Access forms and reports. The web page can be a static page that consists of a straight HTML file with no dynamic querying. Or it can be a dynamic page that queries the database each time the user views the page. In addition to publishing the database results as web pages, you can create a home page that ties together all the data-driven pages.

If you select static pages as the output type, the wizard creates a file containing the entire contents of the report, query, table, or other document, typically formatted as a table. If you select dynamic output, the wizard will create HTX and IDC

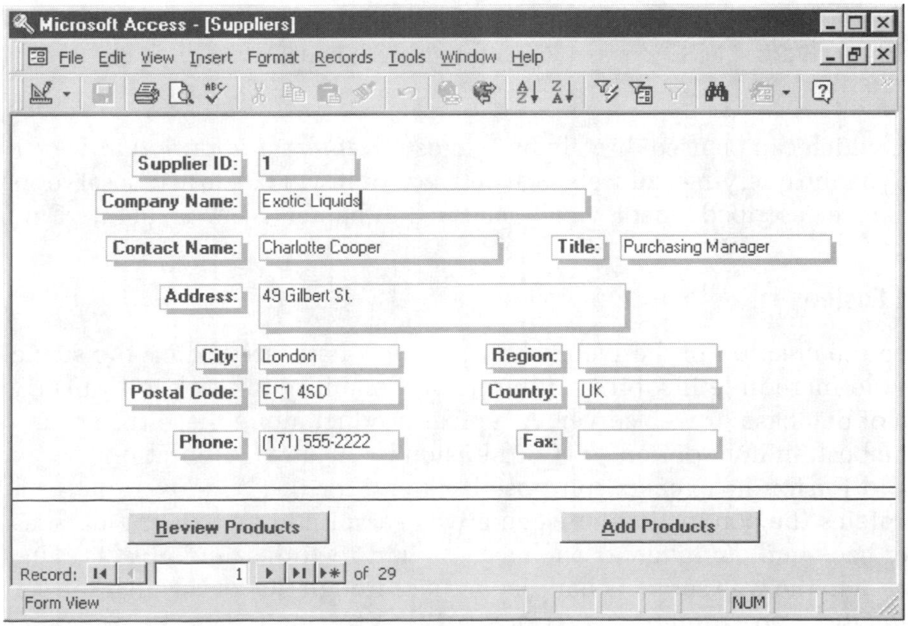

Figure 7.22 Sample data entry form in Access.

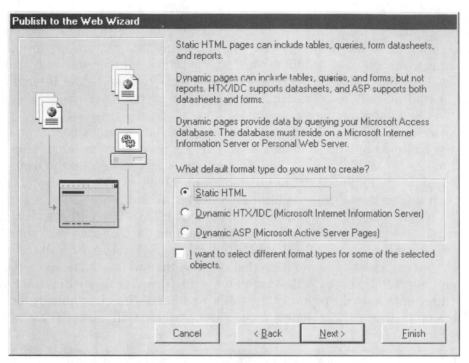

Figure 7.23   MS Access web-publishing wizard.

files, which can be used directly by Microsoft's *Internet Information Server* (IIS) for dynamic querying and web page delivery, or it will create active server pages, which are described in more detail later in the chapter (see "Visual InterDev").

Cold Fusion

Since the creation of the Web, many products have arrived on the scene that provide incredible flexibility in terms of the ability to work with nearly any type of database or web server. A typical product along these lines—and one of the best, in my opinion—is Cold Fusion by Allaire Corporation.

Cold Fusion is a general-purpose back end for the Windows platform that completes the connection between a web server and an existing database, or other back-end components such as e-mail, directories, and objects. The connection to the web server is handled either through CGI or through the server's *application programming interface* (API). You don't have to program anything, however. During installation, Cold Fusion automatically detects the type of server you are using and connects to it in the most appropriate manner. Naturally, this installation occurs on the server machine itself.

Interfacing with the database is handled through Open Database Connectivity (ODBC) and Dynamic SQL, though again the connection method can be partially or totally transparent to the developer. Cold Fusion recognizes the database type; it also installs and uses the appropriate drivers.

The power of tools like Cold Fusion is that they let you do sophisticated database access and query through a markup language like HTML. The web page containing Cold Fusion markup looks a lot like regular markup language. For instance:

```
<!--- Database Query --->
<CFQUERY NAME="CourseList" DATASOURCE="CF 3.0 Examples">
SELECT * FROM Courses
</CFQUERY>
<HTML>
<HEAD>
<TITLE>Department List</TITLE>
</HEAD>
<BODY>
<H2>Course List</H2>
<HR>
<!--- Output of database Query --->
<CFOUTPUT QUERY="CourseList">
(#Number#)</B> #Description#<BR>
</CFOUTPUT>
</BODY>
</HTML>
```

This standard Cold Fusion example shows a regular HTML file (notice beginning and ending <HTML> tags) with two specialized Cold Fusion tags included. The first tag <CFQUERY> defines a standard SQL query against a database called "CF 3.0 Examples." Inside the web page, the <CFOUTPUT> tag provides an output template for the results of the query, which in this case will pull a list of training courses from the database and list the course number and course description for each course. These tags are ignored by the browser but are processed by the Cold Fusion application.

When a user accesses a web page like this one, a special Cold Fusion server does the database lookup, formats the output as a web page, and returns the page to the web server for shipping back to the user. This is just a simple example. But it gives you an idea how easy it is to set up a database application using a tool like this. Like most other web tools, however, recent versions of Cold Fusion have gotten quite feature-filled, and thus quite deep. So, while it is fairly easy to link web pages to database applications using a tool like this, it is also possible to build a minor specialty—if not a career—around the use of these types of tools.

LiveWire

LiveWire is Netscape's solution to the database connectivity puzzle, but it goes a bit beyond that description to provide some other features that many database development tools do not have. Most prominent among these is its built-in Site Manager tool, which includes templates you can use to develop new sites. LiveWire also provides a visual management environment that lets you move pages around through a simple drag-and-drop process (Figure 7.24).

There is also a JavaScript Compiler that compiles web pages containing JavaScript into compressed, platform-independent bytecode, in the same way that Java applications are compiled into bytecode. Web pages compiled this way can be served from a Netscape server and interpreted by Netscape

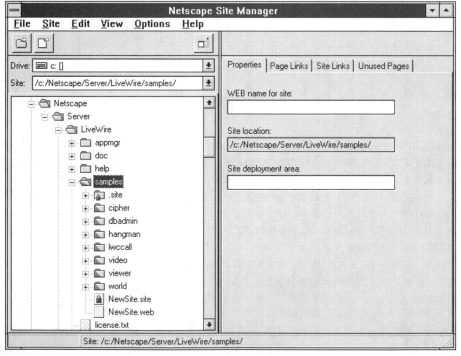

Figure 7.24   LiveWire site manager window.

browsers. LiveWire also allows application developers to embed server-side JavaScript into web pages. Unlike the client-side JavaScript discussed earlier, which operates only within the local browser, server-side JavaScript allows a web page to retrieve application variables and database variables from the server side as part of a LiveWire application. Compiled applications can be managed using the LiveWire Application Manager shown in Figure 7.25.

A key feature of LiveWire is its built-in database connectivity features, which allow direct SQL connection to Oracle, Sybase, and Informix databases. It also supports ODBC connections to many others. Conveniently, LiveWire comes bundled with a single-developer copy of the Informix Workgroup Server, which is a simplified version of the Informix Dynamic Server.

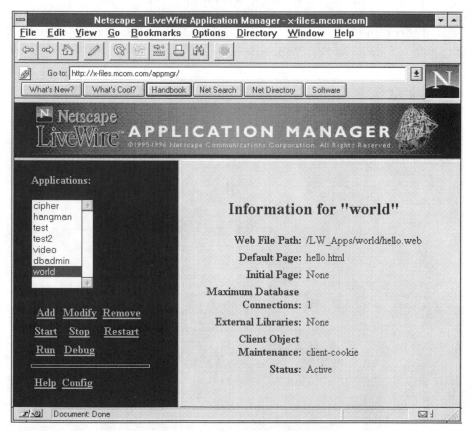

Figure 7.25   The LiveWire Application Manager.

Visual InterDev

Microsoft's Visual InterDev (VI) is that company's answer to the need for more interactive web applications and for more integrated sets of development tools. A nice feature is its ability to interoperate with FrontPage so that a work group with different levels of skill sets can cooperate to build a fully functional interactive site. To this end it includes a copy of FrontPage Editor and a site-management tool similar to what is found in FrontPage Explorer.

The visual development tool allows you to open a "live view" of an existing web site and modify the structure of the site, including adding, deleting, editing, moving, or renaming files and folders (Figure 7.26). Each element of the web site, including all graphic files, controls, and applets, are instantly retrievable and editable. Check-in, check-out features allow multiple developers to work on the same site together without conflict.

But the true power of VI lies in the fact that it is a visual integrated development environment (IDE) that churns out a Microsoft specialty called *active server pages.* A recent feature of Microsoft Internet Information Server (since

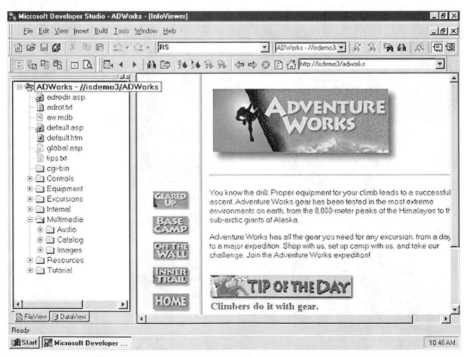

Figure 7.26   Microsoft Visual InterDev.

version 3.0), active server pages are a souped-up version of the standard web page with live database access, state management, scripting, and reusable components built-in. In this example, provided by Microsoft, a simple page with scripting components, such as:

```
<HTML>

<P>
<% FOR i=3 TO 7 %>
<FONT SIZE=<%=i%>
Hello World!<BR>
</FONT>
<% Next %>
</HTML>
```

gets translated into the following HTML as it leaves the server:

```
<HTML>
<BODY>
<P>

<FONT SIZE="3">
Hello World!<br>
</FONT>

<FONT SIZE="4">
Hello World!<br>
</FONT>

<FONT SIZE="5">
Hello World!<br>
</FONT>

<FONT SIZE="6">
Hello World!<br>
</FONT>

<FONT SIZE="7">
Hello World!<br>
</FONT>

</P>
</BODY>
</HTML>
```

which looks like the web page shown in Figure 7.27.

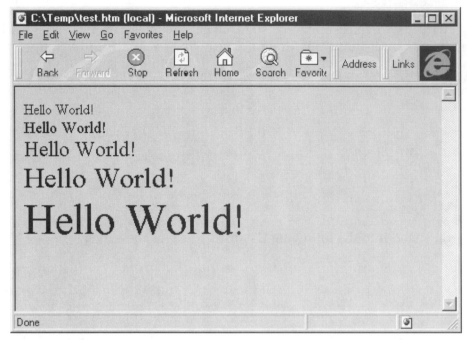

Figure 7.27   Web page resulting from active server page.

Visual InterDev provides easy access to data stored in ODBC-compliant databases such as Oracle, Informix, SQL Server, DB2. Access, and Visual Fox-Pro. VI also boasts interoperability with ActiveX, COM, and Java. An especially valuable feature allows you to preview web pages both in Internet Explorer and Netscape Navigator, to make sure the end result will work in all environments. Microsoft also has something called *Active Data Objects* (ADO), which use ActiveX scripting to establish connections between databases and which provide a sophisticated set of properties for setting cursor options, scrolling, transaction support, error handling, and much more.

A special Data View feature (Figure 7.28) provides a live view of each database being connected to a web site, including the ability to see detailed information on table definitions, field types, key structures, and stored procedures. You can then automatically build queries using VI's built-in Query Designer. A similar Database Designer allows you to set up the structure of Microsoft SQL Server databases. Finally, if that isn't enough, database wizards are available to lead you through the process of creating customized forms. The wizard automatically generates the correct HTML and ActiveX server-side scripts needed to connect the form to the database.

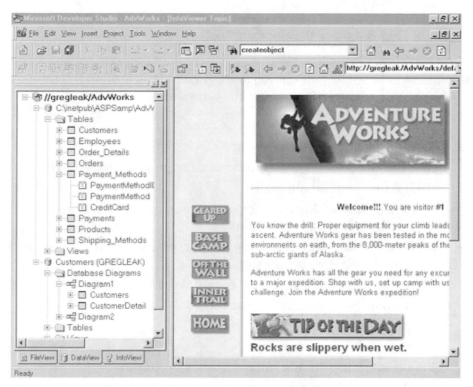

Figure 7.28   The Data View in Visual InterDev.

When you take into consideration the fact that this feature-packed development tool is bundled with FrontPage, Visual InterDev provides just about everything you need to create rich interactive web sites. That includes everything from building simple static Web pages to the most advanced highly scalable data-driven applications imaginable.

Creating Search Operations at Your Site

In my mind, the perfect home page is one that has a Search Field prominently displayed. Instead of clicking through the site—on the odd chance you might find something interesting—you can type in words to describe what you're looking for, then hit the Search button to find what you need. Certainly, by now, you've used the great search engines on the World Wide Web, like Excite (www.excite.com/), Infoseek (www.infoseek.com/), and others. What you may

---

Where to Find Database Development Tools

In this section, I provide several examples of developer tools you can use to build sophisticated data-driven sites. A good look around the Internet, however, will turn up many more. Here are some pertinent URLs:

Active Software.   www.activesw.com/

Cold Fusion.   www.allaire.com/

DB2 Connection.   www.software.ibm.com/data/db2/www/dbWeb

HAHTsite.   www.haht.com/

LiveWire Data Sheet.   home.netscape.com/comprod/products/ tools/livewire_datasheet.html

LiveWire Documentation.   developer.netscape.com/library/docu- mentation/livewire/index.html

Net.Data.   www.software.ibm.com/data/net.data/

NetDynamics.   www.w3spider.com/

Sapphire Web.   www.bluestone.com

Tango.   www.everyware.com/

Visual InterDev.   www.microsoft.com/vinterdev/

WebBase.   www.webbase.com/

WebObjects.   www.next.com/

---

not realize is that many of these same search engines are available for installation on your intranet.

Despite the fact that search engines are some of the most expensive software you may purchase for your intranet, they are also the most valuable. Nothing less than the productivity of your entire workforce is at stake. At the very least you will want to have a search engine for your departmental web site (which you can do, by the way, using the Search component in FrontPage, shown in Figure 7.29). But ideally, you will want a search engine for the entire intranet.

Search tools are a lot like CGI applications, in the sense that they take the input from a web form and process it against a back-end application. The main difference is that the web form is often represented by a single Search field and a Search button that sends the user's desired search keyword to the back-end application for processing. For example, the following HTML code

Database Vendor Solutions

Naturally, no one should be better at providing connectivity to databases than the database vendors themselves. Consequently, each of the major vendors has come up with its own solution over the past two years. Typically, this is in the form of a database server that either handles web requests directly or sits on the back end between the web server and the proprietary database. These work well if you are already using the vendor's database and need a web interface for it. The vendor solutions can be found on the Internet at the following Web locations:

Informix OnLine Servers and Universal Web Connect. www
.informix.com/informix/products/new_plo/plo1.htm

Lotus Domino Server. www.lotus.com/domino/

Oracle Web Application Server. www.oracle.com/st/products/
was/

Sybase Internet Products. www.sybase.com/products/internet/

Java Connectivity

It had to happen. The Open Database Connectivity model (ODBC), which is used by many applications to transparently connect to databases, found itself with a new Java counterpart after release 1.1 of the Java Development Kit. JDBC is touted as the primary API for database access in Java and allows Java classes to control database connections, SQL commands, result sets, and metadata. Like ODBC, the JDBC model uses vendor-supplied drivers to operate different databases. The drivers may be written in Java and downloaded as part of an applet. A special "bridge driver" feature also translates JDBC method calls into ODBC function calls, so that Java applets can work with existing ODBC drivers. For more details on this technology, see the JDBC page on the Web at java.sun.com/products/jdbc/.

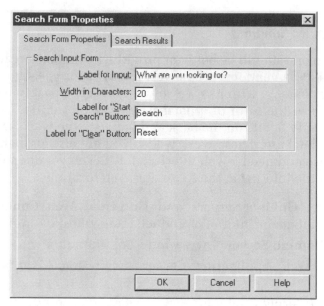

Figure 7.29   Search component in FrontPage.

is used for a Search field on a FrontPage web and produces the display shown in Figure 7.30.

```
<form action="_vti_bin/shtml.exe/search.htm" method="POST">
<input type="hidden" name="VTI-GROUP" value="0">
<p>
<b>What are you looking for?</b> <input type="text" name="search" size="20"
value="web">
<p>
<input type="submit" value="Start Search">
<input type="reset" value="Clear">
</form>
```

Most high-powered search tools use an indexing method in which the content files are searched using a special routine, and then an index file is built.

Figure 7.30   Form result from HTML codes.

The index file is never seen by the user; it only exists for use by the search engine. When the search is conducted, it is done not on the content files, but on the index file. At first this might seem to be an inefficient way to do things, but actually it is more efficient and much faster to search a tightly formatted index than it is to search a loose collection of documents. In fact, the tighter the index format, the faster the search. This is no small consideration, since most users are not going to like it if they have to wait more than a few seconds for the results of their search.

Search indexes are created based on work done by a web crawler or robot that searches the web, following each link to its logical end point and capturing information about all the sites it encounters along the way. Different tools index the resulting information in different ways, but these are the most common:

Keyword indexing lists the most common terms in the documents. Depending on the search tool, this may be limited to headers, titles, or URLs. Or the search engine may allow a "full text" search against most of the key words in each document.

Concept indexing uses artificial intelligence and fuzzy logic to find indexed material related to the user's search keyword.

An important feature of some search tools is the use of Boolean operators such as And, Or, and Not in searches. Depending on the capabilities of the engine, it may be possible to construct quite powerful queries that can pinpoint data precisely. Another important feature is the ability to search across multiple servers and multiple platforms, and to respect the security mechanisms within specific server domains or protected web sites.

You can test drive some of the best commercial search engines on the World Wide Web at places like Infoseek, AltaVista, and others. After typing in a keyword, you get dozens of matching hits in a flash. For a global, corporatewide intranet, you may need something that powerful. If you are developing a local site for an intranet, however, you may be able to get by with something as convenient as the Search component of FrontPage. Also check for search features bundled with your current web server software, or some of the lower-end or freeware solutions listed in the accompanying sidebar.

The Groupware Gospel

Intranets are nothing if not a way for people to share information across large organizations. If you want to really foster sharing—according to many—what you need is something called *groupware*.

Searching for Search Engines

First, the freeware and shareware search engines that are available at many sites on the World Wide Web.

    Excite for Web Servers. www.excite.com/navigate/

    Glimpse for UNIX. glimpse.cs.arizona.edu:1994/

    Harvest for UNIX. harvest.cs.colorado.edu/

    Web Search for Windows. wgg.com/wgg/best/search.htm

Many companies are now going for the added features and flexibility of commercial search engines like Verity and AltaVista. Here's where to find them on the Web:

    AltaVista. altavista.software.digital.com/search/index.htm

    Infoseek. software.infoseek.com/

    InMagic. www.inmagic.com/

    Lycos Spider. www.lycos.com/software/software-intranet.html

    NetResults. www.netresults-search.com/

    Verity. www.verity.com/

Groupware is a nebulous term that has come to encompass everything from e-mail applications to databases. In Chapter 2, I pointed to groupware as the culmination of many trends in the business world over the past decade, particularly the trend toward empowering teams and work groups to take responsibility for business processes. For this reason, the groupware tag could probably be applied to any software that helps work groups communicate better, including e-mail, online forms, online databases, and common document repositories.

Any web system, whether on the Internet or on intranets, could be seen as groupware under that definition. And when web technology first appeared, it was seen that way. For a while, after the Web became explosively popular and the first intranets were created, technology writers regularly hailed this as the magic bullet that would kill off the most popular groupware applications. Writers in *InfoWorld* intoned, "Eight months ago, there were 10 things that [Lotus] Notes could do that the Web couldn't do, now that is down to two." Even IBM, which had purchased Lotus just 3 months earlier, hosted its own networking forum in late October 1995 in which one panelist asked out loud: "Is the Web going to be the death of Lotus Notes?"

Several years later, Lotus Notes is still alive and apparently thriving. What happened?

Many people see Lotus Notes as the quintessential groupware application. Notes combines a document database, a messaging system, and configuration tools that let users create their own custom business applications. Like intranets, it supports the custom design of fill-out forms that can be used across the network to capture user input to a database.

Probably the neatest trick that Notes performs, however—and apparently the hardest feature for others to duplicate—is a feat called *replication*. This means that users should be able to work on multiple copies of the same document or database, and have all of their changes automatically reconciled across the network. Thus, for instance, you might take a copy of a group-authored document on a business trip with you, work on it on the airplane, then bring it back to the network and your changes would automatically be reconciled in all other copies of the document in the network.

For a while, the main beef about Lotus Notes was its price. In early 1996, one U.S. company with 1,000 employees found it could create an intranet system to share information companywide for a total cost of about $50,000, while a similar system using Lotus Notes would have cost $500,000. If there is anything that intranets have done, it has been to bring down the price of Lotus Notes. The client version of the software has dropped in price precipitately, and Lotus's Domino server technology makes it possible to open Lotus Notes databases for viewing by wider audiences through the inexpensive and now common desktop web browser.

Certainly, web technology has trimmed the market share that Lotus would have had otherwise, and it has helped raise a new generation of competitors, too. But it has also helped awaken many companies to the necessity for a groupware approach, and many of those in turn have adopted Lotus Notes as—no less—a complete intranet solution. It is true that if you like the web because of its collaborative features, perhaps you need to start with a truly collaborative tool set instead of random web servers and browsers knit together in an ad hoc alliance.

Communicator as Groupware

Seen in this light, however, competitive groupware tools like Netscape Communicator become more attractive—a way to finally begin creating order in a previously chaotic intranet environment. With Communicator, you finally have bundled together—in one tightly integrated package based totally on open web standards—not only your standard web tools but also some of the major groupware applications that everyone drools for, including:

Messaging through its Netscape Messenger component

Group discussion through its Collabra component

Editing and publishing through its Composer component

Live conferencing, telephony, and whiteboarding through its Conference feature

Online calendar scheduling through its Calendar feature

Add to this a greatly upgraded browsing capability with support for dynamic HTML, cascading style sheets, and even push channels through the Netcaster component—not to mention the attractive price—and even Wild West–style intranet experimenters begin to see the value of taking their intranets toward a more integrated, collaborative model (Figure 7.31).

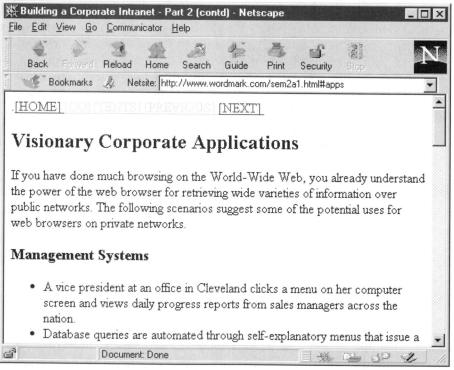

Figure 7.31 Netscape Communicator.

Finding Groupware for the Intranet

If you're interested in finding groupware solutions for your intranet, look no further than the following WWW sites:

InTandem.   www.intraactive.com/

Lotus Notes.   www.lotus.com/notes/

Microsoft Exchange Server.   www.microsoft.com/exchange/

Netopia Virtual Office.   www.farallon.com/product/netopia/

Netscape Communicator.   home.netscape.com/communicator

OpenText LiveLink.   www.opentext.com/livelink/

Radnet's WebShare.   www.radnet.com/webshare/main_webshare.html

ActionWorks Metro.   www.actiontech.com/

Novell GroupWise.   www.novell.com/groupwise/

Oracle InterOffice.   www.oracle.com/products/interoffice/html/

This is not to detract from Lotus or from the many other worthy competitors out there. If you admire the groupware approach to intranets, there are many products competing for your attention. Make sure that any solution you choose takes into account your budget, your corporate goals—and that it leverages as much as possible your existing toolset—and you can't really go wrong.

Where Do We Go from Here?

Now you've done it. You've finished an extensive survey of the three most important applications of web technology that exist. It began in Chapter 5 with online publishing, continued in Chapter 6 with multimedia, and concluded in this chapter with database access, online interactivity, search tools, groupware, and web applications. Do you still have a nagging question in the back of your mind? Are you still wondering what the heck the Internet might possibly have to do with all of this? You may have noticed (other than for the occasional sidebar on WWW sources) that I have largely ignored the role of the Internet in the development of an intranet. But the question still remains: What relation, if any, should there be between the internal intranet and the external Internet? And what other network integration issues are lurking in the background? The next chapter tells all.

PART THREE

THE INTRANET FOR MANAGERS AND PLANNERS

◆ This section deals with the advanced integration issues that must be dealt with at the enterprise level. For that reason it is more likely to appeal to strategic planners, IS, and management. Compare this to the previous section, which dealt with the publishing and data connectivity applications that occur at the business unit level. This section includes a discussion of internet connectivity and firewalls, talks about extranets, and pays considerable attention to integration issues as well as strategic planning of the "pilot intranet."

Chapter Eight at a Glance

Up to now we've talked about the Internet and intranet separately, and hinted about this additional concept called the *extranet*. What is the relationship between the various components of a company's Internet-style communication system—the Internet, intranet, and extranet? This chapter explores the subject by discussing:

- How and what to communicate over the extranet (Internet/ WWW)
- How companies connect to the Internet
- The difference in server models and design approach between the intranet and extranet
- How companies use proxy servers and firewalls to achieve integration between intranets and extranets
- Special ways you can communicate with external customers, dealers, and suppliers

The Internet and the Extranet

The Internet has become so pervasive in our thinking about web technology, it may be hard for some people to understand that it's not even a required component of any of the systems or applications discussed so far in this book. You don't need an Internet connection to make your intranet work. You don't need permission from the Internet authorities, or any kind of an "Internet license" (other than, possibly, a company domain name). There is no magic elixir that seeps through the wires from the Internet to fire up your internal network. The intranet works on its own simply because you have a TCP/IP network—the same way the World Wide Web works on the global TCP/IP network called the *Internet*. You could operate your intranet from now until the year 3,000 without *ever* being connected to the Internet.

Having said this, it's equally important to make a point that is almost the diametric opposite. To have the best intranet, you really *should* be connected to the Internet. Not for technical reasons, but because it makes good business sense. People on your network *should* be able to access sites on the Internet as easily as they access sites in the next room. And you should be looking at ways to start communicating routinely across the firewall with business partners, suppliers, customers, and dealers. Not just with e-mail (as many businesses already do), but with data, published documents, and multimedia.

Why make both points? Because business leaders fall into two categories: those who grudgingly embrace the Internet and those who flail against it. There's still a lot of paranoia about the security problems of the Internet— some of it justified. There's also a concern that if you give employees a direct connection to the World Wide Web, they'll abuse it. Some business managers have a well-developed fear of new technology, or an irrational fear of the unknown. Many just avoid the Internet because they don't understand it. For all these reasons and more, many companies can quote a dozen reasons they *shouldn't* be connected to the Internet. If your company fits that description, fine: You can still use an intranet quite productively within the closed environment of your private LAN or WAN.

Others realize the obvious. Increasingly now and in the near future, the Internet will be a vital and indispensable component of any long-term business communications strategy. No business exists in a vacuum; there are customers, dealers, and suppliers out there in the real world with whom you have to communicate. And that's what the Internet will increasingly help us do—communicate with the rest of the world outside our own private networks in ways we never imagined before.

The Paranoia, the Puffery . . . and the Possibilities

Actually, even if you don't have complete World Wide Web access at the desktop, there's a good chance your business *already uses* the Internet to communicate with external customers and suppliers. Most businesses have e-mail systems that connect to the public data networks either directly or indirectly, so that it's possible to transfer messages from J.P. Morgan to Federal Express, from Microsoft Corporation to Compaq Computer, or from Your Company Ltd. to My Company Unlimited. This e-mail traffic hops a ride on the Internet to make the journey between company A and company B in the world of private enterprise.

It does so—by the way—entirely without the kind of paranoia you see attached to every other use of the Internet, even though most of that traffic flows unsecured and unencrypted through wide-open public channels. Chances are, your confidential message to your key dealers about the pending release of your top-secret product goes cruising out onto the Internet, right past all that pornography and Beatles traffic, past all the X-rated GIFs and all the Cool Sites du jour—without your even realizing it. And unscrupulous hackers who bother to tap into the Internet flow can watch your message scurry by and take all the notes they want. I'm sorry I have to bring this to your attention, but if you want to be paranoid and morally indignant, you might as well know all the facts. I doubt, however, that you will disconnect your e-mail system tommorrow.

Most businesses also use the World Wide Web in a limited sort of way. Any self-respecting company now has its own external WWW site to provide an "Internet presence" to the rest of the world. But most often the external site is a static set piece: A fancy bit of puffery developed by some creative design agency to make your company look like a billion dollars to the rest of the world. Many WWW sites are totally one-dimensional and unidirectional. They spew out marketing information to customers—which is certainly a vital task for any business to accomplish—but ignore many of the other ways that Internet-based communications can be used to enhance business opportunities, productivity, and customer service.

What's missing from the current WWW equation is a fluid, two-way stream of communication that mimics the normal flow of information and commerce in the business world. Instead, that two-way flow is still being handled through all the traditional methods: a sales rep cruising the back roads with a trunkful of product catalogs, a ream of invoices flipping out of a high-speed printer, a sack of bulk mail hefted onto the loading dock, an express mail delivery person striding down the hall, or a room full of customer service reps chattering over the phone.

Though e-mail systems are already used for two-way communication, traditional text-based e-mail systems are really the electronic equivalent of the Post-It note. Only occasionally are they used to send something more substantive, like an attached PowerPoint file. A method called *Electronic Data Interchange* (EDI) is another way that businesses exchange data, but EDI is a complex technology that is limited in scope and not easily accessible to the average user.

The best way to handle that bidirectional stream may be through web technology, because that's the only technology that gives us instantaneous point-and-click access to the full range of rich data types on any computing platform, regardless of where that platform is located or whether it's on a private network or a public one like the Internet.

Assuming that the web will be the communications method of choice for the next generation of systems, the challenge becomes the integration of the intranet and extranets in such a way that they enhance this bidirectional flow and provide seamless access across the firewall. This brings several questions to mind:

- ◆ Is there any crossover between the Internet, intranet, and extranet? What are the things they have in common and what are the differences?
- ◆ How are the servers for internal and external web access set up and configured?
- ◆ Who are the external users for your business; what and how should you communicate with them?
- ◆ Can people on the outside access the inside; can people on the inside access the outside? How does that work?
- ◆ What are the security issues related to the Internet and extranet? Will it ever be completely safe to have an Internet connection?

These are all good questions, which will be answered one by one on the following pages.

The External Side of the Corporate Web

In previous chapters, I've spent a lot of time talking about the intranet, but not much time talking about the Internet and the extranet. Before going any further, let me clarify what I mean by the Internet and extranet components of a business communication system, because it's an important concept to understand. The *Internet* includes the kind of corporate and promotional sites you see regularly on the World Wide Web. For instance, anyone with a web browser and an Internet connection can view the public web sites of Microsoft Corporation, Ford, Merrill Lynch, Chevron, Netscape, Bank of America, Miller Brewing, and thousands of others.

The *extranet,* on the other hand, is a private version of your company's Internet presence. It's a way for your customers, suppliers, dealers, business partners, and outside sales reps to connect to proprietary or privileged company information, whether through a private web site or by using the Internet to connect directly into your intranet. This may include components that are public (such as your company's regular WWW site), components that are private (such as a service protected by password and ID), or components that are semi-private (such as a "shadow" WWW service that is only publicized to dealers or business partners). The purpose of doing this is to produce the well-rounded business model I talked about in Chapter 1 (see Figure 1.9).

Just because web services are external doesn't mean the *servers* are physically located outside your network. They might be external, but they might also be located at various places inside your physical network, with links to the outside. The important thing to understand about the Internet and the extranet is that they can be used to serve a lot more than just the traditional types of information you see on today's commercial WWW sites. Here are some examples of the different types of data you might consider serving. Some might be served on the public Internet, and some on the private extranet. *Which* type of data goes *where* is a business decision that will vary from company to company.

Sales and Marketing Data

Of course, your Internet web site or extranet can, should, and probably already does serve a lot of traditional marketing data, including:

- Product brochures
- Online electronic catalogs
- Product specs and manuals
- Product promotions and discounts
- Real-time product pricing
- Frequently asked questions and answers about products
- Ordering information, or online ordering and billing
- Interactive registration
- List of dealers or sales contacts
- Multimedia demos

Parallel sets of information could be provided for each product, so that a customer interested in the XYZ Widget could get a sales brochure, a complete set of specifications, frequently-asked questions (FAQs), manuals, and so forth. Typically, sites containing sales and marketing information are open to the general public over the Internet. In some instances, however, your business may want to limit its exposure to specific customer audiences (see Figure 8.1).

Customer Support

Customer support will increasingly play an important role on the Internet and extranet. Here is a short checklist of options:

- Contact information
- Release notes and upgrade notices
- Online warranty registration and information
- Online literature request forms
- Troubleshooting and maintenance procedures
- Frequently asked questions
- Viewable/printable product manuals
- Online problem-reporting and evaluation forms
- Customer forums and chat groups
- Catalogs and online ordering forms for spare parts or accessories

Typically, customer support might be provided as a public service. In special cases, however, you may want to limit access to registered customers only,

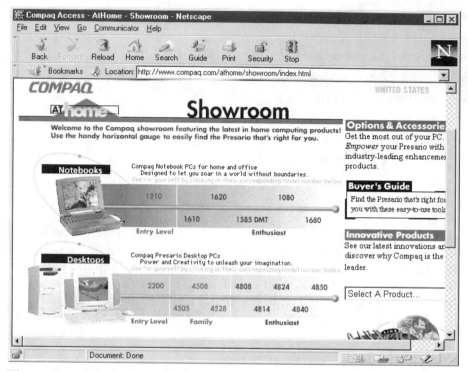

Figure 8.1   Typical marketing-oriented home page.

depending on the type of products you sell and your market requirements (see Figure 8.2).

Supplier/Dealer/Sales Support

An extranet site can help suppliers, dealers, or field reps stay in touch with company operations. It also can provide an excellent way to link customers and sales reps "downstream" directly to supplier information "upstream." The following list shows the types of information you may include:

◆ Contact information

◆ Details on VAR/dealer programs, special promotions, discounts, etc.

◆ Passthrough links to supplier web pages, industry web pages, conferences, or other sites

◆ Product release notes and upgrade notices

◆ Market surveys and focus group studies

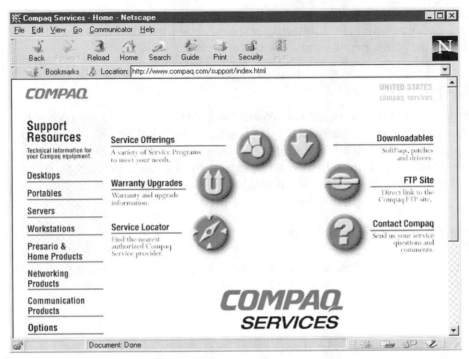

Figure 8.2 Typical tech support page.

◆ Competitive cross-referencing

◆ Links to competitor pages

◆ Wholesale pricing

◆ Downloadable and printable product literature

◆ Downloadable canned presentations

◆ Product troubleshooting and maintenance procedures

◆ Interactive problem-report forms or requests for service

◆ Complaint and feedback forms

◆ Sales report forms

◆ EDI or business-to-business data transfers

The creative part of the extranet comes in designing and implementing ways that this kind of data can be served to exclusive audiences. For instance, such information could be served from internal or external machines, with or without password protection, and with or without IP address filtering. The service could be provided over the Internet using a *virtual private network* or a technology called *IP tunneling.* Or it could be provided through dial-up networking or other private network connections.

Employee Recruiting

Many companies are using the World Wide Web for employee recruiting as a way to save money on classified advertising and other recruiting expenses. Employee recruiting ads or notices may be posted on your own company's web pages (Figure 8.3) or on third-party pages provided by headhunters or employment listing services such as CareerMosaic (www.careermosaic.com/).

Doing Business on the Internet

Assuming you need to do business with the general public on the Internet, the question is how to set up shop. The most common way to do business on the

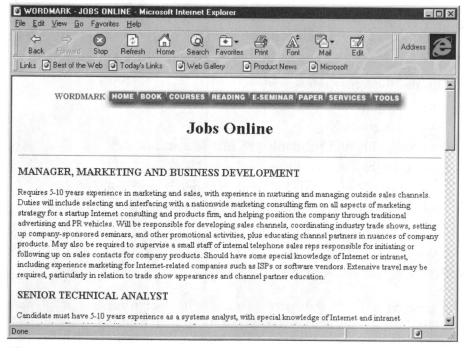

Figure 8.3   Typical employment listing.

Internet is through a public WWW site that is freely accessible to anyone. The way you set up shop depends largely on your organization's internal expertise, capabilities, and goals.

Renting Space: The Simplest Option

Just as many businesses rent their retail space from shopping malls, so many business open shop on the WWW through third-party hosting services. In this case, your company simply rents space on an existing web server that is already connected to the Internet and maintained by a professional organization that is in the business of providing Internet and web services. The organization you will typically rent such a server from is called an *Internet Service Provider* (ISP).

The service itself is physically located at the ISP's site (see Figure 8.4). There is a computer connected to the Internet and (hopefully) monitored 24 hours a day, with your web pages and other content stored on its physical hard drives. To get your content files to your provider's computer, you might use a dial-up Internet connection and the File Transfer Protocol (FTP). The connection you make is temporary—just long enough to upload the files—so there is no serious concern about security.

The host computer could be located anywhere in the world. Your company could be in Miami, for instance, and use a third-party service in Seattle. So, when selecting a third-party host, especially for dedicated web service, it pays to shop around because rates vary considerably. And of course, the best place to shop is on the Internet.

Dedicated Service with Unique Domain Names

When you use a hosted third-party service, you may be one of dozens or even hundreds of other businesses that the ISP hosts. This raises the question of

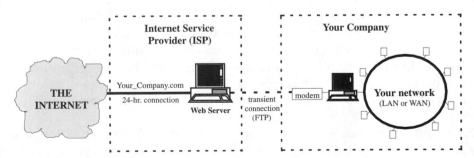

Figure 8.4 Example of a hosted web service.

How to Locate a Web Hosting Service

If you want to shop around for third-party ISPs that provide web hosting services, look no further than your nearest Internet web browser. You may want to start with a look at internet service providers in your area code, on "The List" at:

thelist.internet.com/

However, there are thousands of web hosting services available these days: Practically everyone does it. Some of the biggest web hosting outfits in the U.S. are the following:

BBN   www.bbn.com/
DIGEX   www.digex.com
Cerfnet   www.cerfnet.com/
Webcom   www.webcom.com/

Costs will range from under $50 for an entry-level site, to several hundred dollars a month for a commercial-grade shared server partition, to thousands of dollars a month for a dedicated server.

---

how users will be able to contact the web server in such a way that they access your files uniquely, without interference from all the other traffic at the ISP hosted server. There are several ways to do this, but the best way is through dedicated service with a unique domain name.

For instance, you may have a machine set up at the ISP site that is purchased especially for your company and dedicated to your own use. The machine is connected to an Internet port that is assigned a dedicated IP address. If you have a large audience accessing a large site filled with lots of multimedia and graphics, this is the best way to go. You're not sharing drive access or CPU cycles with other hosted sites—the full power of the machine is at your disposal. Naturally, this is more expensive than other options, but compared to other types of business communication expenses it may still be rather small—from several hundred dollars to several thousand dollars per month.

So how do users reach your dedicated machine? Typically the ISP registers a domain name for you (in the format *your_company.com* or *your_group.org*) through the Internet registration authority called the *InterNIC.* (rs.internic.net). At this point, you may want to consider how the domain name will read. This is a lot like choosing a logo, since Internet users will always think of your company using this name. It should be easy to guess, too, since many Internet users may not know it, but may try to guess it based on your company name. For instance, consider the domain names for Microsoft Corporation (*microsoft.com*) or John Wiley & Sons (*wiley.com*).

A problem may arise if you want a domain name that is already taken. One of the main functions of the InterNIC is to guarantee that all domain names are unique, just as all trademarks are unique. Without unique domain names, conflicts may arise in resolving a request for service, and a request sent to one company may end up at another. If your preferred domain name is already taken, you may have little choice other than to select a different one.

When registering the domain name, the InterNIC wants to know the name and address of your company, the name and phone number of administrative contacts, and the IP addresses for your primary and secondary name servers (DNS). A name server is a computer somewhere on the Internet that knows the ultimate location of your domain name. Often, the name server is a computer on your ISP site. Typically, this information might be located on the name server in a host table that maps specific domain names to IP addresses. For example:

```
www.abc.com     173.28.2.14
ftp.abc.com     173.28.2.15
def.com         173.28.2.16
www.ghi.com     173.28.2.17
www.jkl.com     173.28.2.18
```

Thus any Internet request sent to *www.abc.com* will be routed automatically to the computer with IP address 173.28.2.14. When your service is set up this way, a user can enter your domain name in a URL:

```
www.abc.com/
```

and hit your server directly.

Shared Service

Most ISPs can provide cheaper service if you agree to share the server with other companies. A site on some shared servers can be as low as $50 a month or less. You can still have your domain name point to the server, but—since all the different sites on the server can't share the same server document root—your material may be placed in a subfolder off the document root. That's not so bad, except it makes your URL look like this:

```
www.abc.com/abc/
```

or even like this:

```
www.abc.com/~abc/
```

Increasingly, ISPs are able to work around this problem using a new feature in some servers that provides virtual domain name service. Thus a domain name like:

```
www.abc.com/
```

would be received by the server and cross-referenced to a specific local server folder, such as:

```
/pub/www/abc
```

which contains all the content for your web site.

Advantages and Disadvantages of Hosted Web Services

Regardless of the hosting method used, the idea of letting an ISP host your web service has many intrinsic advantages and disadvantages. Among the advantages are:

- ◆ Smaller learning curve; ability to get a site up faster.
- ◆ No worries about security. All security problems are placed in the lap of the ISP.
- ◆ No need for special on-site equipment, technical talent, or other resources.

In fact, if you want, most ISPs are glad to prepare all your web content and services for you, as well as provide a place to store and serve them. Thus, your own staff would not have to learn HTML, database applications, or web publishing. All that could be outsourced to the ISP.

The disadvantages of using an ISP are not all that great if you plan to have a static service that doesn't change much. The main disadvantage in that case is your having to manually transfer the data to the remote server.

But suppose you want to have a more dynamic service, such as an online catalog where products can be added and subtracted daily, or where catalog pages are assembled from a dynamically changing database on the fly? Suppose you want customers, dealers, or sales reps to be able to access up-to-the-minute information on product pricing or discounts, or connect to other internal corporate data services? Such applications become much more complicated when you have a web hosting service acting as liaison, mainly because there is an open synapse in the data stream between you and the customer. In fact, if you want to provide an advanced, dynamic, and powerful web service, you almost certainly will have to consider bringing your server in-house.

Setting Up Your Own WWW Service

Third-party hosted services are ideal for companies that don't want the hassle of setting up their own web site. However, it may be that you don't like the idea of putting your WWW service in the hands of another company, that you already do have the resources on-site, or that you want more control over your web service—including the ability to dynamically stream data out to external users. In that case, you should set up your own Internet web site.

To set up your own service, you need a full-time Internet connection, a registered domain name, a valid Internet IP address, a web server, and web content that is prepared in a web-compatible format (see Figure 8.5). Since the Internet is a global environment, your server and its informational content should be available 24 hours a day. If you serve a local or regional market, 24-hour access may not be as important, but you should correctly assume that your users may want to visit the site "after-hours and on weekends." Thus, a full-time server is always recommended. To get a better idea of what's involved, let's look at each of the required components individually.

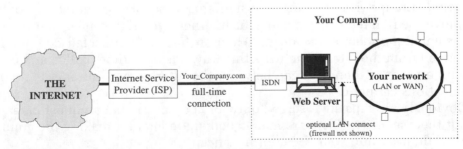

Figure 8.5 Example of an "on-site" web server.

The Internet Connection

When you want to connect to the phone system, you don't just run your own wire out to the nearest telephone pole. You call the phone company, which makes the connection for you, then charges you monthly for your telephone service. Likewise, if you want to connect to the Internet, you'll need to do it through a local ISP, which will provide the physical link and bill you monthly for it.

The actual connection can be achieved in many different ways. It can be made through ordinary phone lines using analog equipment such as a *modem* or digital equipment such as *ISDN*. The technology you use depends on your needs. A modem provides exceedingly narrow bandwidth—about 56 Kbps maximum, which is enough to serve only a few customers at a time. ISDN is a bit faster (56 to 128 Kbps) and can serve 2 to 4 times more information than a plain modem. But if you're serving a large market using rich media—including graphics and multimedia—even dual-channel ISDN may be too slow.

A common way to connect businesses to the Internet is through a partial or full T1 connection, which provides up to 1.5 Mbps service through a leased line. Instead of a modem, this type of service usually requires a special high-speed digital converter called a *CSU/DSU.* Costs may range from under $100 per month for dedicated modem service to several hundred dollars a month for full T1 access. Higher-traffic sites now use bundles of T1 lines. For instance, a dual T1 capacity would be 3 Mbps. You can add T1 lines up to the point it becomes cheaper to just get a full-fledged T3 service, which provides 45-Mbps bandwidth.

Optional LAN Connections

The diagram in Figure 8.5 shows how an on-site Internet connection and web server might work. Notice in this case that the Internet connection reaches all the way into your physical plant, but that *the link to your LAN or WAN is optional.* Companies sometimes install this type of configuration so that employees will have a way of using the Internet, even if they have to use a special standalone machine to do it. When an Internet-connected computer is separated from the internal network this way, it is sometimes called an *air-gap* machine because there is a gap between the Internet and intranet that communications cannot cross.

Obviously air-gaps are reserved only for companies that are most paranoid about their security. There are many good arguments for making the connection all the way into your LAN, for instance:

- ◆ You want to move files onto the web server over the LAN, without having to physically carry files to the web server on a floppy disk or tape.

- ◆ You want your internal users to be able to access the Internet and the World Wide Web from their desktops.

- ◆ You want to provide Internet services to external users (the extranet) from points *inside* your network or on the fringes of your network.

However, if you're truly paranoid about Internet security (and perhaps you should be, as I'll explain later), you can have your cake and eat it too. You can place a web server in-house with a full-time Internet connection, but without connecting it to your LAN. That way, the web server itself is exposed to a security threat, but the LAN isn't. Even if you do this, however, firewall software is recommended at the web server to protect it from attack.

Registered Domain Name and IP Address

For users to reach your on-site web server, you would still have to register an Internet domain name as before (see "Dedicated Service with Unique Domain Names" earlier in this chapter). And the ISP would probably help you do this, as before. Any requests addressed to your company's domain name, such as:

`www.abc.com/`

would be forwarded through the Internet to the port on your ISP's router where the leased line is connected, and thence onward to your web server.

The question arises: If you have your LAN connected to the Internet, do you need to register a separate domain name and IP address for each internally connected computer? The short answer is no. As the later discussion on security will show, you want to limit direct Internet connections to as few nodes as possible. Ideally, there should be only one or two nodes on your network that connect to the Internet, so you can concentrate all your security efforts at that one spot.

Whether your connection point is at a single node or at several nodes, only the nodes on the Internet side need to be directly addressable from the Internet and registered with a reserved domain name and IP address. Nodes on the intranet side may use their own numbering scheme.

Each node on your internal network will have its own IP address—it must for TCP/IP to work—but these do not correspond to reserved IP addresses on the Internet. They look just the same, and in some cases your local machines may actually be using IP address numbers that are already assigned to computers out on the Internet. But since these internal nodes are not visible from the Internet, it doesn't matter.

The Web Server and Content

A web server for external access will typically be installed on the gateway computer(s) connected to the Internet. The web content to be served across the Internet will be placed on this server, including the HTML files, image files, and other components that form the core of your offering. This arrangement will allow users to connect to your World Wide Web site without having to enter your private network.

In addition, if you want your internal users to have access to the World Wide Web, there may be a proxy server sitting on or near the firewall (sometimes it *is* the firewall), which passes requests back and forth from the internal network to the World Wide Web. If an employee sitting inside your company tries to hit the Ford Motor Corporation site, for instance, the request will be fielded by the proxy server, which will send it out to Ford and then ship the resulting web page back to the user. More on this later, in the section on firewalls.

Why Security Is Important

Notice I return again and again to the idea of security. This is because security on the Internet is a constant and serious concern. No matter what kind of private network you operate, you will definitely not want to have it connected to the Internet without at least installing some basic security options.

You can be assured that there are plenty of unemployed, technically proficient people out there (employed ones, too) who have nothing better to do with their spare time than sit around and try to break into private computer networks. Some call them *hackers,* although there are many computer aficionados who like to think of themselves as hackers (in the sense that they *hack out programming code*), yet never try to break into other people's computers. More appropriate, we should call the intruders *crackers,* because they try to crack your system the same way a burglar cracks a safe. Some of these people are quite benign (some might even be your own employees, trying to log in from home). Some may be simply bored or looking for a technical challenge. A few may be malicious vandals or thieves.

Companies that have LANs connected to the Internet will tell you that attempted break-ins are quite common. "We do have firewalls, and we have people every day trying to break in," says one busy network manager. A typical comment: "We see that it happens, but it hasn't been successful *that we've been able to determine.*"

But just because there are guaranteed security problems doesn't mean you should reject the Internet as a way of doing business, or turn away and hide your head in the sand. When you're doing business on the Internet, you might want to accept the fact that security threats are just part of the territory, then plan for them and manage against them. The best way to deal with security threats is to set up rigid defenses and monitor them on a daily basis.

The idea of controlling Internet security is remarkably similar to the idea of controlling security in the real world. Thieves tend to strike at night or whenever there's no one around. And there's never been a security device invented that could keep them out, if they're truly determined. You can install every kind of security device on your house or office building—including burglar bars, padlocks, deadbolts, and alarms—and the thief can break through all of them given enough time, inclination, and lack of vigilance on the owners' part.

Installing Internet security, therefore, is much like installing locks on your doors. Thieves might be able to break through all of them, but the more you've installed, the longer it takes. If you install enough security measures, the thieves may make quick mental calculations, weigh their options, and decide it may be easier to break in somewhere else.

If a break-in does occur, it doesn't mean anything bad will happen to your system. The invaders may have proven their point, gotten their jollies, and logged out. Sometimes, however, crackers do illegal and devastating things. They may steal passwords, tap into confidential employee data, insert viruses, and even erase files or entire hard drives. These are the cases you want to protect against.

It's certainly beyond the scope of this text to serve as a complete guidebook to the installation and use of Internet security devices. There are plenty of other books devoted exclusively to the subject at your local bookstore. But it's fair to give you a basic idea of what's involved—not so you can install your own firewalls, but so that you might understand how you can set up a system to "communicate around them."

Communicating around a Firewall

Generally speaking, a firewall is a mechanism designed to prevent unauthorized access to a private network area. The firewall activity typically occurs right at the *gateway,* the computer on your internal network that is first touched by the Internet connection. Since all the defensive activity is concentrated at the gateway, this machine is sometimes called the *bastion host* after the bastions that formed the most critical points of defense in medieval castles.

Naturally, because the firewall is designed to limit communications, that's exactly what it does. If you have people on your internal network who want to access the Internet, or people on the outside who want to access internal services, the firewall tends to get in their way. However, there are methods you can use to get around the restrictions of the firewall without unduly compromising security. Let's look at a few typical firewall setups and the ways that intranet developers can work with them and around them. Keep in mind, however, that you should never try to work your way around a network firewall without the full consent, cooperation, and assistance of the network administrator who's in charge of the firewall.

Multihomed Gateway

Imagine taking the machine serving as your bastion host (Figure 8.5) and installing two network cards in it: one connected to the internal network and one to the external network (i.e., the Internet). All routing between the two networks is turned off so that any communications from outside or inside terminate at this machine. This is called a *multihomed gateway* (Figure 8.6).

In the past, network communications stopped dead at the first network card and were unable to proceed onto the second network. This was an inconvenience mainly for people on the inside who wanted to use the Internet—they had to log onto the firewall machine and use the Internet from there. This setup also eliminated the possibility that any services might be provided to the outside from inside the network.

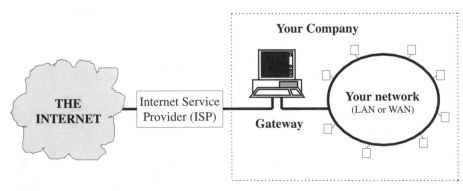

Figure 8.6   Multihomed gateway.

In the last two years, however, several different vendors have created fire-wall software that passes communications between the gaps on the two net-works, but keeps a vigilant eye on the types of traffic passing from one network to the other. For instance, firewall software will filter out e-mail commands known to be a cracker's favorite entree into a network, or will look for over-flowing mail headers, which are often used as a transport for hacker mischief. The firewall denies all transactions that haven't specifically been allowed in its rules.

Often, a third network card is placed inside the gateway, with a separate web-server machine running off of it, connected to the firewall machine by a single crossover cable. This becomes a "third home" on the gateway and serves as the company's web site on the World Wide Web. The firewall soft-ware permits web-related traffic to penetrate from the Internet as far as the web server. But if crackers manage to break into the web server, the most they can do is "hose" it. The firewall software will prevent intruders from breaking through to the internal network.

Screening Gateway

Some companies will take the extra step of installing a special hardware device called a *packet filtering* router. The router can examine each packet of data that comes through the network and determine where it came from and where it's going, then reject various packets if they are bound for forbidden destinations on the network. For example, a router could reject all requests for access to your network except the ones specifically destined for the WWW server (usually port 80). This eliminates other ports that a cracker might use to gain entry to the corporate intranet.

To create a more secure firewall, the administrator can program the router to screen out all communications that are not specifically targeted to the bastion host (Figure 8.7). Anything targeted to an internal machine may be rejected, or the administrator may allow selective communication with certain closely monitored and controlled internal machines. At the same time, the router can be configured so that any requests for Internet service coming from within the network will be passed through without filtering. Thus, internal employees can potentially access Internet services without the use of a proxy server.

Screened Subnet

This configuration is similar to the multihomed gateway, except that an entire subnetwork is built in the gap between the Internet and the intranet (Figure

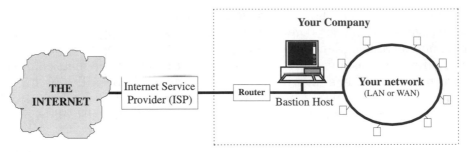

Figure 8.7 Screened gateway.

8.8). This subnetwork might contain several servers needed to interact with internal and external users, such as FTP, mail, a World Wide Web server, or a proxy web server. Screening routers can be added to both sides of this "service network" to filter out unwanted traffic in both directions, and firewall software can also be used to automatically monitor and control communications between each of the three networks (Internet, subnet, intranet).

Proxy Servers

A proxy server is not a firewall, although some companies have been known to use it that way. Instead, it is a special-purpose server that helps people communicate around and through firewalls and that otherwise helps the internal network operate more efficiently. For instance, Netscape offers a proxy server as one of its commercial applications, and the old CERN server has a feature that lets it operate in *proxy mode.*

Proxy servers actually help improve the load on your company's Internet connection, because they allow internal users to easily funnel their requests

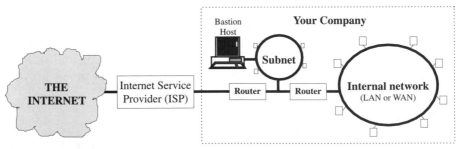

Figure 8.8 Screened subnet configuration.

Where to Find Firewall Solutions

Many vendors offer firewall solutions for the network, ranging from special hardware to special software solutions. Here are a few of the market leaders in providing firewall hardware and software:

Raptor   www.raptor.com/

Checkpoint   www.checkpoint.com/

Trusted Information   www.tis.com/

Cisco   www.cisco.com/

Novell   www.novell.com/

---

through a central caching device that limits the number of repeat accesses to the same site. For instance, if two users request the home page of the *Wall Street Journal* in the same day, the proxy server processes the first request and delivers the requested page back to the first requesting user—meanwhile storing a copy of it in the server cache. Then, if a second user requests *WSJ* on the same day, the proxy server simply retrieves a copy from the cache.

Unfortunately, even though the proxy server reduces the traffic between your company and the Internet, it does little to reduce traffic within your intranet. The same number of pages will flow between the proxy server and employee web browsers, whether the pages are cached or not. Cached pages will serve quicker, but they place no less of a load on the network. To use the proxy server for Internet access, each browser on the internal network must have its proxy options set to the correct server.

Other Tactics

Hardware and software configuration is only a small part of network firewall administration. There are other steps that a trained administrator can take to make the gateway more secure, including disabling some of its internal functions, laying traps for potential crackers, and monitoring certain key processes on a regular basis.

If your organization wants to connect its internal LAN to the Internet, you should hire a qualified network administrator who has thorough training in firewall setup and maintenance and who will be involved in the daily operations of the firewall and monitoring of the site. This kind of network security requires constant vigilance by someone who knows the signs of trouble and who can respond quickly when a problem arises. Never attempt to install or modify a firewall configuration on your own.

Back-Door Access for Special Users

So far, all the discussion has been about giving external users access to the *public entrance* of your web site. If the Internet is like a public highway and your company's domain name is the knob on the front door, then any member of the public can find out where you do business, turn the knob, and walk in. This is fine if you are providing information to the general public. But what about other external users who may require more targeted or even protected information—the field reps, commercial partners, dealers, and suppliers who help make your business a success? This section explores some of the ways you can provide more targeted or limited access for these users.

Hidden Entryways

A simple way to provide limited access to special audiences is to include additional audience-specific material on your World Wide Web site but to set it up in such a way that it is accessed through a different home page. The material would not be visible to the general public because the main home page would provide no links leading to the special pages. For instance, you might create a folder off the main server root called *dealers* that can be accessed through your normal domain name.

Thus, any member of the general public who wants to access your web site would do it like this:

```
www.abc.com/
```

and they would instantly see the main home page with links to all the information available to the general public. Dealers, on the other hand, might be told that they can access special dealer information by entering the following URL:

```
www.abc.com/dealers/
```

and they would be served a special dealer home page that is not accessible any other way. In fact, if you are in a position to supply your dealers (or other special audiences) with web browsers, you could preconfigure their browsers to open automatically to the special home page for their particular group upon starting. Members of the general public would be unaware that your site contained any other material, and thus would bypass the dealer information entirely.

Though this was a viable way of serving unpublicized web content in the past, some of the more intrusive web-search engines are capable of scanning any page on the World Wide Web and adding it to its index. So if you don't want your private dealer pages showing up in someone's Internet search, it may be time to take more secure measures.

Pass Keys

Of course, the previous scenario is not a secure one. Any member of the general public could also access the dealer pages if someone told them about the special URL, or they come across it in a search engine. If you really object to the public seeing the dealer page—especially if you want to keep your competitors out—you could put password protection on the *dealer* folder so that only registered dealers could access it.

Of course, this will require some maintenance on your part. You will have to authorize each individual user the way you do with more traditional password-protected computer applications. You may be able to automate this process somewhat by creating a user registration form in which a CGI script takes the user information and checks it against a database or e-mails the specific user with confirmation. Or, if rigid security is not required, you might assign a single ID and password to everyone.

Once password protection is installed, you could easily add links to password-protected material from the main public home pages (with appropriate forewarnings that a password will be required). The user would click the link and automatically see a login dialog that would accept a user ID and password.

Exclusive Access

If you had some way of knowing the specific IP addresses or domain names of the machines used by people in your special audience, you could potentially restrict a specific site to only people using those machines. In this case, the password mechanism would *deny access to everyone* unless it noticed an incoming request originated on a machine with a certain IP address or domain name.

By the same token, you could make it hard for known competitors to access protected information from their own machines by filtering out their company domain names. For instance, you could specifically allow anyone to access the web site, unless the request originated from your competitors *voracious.com* and *megawidgets.com*.

Admittedly, this isn't a particularly secure method of allowing or denying access, since it isn't specific to individuals. Competitors that you shut out by domain name could still potentially access your site through independent accounts purchased from local service providers. And machines that you have authorized for access could be used by anyone, such as a competitor who happens to be doing business with the same dealer. The ability to accept or deny service based on name/address of the user depends on the server software, of course. Some web servers may not support this feature.

Special Services

Instead of burying hidden material in your existing web sites, you may want to create special web sites or services that are dedicated to a specific function. This is especially useful for high-traffic, high-volume applications that you don't want bogging down your regular server. Netscape, for instance, maintains a special server for its general store (merchant.netscape.com) that is separate from its main home page server (home.netscape.com), though both are equally accessible to the public. Sun Corporation maintains a site for its Java group (www.javasoft.com) that is separate from its regular home page server (www.sun.com). You could conceivably apply all of the restrictions mentioned so far to the special server site, including hidden access, password protection, and IP filtering.

Remote Access Services

Again, all the solutions so far assume access through the Internet to public web servers that would normally be open to the public, but that are controlled in some way. But there is one other solution that you may find useful that many companies use to provide guaranteed secure access to the inner network. That solution is called *dial-up networking*.

If you've ever taken out your own account with a local Internet service provider, you already have experience with dial-up networking. Your computer dials the provider's number, connects automatically, and logs in to the remote computer using a preprogrammed script. At the end of the login process, a connection is made and suddenly your computer becomes a TCP/IP node on the Internet. This allows you to easily run any TCP/IP client application such as e-mail, FTP, or WWW and access any available servers on the Internet.

Now imagine that the same thing happened, but with your own company. External users might dial in and be logged automatically as a node on your intranet. Then they could start up their web browsers and cruise the intranet, just like anyone sitting inside the corporation. Many companies have been providing their remote workers with dial-up capabilities for years, using utilities like the RAS feature in Windows NT Server. The difference now is that workers can connect directly into the intranet and go surfing with their web browsers on the TCP/IP layer of the network.

Extranets and Virtual Private Networks

An extra dimension has been added to the firewall and network security picture with the recent rise in popularity of extranets and virtual private networks. Let's look at these terms individually:

Virtual private network. Some companies have found they can create a private wide area network using the Internet as the carrier, without unduly subjecting themselves to security hazards. In the past, a company with multiple locations in different parts of the world would have to connect its locations with private lease lines, an arrangement that can be quite expensive. Recently, however, companies have found that, instead of spending all that money on lease lines, they can connect each branch of the organization to the Internet, then transmit their private communications across the Internet. The privacy is preserved through a process called *tunneling*. Each packet of data being transmitted between company locations is double- or triple-wrapped inside of other IP packets that can only be unlocked using a digital key. So, even though the packets are traveling across the Internet to get to their destination, and even if someone traps the packets en route, it is virtually impossible to discover the key and unwrap the packets.

Extranet. This describes any use of the Internet to reach the intranet. In effect, it is an extension of the intranet into the public domain, but with protections that allow you to keep it private. The extranet may be used by sales reps, dealers, suppliers, and special customers to get into the network. In some cases, users access a special network port where a hardware-based user authentication device (such as SecureID) must be used to log in. Once the connection is made, all communications are encrypted between the intranet and the remote user, so that anyone watching will not be able to decode what is being transmitted.

The extranet and virtual private networks are some of the last pieces in the Internet puzzle that will allow companies to create an entirely IP-based network for communicating with all of their business partners, suppliers, dealers, and customers throughout the world.

Inside Looking Out: Integrating the Two Sides of the Web

If you ever visit a company with a highly developed intranet, you may notice the almost seamless ease with which links from internal pages cross over into the extranet. The experience can be totally transparent, even though the user is crossing rather rigid network boundaries between the private and public worlds in the process.

For instance, while researching this book, I had a chance to visit with a local salesperson for a major telecommunications firm, who was showing me how he used the company's intranet in his daily work. The man knew his way around the web quite well, but he still didn't understand quite how it all fit together. I watched him move from some of the company's intranet pages, out to the company's World Wide Web page, and then effortlessly out onto the Internet and into the web pages of some of his company's competitors.

All the while, the salesman was under the impression he had never left his company's intranet. He actually thought that the competitor pages had been created by his company for the benefit of the company's sales staff, so that he could easily see the people and products he would be competing against. At that point, I felt obliged to explain that much of his web surfing was happening out on the external Internet. I quickly pointed out the Location field on his browser and showed how he could tell when he was on the Internet and *when he was not.*

Not everyone in your company will need external access to the Internet, but for many it will be a priceless addition to their productivity. Most companies I know provide external access indiscriminately to internal users, but some are cracking down and installing new controls to warn users when they are crossing into the public sphere, so that they will be more conscious of their use of external bandwidth. One company has developed a tracking system that automatically logs and bills all extranet time to individual departments. The time is not that expensive, averaging a few dollars a month per employee. But the system helps discourage unauthorized and inappropriate joy riding on the Internet.

The employees who really need access to the Internet are the ones who are already outward looking in their jobs. Research staff are at the top of the list, since questions that once took days to research can now be resolved in minutes on the Internet. Sales and marketing staff are a fast second, since they need to keep up with the activities of both customers and competitors.

As soon as employees are empowered to access the Internet from their desks, they quickly and invariably find it an indispensible part of their job. With Internet access, information on any topic is just a few keystrokes away; whether it is government regulations, scientific research, stock or commodity prices, competitive data, market studies, proceedings of professional organizations—you name it and it's there. This kind of global reach and instant access to information can do much to boost productivity within your organization and give your company a solid jump on the competition. If you hesitate—and many companies have—then your competition has an ideal opportunity to get the jump on *you*.

Other Aspects of Integration

In this book, I have given most of my attention to web technology, because I see web as the core of the intranet. Even though people have been using e-mail to share information over private networks for years, we didn't start calling the private network an *intranet* until web technology came along.

It's true, however, that other services such as e-mail and newsgroups—or what some people call *discussion forums*—should be an integrated part of the intranet. This is true for several reasons:

- ◆ E-mail and newsgroups are an integral part of the services offered on the Internet, so why not have it this way on the intranet, too?
- ◆ Both of these additional services can operate on the same TCP/IP layer that carries our web communications (though most corporate e-mail systems don't).
- ◆ Web, e-mail, and newsgroups can all have built-in hyperlinks that call each other, if they are integrated properly.
- ◆ In cases where employees have Internet access at the desktop, they should be able to access internal *and* external e-mail addresses or discussion forums simultaneously, in much the same way as they can access internal or external web sites.
- ◆ Both Netscape Navigator and Internet Explorer have built-in e-mail tools and newsgroup readers that are tightly integrated with the web

browser. These can be operated as a suite of applications used for intranet communication (not to mention other bundled applications such as the conferencing and collaboration tools in Netscape Communicator).

To understand the integration issues involved in having e-mail and newsgroups on an intranet, let's take a look at these one by one.

Open versus Closed Standards

Before we talk about the specifics of integrating e-mail and newsgroups, let me make sure you understand what I mean by *open systems* versus *proprietary systems.* As I said before, companies have been using e-mail for years, but most corporate e-mail systems are based on proprietary standards that are not intrinsically "open" in the same way that web systems are.

On a web, for instance, you can use a Microsoft or a Netscape web server to publish web sites, and you can use either a Netscape browser or a Microsoft browser to access the published web sites. That's because all web servers and all web browsers are based on the open standards of the HyperText Transfer Protocol (HTTP) and the HyperText Markup Language (HTML). In fact, you don't have to limit yourself to Microsoft or Netscape web servers. There are plenty of organizations out there making and selling (or giving away) web servers. And you can install any of these competing servers on your network and still use them to serve web content to your end users. It's just that Microsoft and Netscape get all the publicity and attention and have become the acknowledged market leaders in this area—for many good reasons.

A few years ago, likewise, there were dozens of companies offering their own versions of the web browser. You may recall that most popular web browsers since 1993—including both Netscape and Internet Explorer—were based on the original NCSA Mosaic browser source code developed by Marc Andreessen and Eric Bina during their days as students at the University of Illinois. Companies like Spry, America Online, and others created their own browsers based in whole or in part on that original model. And if any of those browsers were still widely distributed, you could probably get one of them and use it on your intranet, as well.

These days, however, it's hard to find any web browsers on the market other than the Netscape or Microsoft products, simply because these two companies have been able to quickly outstrip the competitors in features and sophistication. The browser wars, in many cases, are like a beauty contest. One queen will do just as well as the next, but of course people have their favorites. In the web world, Netscape Navigator and Microsoft Internet Explorer are the reigning beauty queens, and most other contenders have simply dropped out of the race.

Notice that this interoperability between different brands or versions of software is something relatively new. The history of computing is nothing but a history of proprietary systems. In the early days, for instance, both the computer hardware and software were intricately intertwined and totally—incorrigibly—proprietary. The old IBM mainframes would run *only* IBM software. If you bought a machine called a *Displaywriter*, it came with its own built-in word-processing software that was *the only software* you could run on that machine, and word processing was the *only thing* you could use that machine to do.

These days we find such concepts laughable. Even in the early days of the PC, circa 1980, these early desktop computers were open enough that different companies could create different kinds of software to run on them. Yet, even though the hardware and operating system opened up enough to allow different types of software to co-exist on the desktop platform, the software itself remained rigidly proprietary. You could create a document in Microsoft Word 1.0, but it was only much later that other word processors opened up enough to let you open that document in their programs. And when you did, the documents were so incompatible that you would lose most of the formatting.

By comparison, the different implementations of HTML and HTTP—though still not perfectly uniform—are much more in synch from one vendor to the next. If you read my discussion of these standards in Chapter 2, you will recall that both were originally created by international standards-setting organizations, including organizations like CERN, the *Internet Engineering Task Force* (IETF), and the *World Wide Web Consortium* (W3). In many cases, companies like Netscape and Microsoft have rushed forward with new "extensions" to HTML that became de facto standards. But in most cases, these companies later submitted their new extensions to the standards-setting bodies for approval and—even before the approval process was finished—took the trouble to make their own software compatible with the de facto standards developed by their competitors.

There are a few notable exceptions where Netscape browsers don't work well with Microsoft servers, or vice versa. Few of these, however, are related to HTML or HTTP standards. Most arise due to the different ways in which these companies have chosen to implement the non-HTTP technologies, such as Java, JavaScript, ActiveX, and some extensible markup languages. Yet even in these cases, the interoperability is remarkable. There are also some distinctly proprietary aspects to the server-side of web technology, such as Microsoft's active server pages discussed in Chapter 7. But Microsoft's server converts active server pages to HTML on the fly as they are being served, so that they are still readable by any up-to-date web browser at the user's desktop.

Opening the Mail

Against this backdrop of open-versus-proprietary software applications, it is interesting to take a look at the current state of the art in e-mail systems. Unlike web, which came to the corporate intranet as a full-blown open standards–based application just within the past few years, e-mail systems have been around for years—ever since the first LANs were created. And, as a direct result of their age, most of our legacy e-mail systems are proprietary to their bones.

Since most corporate networks started during the mainframe era, most early e-mail systems were mainframe based. A great example of that is a system called PROFS, which was available on many dumb terminals and which provided the ability for employees to exchange messages with each other through the mainframe system.

Later, with the advent of local area networks, many LAN-based e-mail applications were developed, including programs like Lotus cc:Mail and Microsoft Mail. But these were all rigidly proprietary: Each had its own messaging format that could not be natively read by other competing programs. This became an increasing problem as corporate networks grew larger and more interconnected, and the same network might be host to mainframe terminals and PC desktops running several different types of e-mail applications.

The problem of exchanging e-mail between competing products was eased a bit by the development of industry standards like X.400 and other gateways and application programming interfaces. The gateway provided an automatic conversion process, in which messages would be converted to a common format that could be read by programs on either side of the gap. (Imagine, for instance, that web servers used their own proprietary formats and that a special web-based gateway temporarily converted the traffic to HTML so that it could be read by proprietary browsers on the other side. Sounds a little like Microsoft's active server pages, doesn't it?)

E-mail interoperability between the proprietary LAN-based applications was assisted by standards such as Microsoft's *Mail Application Programming Interface* (MAPI) and Lotus' *Vendor Independent Messaging* (VIM). Mainframe and minicomputer-based systems such as PROFS, All-in-One, and SprintMail used the X.400 standard to handle intersystem e-mail operability.

Meanwhile, interestingly enough, companies sending e-mail traffic out over the Internet were using their own set of mail formats and standards. Unlike the proprietary environment of the corporate network, however, people on the Internet knew their systems would have to be interoperable, so they developed a standard set of protocols, such as the *Simple Mail Transfer Protocol* (SMTP), to handle communications between users. Thus, it was possible to create e-mail servers and clients that could easily talk to each other, using the TCP/IP protocol. The IP (Internet Protocol) part actually controlled the format of e-mail addresses. Mail streaming out of corporate networks typically went through a gateway that handled the conversion to and from the Internet format.

As Internet technologies began to penetrate the corporate networks, however, many companies started realizing that their web systems were not totally compatible or interoperable with their e-mail systems. On a web page, for instance, you can have a hyperlink to a mail address, and when you click it, the hyperlink brings up a mail window that you can use to jot off a message. That mail window and the messaging format, however, were originally invented for use on the Internet, not the intranet. So naturally, the people who invented this feature did not even think about all the internal contradictions of corporate e-mail systems. They just used Internet standards for creating the integration between the web browser and the e-mail program.

To handle these incompatibilities, many proprietary LAN-based e-mail vendors started offering SMTP gateways that could handle the traffic being routed through them through the Internet/intranet layer. But wait a minute: Isn't this all getting a little absurd? When you think about it, isn't this constant overlapping of gateways like some kind of massive kluge or Band-aid that we keep applying to our networks to heal all these inconsistencies and gaping wounds in the process? Given the fact that we have this inexpensive, standards-based set of Internet tools, isn't it time to question whether we actually need all these expensive proprietary e-mail systems that are so competitive and hostile that they won't even talk to each other?

Just as you can install low-cost web servers anywhere on your network, and use free or low-cost web browsers to communicate between them, you can also install Internet-style mail servers on your network and use Internet-style e-mail clients to communicate between them. Furthermore, once you convert to an open standards–based Internet mail system, your options in terms of e-mail software are wide open. You can easily pick and choose between the best Internet-style e-mail systems that the market has to offer—and the choices are becoming increasingly better. Furthermore, people can conveniently start using the e-mail tools built directly into their Netscape or Microsoft web browsers (Figure 8.9), so you don't have to worry about the installation of special software.

Once you adopt Internet-style mail standards, you can get everyone communicating on the same wavelength—regardless of the platform they are

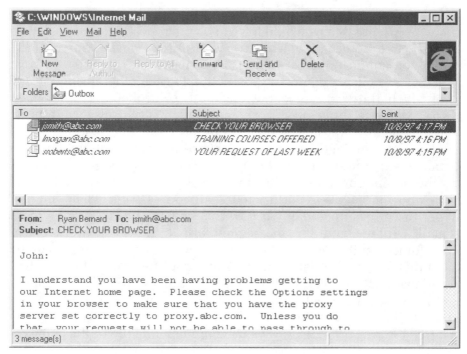

Figure 8.9   The Microsoft Internet mail tool.

using. Furthermore, messages created on internal desktops will be totally compatible with the Internet itself and will not have to pass through a special gateway for conversion.

Beyond the interoperability issue, however, cost may be the true driver. If you don't know already, you might guess that proprietary LAN-based e-mail systems cost a good bit of money, otherwise the companies that created them wouldn't have bothered. By comparison, Internet-based mail solutions are significantly less expensive and could end up saving your company quite a bundle of cash.

To begin adopting Internet standards, you'll need to switch to mail servers that use the *Post Office Protocol* (POP) and *Simple Mail Transport Protocol* (SMTP). Many traditional mail servers are now offering this feature. For example, you can buy extensions or gateways for both cc:Mail and Microsoft Mail to keep legacy mail users happy. But there are also many servers that began life under SMTP that will do the trick as well. Seattle Lab's SLmail is an example of an inexpensive Windows NT-based mail server that costs just a few hundred dollars. Bigger NT suppliers like Microsoft and Digital offer solutions, as well.

If preferred, you can take the total plunge and convert everyone to the new standard, or convert your company division by division. But converting to Internet protocols doesn't necessarily mean that everyone has to convert right away. As I mentioned, most proprietary mail systems now have their own kludgey SMTP gateways that will talk to Internet mail servers, so people can continue using their cc:Mail without interruption. But people who want to make the switch can increasingly use the Internet mail tools embedded in their browsers and desktops. Or they can choose from standalone Internet mail tools like QualComm's Eudora and Pegasus Mail. Pegasus, in particular, works well with both Internet mail servers and the Netware-based *Message Handling Service* (MHS) on Wintel platforms.

Adopting Internet e-mail as your corporatewide standard opens some other possibilities as well—among them the type of mailing list applications you see often on the Internet. On the Internet, a majordomo or *listserv* program can be set up so that a community of users can share messages on a specific topic. For instance, I personally belong to a private mailing list that is used by Internet authors to discuss the sort of things Internet authors like to discuss. Likewise, in your company, you might set up a mailing list for engineers that accommodates their own engineering concerns. Any message sent to the list goes to all users in the list. Responses to a message can be made back to the original author, or to the entire list. This is a quick and easy way to set up ad hoc discussion groups that can increase the collaboration within and between different departments and work groups in your company—at a fraction of the cost of similar groupware programs. Programs such as Revnet's GroupMaster make mailing list management quite easy.

Keeping Up with the News(Groups)

One popular, but often misunderstood, Internet application is something originally called *Usenet,* but now typically called *newsgroups.* In fact, newsgroups of the *alt.sex* variety are responsible for much of the negative press that the Internet has gotten over the years. Newsgroups are where freedom of speech has found its true home, although the kinds of speech being used are often raucous.

When you strip away all the notoriety and bad publicity, however, the Internet-style newsgroup is really a remarkably simple and useful concept—and one which has extensive applications on the corporate intranet. Essentially, the newsgroup revolves around a *news server,* which becomes something like a bulletin board for messages posted randomly by the newsgroup *subscribers.*

For instance, let's say that there is a newsgroup devoted specifically to the topic of engineering designs for the ABC widget. The subscribers of the group

---

Where to Find E-mail Products

Most of the products discussed in this section are available for download and testing from the Internet. In particular, you may want to take a look at the following:

Lsoft's ListServ. www.lsoft.com

Netscape's Messenger. home.netscape.com/communicator/ messenger.html

Microsoft Internet Mail. www.microsoft.com/ie/most/howto/ mailnews.htm

Pegasus Mail. www.pegasus.usa.com

Seattle Lab's SLmail NT. www.seattlelab.com

Qualcomm's Eudora. www.eudora.com

Revnet's GroupMaster. www.groupmaster.com

---

would be—naturally—engineers who are working on that design effort. Any engineer who had an idea about a better design could share it with the other engineers by sending a message to the newsgroup. Instead of going to every member in the group as an e-mail would, however, the message would get "posted" to the server automatically. To view the messages, you would need a special piece of software called a *newsreader.* When you view the newsgroup in the newsreader, it shows all the messages that have been posted to the newsgroup—sort of like a group in-box for mail messages.

If you want to respond to a newsgroup posting, you create a response much as you would normally respond to an e-mail message. Instead, however, the response is posted back to the newsgroup in such a way that it becomes associated with the original message. Thus, users can view the original message and all the messages associated with it in a sequence of postings called a *thread.* The ability to view threads lets you view all the messages on a particular facet of the topic, without having to track them down individually. In fact, the newsgroup reader has typical features that allow you to easily move backward and forward through all the postings in a thread.

Applied to a corporate intranet, the newsgroup feature becomes a way to support discussion forums between various groups in the company. Notice that in many ways, this same discussion feature could be handled through the types of mailing lists discussed at the end of the previous section in this chapter. However, newsgroups have their own set of features that some users may prefer.

The words *user preference* are really important here. There is no way that the people who create the intranet can guess what people will want in terms of newsgroups. Most newsgroups created by a central authority—on the theory that people will want to use them—typically go unused. The newsgroups that really work are the newsgroups that various work teams create for their own purposes on an ad hoc basis.

Thus, the best way to implement newsgroups on your corporate intranet would be as follows. First, make sure people understand what newsgroups are and the possibilities that they hold. This will typically be done through some form of training—whether as part of a classroom regimen or online. You may want to create a model or two to help acquaint people with the concept. There may be some issue of common concern in your company that people have strong opinions about and that can serve as a model for other newsgroups. Once people see a model, they can begin imagining their own uses for it. Thus, there should be some way that people can easily set up and begin using their own ad hoc newsgroups on the intranet whenever they want to.

Of course, if you want to create newsgroups, you will need the proper software at both the server and the client end. You can install news servers on your intranet the same way you install web servers or e-mail servers, and you can also use them to define newsgroups of your own, or on demand from various work teams. To use the news servers, all your users will need newsgroup readers, which, thankfully, are built into both the Netscape and Microsoft web browser offerings. Newsgroup readers are also becoming a prominent part of most intranet-based groupware suites, like Netscape Communicator.

Where Do We Go from Here?

This chapter has covered all you need to know about the different issues regarding access and integration of the Internet, intranet, and extranet. Other than the issues covered here, there is no significant difference in the technologies and techniques that you use to build one or the other—the internal or the external web. What's different is the way we use the technologies to further business goals. Now we move on to the last chapter of the book, in which I explain the different management and control issues related to the development of an intranet.

Chapter Nine at a Glance

Now that you have read about all the technologies related to intranets and all the interoperability issues, you are ready to begin building your new intranet—or improving the one you already have. This final chapter explains the management issues related to corporate intranets. Most specifically:

- ◆ Control issues and control models related to intranets
- ◆ The importance of using the intranet as an enabling technology
- ◆ How to jump-start the intranet, or improve an existing one
- ◆ Why structure and centralized control can sometimes be imposed after the fact
- ◆ How various methods can be used to turn the intranet into an ad hoc corporatewide knowledge base
- ◆ How standards, templates, and work flow designs can be used to minimize disruption to the organization and increase productivity
- ◆ How to achieve buy-in from employees and management
- ◆ Budgeting, licensing, and support issues for intranets

Intranet Management Strategies

"How odd," you may think. Here we are, at the last chapter of the book, and it's only now that the author starts talking about management issues. Aren't we supposed to do our planning up front? Isn't management supposed to lead, rather than follow? If we're going to implement such a potentially massive new information system, don't we first have to whip out our graph paper and our spreadsheets and do feasibility studies and have committee meetings and plan and put together project teams and hire squadrons of programmers and computer network wizards?

In fact, shouldn't we just turn this over to some big-time consulting firm like Anderson or Deloitte & Touche and let them figure it all out? Don't we know from experience that every new wave of computer technology is massively more complex than the previous one, and that it will require massive new layers of infrastructure and massive amounts of expertise to pull it off? Isn't this, after all, what the client-server revolution has taught us?

Well, yes and no. To some extent, management anxiety over planning and strategy issues should be measured against the fact that some of the world's largest and most successful intranets began life as ad hoc web sites or programmer experiments. If you look at the SunWeb in Chapter 3, for instance, you can see that it began with the efforts of a single individual and kind of grew from there. Of course, the Sun intranet is now highly organized, with gatekeepers and templates and all the other kinds of controls that are now common on the large, complex intranets. But those features were added later, after the intranet was already well under way. The planners were able to begin their efforts after the fact and mold what had already been started into an organized whole, without having to go back and reengineer every part of the intranet structure. That's why there's always hope for improvement on an intranet, no matter how amateurish the initial efforts.

A key point to understand is that centralized planning and control is somewhat antithetical to the idea of an intranet. You can try to go through a six-month planning period, making sure all possible problems are identified and dealt with in advance. But, at the current frightening pace of development in Internet technologies, everything will have changed by then anyway. Perhaps the best thing to do is to get started and, to a certain extent, improvise as you go.

Instead of centralized planning and administration, the word "empowerment" should be our mantra, along with our previous slogan of "Keep It Simple." The job of a planner should be to build a vessel that others pour their work into. Above all, it is important to recognize that in the Intranet Era, many of your employees—by and large—may be able to set up servers and develop content and applications by themselves, thank you very much. In this new era, employees will have the power to help themselves, and management may sometimes happen a little bit after the fact.

In most companies that were early web adopters, it was with the tolerance of management, rather than at their urging, that the intranet was formed. Lucky is the manager who fully understands what's going on. Executives traditionally have gotten little help with this from their IS staffs. But even the crustiest old systems analysts in IS are starting to crawl out from under their rocks and wake up to the potential of the intranet.

"IS people were asleep when personal computers happened," one observer told me two years ago, when I wrote the first edition of this book, "and I think they are asleep now on the World Wide Web." Now, if we can believe reports in *Computerworld, Information Week,* and most of the other venerable journals of the IS establishment, the people in IS have their ears perked and in many cases have their sleeves rolled up—with ambitious plans to take full advantage of the new intranet models

Still, empowerment is the key. In companies where employees are truly empowered, people tend to take this technology and run with it in all kinds of unexpected ways. In fact, you might gauge the intellectual health and level of entrepreneurship within your own organization by the speed at which intranets are adopted and grow. In companies where employees are functionally empowered, technologically enabled, and intellectually challenged, web technology may spread very fast. In companies that ration technology and where initiative is stifled by layers of bureaucratic control, you may see some signs of life on the intranet front, but the general rate of adoption may be incredibly slow. The quickest adoption often occurs at companies like Chevron, where savvy managers catch on and help lead the charge.

Intranets will work best when people are given the same freedom to use them that they now have with ordinary business applications like desktop publishing and spreadsheets. It's important to recognize that web technology—at its core—is not rocket science. It's just another business communications medium, as desktop publishing is now, but one in which the network substitutes for paper. But it's also important to realize that web will exponentially increase the speed and immediacy of business communications and that it will eventually suck in all the other information streams—not just words and pictures, but data, multimedia, messaging, conferencing, and applications.

When this happens, watch for a further flattening of organizational structures and drastic changes in the management of information systems. In the Intranet Era, midlevel managers will have an even smaller role as the intermediaries who interpret and transfer information between the bottom and top rungs of the corporate ladder. Executives and rank-and-file workers alike will have a common platform for communication where they can silently (or even audibly) audit each others' web pages, hear each others' concerns, and add their voices to corporatewide discussion groups focused on special topics. The new technology will enhance the communication of corporate goals, performance targets, and employee feedback across the organizational nexus.

IS managers now find their entire world shifting around them once again, as the intranet becomes the dominant environment for delivering data and applications. The entire method of application design and delivery may require a new phase of reengineering with a focus on more modular, applet-based information systems, and a more serious look at ways of integrating the entire information stream, including data, documents, multimedia, and applications. IS will certainly continue to be the guardian of back-end legacy data, but will find more and more of their information being served out directly onto the intranet. Many application programming functions may devolve out to individual departments or information centers, as people create their own form-based interfaces to data sources.

None of this should suggest that an intranet is unmanageable, or that there aren't concrete steps that should be taken to manage it. In fact, there are many management issues that must and should be addressed to ensure that people can use the new technologies in efficient and productive ways. This chapter will discuss the key management concepts and suggest ways that management can cope with the coming web explosion.

The Matter of Control

When you work with the Fortune 500, you find yourself being ushered through the halls and back alleys of some of the world's most massively structured organizations: miles of maze-like corridors opening onto warrens of cubicles, with doors that you need secret codes or passcards to enter. Large organizations love control, and the larger the organization, the more effort they spend controlling things. It's no wonder, then, that one of the key management issues in the intranet world has to do with the concept of control.

This is not a subtle thing at all. In fact, people make no bones about it. I once met with a potential client at a research arm of one of the Fortune 10 who was thinking about setting up an intranet, but with only a single server that could be controlled by the company's computer services group. "Our company likes control," he told me flatly. "We might not want just anyone going out and setting up a web server, or using one of these things."

This is a typical argument for those who haven't yet seen how the intranet works. But think about it. If the company likes controls so much, where are the controls on the telephone and e-mail systems? Who controls the desktop publishing and interoffice mail systems? All company employees can use a word-processing program to prepare a document, print as many copies as they want, and drop all those copies into interoffice mail to be distributed throughout the company with *no questions asked!*

"We can't control every word processor or copying machine," these people may argue. "That would be impossible. Everybody needs those tools to do their job."

That's my point exactly! You don't mind employees wasting money to print all this paper and hand deliver it to locations worldwide. They can do *that* without restriction. But if employees want to use the network to bypass these archaic information distribution systems, they have to ask for permission first. Does that really make sense?

Of course, at this point in the book, we all understand that the control issue is a vestigial part of the old information systems models. In traditional computing environments, you start with the idea that *everything is prohibited* unless someone in power enables it. Thus, people who want access to computer resources are typically given access only when someone approves it.

With intranets, assuming everyone has a browser on his or her desktop, access to information is typically granted *unless it is specifically restricted.* In other words, in the first intranet systems, employees started with full access and then were restricted from key applications only where that type of control was absolutely necessary (such as with highly confidential product designs, personnel records—that sort of thing).

This is a good model to follow, since it applies the bureaucratic strictures of control only to those applications where they are absolutely needed. The Holy Grail of intranet success—what any intranet should strive to achieve—is total employee participation across the entire organization. You are not going to get people to participate, however, if you put obstacles in their way.

Understanding the Web Control Model

That's not to say that control is not a legitimate issue. There must always be some amount of access control, even in an open system like a web. It's just that the control model has changed; almost inverted. On its face, a web server is the epitome of control. With web, however, the controls are totally nonintrusive, built-in, and decentralized.

Think about it: If I install a web server today and create documents and data to be accessed through that web server, then—by default—any user on the same network can see that information instantly without having to log in or even knock on the door. A simple click is all it takes to whisk the information away to the user's machine. In a system like this, you might think there's no control at all.

But look at what's really happening. Can anyone access just *any* information on the web server? No. The people who are looking at my web site see *only the information I want them to see.* In other words, I—the individual, the author and provider of the information—can exercise control over who sees what by moving it into my own web-server document folders. No one (unless he or she is a somewhat bored and very talented hacker) can see any other information on a web server unless the authors physically move it to the server folders. So the authors exercise control by choosing what they want to publish.

The bottom line is this: If I want people to see certain information on my computer, *I am the one who makes that decision—little old decentralized me.* Furthermore, I have the ability to let people view my information without the help of a network administrator. And, if I don't want people to see certain *other* information on my computer, again I am the person in control.

In either case, it's a win-win situation both for me *and* the network administrator. I don't need the administrator's help authorizing each individual user of my personal client-server system. And the administrator doesn't have to constantly manage user access to every server in the network. To put it in computer industry terms, you might say that after all the hype about open systems, client-server is finally moving to a truly open, distributed, and decentralized model, because in a web some of the old models of network administration have suddenly evaporated.

On an intranet, the control model is split the same way that the viewer-author model was split in online publishing (as previously discussed in Chapter 2). There are now two levels of control involved, which could be called *author* versus *viewer control,* or *server-side* versus *client-side control.*

The diagram in Figure 9.1 shows what I mean. Think of the web server as sort of neutral territory being visited from both sides by two opposing camps.

On one side are the authors of the information, who are mainly responsible for publishing it and keeping it up to date. On the other side are the users of the information, who are mainly responsible for browsing through it, learning from it, and occasionally interacting with it. Here's how the control systems work on both sides of the equation.

Server-Side Control

On the author/server side, we have the issue of who will be able to create new information and deposit it inside the web-server directories, who will be able to update the information, and who will be able to tamper with the configuration of the file systems or other aspects of the server host computer.

If department or division has installed its own web server, then this issue should be left up to the local group to decide. The nice thing about an intranet is allowing any department to set up a web server and be responsible for its own content and server configuration. The entire approach of this book is empowering people to use the network as an information dissemination tool for their own purposes, the same way they currently have unlimited use of the phone and interoffice mail system. Though unlimited and unregulated growth of individual servers would have been unthinkable, impermissible, and undesirable in older networks with limited bandwidth and centralized administration models, they will be increasingly feasible in the high-speed, mass-audience, wide area networks of the future where the network is suddenly too far-flung to treat as an empire and too high-speed for anyone to quibble about individual traffic burdens.

Some companies, however, still choose to provide a centralized server or group of servers—on the premise that many departments will not want to bother with installing, configuring, and maintaining their own. This works too, of course. It's a testament to the flexibility of the intranet that both models can

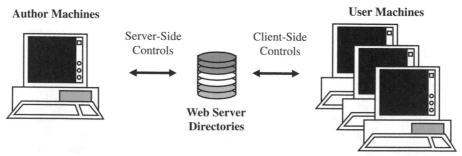

Figure 9.1 The web-server control model.

coexist fluidly side by side: a centralized group of servers controlled by IS and any number of distributed servers controlled by network-savvy developers and authoring groups scattered throughout the organization.

Traditional control models work well with servers that are shared by a large group of authors and developers. The web server can be installed like a network file server, with the server directories mounted as a local file system on each contributor's machine (Figure 9.2). That way, each author can directly access and edit the information just as though it were stored on a local hard drive. In this case, permissions would be set on the server side to make sure that only members of the group could access the server folders to change their content. Or an automated process could be used to transfer and convert web content in a shared work-group directory to a set of production server directories controlled by a webmaster.

On a wide area network with built-in Internet software, access to the server directories could be provided in other ways, including FTP through the network or through a dial-up connection. Thus, for example, authors might create and manage the content on their own local computers, then use FTP to transfer the completed files over to the web server. A time-triggered "cron" job could be set up as a batch process to automatically move regularly updated document sets to the server on a regular schedule. FTP is used widely on the Internet to transfer web site–content updates to third-party hosted sites. In general, FTP access is not as desirable as direct access, but it provides an alternative when direct server mounts would be difficult or inappropriate.

Client-Side Control

Access control issues are entirely different on the browser or client side of the web model (Figure 9.1). Here we start with the idea that there is no control at all, other than read-only access. In other words, anyone on the network can hit

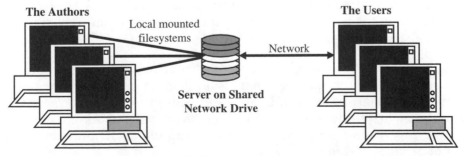

Figure 9.2   Work-group web server.

the web site and extract the contents, but no one can edit or change the contents at the site. That's for starters.

Beginning with this open model of universal read-only user access, we then have other levels of access control:

Read-write access to selected materials.   The authors or developers of the web site can selectively provide users with both read access and write access to certain materials. For instance, the authors might include interactive forms that can insert or update records in a database at the author's site. Though rarer, its not hard to imagine that future server-side applications will be used to pass edited documents back and forth from authors on the server side to collaborators on the client side. Chapter 7 discusses how two-way interactivity can be enabled on a web site.

IP address filtering.   The authors or developers of a web site can selectively allow or deny access from specified IP addresses. Most likely, this would be used to limit access to certain audiences, such as people in the same department or work group, or to certain classes of users such as dealers or sales reps.

User authentication.   If desired, web authors and developers can take their sites all the way back to the old login model where everyone who accesses the site must have a user ID and password. Naturally, this increases the administrative burden considerably, since each user ID and password must be set up individually at the web server. But some web authors and developers may want to use this feature interactively to "register" people for their sites. A form could be provided so that people can register their own user ID and password the first time they enter the site. A CGI program could be used to append the user IDs and passwords automatically to the site's password authorization file so that they don't have to be maintained manually. Using this method, the site authors have a way to capture a real snapshot of their potential user audience. Furthermore, user names and e-mail addresses captured on the registration form could be used as a mailing list to notify registered users of changes to the site.

Though access issues may seem a somewhat arcane subject, they are really at the core of the entire management issue. Though the intranet comes with certain access controls built in by default (read-write on author/server side, read-only on user/client side), much of the creative work in developing intranets revolves around how access is manipulated to provide different kinds of services and functionality.

Jump-Starting the Intranet

So we've studied all the technologies, we've looked at integration issues, we've talked about empowerment and access control—but how about getting the intranet started? We've come this far; are we saying the intranet just starts itself? What about all those intranets that started as experiments by small ad hoc groups and never went anywhere?

The traditional answer to these questions is something typically called a *pilot project.* This is a pump-priming mechanism designed to jump-start the intranet by defining the tools, best practices, standards and guidelines, typical content, and structure of the budding intranet. What's more, a pilot project can help your company develop a core of expertise that can serve as a basis for expanding the intranet. This isn't just a good idea for budding intranets where you are building things from scratch. Many corporate intranets that were not built using the pilot method eventually found themselves floundering. That's because not enough was done to provide employees with good models and best practices—the kinds of things that a pilot team can best handle.

Pilot Team Goals

The pilot can be a bridge between an intranet that is little more than a proof of concept and something more substantial—something that has the full approval and imprimatur of the organization. It begins with a project team carefully chosen from among the different departments and divisions of your company. It isn't necessary to have a bunch of Java and HTML experts—although a few of those would certainly be nice.

What's most important is that you have a team of relatively computer-savvy individuals who represent a good cross section of the company, and who are typically involved in publishing, database, or development projects within their own departments. By your selection of a team you are, in effect, saying: "These are the kinds of people who will be creating information on our intranet on a regular basis, once it is underway." These people should provide a role model to their own departments of what an intranet developer or publisher looks and acts like. In fact, expect these people to go back to their departments, tell exciting stories about what's going on, and eventually help spread around the expertise that will be needed when it comes times for everyone to get involved.

The people you select should be prepared to work part-time on web-development projects for a period of three to six months, in addition to their regular assignments. Most of their time will be spent in meetings, doing research on various aspects of intranet development, and in actual development time on key content areas.

The ideal team size is probably at most one or two dozen people, to keep it manageable. Here are the goals the team should aim to accomplish:

1. **Determine the content.**   One of the first actions a team takes is deciding on a set of ideal content that will get the intranet off to a good start. If the intranet is already started but not used widely, then the pilot team should take up the question: "What does this intranet need to make it truly vital to our organization?" This might include engineering reports, departmental newsletters, benefits information, product information, technical manuals, executive decrees, training materials, help desk information, database queries—you get the picture.

2. **Search for killer apps.**   The team should also look for some truly important applications—what we often call *killer apps*—that everyone in the organization will want to use, and that will thus make the intranet an indispensable part of daily office routine. You shouldn't have to look long for that kind of application. How about the company phone directory for instance? If you really want to get everyone's participation (and, of course, assuming you have a very high ratio of desktop computer users), you may want to consider making phone information easier to get online and harder to get in paper. If you haven't already, maybe now is the time to begin storing that information in a database and allow everyone to always get up-to-the-minute information on phone numbers, employee locations, and more, without having to wait for the next paper version to be printed. In fact, you could potentially allow employees to update their own information, or have the information automatically updated as part of a work order process whenever an employee is moved or reassigned. Employee benefits are another popular application on intranets, especially if the information is data-base driven and allows employees to look up details on pensions or other programs (password-protected, of course). Don't forget the kind of killer apps that may be more department specific, such as a "quote generator" for the sales department.

3. **Define a format.**   By putting all this representative content online, the team will provide a model for the intranet. Not only something that people can point to and say "this is great," but that also makes the statement: "This is the kind of information we should put on the intranet, and when we put it on there, this is how it should look." It

is especially important to define standard page layout elements that have the net result of making it easy for the end user to navigate through the intranet and determine whether the information being viewed is authoritative and up-to-date. This includes items such as the positioning, format, and appearance of navigation bars, corporate logo elements, revision dates, and contact information, such as the author's phone extension or e-mail address. This format will become part of your "standards and guidelines," as discussed later.

4. **Define standard tools.**   The team should be able to make some valuable decisions about the most productive set of tools to use for setting up web pages and developing web applications. Having a standard toolset is important because it will be easier for groups like help desk, purchasing, and training to support a limited set of tools, rather than support any tool that strikes anyone's fancy. This is why most large companies already have a "tech set" of officially supported software products. In effect, having already defined the best types of content and layout for intranet pages, the team is now saying: "These are the types of tools we should use to develop the content, and these are the methods we will use to develop the content."

5. **Define best practices.**   Each tool defines its own ideal work flow, just as each work flow demands an appropriate tool. Thus, a major result of tool selection and implementation will be to decide "best practices" for producing web content and migrating it to the intranet. If you read Chapters 5 through 7 of this book carefully, you should already have some good ideas about publishing tools, work flows, organizational structure, and application-development models for your intranet. The best practices defined by the pilot group may end up as a published set of standards and guidelines, which will provide a clear path for others to follow. It also helps if each author or developer in the pilot team writes up a report explaining "how I did it" so that others can see not only the model content, but also the model procedure for getting it online. The best way to deliver this information, of course, is in a prominent spot on the intranet itself, where would-be authors and developers can go for assistance.

6. **Define architecture.**   While you're at it, why not let the team decide how the intranet is to be set up and configured? There are many architectural issues to be decided: How many web servers should there be, and where should they be located for easiest access? Should employees be allowed to install their own ad hoc servers? How should server folders be organized and structured?

How should the top-level menus of the corporate intranet look and work? What browsers and plug-ins should be supported on the desktop? How will new content be integrated into the top-level menus? What kind of search engines should be included? Should the intranet support newsgroups and collaborative features? Team members may also want to handle more general infrastructural requirements, such as creating a common image library (GIFs and JPEGs) that everyone can use.

Assuming you have selected a diverse set of employees for the pilot team, the team members really are the best candidates for deciding all of these issues because, hopefully, they bring experience from their local departments to the table. They should have a gut feel for what will work and what won't work; what *is* worth the trouble and what *isn't* worth the trouble. Because they—not the director of IS or any individual expert—are in the best position to understand the publishing and application needs of their individual departments and the most productive work flows and tool sets that their own people will be able to handle.

Remember that the intranet ideally should be a participatory experience that involves nearly everyone generating information companywide. But you are not going to get people to participate unless you keep it simple through your selection of appropriate tools and your design of appropriate work flow. And you are not going to keep it simple unless you have peer groups defining what simple is.

While the pilot team is going through the process, it's fascinating to watch them grow in sophistication and self-assurance. Once the pilot is finished, you may suddenly realize that your awkward group of intranet novices is now a knowledgeable cadre of internal experts who can spread the logic and methodologies they've learned to their own individual departments, by providing training and support to others who try to follow in their footsteps.

Pilot Team Limits and Budget

When designing a pilot project, the don'ts are often just as important as the do's. The following are among the most important things *not* to do. If you have a failed or floundering project, or your pilot seems to be taking you nowhere, perhaps you can blame it on one of these problems:

Don't make the team too large.   One client of mine suggested maybe the pilot team should include hundreds of people, including many people on a secretarial level. How are you supposed to manage a group that large? Remember that the pilot project is something you manage, but the eventual result—the working intranet—is supposed to manage itself. So keep the initial group a manageable size. Then if the results are successful, you will have a model that hundreds or thousands of people in your organization can emulate.

Don't try to put everything on the intranet all at once.   The intranet is not something you create from scratch, then wipe your hands and walk away. It is an ongoing project. There will be time to add in everything you want eventually, but much of it can be added after the pilot is over and people in your company have examples that will allow them to understand how to get content online. Trying to lump everything into the pilot project will create what we call "the Big Bang." You don't need a Big Bang, nor the potential for chaos that it can create.

Don't get overly ambitious with any one component of the pilot project. It's important not to hold up the entire train to wait for a single application to come on board, or to bet the success of your intranet on any single all-important application. The value is in having a broad array of different content that users can select from. Since not everyone will go to the intranet for everything, there should be a little something for everyone. So you should focus on getting it started, giving people something to hang their hats on, and the most difficult, ambitious projects can still happen later.

Don't let the schedule drag.   The maximum time frame for the pilot project should be three to six months. Any longer than that, and people will lose patience—or lose faith in the project.

Don't spend more than you have to.   For example one client of mine with over one-thousand employees spent about $160,000 for the pilot, including the time of all the volunteer teams members. Incredibly, over half of the expense was charge-back from the company's computer services group for installing and tuning the servers. Outside consultants were about 25 percent of the total. The rest was the cost of software (a Netscape server) and the cost of team member time.

Perhaps the biggest "don't" relates to the last item. Don't expect outside consultants to come in and do it for you. At best, outside consultants can help by steering your organizational efforts and providing special expertise in certain fields like Java or IIS. If you fail to develop a cadre of internal experts, your intranet has a much smaller chance of succeeding in the long-term.

Don't Forget Rollout

The old saying, "don't hide your light under a bushel basket," applies in spades to the intranet. Creating a pilot intranet is just the first step. The next question is, "How do we get from point A to point B with this project?"

Take a cold hard look at the facts. If you've done your work right up to this point, you have a very useful pilot intranet already started. Now the problem is getting someone to use it. Just because you think the intranet is a great thing doesn't mean that everyone else will automatically agree with you. To get to point B in your intranet-development project, it's time to go through the phase called the *rollout.* For a period of days or week, there will be this tense pause between the quickly ending efforts of the pilot team and the time when people begin to use your intranet.

What you do within that period can make all the difference in the world to the ultimate success or failure of your project. Here are some suggestions:

Get management buy-in.　People will pay more attention to the intranet if upper management makes it known that this will be *the way that everyone will communicate in the future.* Employees have to know management thinks this is a good idea and that this is a key strategic focus for improving company operations.

Plan carefully.　Make sure that all the key rollout events are mapped out in advance so they proceed without delay. In fact, it should probably be the responsibility of the pilot team to plan and help conduct the rollout.

Promote and publicize.　Some companies throw parties equivalent to a major product launch. Try having an "Intranet Day" with short seminars, demonstrations, and a trade show atmosphere. Build anticipation and excitement for the new communication model. Add notices to all company newsletters and issue special bulletins. Put signs and posters on the walls for about a month, with intranet slogans on them.

Train, train, train.　Just because you find intranets understandable doesn't mean everyone will. And people will not believe in something they barely understand. You should offer all the depth of training that people might want, plus the flexibility of online training like that at www.intramark.com/. Remember that if you designed your work flow and selected your tools wisely, there should be minimal training involved.

Support and encourage.　Once you've done all the above, it doesn't necessarily mean that people will just hop in smiling. Expect a little chaos, and make it more tolerable through professional support and encouragement. Here is another place where former pilot team members can lend a hand. There should also be someone on your help desk who specializes in intranet questions.

Get rid of paper, where possible.   If some of the pilot intranet material duplicates information already on paper, warn people that the paper version will be phased out by such-and-such a date. People will stick with what they know, and if the same information is available on paper versus online, guess which one most people will choose? Again, this may be a training problem, since most people may not understand right away how up-to-date the intranet can be when compared to the paper version.

It's impossible to overstate the importance of doing the rollout right. Nothing less than the safety of your investment hangs in the balance.

Future Roles for the Pilot Team

Once the pilot is over and the rollout is underway, is it time for the pilot team to call it quits? Not necessarily. Pilot team members may have been inspired with even more ideas while doing the pilot, and may be ready to help deliver a slew of new applications. Once the rollout is finished, it may be wise to call the pilot team together for an occasional meeting to assess the results and see if there are more applications that could be brought online. In effect, the pilot team at this point becomes a *steering committee* or support team for the intranet.

The best use of such a support team is to have the members function as consultants and advisors on web technology to the rest of the organization. The responsibilities of this team could be quite diverse but would probably include some of the following, which could be handled part-time or full-time by pilot teamers or full-time staffers groomed for ongoing support roles:

◆ Promoting the use of web technology within the organization through seminars, workshops, and special events

◆ Helping with ongoing training of employees in Internet/intranet technologies

◆ Evaluating and critiquing the contribution of different departments to the overall Web

◆ Assisting with migration of content to the web within their individual departments (web administrator function)

- ◆ Advising departments on innovative ways to apply web technology to specific applications

- ◆ Providing the technical expertise where needed to develop more advanced applications such as interactive forms, CGI programs, and database integration

- ◆ Assisting in managing the overall Web, including broken-link analysis and usage reporting

An internal consulting group set up to perform these tasks can help promote organization goals without creating a centralized bureaucracy. Notice that many of these are also ideal tasks to hand to external consultants who will work with your company on a regular basis.

Why It's Never Too Late

Perhaps you've already undertaken a pilot project or have an intranet already underway and—well, let's just say the results are less than spectacular. Should you give up hope? That's a little like riding down the highway in 1920, finding a guy sitting by the side of the road in a broken down Ford Model T, and asking whether it wouldn't be better to just forget this whole car thing and go back to using a horse. No one thinks twice about using a car anymore, nor—in a year or two—will any company think of being without an intranet.

If you read the case studies carefully in Chapter 3, you may realize that some companies have redesigned their intranets more than once since getting started. Despite the massive size and complexity of the intranet, redesign is relatively easy, thanks to two little buzzwords I invented, but which refer to some very real features of the intranet. The buzzwords are *virtual centralization* and *planning after the fact*. Sit back while I explain what they mean.

As you're probably thinking by now, the fact that we let people go off and do their own thing on an intranet can potentially lead to chaos. Web sites proliferate somewhat haphazardly out on the network, without any guarantee that people will follow the company guidelines.

With an intranet, however, it's quite easy to point to new content simply by adding hyperlinks to your top-level menus. In fact, you can build and rebuild the main menus of your intranet as often as you please without changing the underlying content. And you can provide search tools that automatically connect users to the information they need in a flash. So even if your intranet came into being without a whole lot of planning, you can put a new face on the system that makes it look as though it had been *planned that way all along*.

This is what happened at Sun Microsystems and other companies in the Chapter 3 case studies. Even though planning is recommended, it is not always necessary to have every factor under control in a fast-growing intranet system. Consider this awe-inspiring fact: If the Internet had been planned, it would never have happened at all. The beauty of the Internet model—especially the hypertext features of the WWW—lies in your ability to impose a structure on it *after the fact*. On the Internet, that structure is imposed by ad hoc "best links" sites, web directories like *Yahoo!* (www.yahoo.com/), and web search/cataloging engines like *Excite* (www.excite.com/).

Often enough, people at the department level, or even the team level, do their best to populate the intranet with content without having anyone worry about how it will fit into the overall structure. Then you can come behind them and create a centralized directory structure (top-level home page and submenus) for your intranet, and arrange the top-level menus in any way you please. The intranet now appears to be centralized, when in fact it is completely decentralized (thus the term *virtual centralization*). And it appears to have been planned, when in fact nothing of the sort occurred (thus the idea of *planning after the fact*).

So you really have the best of both worlds: employee empowerment—people doing their own thing, yet with a management technique that captures what they're doing and makes this information accessible to the average user. You get to sit back and let people put the technology to its best uses, then come behind them and paste a big smiley face on the whole mess. It's kind of like the ultimate manager's dream, isn't it?

The 80/20 Rule, in Spades

You've heard about the 80/20 rule. It applies to many things: 80 percent of the money is earned by 20 percent of the population; 80 percent of the pizza is eaten by 20 percent of the gluttons; 80 percent of the complaints received by your company are made by 20 percent of the customers—that sort of thing. In this case, the 80/20 rule applies to information systems.

One of the key moments in computing history was probably the day—sometime back in the 1970s or early 1980s—when the name of most corporate computer departments changed from "data processing" (or DP) to "information systems" (or IS). This change recognized that computers could be used to deliver more than just raw data in the form of mind-deadening numbers, that instead they could be used to provide people with useful *information*.

The job of computer departments, then, was to capture information, process it, and present it to users in an automated way. And they've done an admirable job, considering what they've had to work with. Back in the days of *data processing,* the computer room was like Dr. Frankenstein's lab. The old CRT displays were covered with gibberish. Today, your very own personal computer is more likely to greet you with a smile, a catchy tune, or even visions of flying toasters romping in outer space.

But the job of automating information systems is far from complete. Even today, with all their growth and technical sophistication, corporate information systems only handle about 20 percent of the total information available in the enterprise. The other 80 percent falls under the category of *miscellaneous.* Information systems are great at handling all the mission-critical data, including customer information and accounting records, but not all the other stuff, such as reports, memos, catalogs, specifications, manuals, budgets, project schedules—you name it.

Nowadays, these various bits of information are *prepared* on computers, of course. But then they often get transferred straight into the *old* information system: the copier, mail room, and filing cabinet systems that handle tons of paper every day. Normally, you can't see these documents online unless you're the one who authored them. Or if they are online, they're online in an inaccessible way: in certain people's in-boxes, on certain network file servers that can only be accessed by certain groups at certain times, locked in PC Win-Help systems, and so forth. There hasn't been a way to take all of this information and catalog it in the same way you can catalog information in a database. Raw information is a messy business that doesn't easily submit to neat solutions the way raw data does.

The problem of automating the other 80 percent of corporate information, therefore, has been partly due to a lack of suitable technology. That's no longer true with the intranet. First, people put their information online using web-publishing tools, conferencing tools, and messaging tools—instead of putting it on paper with the old desktop-publishing tools. Then a search engine comes behind and makes it all accessible enterprisewide within seconds.

The feat you accomplish with virtual centralization is a little like what might have happened if you had deliberately set out to bring online the other 80 percent of data that remains untouched by the corporate IS function. But instead of years of dogged efforts by squadrons of bleary-eyed IS people and contract programmers, it can all happen fairly quickly.

Imagine being able to catalog and have at your fingertips every message, memo, report, or other document produced by any person in the company. Sounds incredible doesn't it? If you don't believe it can be done, go to Excite on the WWW (www.excite.com/) and enter a query for "Ryan Bernard." You'll instantly see a list of most of the places on the World Wide Web where my name is mentioned (over 100 at last count), including many of my own pages and messages that I posted to random Internet newsgroups as far back as fall 1994. How embarrassing; but also, how incredibly amazing. If you can do this kind of search for any subject or name across a global network with hundreds of thousands of servers, imagine what you can do in a more limited corporate network environment.

The Importance of Standards

Another area where management can make a difference in the development of an intranet is by promoting standards for development, design, and production of the new systems. There are basically two ways your company can deal with an intranet: (1) Employees can reinvent the wheel every day and do things in the hardest possible way, or (2) employees can benefit from a set of standards, guidelines, and tools that will help them work smart and be as productive as possible. Admittedly, these are two opposite extremes of the spectrum. There are gray areas in the middle, somewhere. But it pays to examine both the worst case and the best case to make a point.

Worst Case: No Guidance, No Standards

Let's look at the worst case first. Assume that all users are on their own without any standards, guidelines, or training to help them. First, they will have to go off and learn about web technology on their own. They'll have to read books like this one (actually, not a bad idea) or do about a year's worth of thinking and study on the subject before they realize how web-based communications can benefit the entire organization. Then they'll have to find it in their hearts to put the organization's best interests ahead of their own lethargy and start using the intranet. Not too likely, right?

Next, they'll have to locate some tools, or accept the tools selected by others in their group. Assuming the worst case—that someone in their group is already an HTML whiz and just adores using HTML editors—they'll probably start with an HTML editor, too. This will triple or quadruple the time they have to spend learning how to publish on a web, and each document they produce will be hacked together with about 5 times the effort it would have taken otherwise. The documents will be full of coding mistakes, may look rather like something the cat coughed up, will be difficult to navigate, and may have broken icons every place an illustration was supposed to occur. Instead of making things easier, the web suddenly made them harder.

To do database publishing, web authors will have to take the same path: learning what it is, finding the tools, and so forth, on their own. With multimedia it will be the same. Instead of helping people in their jobs, the intranet will hinder people and make their jobs harder. Instead of using the intranet to carry important communications, they will turn back furtively to the old methods, frustrating your goal of bringing the entire organization online.

The Ideal Scenario

Now let's look at how a well-designed set of standards, guidelines, tools, and work flows can help an organization. The first step is: *Everyone freeze!* Hands off the HTML editors. Let's get the following straight right from the beginning:

- Nobody changes tools.
- Nobody learns a stitch of HTML.
- Nobody does anything different, with a few key exceptions.

Here are the exceptions:

- If you already use Microsoft Word, here's a set of templates you can use for various types of documents: memos, manuals, reports, newsletters.
- If you already use FrameMaker, here's a set of templates you can use to do the same thing.
- If you already use "whatever," here's a set of templates for that.

Now everybody can go on about their business, using these templates whenever you want to create documents. When you're finished, save your work in this set of directories.

The templates would contain a set of *style tags* (also called a *style sheet*) that everyone should use to format their documents: *Heading 1* for major headings, *Heading 2* for subheadings, *Bullet* for bullets, *Body* for body text, and so on. To use the style tags, just point at the paragraph you're typing and select the correct tag from the style menu. This new method of preparing documents is a little disorienting the first few times, particularly for those people I call "creative formatters"—but you get used to it. You can distribute the templates as hyperlinked directly from a web page and include online instructions on how to use them or a full-fledged online style guide.

Some people quibble about this. You talk to companies that have never used templates, and they say it can't be done. Then you talk to companies that use them all the time and they say it's no big deal. The fact of the matter is this: When it comes to web publishing, you can either ask people to change their habits slightly by adopting a new workflow, ask everyone to learn new tools, or have someone who reformats and styles every paragraph of every document that needs to go onto the intranet.

Personally, I think it's easier to distribute the workload in such a way that everyone cooperates in maintaining a publishing standard. This helps avoid the retraining that would be involved in a move to new tools, or the rework and doubling of effort required to reformat everything that everyone writes. Style sheets are not hard to use: In fact, they will make everyone more productive even if you aren't doing web publishing.

The nice thing about style sheets is documents going up on the intranet in seconds—if you can get everyone using them correctly (and that's not really such a big *if,* assuming they're well-designed and people understand why they're important). For each set of templates, there will be a set of map files and a tool like HTML Transit or WebMaker that can suck the documents right out of their folders and turn them into a published web site on the fly (see Chapter 5 for an extensive description of the tools). It is important that the templates and map files be designed to work together by someone who understands style sheets, HTML conversions, the tools involved, and the formatting requirements of the web.

Once all the elements in a template-based work flow are set up and meshed properly, the conversion process is so easy that a single administrative assistant (or webmaster) could easily handle all the conversions required by a work group—or even a set of work groups—without seriously breaking stride (Figure 9.3). The only steps required for each set of documents would be to open the conversion program, specify the files to be converted, specify the conversion map file to use, and let the conversion run itself (see HTML Transit conversion examples in Chapter 5). If any given set of documents changes often, you may

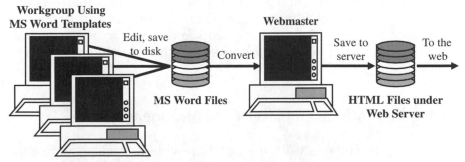

Figure 9.3   Work Group model using standard templates.

want to find ways to set up the conversion as a time-triggered batch process that runs automatically either nightly or weekly (depending on frequency of updates)—converting the same set of files regularly on a fixed schedule.

The Alternatives

If you feel that work groups shouldn't be required to use templates, it's still not a major problem. However, for each new document that comes down the pike, the person designated as webmaster will have to create an entirely new conversion map, or may have to go in and edit the documents manually. If you have an extra person to spare, this may be an acceptable way to go. But keep in mind that handling all the editing and conversion needs for an active work group may be a full-time job.

If you are strictly opposed to the idea of templates and style guides, and you don't want to dedicate a full-time webmaster to edit documents, the next option is to have your work group members drop all their current tools and retrain on web-publishing tools. In that case, I recommend WYSIWYG editing tools like Netscape Composer, FrontPage, or NetObjects Fusion, among many others (see Chapter 5).

The idea of serving data and multimedia is a little more tricky, but easily dealt with. If you set up a web advisory group in your company, it should be the job of that group to locate tools that are compatible with the database platforms most commonly used on your network (see discussion of database access in Chapter 7). Once these tools are selected, a person trained as a webmaster could create the forms and database hooks needed to set up interactivity. Compared to ongoing document publishing efforts, the need to create new database access applications is relatively rare. Someone who is good at this might spend a day or two a week filling the needs of several work groups.

Multimedia is not a problem if the work group is already familiar with illustration and multimedia tools. If you're going to do sound or video on a web, it will typically be done by some group in your organization that was already using these. The intranet advisory group can choose the appropriate multimedia conversion tools and give the work group the appropriate training needed to use them and to embed multimedia into web documents (see Chapter 6 for a discussion of multimedia).

Achieving Buy-in from Employees and Management

If you're going to create a truly organization-wide intranet, you're going to need participation from everyone. That means not only identifying mission-critical applications and creating teams to develop them, but allowing people to use the intranet as a standard conduit for their critical information.

One of your greatest challenges in doing this will be helping people understand the benefits of the new communications model. Just because you find this technology powerful and productive, you shouldn't assume everyone will share your feelings automatically. To get everyone working on the same channel, it's necessary to achieve buyin from both the executive level and the rank-and-file employee level. To bring benefits to the entire enterprise, the intranet must achieve a certain level of saturation within the organization.

Preliminary reports back from the front say that it's not easy to impress rank-and-file employees with the benefits of this technology unless several things happen:

- Upper management makes it clear that it supports the effort and that it considers an organization-wide intranet to be an important strategic tool of the organization.

- The intranet contains a critical mass of important applications that people need in their daily work and that are essential time-savers. That means not just documents but crucial up-to-the-minute data, like the profit-and-loss statements Chevron maintains for each team (see Chapter 4).

- Rank-and-file employees get the tools and training they need to make web publishing easy—and even fun.

Never underestimate the enthusiasm of empowered employees. In places where employees have been given the right tools, the right models, the right emphasis on benefits, and the right training, the intranet has achieved critical mass and taken off. In some places, the intranet is so popular that other problems arise: keeping people from doing too much with it and using it for inappropriate purposes, such as putting up pictures of their children and dogs.

In places where employees don't get the proper tools and training, where management imprimatur is absent, or where the intranet is still in an experimental or stripped-down stage, the task will be harder. People may applaud the new technologies, then turn around and go right back to doing things the old way.

Of course, no matter how much you try to train and promote the intranet, there will always be some people who just won't "get it." After all, we are still trying to convince some people of the benefits of *e-mail* for Pete's sake. For people who fail to see the shortcomings of the old technologies, there's probably little point in trying to explain new communications models like the intranet.

In the end, you shouldn't have to force people to use web-publishing tools any more than you have to force them to use desktop publishing. People already use desktop publishing as a matter of convenience, to help rapidly develop the standard written communications required in every job. They should use web publishing the same way, but also for its added benefit of allowing document distribution without the hassle of printing and distributing paper documents. When people see the benefits of the intranet fairly presented—that it can speed up their communications and take the drudgery out of distribution, it should be sufficient to turn them on. But that doesn't mean it necessarily will.

Budgeting the Intranet

As I continue writing this chapter, I keep hearing the low murmurs from all you bottom-line managers out there: "Yeah, sure. So how much will it cost?" A few more paragraphs go by, and again I hear that insistent muttering in the background: "Yeah, yeah. So what's it going to cost me?"

Naturally, any time you adopt new methods and tools, there are going to be new costs. But change is now a constant in the business world, and the cost of change is always with us. Changing tools to keep up with the technology curve makes good business sense, because it increases productivity, which lowers costs. If new tools don't do this for us, we should reject them.

The costs of developing new intranets will show up in two main areas: the cost of retooling and the learning curve. Let's look at these one at a time.

The Cost of Retooling

There are several different types of tools you will have to adopt to make the internet work that didn't exist before. This is mainly in the area of servers and clients (browsers), but also may involve some authoring tools as well. What's incredible is how many of the new tools will be available at no additional cost. From servers, to web browsers, to authoring tools, there are low-cost or no-cost options available:

Browsers.   In this category, your current choices are Netscape Navigator, near $50 per seat, versus Microsoft Internet Explorer for free. Many companies think this is a no-brainer. Why pay for something when you can get a product of equal or better quality for free? (Let's ignore for a moment whether it was fair for Microsoft to compete against Netscape by giving away its web clients and servers, when in fact web client and server software is all that poor Netscape has to sell.) In most intranets I have seen, Internet Explorer will be the default browser in the foreseeable future. Netscape was the strongest contender—and people were willing to pay extra for it—until Internet Explorer 3.0 was launched. Since then, Internet Explorer has equaled or surpassed Netscape in every feature category. In the future, Netscape will be used mainly on mixed-platform Intranets that have a strong UNIX component, or for special purpose applications that have Netscape components on both the server and client side. In fact, during the 1998 to 1999 time period—barring intervention by the U.S. Justice Department or a major change in business strategy at Netscape—I predict that Netscape's share of the browser market will plummet from its previous 80 percent level to around 25 percent or less, mainly due to its weakness in the intranet market.

Servers.   Again, the choice is similar. Do you want to pay for Netscape servers like SuiteSpot and FastTrack, or do you want to get Microsoft's Internet Information Server (IIS) for free? "For free" means you are actually purchasing Windows NT Server, of which IIS is a free component. If you were using NT anyway as a network operating system, then IIS will cost you nothing more. On a UNIX platform, Netscape is a better argument, but again there are several free servers on the market, including the old NCSA server and the perennially favorite Apache server (www.apache.org/). Naturally, the number of servers required to support a web might be quite low—in the dozens, depending on your company size. And, if you pay extra for them, the costs of each server may be anywhere from $500 to $1,500—not exactly a budget-breaking investment.

Authoring tools.   On the authoring side, again, you will find many free alternatives. If your workforce uses Office 97 or any of the most recent office suites, users will find the ability to create web pages already built-in. If you shell out money to put Netscape Communicator at the desktop, you will find Netscape Composer already available. If you don't have Communicator, for productivity's sake, you may want to consider investing in an advanced WYSIWYG editing tool like FrontPage for certain authoring groups who primarily publish to the intranet. Costs for these tools are in the $150 to $500 range per author.

Developer tools.   Development tools are another story. It is quite possible—and actually quite common—to develop Java, JavaScript, or CGI/

Perl applications using nothing more than a text editor. Of course, plenty of visual development environments exist as well, which range from inexpensive to pricey. Again, productivity is the determiner here. If developers can save time with special tools, they are probably worth the investment.

Even though most of the tools for intranets are free or low cost, it's still a good idea to make sure that people aren't retooling unnecessarily—since that takes its own toll in terms of lost work time and productivity drain. This is one area where a good set of standards, templates, and work flow models can save people from retooling, by making sure that web content can be generated from standard office documents and that only a few specialists will be needed to handle the technical requirements of HTML coding or web-application programming.

As part of the cost of retooling, consider the efforts required to roll out the new tools. As part of its push to standardize the entire company on a single browser, one company developed standard toolset configurations for its Mac, PC, and UNIX platforms, then enlisted the help of its marketing and PR departments in spreading the word among internal employees. To save time, confusion, and support costs, the browser software was configured in such a way that—upon installation—it automatically referenced the proper proxy servers for Internet access and also opened automatically to the standard internal home page that centralized access to all the top-level resources, as well as most lower-level servers.

The Learning Curve

With the cost of retooling comes the cost of retraining. If you have used computers much over the past decade, you already recognize that retooling and retraining did not start with the intranet. The main cost of retraining should be in the areas of:

◆ Introducing rank-and-file employees to the intranet and use of the web-browser tool

◆ Showing key development groups how to set up and maintain servers

◆ Training in web-publishing techniques, where required

The steepness of the learning curve—and the training costs involved—will be directly related to how sophisticated your intranet is and how well you were able to avoid certain key stumbling blocks. For instance, the web browser itself requires practically no training, since all you have to do is point and click. Extra training may be required, however, in the concept and benefits of an intranet—why it works the way it does, and why it is better than some of the old tools used for publishing and data delivery.

If the intranet includes newsgroup-style discussion threads, your training may need to include the newsreader features of the browser. If it includes Internet integration, your training may need to expand to include Internet concepts in general and a tour of key WWW sites and directory services.

More training will be needed on the authoring and development side for key groups of content providers. If your organization already uses style guides and templates for document publishing, or if you plan to use them, there may be very little training required, since most people can continue using their standard publishing tools. The training burden will increase as you move away from that ideal to the idea of people learning new WYSIWYG editing tools or even raw HTML coding.

Assuming you've already done training before for other types of computer systems, you should already know how much training costs will run in your area. In the U.S., training costs can range from $100 to over $300 per employee for each day of training. This, then, will be your biggest cost, which is why it is important to minimize the retraining required. Low-cost online alternatives are available, like the IntraMark product at www.intramark.com/.

Software Licensing and Support Issues

A key point to remember, of course, is that many of the tools you may need to build or maintain an intranet are available over the Internet as freeware or shareware. When using these types of tools, it's important to understand the difference between the various software licensing options, as well as the quality and support issues involved. First a definition:

Freeware is just that: programs offered for free in the public domain without licensing restrictions.

Shareware is trademarked and copyrighted software that is initially offered for free during an evaluation period but that requires a registration or licensing fee if used in an ongoing basis.

Freeware often includes programs created by universities or nonprofit organizations that may be offered for free to other similar institutions but that may not be free to commercial for-profit organizations. For instance, the original

NCSA Mosaic product was issued with such stipulations. However, the freeware category includes sophisticated commercial products offered by highly respected software vendors, including Microsoft's Internet Explorer or Adobe Corporation's Acrobat Reader product. Often the big software vendors offer freeware as an extension to their regular line of products. For example, Word Viewer makes Microsoft Word files available to a wider audience by allowing anyone to view Word files online. Similarly, Acrobat Reader allows anyone to view PDF files created using other Adobe products such as Acrobat Exchange or Distiller.

Shareware includes programs offered by individual programmers, small programming shops, small companies, or even respected commercial vendors. Many software developers turn to shareware as a method for distributing software because, although it increases the risk of piracy or abuse, it also lowers marketing costs to almost nil. Increasingly, companies are offering beta versions of their products over the Internet as shareware or evaluation versions that have built-in time limits.

Netscape, for instance, regularly offers the latest beta version of its Navigator browser for free downloading over the Internet, but builds in a time lock that disables the program after a certain date. Commercial versions without a time lock can be purchased from Netscape on a per-copy basis, or as a site license. Most of the other popular web tools are offered for downloading from the WWW on a free-trial basis for a limited period of time.

Freeware and shareware often suffer from the perception that they are inferior products simply because they are inexpensive or easily obtained. While this may be true for certain isolated products, this is not necessarily true as a rule of thumb. If there is any inferior aspect to freeware and shareware, it is their tendency to be unsupported products, in the sense that you are not likely to receive human assistance in case you have trouble. Increasingly, the only support offered are documentation and troubleshooting tips, lists of frequently asked questions, and the occasional product-related newsgroup where you can ask other users questions, or e-mail support where you can mail in questions and receive mailed answers.

If you plan to offer shareware or even freeware as standard equipment to users on your network, you should consider both the licensing and support issues involved. Licensing is especially important in a commercial environment because you may expose your company to liability if you fail to live up to the terms of the licensing agreement and fail to pay the registration fees associated with a product.

Always read and be prepared to comply with the fine print in the README files that come with the product before authorizing it for widespread use on your network. A careful virus scan on the original copy of the product is also a good idea. You should adopt freeware and shareware only with eyes wide open to the potential support issues involved. If documentation and technical support are *not* offered with the product, your organization may have to provide them to users, which may add to your cost. In that sense, shareware may not always be the deal it is cracked up to be, and it may actually be cheaper overall to invest in a more expensive commercial product that *does* offer actual support and documentation.

Where Do We Go from Here?

This concludes the main body of the book, and the survey of the tools, technologies, and techniques used in developing and building an intranet. I hope you are able to put these all to good use within the context of your own organization, to bring a new level of immediacy and functionality to your networked environment, and to improve communications across your organization. Good luck in your web-building chores, and watch for future editions of this book that will track the ongoing development of new technologies within the intranet environment.

For information on seminars or training materials related to this book, see the Wordmark.Com, Inc. home page at www.wordmark.com/ and the Intra-Mark home page at www.intramark.com/.

What's on the Web Site?

The companion web site for *The Corporate Intranet, Second Edition* can be found at www.wiley.com/compbooks/bernard. It contains various information and resources you may find useful:

A book summary and a lengthy excerpt from Chapter 1 of the book. This information is provided mainly for use by those who have not yet purchased the book, but who want to learn about the book by browsing through the web site.

A sample intranet containing some simple examples of the types of information typically found on intranets. This is not an extensive model, nor does it show any of the complex applications that can be developed for intranets. However, it can help give an idea of what an intranet may look like to those who have not yet come into contact with them. It can also be used as a simple prototype, if you want to quickly demonstrate to others in your company what an intranet looks and feels like. The sample intranet is provided in a zipped format, so you can easily download it, unzip it, and transfer it to your in-house web server for demonstration purposes. On the sample intranet you will find:

- A home page with a clickable image map (Figure A.1)
- A sample "What's New" page providing an overview of site content
- An employee phone directory
- A quick tour of the fictional company called TSM Incorporated
- A rudimentary document library with sample documents in HTML format

♦ An employee bulletin board with examples of several forms, which simulates the operation of forms (actual back-end application not connected)

♦ A search page, which simulates an online search (actual search engine not connected)

Links to other resources, such as a training product based on *The Corporate Intranet,* Second Edition (http://www.intramark.com/) and various resources at my web site, including:

♦ Reviews of this book

♦ Reader testimonials about the book (write me at rbernard@ wordmark.com if you want to add your own testimonial)

♦ Links to vendor sites for key Internet/intranet tools that you can use to create or improve your own intranet

Of course, this is only the beginning. I will keep updating the site from time-to-time as more information and resources become available.

Figure A.1   Sample Intranet Home Page.

Hardware and Software Requirements

To use the web site, you will need a reasonably up-to-date computer (486 PC or better), an Internet connection, and a copy of Internet Explorer (version 3.0 or higher) or Netscape Navigator (version 2.0 or higher). The web site contains simple hypertext links and tables. However, earlier browsers may not be able to correctly read the information at this site. If you do not have a current web browser, you can download one from the Internet at home.netscape.com or at www.microsoft.com/ie.

User Assistance and Information

The web site and its accompanying information are being provided "as is," without warranty or support of any kind. Should you require assistance accessing the web site, please call this Wiley product support number at (212) 850-6194 weekdays between 9 A.M. and 4 P.M. Eastern Standard Time. Or, we can be reached via e-mail at: **wprtusw@wiley.com.**

To place additional orders or to request information about other Wiley products, please call (800) 879-4539.

glossary

active server pages (ASP). A way of storing information on a web server that uses server-side scripting to deliver finished pages to the web browser. The script runs at the time the page is called and delivers finished HTML to the browser. ASP was designed by Microsoft for use with its servers, but it can deliver pages for viewing in any up-to-date web browser.

active streaming format (ASF). A format developed by Microsoft Corporation that allows you to develop streaming multimedia presentations using sound, video, and other formats.

ActiveX. An updated version of Microsoft's original Object Linking and Embedding (OLE) technology, which allowed components of one program to be embedded in another. This allows various *controls* to be added to web pages that perform application-style functions.

animated GIF. A GIF file that contains multiple images, which are swapped out in a sequence that produces an animated effect. See also GIF.

anonymous FTP. A way of connecting to an FTP server without a unique user ID and password. If an FTP server is set up for public use, you can log in with the user ID *anonymous* and use any set of characters as the password. People who log in this way are usually limited to a fixed set of public directories.

API (application programming interface). A set of features that allow a software program (application) to control, or be controlled by, other applications.

applet. A small program, usually written in the Java programming language, that is intended for delivery over a network to a Java-enabled client such as a web browser.

application. Any computer program designed to accomplish a specific task or related set of tasks.

backbone. The main trunkline of a network, which supports all the branches (subnetworks). Usually faster than the other parts of the network, it can easily handle communications between all the outlying parts of the network.

back end.   Processes or applications that run behind the web server, from the point of view of the user or client. For example, a web server might use Oracle as a back-end database for serving data to users.

bandwidth.   The data transmission capacity of a network connection, usually expressed in kilobits per second (Kbps), megabits per second (Mbps), or gigabits per second (Gbps). For instance, the bandwidth of a typical consumer modem is between 14.4 and 56 Kbps. Parts of the Internet backbone, on the other hand, have bandwidths in excess of 1 Gbps. Data transfer volumes and speeds increase as the bandwidth increases.

browser.   Any software program that allows you to visually display and navigate through information stored on a local drive, an intranet, or the Internet. See also web browser.

bytecode.   A generic, compiled format for Java and other program code that can be interpreted by any compatible browser.

cable modem.   A way of connecting computers to the Internet using cable TV technology.

cascading style sheets (CSS).   A feature of HTML available in the 4.0 or later versions of Netscape Navigator and Internet Explorer. CSS allows you to redefine HTML tags to include specific font changes, spacing, or indentation, then to apply those styles across multiple pages through linked references. In theory, the page layout style of an entire web site (or intranet) can be controlled entirely from a single point in the network.

CERN.   The European Particle Physics Laboratory in Geneva, Switzerland, where the original protocols for the World Wide Web were first developed and implemented.

CGI (Common Gateway Interface).   A standard communications interface that allows web servers to communicate with back-end processes, such as databases or other servers. CGI was widely used in the early days of the Web but is now often seen as too low-performance for most high-traffic business applications.

CGI script.   A short, uncompiled computer program written using a scripting language (typically Perl) that handles the communication between web servers and other applications. For instance, when a user fills out an online form, a CGI script might be used to process the user input, extract key data, and then do something with it. The script might store the data in a local file on the server, forward it in the body of an e-mail message, or insert it into a database.

channel.   See push channels.

channel definition format (CDF).   A format developed by Microsoft Corporation that allows web-site developers to define push channels.

client.   The part of a client-server application that runs on the user's local machine and interacts with remote servers located on other parts of the network. For example, Netscape Navigator and Microsoft Internet Explorer are client programs designed to obtain data and files from remote web servers.

client-server.   A way of designing software applications that divides the work between two separate but linked components. The *client* software typically runs on the user's local workstation, helps the user request data from the server, and displays the requested data appropriately on the user's screen. The *server* software typically runs on a remote computer located elsewhere on the network, handles requests from multiple clients, processes the data as requested, and returns requested data to the clients. See also server and client.

database.   Any file or set of files containing data stored in an organized format.

database management system.   Computer software that manages databases.

DBML (database markup language).   A language used to embed database access commands inside of HTML documents, the same way HTML is used to embed document-publishing and hyperlinking commands inside of plain text documents.

desktop.   The local computer environment that sits on a user's desk. Also, the set of applications available on a user's local computer, including the operating system.

directory.   The term used in UNIX and early PC operating systems to describe a location on a hard drive where files are stored. This is equivalent to the term *folder* in Mac and Windows 95 systems.

domain.   A way of organizing the Internet, characterized by the suffix of the domain name. For example, *.com* is the commercial domain that includes organizations like *microsoft.com* and *fedex.com; .edu* is the educational domain that includes entities such as *rutgers.edu* and *harvard.edu.* Other domains include *.org* (organizations), *.mil* (military), *.gov* (governments), and *.net* (networks). Special geographical domain suffixes are provided for Internet services that are specific to a country, such as *.us* for the United States, *.ca* for Canada, *.fr* for France, or *.de* for Germany.

domain name.   An easy-to-remember name that can be used to address a specific computer over the Internet. Typically, the domain name is associated with a specific IP address and can be used interchangeably with its assigned address. For example, if the domain name *abc.com* is assigned to the computer at network address 192.2.123.45, you can use either *abc.com* or 192.2.123.45 to address the computer. See also host name and IP address.

download. To transfer data from a remote computer (host) to a local computer. See also upload.

DSL (Digital Subscriber Line). An advanced digital format for communicating over phone lines. It is expected to be a major way that users will connect to the Internet in the future.

dumb terminal. A type of computer display used with mainframe systems that has no computing power of its own. All the work is done by the mainframe computer. The dumb terminal displays data locally and captures the user's keyboard response.

dynamic HTML. New features added to HTML with the 4.0 version of Netscape and Internet Explorer that allow finer control over the layering and positioning of objects on a web page. Dynamic HTML also allows scripts to be embedded in the web page, which cause the page to change based on user actions, without requiring additional calls to the server.

environment. A set of conditions or components that control the operating requirements of a computer system. For example, the "Windows environment" typically includes the Microsoft Windows operating system running on Intel-compatible chips. See also platform.

Ethernet. A bus-based network technology used to connect computers. Traditional Ethernet bandwidth is about 10 Mbps, though many networks now run at 100 Mbps or even faster speeds.

extensible markup language (XML). A markup language that can be used, like HTML, to display certain types of data across the Internet or intranet. For instance, Virtual Reality Modeling Language (VRML) is an extensible markup language that allows you to simulate 3-D objects in a browser display.

extranet. A way of connecting authorized external users—such as customers, dealers, suppliers, and business partners—to a private intranet, typically using the Internet as the data channel.

file server. A traditional type of LAN service that allows files to be stored on the hard drive of a remote computer and accessed by authorized users through the network. Storing and accessing files this way allows users to expand their storage space and file-exchange capabilities by sharing a large and powerful hard drive, which is typically called a *network drive.*

firewall. A control mechanism placed on a private network to prevent unauthorized access. Typically a gateway machine that uses some type of software to examine packets being transmitted.

folder. A term used in Mac and Windows 95 environments to describe a location on a hard drive where files are stored. This is equivalent to the term *directory* or *subdirectory* in UNIX and PC systems.

form. A hypertext document containing various GUI-style fields and devices, including text boxes, pull-down menus, pushbuttons, radio buttons, and check boxes.

freeware. Software that is distributed free of charge, usually through the Internet or through more traditional computer bulletin boards.

front end. The client interface. In other words, the "front" side of a client-server application that directly communicates with the user. Compare back end.

FTP (File Transfer Protocol). An Internet-based client-server application that lets you exchange files with other computers. You can log in to a remote FTP server and display lists of files, just the way you do on your local computer. Then you can use your own computer to *get* files, transferring them from the host computer to your computer. In some cases, you can also *put* files, transferring them from your computer to the host computer. The first web browsers included the ability to download files from FTP servers. See also anonymous FTP.

gateway. An interface between different types of networks or applications, which may control access to the network and automatically convert the data from one format or protocol to another.

Gbps. Gigabits per second. A way of measuring network capacity or *bandwidth* that shows how many units of data can be transmitted each second.

GIF. A graphics file format developed by CompuServe to be used for transmitting pictures and diagrams across online computer networks. Used as one of the native graphic formats for web pages. See also JPEG.

groupware. Software that allows multiple users to work as a group on the same set of data or documents. Groupware often includes integrated e-mail, scheduling, and other group-oriented communication features.

GUI (graphical user interface). A way of displaying information on the computer screen in a graphical format, using windows and a mouse. Compare to the old character-based interfaces (including the DOS and UNIX operating systems, which only displayed text characters and could only be manipulated from the keyboard).

helper application.   A program used to play back special file types. See also plug-in.

home page.   The opening page or main menu of any web site. Normally, this page appears by default if you do not request a specific file.

host name.   An easy-to-remember name that can be used to address a specific computer on an internal network. On a TCP/IP network, the host name is typically associated with a specific IP address and can be used interchangeably with its assigned address. For example, if the host name *hrweb* is assigned to the computer at network address 192.2.123.45, you can use either *hrweb* or 192.2.123.45 to address the computer. See also domain name and IP address.

HTML (HyperText Markup Language).   A standard way of marking up text so that it can be displayed online in a web browser. HTML includes not only style tags for headings, bullet lists, and the like, but also provides ways of creating *hyperlinks,* online forms, multimedia, and embedded applications.

HTMLHelp.   One of two competing standards for displaying traditional WinHelp-style online help through web browsers. See also NetHelp.

HTTP (HyperText Transfer Protocol).   The standard protocol used to communicate between web clients and web servers, specifically by using hyperlinks containing URLs.

hyperlink.   A coded link in hypertext that causes new information to be retrieved. The hyperlink makes use of a URL to retrieve the correct information from the correct computer.

hypertext.   Any text that contains hyperlinks to other sources of information.

imagemap.   An image that contains multiple embedded hyperlinks. You can click on different parts of the image and it retrieves different web pages, such as a map of your region that retrieves information for each city you click on.

information center.   Any division, department, business unit, group, or individual in a company that has information to share with others. Also, the web service used to publish that information.

interlaced GIF.   A GIF file that is formatted in such a way that the image "fades in" a little at a time. This format helps speed up the loading of web pages by giving the user an instant idea of what the graphics will look like, even before they are fully loaded. See also GIF.

Internet.   A global collection of private networks that are interconnected through public links.

InterNIC.   The Virginia-based organization responsible for registering top-level Internet IP addresses and domain names.

intranet.   A set of Internet-style services installed on a private network. The intranet typically uses the TCP/IP networking protocol to provide web services, e-mail services, newsgroups, and even file transfer.

IP address.   A string of numbers, such as 192.2.123.45, that identifies a specific computer on a network using the TCP/IP protocol. See also TCP/IP and domain name.

IP filtering.   The ability to limit server access to certain IP addresses, or to exclude certain IP addresses from server access.

ISDN (Integrated Services Digital Network).   A communication technology used to transmit relatively high-speed digital data over ordinary telephone lines. ISDN speeds range from 56 to 128 Kbps, depending on the number of channels used.

Java.   A programming language created specifically for the web environment. As opposed to traditional programming languages like C, which must be compiled into versions that can only run on specific platforms, Java is designed to be delivered in a generic "bytecode" format and "interpreted" at the web client end. This makes it completely platform independent. Compilers are also available as an option.

Java Database Connectivity (JDBC).   A method of connecting web applications to databases using special drivers and Java components.

JavaScript.   A scripting language developed by Netscape Communications that can be added to web pages to perform special programming functions. Microsoft created a similar language called *JScript*.

Javastation.   A type of computer that uses Java for the operating system and also as the native language of all its applications.

JPEG.   A graphics file format developed by the Joint Photographic Experts Group as a highly compressed way of storing photos on computers. Used as one of the native graphic formats for web pages. See also GIF.

Kbps.   Kilobits per second. A way of measuring network speed or *bandwidth* that shows how many units of data can be transmitted each second. Also used as a way of measuring modem speed. For instance, some modems transmit data at a rate of 28.8 or 36 Kbps.

legacy data.   Data stored on older computer systems or in older file or database formats that often remains behind as the *legacy* of older technologies. Often, this data presents a challenge to client-server developers because it is still useful, but not always easy to integrate into more current systems.

local area network (LAN).   A set of computers in a local area that are linked together using network cables.

machine name.   See host name.

Macintosh or Mac.   A brand of computer produced by Apple Computer Corporation.

mainframe.   A large floor-mounted computer system that serves as the main data processing unit in most large to mid-sized companies.

Mbps.   Megabits per second. A way of measuring network speed or *bandwidth* that shows how many units of data can be transmitted each second. For instance, most Ethernet networks run at 10 Mbps. Also used as a unit of measurement for some high-speed connectivity devices, such as cable modems.

modem (modulator-demodulator).   A device used to transfer data between computers by converting the data stream into a burst of sound that can be transmitted over a phone line and then returned to its original state at the other end.

Mosaic.   The first full-featured windows-based graphical browser for web applications. Mosaic was originally developed by the National Center for Supercomputing Applications (NCSA). An enhanced version was developed by Spyglass Inc. under license to NCSA, and this version provided the original technology for both of the most popular web browsers, Netscape Navigator and Microsoft Internet Explorer.

NCSA.   Usually refers to the National Center for Supercomputing Applications at the University of Illinois. Also refers to the National Computer Security Association.

NetHelp.   One of two competing standards for displaying traditional Winhelp-style online help through web browsers. See also HTMLHelp.

network.   A set of wires that connect computers and allow them to communicate and exchange data. Also, the collection of computers and applications that are networked together.

NetPC.   A type of desktop computer that runs the Windows operating system, but that also gets some of its applications or functionality from servers located on a network.

network computer (NC).   A type of desktop computer that relies in whole or in part on network servers for its ability to operate. This term is typically associated with devices that do not use the Windows operating system and are promoted by companies like Sun Microsystems and Oracle Corporation. Compare to personal computer.

newsgroup. A computerized bulletin board that contains messages posted by various users who subscribe to the newsgroup. Often used for discussion forums on the corporate intranet.

newsreader. Software used to read the information posted to a newsgroup.

NT (New Technology). A version of the Microsoft Windows operating system designed for use on servers and workstations in a networked environment.

ODBC (Open Database Connectivity). A method of communicating with databases through a "driver" interface that works on the same principle as a printer driver. This way, if you want an application to control a certain type of database, you select the ODBC driver for the database and the control mechanisms are handled automatically.

online publishing. Publishing information in such a way that it can be viewed online. Also see web publishing.

on the fly. Created at the moment it is requested. For instance, some web pages do not exist until the moment that the user requests them. Then certain scripts or programs on the server create the web page instantaneously based on user inputs, queries, templates, and/or built-in page description parameters.

operating system. Software used to handle the underlying infrastructure of a computer. The operating system provides a way of running other computer applications, and accessing disk drives and other peripheral devices

packet filtering. A method used by some firewalls to examine each data packet arriving at a computer or router, and then to approve or deny access based on each packet's characteristics.

PDF (portable document format). A platform-independent file format developed by Adobe Corporation for use with its Acrobat line of products. PDF is a standardized format that can be used to display published documents online.

peripheral. A device connected to a computer, such as a disk drive or printer.

Perl (Practical Extraction and Report Language). A scripting language commonly used to handle the input from web forms in early web systems. Perl scripts can accept data from web servers through the Common Gateway Interface (CGI), process the data, and deliver the results back to the web server through CGI.

personal computer (PC).   Originally, any computer that contained all the memory, processors, peripheral devices, and other components that made it capable of operating in a standalone mode. Now typically used to describe desktop computers running the Windows operating system. Compare to network computer (NC).

pilot.   A type of team project traditionally used to provide the initial content and applications for an intranet.

platform.   A specific combination of operating system and hardware that dictates the operating requirements of a computer application. See also environment.

plug-in.   A program designed to play back special file types directly inside the browser window.

PostScript.   A printer language developed by Adobe Corporation as a way to transfer graphical information, such as fonts, curves, lines, shading, and more, to the printed page.

PPP (Point-to-Point Protocol).   A communications protocol commonly used to connect computers across a serial line on a TCP/IP network.

PPTP (Point-to-Point Tunneling Protocol).   A communications protocol used to connect computers across a a TCP/IP network while actually tunneling through the security mechanisms on a firewall.

print server.   A computer used to store and route print jobs being sent to network-based printers. Print servers allow user groups to share printers, rather than having a separate printer on each user's desktop.

protocol.   A standard way of communicating data across a network. There are many network protocols available that work with different types of hardware and computing systems. There are also many levels or layers of protocols that may operate simultaneously as part of the same network application.

provider.   In Internet terminology, the person, group, or organization that provides information or services to end users. For example, a *content provider* is someone who provides formatted information or data to end users. An *Internet Service Provider* (ISP) is a company that provides Internet connections to people and businesses.

proxy server.   A server that forwards requests from internal users out to the Internet for retrieval. For example, if you are sitting on an intranet and request a page from the *Wall Street Journal,* your request might go to a proxy server on your intranet. The proxy server in turn will make the request for you on the World Wide Web. Once the requested page is received, the proxy server forwards it to your browser. Meanwhile, the proxy server stores the page in a cache where it can be easily retrieved if requested by other intranet users.

push channel. A web site accessed using push technology and a subscription process. The user can typically view a list of available push channels and then subscribe to the desired channels. Subscribing to a channel causes the associated web site to be updated automatically on the user's local machine.

push technology. A way of automatically updating browsers, background information displays, and/or caches on a user's desktop.

QuickTime. A multimedia format typically used to store video clips.

rollout. The cultural process used within an organization to make users aware of the presence of a new intranet.

router. A hardware device used to route traffic through a network.

search engine. A program that allows users to search a web by running keyword matches against an index. The index is created by a robot or web crawler that reads web pages and indexes the content into a searchable format.

server. A term used in various ways to describe the central component of a network application. From a hardware standpoint, it may refer to a specific hard drive or dedicated workstation that is used to store common data and applications shared by multiple users. From a software standpoint, it is typically the half of the client-server application that handles the processing and storage of data. The term "web server" can refer to the software that transfers files to web browsers on request, or the machine that the web server software is installed on. See also client-server and web server.

shareware. Software that is distributed free of charge for evaluation purposes, but which usually requires a registration fee after a trial period.

SLIP (Serial Line Interface Protocol). A communications protocol used to connect computers across a serial line on a TCP/IP network.

SMTP (Simple Mail Transfer Protocol). A common protocol for handling e-mail messages over TCP/IP networks.

streaming audio/video. A method of delivering multimedia data so that it can be read or played back in near real time, while the data is still being downloaded.

style sheet.   A method of defining certain page layout elements, such as headings, body text, numbered lists, and bullet lists, so that they can be easily applied by assigning a style tag to each paragraph. For instance, if you apply the *body text* style tag to a certain paragraph, it looks like body toxt. If you apply the *numbered list* style to the same paragraph, it becomes an element in a numbered list. See also cascading style sheets.

subdirectory.   A term used in UNIX and early PC operating systems to describe a location on a hard drive where files are stored. This is equivalent to the term *folder* in Macintosh and Windows 95 systems.

T1, T3.   Network connections that range from 1.5 to 45 Mbps.

TCP/IP.   A dual-purpose network protocol that serves as the conveyor belt for Internet services. TCP is the Transmission Control Protocol that handles the packaging and sequencing of data. IP is the Internet Protocol that handles the addressing and routing of data to specific computers on a network.

thin client.   A type of computer that gets most of its functionality from the network. Instead of having large programs stored on a local hard drive, the thin client would use applications stored on remote network servers. In some cases, this would make it possible to have computers without hard drives or other peripherals. The use of web browsers and the Java programming language has given new life to the thin client idea, as witnessed by the advent of Java-driven platforms such as the NetPC and the network computer.

transparent GIF.   A GIF image in which the internal background color is dropped out, producing a transparent effect and causing the image to float against the overall web page background. See also GIF.

UNIX.   A type of computer operating system used most often on high-end workstations, such as those used in engineering or financial applications. Often used as a generic term to describe more specific commercial implementations of the generic UNIX code, such as Solaris (Sun), AIX (IBM), or IRIX (Silicon Graphics). UNIX was also the native platform for the early Internet and most early intranets.

upload.   To transfer data from a local computer to a remote computer (host). See also download.

URL (Universal Resource Locator).   A string of information used to send a request to a web server, which identifies the path required to retrieve the information. The most common URL format for retrieving a web page on a remote server is http://server_name/path/filename.ext. However, a URL can also be used to pass data or queries to the server, or to communicate with other types of servers. For instance, to download a file from an FTP server, you could use the URL ftp://server_name/file.ext.

user authentication.   The process of requiring a user to enter an authorized ID and password before entering a web site.

VRML (Virtual Reality Modeling Language).   A formatting language used to display and dynamically manipulate 3-D objects within a browser.

web.   Any collection of online documents or forms that are hyperlinked to each other, especially through HTML and HTTP. The term "web" comes from the fact that the documents are connected through hyperlinks, forming a weblike information network.

web browser (client).   A software program designed to help users request information from web servers and display the information once it is returned. The term *browser* is a popular way to refer to a web client, since it lets users easily browse through large sets of information stored on any number of web servers worldwide (on the Internet), or networkwide (on an intranet).

web publishing.   A form of publishing akin to desktop publishing, but where the finished document is displayed on the web instead of on paper.

web server.   A software program designed to serve files and data to web clients (browsers) such as Netscape Navigator or Microsoft Internet Explorer. Also may refer to the complete set of server software, server content, and server hardware.

web site.   A set of information accessed through a web server, which is available to any user with a web browser, no matter where the user is located on a network. This can be used as a generic term to refer to sites on an intranet or on the Internet.

web system.   A set of web servers and clients that are configured to work together as a system.

webtop.   A background display with web features, such as the Active Desktop in Internet Explorer 4.0 and later browsers. This looks and acts a lot like our current *desktop* with its familiar background pattern and program icons, but it also may contain embedded hyperlinks and dynamic push broadcasts.

wide area network (WAN).   A widely dispersed set of computers or local area networks (LANs) that are linked together, typically using leased lines.

Windows.   A commercial operating system designed by Microsoft, typically for use on personal computers using chips manufactured by Intel or others. The first widely used version of Windows was Windows 3.1. Current versions of Windows include Windows 95, Windows 98, and Windows NT. See also NT and Wintel.

WinHelp.   The online help application built into the Microsoft Windows operating system, traditionally used to provide online help for most Windows applications. See also NetHelp and HTMLHelp.

Wintel.   A term used to describe the Windows operating system running on Intel (or similar) chips.

World Wide Web (WWW).   The worldwide public network of web sites available on the Internet.

WYSIWYG (What You See Is What You Get).   A common term used to describe an online display that bears a close resemblance to the way the information will look when it is printed. May also refer to web-authoring software such as FrontPage, that allows you to edit web pages in a display that bears a close resemblance to the way it will look when it is online.

WYSIWYG web editor.   An HTML editor such as Netscape Composer or the FrontPage Editor that lets you edit a web page inside a display that looks exactly like the final online document. Compare this to an ordinary HTML editor, which shows the text with embedded HTML codes. The WYSIWYG editor hides the codes completely from the author or editor, yet still includes them in the final HTML file that produces the displayed web page.

XML.   See extensible markup language.

index

Corporate INTRANET
ONLINE TRAINING

IntraMark™
Corporate Intranet
Online Training

A Comprehensive Set of Web-Based Training Modules for Self-Paced Study in an Online Environment

IntraMark is a total solution for your intranet training needs.

The Learning Center installs on your intranet as a self-contained web site, providing thousands of pages on all aspects of Internet and intranet technology, for self-elected self-paced training by all employees in your organization.

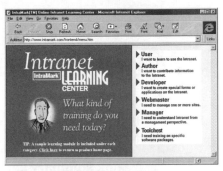

The IntraMark main menu easily integrates into your existing intranet.

The IntraMark Learning Center is the first training about the intranet to be delivered over the intranet. Today, there's too much to learn and not enough time to learn it in. Let IntraMark give your employees just what they need, exactly when they need it. See our web site for prices and information.

The IntraMark On-line Training CD makes installation quick and easy.

As the technology changes, the Learning Center changes with it. An annual subscription buys regular quarterly updates with new material on the latest versions of Netscape, Microsoft, and other industry leading tools. Or buy the single-user version for your local hard drive.

- **Extensive training for users, authors, developers, webmasters, and managers**

- **All pages viewable through standard web browsers; no special software or "plug-ins" required**

- **Ideal for "just-in-time training" and online performance support**

- **Low starter fee, add users as your intranet grows**

- **Includes evaluation copies of key intranet tools**

- **Customization option for large installations**

- **Some material based on "The Corporate Intranet" (John Wiley & Sons)**

Wordmark.Com, Inc.

info@wordmark.com   **http://www.intramark.com/**

What's on the Web Site?

Visit the companion web site for this book at www.wiley.com/compbooks/ bernard. There you'll find:

A book summary and a lengthy excerpt from Chapter 1 of the book.

A sample Intranet containing some simple examples of the types of information typically found on intranets:

- ◆ A home page with a clickable image map (see Figure A.1 in the Appendix).
- ◆ A sample "what's new" page providing an overview of site content
- ◆ An employee phone directory
- ◆ A quick tour of the fictional company called TSM Incorporated
- ◆ A rudimentary document library with sample documents in HTML format
- ◆ An employee bulletin board with examples of several forms, which simulates the operation of forms (actual back-end application not connected)
- ◆ A search page, which simulates an online search (actual search engine not connected)

Links to other resources, such as a training product based on The Corporate Intranet (www.intramark.com/) and various resources at my web site, including:

- ◆ Reviews of this book
- ◆ Reader testimonials about the book (write me at rbernard@ wordmark.com if you want to add your own testimonial
- ◆ Links to vendor sites for key Internet/intranet tools that you can use to create or improve your own intranet